THE TOWN LABOURER:
The New Civilization, 1760–1832

Asa Briggs is Professor of History at the University of Sussex. His books include *Victorian People*, *The Making of Modern England, 1784–1867*, *The Age of Improvement*, and *Victorian Cities*.

THE TOWN LABOURER:
The New Civilization
1760–1832

BY J. L. AND BARBARA HAMMOND

PREFACE BY ASA BRIGGS

GLOUCESTER, MASS.

PETER SMITII

1975

Reprinted, 1975, by Permission of
Doubleday and Company, Inc.

ISBN: 0-8446-2197-8

Anchor Books edition: 1968

TO

LEONARD TRELAWNY HOBHOUSE

AND

JOHN ATKINSON HOBSON

PREFATORY NOTE

Chapter XIII has been partly re-written in the light of the knowledge provided by Dr. R. F. Wearmouth's important researches into Methodist history. His book *Methodism and the History of Working Class Movements* was published by the Epworth Press in 1937.

PREFACE TO THE ANCHOR EDITION

Many books have been written about the British industrial revolution of the eighteenth and early nineteenth centuries, the first of a sequence of industrial revolutions which have transformed the world.

During recent years the main emphasis has been placed on the quantitative analysis of economic growth and the arduous effort to discover critical relationships between different sets of economic variables. Sociological research has never been completely neglected, but it too has become more severely analytical and concepts and models derived from theoretical sociology have been employed more frequently than in the past.

The Town Labourer reflects different preoccupations and older modes of scholarship. There are very few statistics in it. The great burst of economic growth in late eighteenth-century Britain, unprecedented in scale, is taken as a datum. The work as a whole is an attempt at a synthesis rather than an analysis, and its sub-title is comprehensive—'the new civilisation'. There is no reliance on technical language, and the book is designed to appeal—as it did, like other books by the Hammonds, with great success—to the general reader as much as to the specialist.

It begins with an account of the influence of steam power on people's lives. The Hammonds emphasised that 'the Industrial Revolution separated England from her past as completely as the political Revolution separated France from her past'. They took off here from what Arnold Toynbee had said in his well-known lectures on the industrial revolution, published in 1884, and what the French historian Paul Mantoux had written in his monograph on the eighteenth-century industrial revolution, which was published in French in 1906. The industrial revolution for the Hammonds, as it had been for Toynbee and Mantoux, was 'a social revolution, creating a new civilisation with problems and a character of its own'. They tried to identify those problems and to establish that character, dealing throughout with people rather than with statistics or concepts, with environment and experience rather than with national energy, wealth and power. In an earlier book, *The Village Labourer*, published before the War in 1911, they had dealt with traditional rural life and its disruption. In *The Town Labourer* they turned to the new forces unleashed by industrialisation and to unfamiliar struggles expressed in novel terminology. 'Unless these new forces could be brought under the control of the common will', they concluded their first chapter, 'the power that was flooding the world with its lavish gifts was destined to become a fresh menace to the freedom and the happiness of men.'

The term 'the common will' meant a great deal to the liberal-minded Hammonds, who in all their books were sharply critical of all kinds of forced social division. 'Unity', they remarked in their Preface, 'is only possible in a society which pursues a common aim, in which all men and women have a recognised and equal share. Such an aim must have some relation to human qualities and human needs.' This approach is well illustrated in the third chapter of their book on 'the new town'. 'The idea of the town as a focus for civilisation', they remarked, 'a centre where the emancipating and enlightening influences of the time can act rapidly and with effect, the school of the social arts, the nursery of social enterprise, the witness to the beauty and order and freedom that men can bring into their lives, had vanished from all minds.' What was missing was psychologically as well as aesthetically or culturally significant—the corporate sense, the hope, the pride, the ambition which would have made the new men of wealth concern themselves not only with making money but with the quality of life in the new urban environment. To reinforce their point the Hammonds compared the new towns of the industrial revolution with Athens, Florence and Siena or with nineteenth-century towns in Europe where there had as yet been no industrial revolution.

Many qualifications to this chapter must be made and have been made by later historians who have noted aspects of the town which the Hammonds neglected. Likewise, qualifications have to be made both to Chapter I and to Chapter II on 'the new discipline' in the factories. Yet the work of the Hammonds made it impossible for any sensitive writers who came afterwards to ignore the human and moral aspects of early industrialisation. The questions were fundamental. Did early industrialisation depreciate human life? Did it contract cultural horizons? Only historians who can offer a different synthesis have any chance of being able to overturn the Hammonds: mere cataloguing of qualifications is useful and necessary but not decisive.

The main argument of the Hammonds is clearly stated in Chapter III—that as a result of the great economic changes associated with industrialisation 'for the first time there existed a vast proletariate with no property but its labour, and therefore in the eyes of its rulers bound by no ties to the society in which it lived except by the ties that discipline could create'. Given this brute fact, it was inevitable that the early nineteenth century, to borrow a later term of the Hammonds, should be a 'bleak age'. Their successive chapters on 'justice' and 'order' present a very grim picture indeed. 'It is not too much to say . . . that none of the personal rights attaching to Englishmen possessed any reality for the working classes.' 'The art of politics was not the art of keeping the attachment of a people who cherished their customs, religion and the general settling of their lives, by moderation, foresight and forbearance: it was the art of preserving discipline among a vast population destitute of the traditions and restraints of a settled and conservative society, dissatisfied with its inevitable lot and ready for disorder and blind violence.' The perspectives are not entirely convincing, but once again the overall conspectus presented by the Hammonds with great imaginative power needs to be countered by an equally powerful alternative conspectus if their work is really to be challenged. Comparative history will probably have to be brought into the reckoning, with studies of the differences between British society and the society of other countries either during the same period or within the same context of early industrialisation.

Chapter VI on 'economic conditions' is a most unconventional chapter, given its conventional title. It is also the weakest chapter in the book, since little real attempt is made in it to substantiate any of its generalisations or to distinguish between different phases of time or different parts of the country in the process of industrialisation. During the last few years there has been a vigorous debate between 'optimists' and 'pessimists' among historians of early British industrialisation, and the Hammonds have been taken to be 'the classical exponents of "pessimism"'. In fact, they made no serious attempt to examine critically the relationship between quantitative information and qualitative judgements, and did little research of their own on wages and prices. The main interest of this chapter is that the Hammonds refused in it to separate politics and economics. Unlike G. M. Trevelyan, who in his best seller *Social History of England* (1940) was to treat social history as 'history with the politics left out', the Hammonds stressed that 'a complete social history of the times would embrace the history of the movement for Parliamentary Reform, as well as the history of a battle for the standard of life'.

Their approach to social history has been favourably commented upon by subsequent Marxist historians who share their 'pessimism' and admire their power to trace connections between different categories of social phenomena while rejecting their liberalism of outlook.

Chapter VII on 'the war on trade unions' shows the influence on the Hammonds of the other famous partnership, that of the Webbs, whose two famous books on trade unionism—*The History of Trade Unionism* and *Industrial Democracy*—both appeared in the years 1894–97, the first just before and the second two years after J. L. Hammond had graduated from Oxford. It shows also, like many other chapters, how keenly the Hammonds had browsed through official Home Office papers. 'The Home Office Papers, now accessible to students in the Public Record Office', they wrote in their first Preface, 'provide new and important material for the study of the period, and considerable use has been made of them in preparing this book.' The papers have subsequently been used by large numbers of historians, who have produced surprisingly varied extracts and conclusions. Certainly the Hammonds' interpretation of the Combination Acts requires modification.

The two following chapters on 'the employment of children' are emotionally amongst the most powerful in the book, concerned as they largely are with alarming details of a number of particular cases, but the most distinctive argument comes in six extremely interesting chapters which round off the book and give it a sense of symmetry. 'The Mind of the Rich' and 'The Conscience of the Rich' are more than balanced by 'The Defences of the Poor', 'The Mind of the Poor' and 'The Ambitions of the Poor'. The first of these chapters, with a very narrow interpretation of its theme, concentrates on the role of political economy, the new science of the period, and does not do justice to the thought of the times. Nor does the account given in it of the attitudes of the aristocracy avoid a certain element of caricature. Similarly, the second chapter on 'the conscience of the rich' leaves out much of the necessary detail of charitable effort, while including such memorable general judgements on Evangelicalism—rather in the style of R. H. Tawney—as 'it was perhaps not unnatural that an [Evangelical] religion that seemed to reconcile men and women to the hardships of life by promising them a happiness that (far from being prejudiced) was actually enhanced by their disadvantages in this world, came to be thought of by the upper classes, when the French Revolution broke into their peace of mind, as designed for this very purpose'. Evangelicalism was also to provide a theme for the subsequent biography of *Lord Shaftesbury*, the great Evangelical leader, which the Hammonds brought out in 1923. For the Hammonds the limitations of Evangelicalism were not simply set by social and economic or political factors. In both these chapters of *The Town Labourer* there are cross references to the classical world, a familiar aspect of the Hammonds' writings as a whole. Tiberius is the subject of an anecdote and Julian the Apostate of a footnote. Hammond had been a classical scholar at Oxford, and he obviously preferred Greek ways of thinking to Evangelicalism, just as he preferred the ways of life within the Greek *polis* to those within the Victorian city.

The chapters on the poor also begin with a classical reference and touch *en passant* with Greek religion. They are perhaps the most interesting in the book, however, and should be set alongside the more recent and fuller account, as controversial as that of the Hammonds, in E. P. Thompson's brilliant book *The Making of the English Working Class* (1963). 'Many histories', they wrote in a different context, 'have been written of the governing classes which ruled England with such absolute power in the last century of the old regime.' The last chapters of *The Town Labourer* turn boldly and searchingly to the history of the alienated classes which had to fend for themselves, developing new conceptions of solidarity and union and creating new economic and political associations and institutions. The Hammonds were to push the study further in their highly original book *The Age of the Chartists* (1932), and they remained interested in the processes whereby the excesses of early industrialisation were eventually eliminated. They were to direct attention to the Factory Act of 1847, the Public Health Act of 1848 and the Education Act of 1870. In the period covered in *The Town Labourer*, however, there was—according to the Hammonds—no alleviation. 'The new industry, instead of guiding mankind to a new experience of freedom, common to all classes, confirmed the power of the few, and made the mass of men still less their own masters.' Even more devastating were the final words of the book. 'Amid all the conquests over nature that gave its triumphs to the Industrial Revolution, the soul of man was passing into a colder exile, for in this new world, with all its wealth and promise and its wide horizon of mystery and hope, the spirit of fellowship was dead.'

No guide to the successive chapters of *The Town Labourer* can give a full idea of the appeal of the book. From the start it was very widely read and it went through eleven reprints between 1917, when it first appeared, and 1949, when a printing of 26,000 copies was ordered. Although its text had almost been completed by the summer of 1914 when Britain and Germany went to war, when it was published three years later the times were even more propitious for an interested reception. The Hammonds themselves stated in their first Preface that 'the subject it discusses has a direct bearing on problems that were beginning to engage the attention of the nation as the war draws, however slowly, to its end'. Readers shared the view. Not only did its message of 'common purpose' chime in well with the mood of war time—the Hammonds were members of the Ministry of Reconstruction set up by Lloyd George—but after the war, as industrial unrest mounted, what the Hammonds had to say about industrial relations, like what R. H. Tawney had to say, seemed to be as relevant as it was interesting. A review in *The Times Literary Supplement* paid tribute to the prophetic power of the Hammonds who had 'helped towards a better understanding, not only of the early nineteenth century, but of the problems of today'.

To understand this historiographical aspect of the Hammonds' work, it is necessary to examine more closely their biographies and the place of *The Town Labourer* in their total achievement. John Lawrence le Breton Hammond was born in Bradford, Yorkshire in 1872, so that he was forty-five years old when *The Town Labourer* appeared. He was the son of a clergyman and, as we have seen, a classical scholar—at St. John's College, Oxford—before he became a historian of the eighteenth and nineteenth centuries. He married Lucy Barbara Bradby in 1901, and they worked very closely thereafter in an academic partnership which lasted until Hammond's death in 1940. Their first joint book was *The Village Labourer*, which appeared in 1911, one of a group of books devoted to rural questions which were published about this time, when the 'land question' was a key issue in British politics. *The Town Labourer* should certainly be studied alongside *The Village Labourer*, for it was written immediately afterwards. It should also be studied alongside its companion volume, *The Skilled Labourer*, which first appeared in 1919. Originally, indeed, the two books were planned as a single volume, and, as R. H. Tawney shrewdly wrote in an obituary notice of J. L. Hammond, 'the reader noticing in the former an apparent error or omission will be prudent, before voicing his criticism, to make sure that the latter does not make the seeming defect good'. Whereas *The Town Labourer* scales the heights, however, and views industrialisation as a whole,

The Skilled Labourer descends into the valleys and examines sympathetically and at close hand the fortunes of particular groups of workers and the economic and political activities in which they were engaged.

The reading of these books should be further supplemented by a reading not only of *The Age of the Chartists* but of *The Rise of Modern Industry* which appeared in 1925. This book seeks to set the Hammonds' earlier works in perspective. It returns to the Ancient World, deals vividly, if briefly, with the 'commercial revolution' which preceded the rise of industrialisation, surveys the processes of industrialisation once more, and ends by linking directly what had happened in the nineteenth century with what was happening in the twentieth. 'The place Great Britain held after the Napoleonic Wars is held today by the United States. Her technique and invention, her engineers and her bankers, are forming and transforming the habits of mankind.' The last sentence of the book maintains the note of challenge which the Hammonds always tried to strike. 'When a people with such a history [the American people] steps into the first place as a world power, it is not easy to acquire at once a world outlook. The future of mankind seems to depend today on the answer that the United States gives to that sudden and disturbing summons.'

Why did the Hammonds treat history in this broad synoptic way, asking leading questions even when they could not give full answers? The first reason was that they inherited the critical and at the same time ecumenical outlook of nineteenth-century British liberalism, which at its best involved a persistent effort to relate facts to principles in all countries and in all ages. One of Hammond's outstanding books—he wrote it on his own—was *Gladstone and the Irish Nation*, which appeared in 1938. It dealt extremely sympathetically with the great hero of Victorian liberalism, emphasising his broad horizons, his keen interest in the Ancient World, his conception of Europe as a family with a rich past, his appeal to human dignity as the basis of self-government. 'Gladstone', Hammond concluded, 'became the greatest popular leader of his age, although he never mastered or seriously studied great social problems, because he offered the working classes something that satisfied their self-respect.' The 'age of Gladstone' spanned the period covered in *The Town Labourer* and the Hammonds' own lifetime, but, unlike Gladstone, they were liberals who were profoundly interested in 'great social problems'. They were, in fact, 'new liberals' who regarded the social content of liberalism as a necessary extension of Gladstonian liberalism. *The Town Labourer* is dedicated to Leonard Hobhouse and J. A. Hobson, two of the prophets of the 'new liberalism', whose writings influenced the foundation of party programmes and, even more important, helped to create a new mood in Edwardian liberal thinking.

Yet a second element in the Hammonds' experience is as relevant as their liberalism. They were in no sense professional historians, and while they were writing about the past they were also—regularly and in this case professionally—writing about the present. On leaving Oxford, Hammond became a journalist, and as editor of the *Speaker,* a left-wing liberal periodical, which was absorbed into the *Nation* in 1907, he was even more concerned with the Boer War than he was with the wars against Napoleon. After a spell outside regular journalism he became special correspondent of the liberal *Manchester Guardian* reporting the Peace Conference at Paris from December 1918 to April 1919. He continued his connection with the *Manchester Guardian* for the rest of his life and in 1934 published an interesting study of *C. P. Scott of the Manchester Guardian,* the greatest of liberal newspapermen. It was perhaps through journalism that the Hammonds learned to write as they did—pungently, trenchantly, with key phrases, headlines and leading questions. Certainly they could write in no other way, and they thought of themselves as disseminators of ideas and as educators of opinion rather than as specialist historians.

The Town Labourer can best be appreciated if the background of its authors is understood. Yet it is not the least of its merits that it can also be appreciated if this background is not known. It speaks for itself. Moreover, it offers readers a persuasive invitation to speculate not only about Britain in the late eighteenth and early nineteenth centuries but about life and thought in any country and in any age. As the Hammonds stated in their first Preface:

> 'The more closely any period of history is studied, the more clearly does it appear that the mistakes and troubles of an age are due to a false spirit, an unhappy fashion in thought or emotion, a tendency in the human mind to be overwhelmed by the phenomena of the time, and to accept those phenomena as the guide to conduct and judgement, instead of checking and criticising them by a reasoned standard of its own.'

PREFACE

The Industrial Revolution is apt to leave the light of history for the shadows of politics. Books in which it is discussed in one or other of its aspects are therefore liable to excite sympathies and animosities, not so much by what the writer says, as by what the reader finds between the lines. It is perhaps not out of place, in view of the course that controversy on this subject has taken since this book was first published, to describe the general outlook from which it was composed.

A civilisation is the use to which an age puts its resources of wealth, knowledge, and power, in order to create a social life. These resources vary widely from age to age. The Industrial Revolution brought a great extension of material power and of the opportunities that such power bestows. The first result, so this book contends, was deplorable, for, instead of creating a happier, wiser, and more self-respecting society, this revolution led to the degradation of large masses of people and the rapid growth of a town life in which everything was sacrificed to profit. The English people did not accept these consequences as its final contribution to the order and freedom of the world. The history of the nineteenth century is the history of its efforts, wise and foolish, brave and timid, to escape from this disorder.

This reading of history is challenged by critics who argue that as there had been a striking development of humanitarian feeling in the eighteenth century, social conditions could not have deteriorated. The first fact is not disputed. The England that allowed Fox to destroy the Slave Trade in 1806 was more sensitive than the England which took the lion's share of that trade at the Treaty of Utrecht in 1713. But the inference that social conditions can never become worse, in a world where pity and concern for injustice and suffering have extended their range, is false to experience. A single illustration will make this clear. Nobody who has studied the fate of the English agricultural labourer between 1760 and 1834 will doubt that he went sharply downhill. Lord Ernle, in *English Farming, Past and Present*, spoke of the peasantry as stupefied for half a century by the shock of the agrarian and industrial revolutions. His well-known judgment was not passed on some obscure and unimportant corner of English life; it related to the mass of the inhabitants of the southern villages, a considerable proportion of the English people. It seems therefore unreasonable to argue that, because there was more humane feeling in England in 1800 than in 1700, the lot of great numbers of Englishmen could not have become worse.

It is contended again that the Industrial Revolution is apt to be blamed for its virtues, because evils which were more acute, but less public, in earlier days, came into general notice and under general censure. There is an element of truth in this contention; it is true of many abuses that they were at once more evident and more manageable in the factory than in the domestic workshop. But those writers who dwell on the horrors of sweating in domestic industry are apt to forget that those industries did not disappear. There were more hand-loom weavers in Lancashire in 1830 than in 1750, and these handloom weavers lived in greater distress under more powerful masters. For half a century after the introduction of steam power, domestic industry, as well as factory industry, was increasing, and the condition of the people engaged in it was growing worse.

It is argued again that family earnings tended to increase with the introduction of the factory, and this estimate is probably well founded. But an increase of family earnings is not the only or indeed the chief test of the happiness of a society. A poor man, under one system of life, may be happier than a man who is less poor under another, for civilisation is the complex of all the forces and conditions that inspire and govern imagination and conduct. At the Industrial Revolution civilisation in this sense was saddened by new evils. They were new evils, for they were the consequences of sudden disturbance: the disturbance inevitable when the customs of a community are destroyed, and new forms of power and new relationships change the setting of its life. Those who think that these evils are commonly exaggerated by writers on the Industrial Revolution point to the improvement that took place at this very time in London, described by Mrs. George in her admirable study, *London Life in the Eighteenth Century*. But anybody who turns to the case of London will see that the contrasts with Lancashire are more important than the resemblances, and that the improvement in London and the deterioration in Lancashire, instead of presenting a puzzle, follow one and the same law.

For London was scarcely touched by the Industrial Revolution. The structure of the London trades was little affected: the typical London artisan in 1830 was very different from the typical Lancashire worker of that time: laws like the Ten Hours Act or the Mines Act, which mattered a great deal to Lancashire and Yorkshire, mattered very little to London. The great disturbance which came to the North of England with the Industrial Revolution had come to London two centuries earlier with the Commercial Revolution that followed the discovery of the Atlantic Routes. It was Columbus and not Watt who had started London on a career of rapid and headlong expansion. Mrs. George traces the great slum problems with which London was trying to grapple in the eighteenth century back to the time of Elizabeth and the legislation of the Stuarts, to the days when the spoils of India and the profits of the new overseas trade had increased so rapidly the wealth, the business, and the population of the Capital.

What London suffered at that time Lancashire suffered at the end of the eighteenth and at the beginning of the nineteenth century. Districts where men, women and children worked at home, partly at agriculture and partly at textile production, were changed into thickly populated towns where factories were set up and streets and houses thrown together by profit-seeking builders without care or supervision. It may be argued that some writers, leaning too much on Bamford and Ratcliffe, have drawn too favourable a picture of the earlier conditions. The generation which saw the factory system introduced may well have cherished memories that were too indulgent of the happiness of the workers when weaving and spinning were still done at home. But this change created problems in town life at least as serious as those created in London in the sixteenth century, and to deny that those problems were grossly mismanaged is to ignore all the evidence collected by Chadwick and others for the Committee of 1842 on the Sanitary Condition of the Working Classes, and for the Commission of 1844 on the Health of Towns. The reports of those Bodies are the most trustworthy evidence we have of the effect of the Industrial Revolution on town life, and their verdict is conclusive.

The writers do not find in the discussion that has taken place on these topics any reason for modifying their general picture of this society. But there are two special subjects which deserve some comment.

It may be held that a study which borrows most of its colour from the life of the textile industries is in danger of giving too sombre a picture of the Industrial Revolution. The great extension of the use of machinery brought, of course, numberless opportunities for the enterprising mechanic. If the rank and file of labour was depressed by the new power of capital, men of exceptional skill or industry could step out of their surroundings more easily than at any previous time in history. Violent revolutions have often opened doors to violent men: this was a peaceful revolution opening doors to the man of thrift, of perseverance, with sharp and nimble eyes for the chances that fell to him. This aspect of the Industrial Revolution is not ignored in *The Town Labourer*, but critics may perhaps contend that it receives less emphasis than it demands.

There was an old view that everything would have gone well with the Industrial Revolution if there had been no war; this view has been urged recently by writers whose researches have earned respect for their opinions. It is a view on which no one can pass a final judgment, just as nobody can say what Europe would be like at this moment if there had been no war in 1870 or in 1914. The war was disastrous to England because it led to too rapid an industrial success, and it gravely complicated all the social problems brought by the Industrial Revolution; the French Revolution was disastrous to England because of the embittered temper caused by the Jacobin scare. War, a catastrophe at any time, was specially a catastrophe at this time. So far there can be no difference of opinion. But those writers who go further, who isolate the war from the conditions of the time, and hold that it ruined what was a brilliant prospect of social readjustment, seem to the authors to fall into an error of perspective. The society which had to meet the grave summons of the Industrial Revolution was, after all, a society that valued the profits of the Slave Trade, and the harsh tone of upper class thinking and speaking on social relations at the time was not new; it had been the fashion for at least a century. The Parliamentary discussion on the Combination Laws is in this respect an instructive study. Some writers compare this legislation to the restrictions imposed under D.O.R.A. in the recent war. But if this analogy were a good one we should surely find Pitt, Wilberforce and the other supporters of the Bills of 1799 and 1800 pleading the needs and circumstances of the war in asking Parliament to pass them. When we turn to the debates, we find that they made no single allusion to the war, and that they relied solely on the general hostility to trade unionism that inspired their age and class.

Hemel Hempsted, August 1925

EXTRACT FROM PREFACE OF
FIRST EDITION

This volume is the first part of a study of the Industrial Revolution. It attempts to describe the general features of the new civilisation. The second volume will give in detail the history of the workpeople in various industries, with a full account of the disturbances known as the Luddite Rising, and of those connected with the adventures of Oliver, the famous *agent provocateur*.

The Home Office Papers, now accessible to students in the Public Record Office, provide new and important material for the study of the period, and considerable use has been made of them in preparing this book.

The writers have to thank many friends for help and criticism; among others Mr. A. Clutton Brock, Mr. G. D. H. Cole, Mrs. M. A. Hamilton, Professor L. T. Hobhouse, Mr. and Mrs. F. H. Lucas, Professor George Unwin, and Miss L. Finch who has helped with the index. Miss M. K. Bradby and Mr. R. H. Tawney have read the book through in proof and made a number of most useful suggestions, while Professor Graham Wallas has given the writers the most generous assistance at every stage of their work.

Hemel Hempsted, May 1917

Researches recently published have shown that the growth of the population in the early nineteenth century, which was attributed by most observers at the time to an increase in the birth-rate, was due in large part to a fall in the death-rate. The writers have taken advantage of a new impression to rewrite the passages that refer to this topic in the light of this new knowledge.

Hemel Hempsted, March 1928

CONTENTS

CHAPTER I

THE NEW POWER

"Our fields are cultivated with a skill unknown elsewhere, with a skill which has extracted rich harvests from moors and morasses. Our houses are filled with conveniences which the kings of former times might have envied. Our bridges, our canals, our roads, our modes of communication fill every stranger with wonder. Nowhere are manufactures carried to such perfection. Nowhere does man exercise such a dominion over matter."

In this passage, part of a powerful contrast that Macaulay drew in the exciting debates on the Reform Bill between the standard of English government and the standard of English life, we have a vivid picture of the effect produced on the imagination of the cultivated classes by the miracles that had been accomplished within the lifetime of most of the members of the last of the unreformed Parliaments of England. It is not surprising that this revolution produced a profound impression on the generation that had witnessed it. Even to-day, when the most fantastic of Mr. Wells's dreams seem to tumble into life before one's eyes in quick succession, the story of the changes that transformed travel, transport, commerce, manufacture, farming, banking, and all the various arts and means of social life, reads like a chapter from the *Arabian Nights*. The blind Metcalf had introduced the art of making roads; the illiterate Brindley, the art of building aqueducts; Telford, a shepherd's son, had thrown a bridge across the Menai Straits; Bell, a millwright's apprentice, had launched the first steamer on the Clyde; Stephenson, the son of a fireman, had driven his first railway engine; while a long line of inventors and organisers—Watt, Arkwright, Wedgwood, Crompton, Hargreaves and a hundred others—by their patience and their courage and their imagination, had between them made England the workshop of the world. When George the Third came to the throne, woollen goods were the chief manufactures sold by England, her cotton exports were unimportant; when Macaulay spoke, her cotton exports were worth some eighteen millions, her total exports had risen from fourteen to over sixty millions, her imports from

nine to over forty millions;[1] a nation that had been poor and
even backward in her roads now possessed three thousand miles
of navigable canals besides her infant railways; the new Stock
Exchange had been founded, and in two years alone no less a
sum than a hundred and seventy millions had been subscribed
for joint-stock companies. The men to whom Macaulay spoke
had seen the dazzling birth of modern England.

It is not the aim of this book to describe this revolution, to
trace the long struggle of inventors, or the rapid triumphs of
the leaders of enterprise, to examine the result of all this energy
in terms of national power and national wealth. That subject,
though not exhausted, perhaps inexhaustible, has been the
theme of a hundred important volumes. These pages are concerned with the fortunes of the mass of the people engaged in
the industries that produced this wealth. The Industrial Revolution was a social revolution, creating a new civilisation with
problems and a character of its own. What were these problems,
what solutions were proposed, what was the result of the spirit
in which this revolution was guided, or left to guide itself, upon
the life, quality, prospects of this new society; what did this
dominion of man over matter look like to the great population
taking part, if a blind part, in its establishment and its exercise?
Other aspects of the revolution will only be discussed in so far
as they seem necessary to a full understanding of the circumstances and conduct of the world that had been shaken into life
in the violent birth of modern England.

A word of caution is needed at the outset of such an inquiry.
It is as true of the industrial world as of any other that there
is a sense in which it is impossible to explain anything without
explaining everything. It is true, again, that there is an element
of risk in any general statement about the Industrial Revolution.[2] Many forms of life and control that are associated with
that revolution were not novel. The normal worker before the
Industrial Revolution was not an independent producer in the
full meaning of the term. There were persons working in factories before this period; there were many more working for
capitalist merchants, on whom they were entirely dependent for

---

[1] Cunningham, *Growth of English Industry and Commerce*, ii. pp.
694 and 695.

[2] See Professor Meredith's analysis in his *Economic History of
England*.

the supply of raw materials and the marketing of the product.[3] M. Mantoux has put it in his classical book[4] that Large Scale Industry did not create the proletariate or capitalist organisation, it completed their evolution.[5] The Industrial Revolution did not sweep away an England in which there were no employers and no employed and none of the problems that arise between master and men. Adam Smith said, in the *Wealth of Nations*, that in every part of Europe twenty workmen serve under a master for one that is independent. But the Industrial Revolution separated England from her past as completely as the political Revolution separated France from her past. For we understand by the characteristics of a society its governing facts and conditions: the classes, institutions, and atmosphere in which its life expresses and arranges itself. These features are quite definite and manifest in the civilisation that had its origin in the changes that came over England between the accession of George the Third and the passing of the Reform Bill. The new classes and the new institutions were not new in the sense in which the spinning-jenny was new or the power-loom was new. The atmosphere of a capitalist society had already crept over certain industries,[6] but it makes all the difference whether this or that feature is an accidental or an essential mark of an age, whether this or that grouping or relationship finds itself here and there in a society, or whether it is the most obvious and significant fact about that society. The view that the English people were the same in 1830 as in 1760 would be rejected as no less contrary to reason than the view that English manufactures were the same, or that they still travelled along the same roads, to the same markets, to reach the same customers.

The most striking fact about the Industrial Revolution, if we look at it as a chapter in the history of men and women, is the rapid rate at which the population grew. Within this period

---

[3] The Yorkshire woollen domestic producer had kept his independence in these respects. See Professor Ashley, *Economic Organisation of England*, p. 142.

[4] *La Révolution Industrielle au XVIIIe Siècle en Angleterre.*

[5] As early as the thirteenth century there were small weavers hiring looms from master weavers in London. See Professor Unwin's important book, *Industrial Organisation in the Sixteenth Century.*

[6] Notably the woollen and worsted trades in the south-west and in the east. Defoe had found the beginnings of the factory system in Norwich, Frome, Taunton, Devizes, and Stourbridge.

the population of England nearly doubled itself.[7] This growth was not uniform or general. It marked a redistribution of the inhabitants. In 1700 the five most populous counties are believed to have been Middlesex, Somerset, Gloucester, Wiltshire, and Northampton. In 1800 they were Middlesex, Lancashire, the West Riding, Staffordshire, and Warwickshire. In the counties that were the theatre of most of the struggles described in this book, the increase was gigantic. In the twenty years from 1801 Lancashire grew faster than Middlesex.[8] This increase represented not only the growth of great towns like Manchester[9] and Liverpool,[10] but the flooding of smaller towns.[11] There was a similar though less violent development in the other manufacturing counties.[12] The cotton towns grew the fastest, then the iron towns, then the woollen.[13] A great feature of the new civilisation was the rapid settlement of a dense working-class population outside the narrow limits of the existing towns.

This alteration in the map of England was caused partly by the change from an agricultural to an industrial society, partly by the growth of new industries, and partly by developments in the method and nature of old industries. If the general change is to be described in a sentence, we may say that England was hastening towards that industrial specialisation which more than anything else distinguishes modern social life from social life before the eighteenth century. Defoe considered that the West

---

[7] Toynbee put it: "Before 1751 the largest decennial increase, so far as we can calculate from the imperfect materials, was 3 per cent. For each of the next three decennial periods the increase was 6 per cent.; then between 1781 and 1791 it was 9 per cent.; between 1791 and 1801, 11 per cent.; between 1801 and 1811, 14 per cent.; between 1811 and 1821, 18 per cent." (*Industrial Revolution*, p. 67).

[8] From 672,000 to 1,052,000. See Baines's *Lancashire*.

[9] In 1774 Manchester had 41,000 inhabitants; in 1801, 102,000; in 1821, 187,000. See Baines.

[10] Liverpool had a population of 77,000 in 1801, of 118,000 in 1821. See Baines.

[11] Bolton sprang from 29,000 to 50,000; Blackburn from 33,000 to 53,000; and Oldham from 21,000 to 38,000. See Baines. M. Mantoux says Oldham had 300 or 400 inhabitants in 1760.

[12] Bradford was a little town with grass-grown streets in 1794, and by 1831 she had a population of 23,000; Leeds meanwhile had grown to 123,000, her population having been less than half that figure in 1801. Sheffield increased in the same period from 45,000 to 91,000; Birmingham, from 73,000 to 146,000.

[13] Mantoux, *op. cit.*, p. 372.

Riding was the only part of England that specialised in manufacture at the time of his tour (1724), but there were already
the beginnings of concentration in particular industries, and
each discovery brought with it some new reason why this or
that industry should make its home in one country rather than
in another. Thus, to take one example, in the early part of the
century the production of iron had decreased, owing to the
scarcity of fuel, but when inventions made it possible to use
coke fuel instead of charcoal, smelting and all iron processes
depended on the supply and neighbourhood of coal, and no
longer on the supply and neighbourhood of timber. This, in its
turn, gave a great impetus to coal mining, and as one discovery
after another made iron a more useful material than wood or
stone, the new industry of iron smelting grew fast in the neighbourhood of coal mines. The iron trade in consequence left the
south and travelled to the north and the Midlands.[14]

It was natural for the cotton industry to find a home in Lancashire, with its little streams flowing from the hills into the
Ribble and the Mersey, because water was needed to drive
Arkwright's machinery. The steam engine, which was first used
in this industry in 1785, led to concentration, and many a water
mill became a picturesque ruin. The new industries suited Lancashire as well as the old.[15] Then, of course, transport played
a decisive part in the destinies of this or that district. The Five
Towns were the Potteries in 1700, and they were the Potteries
in 1830. Burslem had coal and clay, and a race of enfranchised

---

[14] Sussex had been at one time the most important centre of the
production of iron: in 1740 there were ten furnaces in that county,
more than in any other county; by 1796 the output in Sussex had
dropped to 173 tons, and by 1830 the industry had settled in its
present home, Staffordshire possessing no less than 123 furnaces, or
more than all the other English counties together. Wales was not far
behind with 113. See Report of Midland Mining Commission, 1842.

[15] In 1788 there were 143 water mills in the United Kingdom, of
which 41 were in Lancashire; by 1838, of 220,000 cotton workers in
England and Wales, more than 150,000 were in Lancashire. Special
properties of climate and atmosphere had reinforced the advantages of
situation. Professor Chapman sums up the advantages of Lancashire:
(1) The port of Liverpool, (2) cheap coal, (3) a damp climate.
"The spinning districts of Lancashire are so suitable because they lie
on the slopes of hills facing west, upon which the damp breezes from
the Atlantic discharge their moisture, as they are driven to higher
levels by the slope of the ground." See Chapman, Cotton Industry,
pp. 149 and 153.

copyholders, men of initiative and enterprise. These initial advantages were crowned by the piece of good fortune that gave the Five Towns, in Josiah Wedgwood, a leader with the will and energy to drive the Bill through Parliament that made the Trent and Mersey Canal.[16]

But our business is with the people engaged directly as employers or employed in the industries that became important or were called into life by these developments. Who were they? Where did they come from? What were the new classes forming the new society?

Before the Industrial Revolution the rich classes in England were landed proprietors, a small class of bankers and money-lenders, and merchants.[17] The merchants were sometimes manufacturers as well, but there was no regular class of manufacturers in the modern sense of the word. To Adam Smith and Arthur Young that term denoted a person working with his hands. "It was indeed the merchant, and not the manufacturer, who represented the most advanced form of capitalism in the eighteenth century. Long before Dr. Johnson's discovery that 'an English merchant is a new species of gentleman,' Defoe had noted the rise of merchant-princes in the Western clothing trades, observing that 'many of the great families who now pass for gentry in these counties have been originally raised from and built out of this truly noble manufacture.'"[18] These merchant princes were merchant middlemen. At this time there was little capital laid down in fixed plant except in shipping, canal transport, and agriculture. Joint capital found its field chiefly in chartered companies for foreign trade, such as the East India or the Hudson's Bay Company. The machinery of finance and credit was very slight, and in 1750 there were not more than twelve bankers' shops outside London.[19]

The Industrial Revolution produced a new powerful rich class, the class of the capitalist manufacturer. The great mass of people collected in Lancashire, Cheshire, and the western borders of Yorkshire were working in 1830 not for a multitude of small masters, but for a comparatively small number of large masters. The dominant fact about the districts that now became densely populated was the rapid rise of these larger employers.

---

[16] Wedgwood, *Staffordshire Pottery and its History.*
[17] Mantoux, *op. cit.,* p. 376.
[18] Hobson, *Evolution of Modern Capitalism,* p. 62.
[19] Burke in "Letter on a Regicide Peace." Quoted by Toynbee, *op. cit.,* p. 32.

Where did this new class come from? It did not come, as might have been expected, from the ranks of the merchant manufacturers of the east and south-west. Nor did it come from the landlord class. The Industrial Revolution had in one respect an effect exactly contrary to that of the agrarian revolution. Enclosure eliminated the opportunities of the small man; the Industrial Revolution threw open the doors to adventure, enterprise, and industry, and the men who pressed in were spinners, weavers, apprentices, any one who could borrow a little money and was prepared to work like a slave and to live like a slave master. Many of them came from yeoman stock: Peel, Fielden, Strutt, Wilkinson, Wedgwood, Darby, Crawshay, and Radcliffe among others. Radcliffe, whose family, like Fielden's, had been ruined by an Enclosure Act, started without any capital, and so did Watt's friend, Kennedy. Robert Owen was apprenticed to a retail shopkeeper, and he set up in business with a hundred pounds that he borrowed of his brother. Brotherton, father of the member for Salford in the first Reformed Parliament, had been a schoolmaster and an exciseman before he started a cotton mill. Gaskell remarks that few of those who entered the trade rich were successful: ". . . the men who did establish themselves were raised by their own efforts, commencing in a very humble way, and pushing their advance by a series of unceasing exertions, having a very limited capital to begin with, or even none at all save that of their own labour." He gives a dark picture of the life and character of these early employers: "uneducated, of coarse habits, sensual in their enjoyments, partaking of the rude revelry of their dependents, overwhelmed by success, but yet, paradoxical as it may sound, industrious men, and active and far-sighted tradesmen."[20] But the phase thus described, whether the description is just or not, soon passes. The employers become an order; by 1830 the more important of them had been born, as M. Mantoux puts it, in the cotton or the wool, and a wide distance separated them from their workmen. The workman, however much he hated the early master, was in personal touch with him and understood him, but the gulf between the workman and an employer whose father has been a workman, may be as wide and isolating as the gulf between men whose families have been apart for generations.[21]

---

[20] Gaskell, *The Manufacturing Population of England*, pp. 45 and 55.
[21] See Chapman, p. 216. Bamford describes the change, *Early Days*, chap. xii.

There was indeed one industry in which the capitalist class came in part from the aristocracy. If the chief opponents of Lord Shaftesbury's Factory Bills were cotton spinners, the chief opponent of his attacks on the scandals of the mines was a colliery owner who was also a peer, the third Lord Londonderry. Several aristocratic owners are mentioned in the early Reports as working their own mines, among others, besides Lord Londonderry, Lord Durham, Lord Fitzwilliam, Lord Dudley, and the Duke of Portland. But owners did not as a rule work their own mines.[22] The great development of coal mining enriched many landowners directly, and the Enclosure Acts of the period show that the lords of the manor kept an alert eye on the possibilities of enterprise of this kind. Under the Wakefield Act arrangements were made for the prosecution of coal mining that were very satisfactory to the Duke of Leeds,[23] and another landowner took even ampler precautions in the case of an enclosure in the promising county of Stafford.[24] And of course it was not only the landowners who had coal on their estates who were enriched by the success of the new industries. The manufactures of Lancashire are said to have raised the rental of land in some cases 1500, and in others as much as 3000 per cent.[25]

Although the aristocracy seldom became actual employers, they helped the Industrial Revolution by promoting internal

---

[22] Buddle told the House of Lords Committee on the Coal Trade in 1829 that only five out of the forty-one collieries on the Tyne, and only three out of the eighteen on the Wear, were worked by the proprietors, the rest being in the hands of lessees or adventurers. Leases were generally for twenty-one years, and the lessees generally received 10 per cent. and their purchase money back; in very risky undertakings, 20 per cent. The proprietors protected themselves by stipulating for a fixed rent, in addition to a percentage. When the lease expired, the lessor usually had the right to take the machinery on an independent valuation. In some districts, notably in Staffordshire, small pits were let to contractors who were known as "Butties" and were very harsh masters.

[23] *Village Labourer*, p. 383.

[24] Midland Mining Commission, 1842, Appendix, p. 53.

[25] Cooke Taylor, *Tour in the Manufacturing Districts of Lancashire*, p. 167. See Webb, *Manor and Borough*, p. 113n. In 1846 the town of Manchester bought the manor and all the rights and incidents from Sir Oswald Mosley for £200,000. In 1596 a Mosley had bought it for £3,500, and in 1808 the town might have bought it for £90,000.

development and communication. Nothing struck Voltaire[26] more about England than the freedom of the English aristocracy from the prejudice against commerce that kept the French aristocrat out of every trade less reputable than the trade of living openly on the public. If the name of any single patron is to be linked with the progress of canals, which explains so much of the growth of Lancashire and Yorkshire and the Midland counties, the hero of that revolution is by universal agreement the Duke of Bridgewater. There is a heroine too in the story. The Duke was to have married the younger of the two famous Irish sisters, the Gunnings, the widow of the Duke of Hamilton, but at the last moment his peace of mind was disturbed by rumours of the levity of her sister, Lady Coventry. He desired his future wife to break off relations with her sister, and as she gave the only reply that was possible to a woman of spirit, they separated. The lady found a less exacting husband in the Duke of Argyll. The Duke of Bridgewater renounced society and found consolation and distraction in carrying out his father's project of making a canal to connect his mines at Worsley, near Manchester, with the Irwell. For this purpose he employed Brindley, and Brindley's success in this difficult enterprise emboldened the Duke to devote his vast income to building a canal between Manchester and Liverpool. He risked his fortune, but in the end he acquired vast wealth as well as wide renown. The success and results of his great scheme encouraged others to embark on similar projects; a network of canals soon covered the face of Lancashire and Yorkshire; the Duke became the proverbial type of princely benefactor, and Sir Spencer Walpole was able to say of him that he "did perhaps more to promote the prosperity of this country than all the dukes, marquises, and earls combined, who before his time had been born into the world."[27]

It is not difficult to understand how it was that the Industrial Revolution discovered the capital and the enterprise needed for the new industry at a time when profits were made with lightning rapidity. The supply of labour is more puzzling. It looks as if the Peels and the Arkwrights had only to stamp on the ground to turn empty valleys into swarming hives of workpeople. Where did the mass of wage earners in South Lancashire come from?

Before answering this question it is necessary to see what classes made up this population. At the beginning of this period

[26] Morley, *Voltaire*, p. 75.
[27] *History of England*, i. p. 79.

the two main classes of work were spinning and weaving. Both were done by hand, spinning for the most part by women and children, weaving by men, and weaving was considered to carry the higher status. When Samuel Crompton was married at Bolton in 1780, he put himself down as a weaver, although he had already invented his spinning machine or mule.[28] During this period, spinning, with its subsidiary processes, passed into the factories, and weaving in great part remained outside. The two occupations, by 1830, had changed places, spinning (though not its subsidiary processes) being now a comparatively well-paid employment, whereas the weavers were the most miserable people in Lancashire.

How was the factory population assembled? The people working in the factory were children, women, and in a much smaller proportion, men. The millowners began by getting children from the workhouses, and this system of serf labour carried the mills over the first stages, until there was a settled population, able to provide women and children. The men came from all parts, the only class that did not make any considerable contribution being the hand-loom weavers. We have a description of the immigration given by a Bolton witness to the Factory Commissioners in 1833:—[29]

"When power spinning came in, did it throw the hand spinners out of employ?"—"No; spinners were very scarce then: families had to come in from different places and learn to spin, and whole families together were sent for by masters."

"You have been a witness of the operative class in these parts; you have seen it grow from nothing into a great body in the space of a few years: how was it recruited? Of what was it composed? What were the spinners taken from?"—"A good many from the agricultural parts; a many from Wales; a many from Ireland and from Scotland. People left other occupations and came to spinning for the sake of the high wages. I recollect shoemakers leaving their employ and learning to spin; I recollect tailors; I recollect colliers; but a great many more husbandmen left their employ to learn to spin; very few weavers at that time left their employ to learn to spin, but as the weavers could

---

[28] French, *Life of Crompton*, p. 59n.
[29] Factory Commission, Supplementary Report, 1834, part i. p. 169.

put their children into mills at an earlier age than they
could put them to looms, they threw them into mills as soon
as possible, and many of the weavers' children stopped in
the mills and learnt to spin; but during the last twelve
years wevaers have put almost all their children into mills
since hand-loom weaving has got so bad."

"Do you ever hear of people leaving other occupations
now to learn to spin?"—"No; the masters don't take men
from other occupations now."

"How long is it since that influx of grown-up men into
the spinning branch began to cease?"—"It did not break off
at a time, but I should say it had ceased for fifteen or
twenty years."

The weaving population outside the factories was recruited in
much the same way. It was not difficult to learn to work a hand-
loom, and for a few years the profits were high. Agricultural
labourers swarmed into it, and as they had been accustomed to
low wages, the master spinners found them ready to work at an
inferior price, and so discovered an outlet for their extra quantity of yarn. "This at once led to a great depreciation in the
price of hand-loom labour, and was the beginning of that train
of disasters which has finally terminated in reducing those who
have clung to it to a state of starvation."[30] A great number of
the immigrants came from Ireland. During the riots against
power-looms in 1826 there were said to be as many as thirty
or forty thousand Irish weavers in Manchester alone. The Poor
Law Commission Report of 1833[31] contains a graphic picture
of the destitute Irish families continually arriving at Liverpool
to seek employment in the manufacturing districts.[32]

There were three main disturbances of the regular life of the
time to account for the great stream of population into Lancashire and the adjacent counties. There was, first, the agrarian
revolution in England, dispossessing a large number of small
agriculturists and breaking down the life and economy of the
old village.[33] There was, secondly, the congestion of Ireland,

---

[30] Gaskell, op. cit., p. 47.
[31] Extracts from Information received, p. 349.
[32] An Irish Catholic priest in Manchester stated to the Factory
Commissioners that this Irish population kept to itself, and did not
mix with other workmen. Factory Commission, Second Report, 1833,
Dr. Hawkins, p. 15.
[33] A witness, Thomas Smith, before the House of Commons Committee on the Cotton Weavers' Petition in 1811, said that as farms

and the acute distress caused by the exactions of an absentee landlord-class. There was, in the third place, the long war; the disbanding of a huge army let loose a flood of men, whose ties with their old homes were broken. The building of canals and bridges must also have helped to make labour more mobile, and these enterprises drew workpeople to the districts where labour was wanted for the factories.

These causes explain the rapid redistribution of the population that accompanied the Industrial Revolution, but the growth of the population is as striking a fact as this resettlement. It was the general belief of the time that this rapid growth was due to a great increase in the birth-rate. "When employment is plentiful," wrote Arthur Young, "and time of value, families are not burdens, marriages are early and numerous." The first Sir Robert Peel said in 1806, "In the cotton trade, machinery has given birth to a new population; it has promoted the comforts of the population to such a degree that early marriages have been resorted to, and a great increase of numbers has been occasioned by it, and I may say that they have given rise to an additional race of men."[34] After the publication of Malthus' famous work opinion changed, and this increase was regarded as a danger. It was still believed to be due to an increase in the birth-rate, and the Speenhamland system, which gave allowances according to the number of children, was blamed as an active cause. This system was chiefly associated with the village life of the South, but it was in force in the weaving districts of South Lancashire. The Census Report of 1831 took the same view as Sir Robert Peel had taken, that the new factory system encouraged population.[35]

This explanation of the great increase of population has been challenged by recent writers, who have done good service in calling attention to the great improvements in medicine and the consequent fall in the death-rate. Sanitary science had its beginnings at this time, and it found energetic advocates in great doctors like Percival, Ferriar, and Currie, in Manchester and Liverpool. The statistics available are difficult to interpret, but it is certain that there was a striking fall in the death-rate. This

---

were thrown together, cottages were pulled down, and the people were obliged to retire to the towns.

[34] See Toynbee, *Ind. Rev.*, p. 67n.
[35] See 1831 *Census*, I. Preface, p. xlvii.

fall in the death-rate was an important contributory cause of the great increase in the population.[36]

As the cotton industry expanded faster than the woollen and worsted industries,[37] population grew faster in Lancashire than in the West Riding. In both cases the English immigrants came as a rule from the neighbouring counties, though the Yorkshire factories attracted some textile workers from Norfolk and the South West. The Irish immigrants in the textile industries were found mainly in Lancashire and Scotland.[38]

For the working classes the new system meant, then, that a large population was brought together to satisfy the needs of a new power. That power employed steam as well as hands, machines as well as men and women. The event on which the imagination is apt to fasten as representative of the history of the working classes during this period is the Luddite rising. Byron's famous speech and Charlotte Brontë's more famous novel give to most people their idea of the misery of the time, and of its cause, the displacement of hand labour by machinery. This, however, is only part, and a small part of the truth. At the close of this period there were still great numbers of workpeople working in their homes. It was not the introduction of power-loom weaving that ruined the hand-loom weavers, and the revolt of the framework knitters in Nottinghamshire is mistakenly conceived, if it is conceived as an uprising against machinery. The real conflict of the time is the struggle of these various classes, some working in factories, some working in their homes, to maintain a standard of life. This struggle is not so much against machinery as against the power behind the machinery, the power of capital. There were a number of persons who suffered when machinery superseded hand labour, or one machine superseded another; there were more who expected to suffer; but the incidence of the new power was not local or particular, but universal. The whole working-class world came under it. The miner, who had never been a domestic worker,

---

[36] See G. Talbot Griffith, *Population Problems of the Age of Malthus*. M. Buer, *Health, Wealth, and Population in the Industrial Revolution*. J. H. Clapham, *The Early Railway Age*. J. Brownlee, Articles on Birth and Death Rates in England in *Public Health*, June and July, 1916 The writers have had the advantage of seeing the advance proof of an important paper on the subject prepared by Mr. T. H. Marshall.

[37] See an important table, Lloyd, *Cutlery Trades*, p. 399.

[38] See Redford, *Labour Migration in England*, 1800–1850.

and the hand-loom weaver, who remained a domestic worker, were just as sensible of this power as the spinner who went into the factory to watch a machine do the work that had been done in the cottage, or the shearman who tried unavailingly to keep out the gig-mill.

Thus the new world has two aspects. Those who lived under the shelter of property welcomed the new wealth that multiplied their enjoyments, embellished their homes, enriched their imaginations, increased their power, and gave an astonishing range and scope to the comforts and the arts of life. They felt about it as Dryden had felt about his age, and the founding of the Royal Society, and the boundless hopes of the new science:—

"Then we upon the globe's last verge shall go,
And view the ocean leaning on the sky;
From thence our rolling neighbours we shall know,
And on the lunar world securely pry."

For the working classes the most important fact about that wealth was that it was wealth in dangerous disorder, for unless these new forces could be brought under the control of the common will, the power that was flooding the world with its lavish gifts was destined to become a fresh menace to the freedom and the happiness of men.

CHAPTER II

THE NEW DISCIPLINE

In 1831 the Society for the Diffusion of Useful Knowledge published a volume called *The Results of Machinery,* addressed to the working men of the United Kingdom. The little book gives a glowing picture of the glories of invention, of the permanent blessings of machinery, of the triumphant step that man takes in comfort and civilisation every time that he transfers one of the meaner drudgeries of the world's work from human backs to wheels and pistons. The argument is developed with great animation and vigour, and the writer, as he skirmishes with the workman's prejudices, travels over one industry and one country after another. Almost every page offers a graphic illustration of Macaulay's proud verdict on English industrial life, "Nowhere does man exercise such dominion over matter."

If we study the speeches and writings that represent working-class feeling we shall notice very specially one aspect of the new system. The system threatened the employment and livelihood of a large number of people, and complaints to that effect are, of course, constant and general. The fear of this fate or its actual experience was the cause of violence against machinery and of violence against persons. But there appears in the protests and remonstrances of the time a spirit that was quite independent of these anxieties and resentments, a feeling of hatred and terror that no magician among economists could have dispelled by the most convincing demonstration that machinery could not hurt the poor.[1] This spirit finds its most articulate expression, after our period, in the Chartist movement and the passionate response of the working men and the working women of the north of England to the mobilising rhetoric of Stephens and Oastler. The men and women of Lancashire and Yorkshire felt of this new power that it was inhuman, that it disregarded all their

---

[1] See, for example, *The Voice of the People,* which expressly repudiates hostility to machinery, but lays great stress on the servitude to which the working classes had been reduced by its means from their want of power. "Every successive improvement which is introduced tends only to deteriorate their condition" (Jan. 22, 1831). At a meeting at Ashton it was declared that the negroes were slaves in name, but the factory employees were slaves in reality.

instincts and sensibilities, that it brought into their lives an inexorable force, destroying and scattering their customs, their traditions, their freedom, their ties of family and home, their dignity and character as men and women. If one sentence can sum up this impression, we might say, transposing Macaulay's words, "Nowhere does matter exercise such dominion over man."[2]

Scarcely any evil associated with the factory system was entirely a new evil in kind. In many domestic industries the hours were long, the pay was poor, children worked from a tender age, there was overcrowding, and both home and workshop were rendered less desirable from the combination of the two under a single roof. In many, not in all, for there were home workers who were very prosperous, and in his halcyon days the hand-loom weaver was in the enviable position of a man who had something valuable to sell and could make very comfortable terms for himself. But the home worker at the worst, even in cases where to those who examine the economic forces on which his livelihood depended, he seems to have been at the end of a shorter chain than he realised, was in many respects his own master. He worked long hours, but they were his own hours; his wife and children worked, but they worked beside him, and there was no alien power over their lives; his house was stifling, but he could slip into his garden; he had spells of unemployment, but he could use them sometimes for cultivating his cabbages. The forces that ruled his fate were in a sense outside his daily life; they did not overshadow and envelop his home, his family, his movements and habits, his hours for work and his hours for food.

What the new order did in all these respects was to turn the discomforts of the life of the poor into a rigid system. Hours were not shortened, the atmosphere in which they worked was not made fresher or cleaner, child labour was not abolished. In none of these respects was the early factory better than the home, in some it was worse. But to all the evils from which the domestic worker had suffered, the Industrial Revolution added discipline, and the discipline of a power driven by a competition that seemed as inhuman as the machines that thundered in fac-

---

[2] "A steam engine in the hands of an interested or avaricious master is a relentless power to which old and young are equally bound to submit" (a factory inspector, quoted by Fielden, *Curse of Factory System*, p. 43).

tory and shed. The workman was summoned by the factory bell; his daily life was arranged by factory hours; he worked under an overseer imposing a method and precision for which the overseer had in turn to answer to some higher authority; if he broke one of a long series of minute regulations he was fined, and behind all this scheme of supervision and control there loomed the great impersonal system. Let anybody think of the life of Bamford's uncle at Middleton, who used to retire into his house every morning and every afternoon to enjoy a pipe,[3] or of the account of his early days given by a Nottingham stocking maker, mentioned by Felkin, where every other Saturday was taken off for gardening,[4] and then let him enter into the feelings of a spinner at Tyldesley, near Manchester, who worked in a temperature of 80 to 84 degrees, and was subject to the following penalties:—[5]

	s.	d.
Any spinner found with his window open	1	0
Any spinner found dirty at his work	1	0
Any spinner found washing himself	1	0
Any spinner leaving his oil can out of its place	1	0
Any spinner repairing his drum banding with his gas lighted	2	0
Any spinner slipping with his gas lighted	2	0
Any spinner putting his gas out too soon	1	0
Any spinner spinning with gaslight too long in the morning	2	0
Any spinner having his lights too large for each light	1	0
Any spinner heard whistling	1	0
Any spinner having hard ends hanging on his weights	0	6
Any spinner having hard ends on carriage band	1	0
Any spinner being five minutes after last bell rings	1	0
Any spinner having roller laps, no more than two draws for each roller lap	0	6
Any spinner going further than the roving-room door when fetching rovings	1	0

[3] Bamford, *Early Days*, p. 103.
[4] Felkin, *History of Machine-Wrought Hosiery and Lace Manufactures*, p. 451.
[5] *Political Register*, August 30, 1823.

	s.	d.
Any spinner being sick and cannot find another spinner to give satisfaction must pay for steam per day	6	o
Any spinner found in another's wheel gate	1	o
Any spinner neglecting to send his sweepings three mornings in the week	1	o
Any spinner having a little waste on his spindles	1	o

This list of fines was given by the spinners during a strike, in a pamphlet published at Manchester. The pamphlet adds, "At Tyldesley they work fourteen hours per day, including the nominal hour for dinner; the door is locked in working hours, except half an hour at tea time; the workpeople are not allowed to send for water to drink, in the hot factory; and even the rain water is locked up, by the master's order, otherwise they would be happy to drink even that."

In the modern world most people have to adapt themselves to some kind of discipline, and to observe other people's time-tables, to do other people's sums, or work under other people's orders, but we have to remember that the population that was flung into the brutal rhythm of the factory had earned its living in relative freedom, and that the discipline of the early factory was particularly savage. To understand what this discipline meant to men, women, and children, we have to remember too that poor people rarely had a clock in the house. Sadler said that you could hear the feet of children pattering along the dark streets long before the time for the mills to open.[6] No economist of the day, in estimating the gains and the losses of factory employment, ever allowed for the strain and violence that a man suffered in his feelings when he passed from a life in which he could smoke or eat, or dig or sleep as he pleased, to one in which somebody turned the key on him, and for fourteen hours he had not even the right to whistle.[7] It was like entering the airless and laughterless life of a prison. Unless we keep this moral sacrifice in mind, we shall not understand why the hand-loom weavers refused to go into the power-loom factories, where

---

[6] *Memoirs of Life and Writings of Sadler*, p. 374.

[7] An Englishman went to Rouen to superintend a factory there, and when he tried to establish the English discipline among workmen who were accustomed to leave their work as they pleased, there was a strike, and the soldiers had to be called in. See Evidence of Mr. Wm. Smith before Sadler's Committee.

they would have earned much higher wages: a refusal that is an important fact in the history of the cotton industry.[8] Moreover, although to the authors of the books on the advantages of machinery, invention seemed to have lightened the drudgery of men and women, it had introduced a wearing tension: the nervous strain of watching machinery and working with machinery aged men and women faster than the heaviest physical exertions. The machinery never tired. "Whilst the engine runs the people must work—men, women and children are yoked together with iron and steam. The animal machine—breakable in the best case, subject to a thousand sources of suffering—is chained fast to the iron machine, which knows no suffering and no weariness."[9]

The hours at Tyldesley were exceptionally long, but the normal working day in Manchester and the neighbourhood in 1825 varied from twelve and a half to fourteen hours,[10] and mills, like mines, sometimes worked day and night. Moreover, under the system there was a strong pressure for a longer day. A master spinner, who was a member of an association formed at Manchester in 1831 for the purpose of securing the observance of the earlier Factory Acts, gave it as his opinion that if there were no Factory Acts, the tremendous competition in the industry would make masters work their mills for the whole twenty-four hours with no relief except for meals.[11]

In 1824 the Macclesfield masters tried to lengthen the working day in the silk mills. The story was told by a silk spinner before the Committee on Artisans and Machinery.[12] The hours were from 6 A.M. to 6 P.M., and the masters published a paper signed by forty-five firms, stating that in future the hours in Macclesfield would be the same as those in the neighbouring towns, namely, from 6 A.M. to 7 P.M. The men refused to agree

---

8 See Chapman, p. 46: "Only the direst necessity, however, could drive the typical hand-loom weaver into a steam factory, and not infrequently he preferred to fight famine at close quarters rather than surrender his liberty."

9 *Moral and Physical Conditions of the Operatives employed in the Cotton Manufacture in Manchester*, by James Philip Kay, 1832, p. 24, quoted by Hutchins and Harrison, *History of Factory Legislation*, p. 50. Greg said that the work of a spinner was almost the most laborious work known (Fielden, p. 33).

10 Hutchins and Harrison, *op. cit.*, p. 30.

11 Factory Commission, Second Report, 1833, Mr. Tufnell, p. 50.

12 Pp. 582–6.

to this, and after several ineffectual meetings the masters withdrew their proposed rule. Each side appealed to the public. "It is a well-known fact," said the men, "that children very young are employed in the above branch; and can we as men submit to a proposition so highly indecorous, as to increase the hours of labour, knowing that it would not only greatly affect the present age, but ages yet unborn? You are well aware that we have of late obliged them, by working night and day for their peculiar interest." The masters, in announcing their decision not to press their demand, told the public "that it is deeply to be regretted, that the orderly, quiet, and peaceable working classes of this town and neighbourhood should so far have lost sight of their true interest, and given way to the representation of the vicious and designing amongst them, as to reject the proposition of the masters, for working twelve hours to the day, with a proportionate addition to their wages." The witness told the Committee that the increase of wages was an afterthought, and that the men knew well enough that if it were granted, it would soon be withdrawn, on the pretence of trade stagnation. Moreover, there were children in the Macclesfield mills who were under five years of age. "We told them they had made cripples enough already in Macclesfield."[13]

It was not only the life of the men that was swallowed up in the factory. Women and children were shut out from the daylight as well.[14] The home life of Lancashire is described as fol-

---

[13] It is interesting to note that in 1833 the manager of some silk mills in Macclesfield referred to this incident, dating it 1825, representing the proposal of the masters as a proposal to reduce the working day, and the men as standing out for thirteen hours. See Factory Commission, Second Report, 1833, Mr. Tufnell, p. 31. The witness wished to confirm his argument that a shorter working day would be unpopular.

[14] It was calculated in 1833 that the cotton mills employed 60,000 adult males, 65,000 adult females, 43,000 boys under eighteen, and 41,000 girls under eighteen. About half of those under eighteen were less than fourteen years old (Factory Commission, Supplementary Report, 1834, part i. p. 138). Of the factory operatives in 1839 rather less than a quarter were men over eighteen (Engels, Condition of the Working Class in England in 1844, quoting Ashley, p. 142). A manufacturer gave statistics to show that there were 10,721 married women employed in Lancashire factories; of the husbands of these women half were also employed in the factories, 3,927 were otherwise employed, 821 were unemployed, and information was not forthcoming as to 659 (Engels, p. 147).

lows[15] at the end of our time. The factory woman has had no time, no means, no opportunities of learning the common duties of domestic life. "Even if she had acquired the knowledge, she has still no time to practise them. In addition to the twelve hours' labour is an additional absence from home in the going and the returning. Here is the young mother absent from her child above twelve hours daily. And who has the charge of the infant in her absence? Usually some little girl or aged woman, who is hired for a trifle and whose services are equivalent to the reward. Too often the dwelling of the factory family is no home; it sometimes is a cellar, which includes no cookery, no washing, no making, no mending, no decencies of life, no invitations to the fireside." This point had been put in a letter to the Home Office from a Manchester correspondent as early as 1800.[16] "The people employed in the different manufactures are early introduced into them, many at five and six years old, both girls and boys, so that when the former become Women they have not had any opportunity of acquiring any habits of Domestic economy or the management of a family . . . The greater part of the Working and lower class of people have not wives that can dress a joint of meat if they were to have it given them. The consequence is that such articles become their food that are the most easily acquired, consequently their general food now consists of bread and cheese." The writer goes on to mention that in a family known to him, 24s. out of 26s. or 28s. a week earned by its members are spent on bread.

The same sense of an inexorable and inhuman power overshadowed the mining population. Their living was gained in the midst of dangers and hardships of the most terrifying kind, for the age of great accidents and deeper mines had begun, and there was nothing in the administration of the system that seemed to take any account of their feelings.[17] The most brutal and direct illustration of the light in which they were regarded was the policy of intimidation and concealment practised by the coalowners when lives were lost in the mines. "As so many deplorable accidents have lately happened in collieries," said the *Newcastle Journal* in 1767, "it certainly claims the attention of

---

[15] Factory Commission, Second Report, 1833, Dr. Hawkins, p. 5.
[16] H. O., 42 53.
[17] In one mine men were paid an extra allowance of 6d. a day for working in a temperature of 130 degrees, but 2d. was deducted for every hour lost (*A Voice from the Coal Mines*, 1825).

coal owners to make a provision for the distressed widows and fatherless children occasioned by these mines, as the catastrophes, from foul air, become more common than ever; yet as we are requested to take no particular notice of these things, which, in fact, could have very little good tendency, we drop the further mentioning of it."[18] Down to 1815 it was not the custom to hold inquests on the victims of accidents in the mines of Northumberland and Durham.[19] That public attention was drawn to the facts was due to two men, a judge and a parson. The judge was Sir John Bayley, who made very strong representations at the Assizes at Newcastle in 1814 on the scandal of omitting all inquiry into the circumstances under which hundreds of persons had lost their lives, and the parson was John Hodgson, Vicar of Jarrow, who, "braving the displeasure of the affluent Brandlings," wrote and published an account of the accident at Felling, in which ninety-two of his parishioners had perished. Hodgson's action led to the establishment of a Society at Sunderland for preventing accidents,[20] and it was in answer to an appeal from this Society that Sir Humphry Davy visited Newcastle and gave his mind to the problem.[21]

Unfortunately even the alleviations of science were turned to the miner's disadvantage. The Davy lamp, for which the inventor refused to take out a patent, renouncing an income of £5,000 or £10,000 a year, "his sole object to serve the cause of humanity," was used in many cases to serve the cause of profits. Deeper and more dangerous seams were worked, and accidents actually increased in number.[22] The writer of A Voice from the Coal Mines, a pamphlet published by the Northumberland miners in 1825, stated that since the introduction of the lamp the miner had had to work in still higher temperatures, under conditions that caused him physical agony. The Children's Employment Commission[23] reported in 1842 that in the West Riding the lamp was often made a substitute for ventila-

---

18 Newcastle Journal, March 14, 1767.
19 Boyd, Coal Pits and Pitmen, p. 67.
20 Galloway, History of Coal Mining, pp. 157 and 179.
21 Evidence of Founder of Society (Wilkinson) before Select Committee on Accidents in Mines, 1835.
22 The Select Committee on Accidents in 1835 reported that there were 447 deaths in Northumberland and Durham in the eighteen years before 1816, and 538 in the eighteen years following.
23 See First Report of Commission for inquiring into employment of children in mines and manufactures, 1842.

tion, that in South Staffordshire accidents were so common that the people talked as if the whole population was engaged in a campaign, and that in Northumberland and Durham the mining population had become absolutely indifferent to its danger. The indifference of the coalowners scandalised this Commission, and commenting on the accidents that had occurred from negligence in the pits belonging to Curwen and Lord Lonsdale, they observed "when such management is allowed in the mines of two of the most opulent coal proprietors in the kingdom, we cease to wonder at anything that may take place in mines worked by men equally without capital and science." The Commission were severe on the conduct of coalowners and their agents, in throwing all the blame on their workpeople and making them responsible for chains and tackle, but they were most severe about the tasks on which children were employed. In Derbyshire, and some parts of Lancashire and Cheshire, especially around Oldham, it was the custom to employ children to let down and draw up the workpeople. The Chief Constable of Oldham mentioned a case in which three or four boys were killed because the attention of the child of nine years who was in charge of the engine for drawing up the cage was distracted by a mouse. But in all mines children were employed on most responsible work, and the Commission concluded that it was astonishing that accidents were not more frequent, seeing that all expedients for safety might be counteracted by allowing a single trap door to remain open,[24] "and yet in all the coal mines, in all the districts of the United Kingdom, the care of these trap doors is entrusted to children of from five to seven or eight years of age, who for the most part sit, excepting at the moments when persons pass through these doors, for twelve hours consecutively in solitude, silence and darkness."[25] Sir J. C. Hippisley, a Somerset magistrate, wrote to the Home Office in 1817: "At the great colliery of Clan Down . . . from 100 to 150 men are employed in the veins at a perpendicular depth of above 1200 feet, and it is in the power of an idle or mischievous Engine Boy to drown

---

[24] The whole system of ventilation in mines depended on the shutting of the trap doors.

[25] Mr. Buddle told the Lords Committee on the Coal Trade in 1829 that there was no provision for the victims of accidents except parochial relief and the generosity of the employers. He had never known an employer turn out a widow after an accident, and often if she had a boy he was "indulged with some employment at advanced wages."

the whole of them without destroying or injuring the Fire Engine."[26] The magistrate noted this as an argument, not for prohibiting the employment of boys in such responsible work, but for making the punishment for damaging collieries more drastic.

The population that lived thus on the brink of the mines and the brink of the next world became an hereditary race. In some parts of England the women worked as well as the men. Women were employed in Durham at the beginning of the eighteenth century, for there were women killed in explosions in Gateshead (1705) and Chester-le-Street (1708), but the practice died out there before the end of the century.[27] Women were also said to have been killed in an explosion in Whitehaven. When the Children's Employment Commission reported in 1842, women were working in the pits in the West Riding, in Cheshire, in some parts of Lancashire, and in South Wales. The custom had strict local frontiers, as a miner found when he went from Wigan, where women were so employed, to Oldham, where the feeling was strong against it. Women were apparently not employed down the Lancashire mines east of Manchester. They were generally employed as "drawers," *i.e.* in carrying or pushing the corves containing the coal "won" by the hewers, for the men liked women in this capacity, finding them easy to manage, and yet too spirited to let others pass them. Also, though women coal-getters were not unknown, they were rare, and therefore the danger of competition for employment was diminished by using women for "drawing."[28] A witness told the Commission of 1842 that a married woman miner worked day and night, the day being spent in the mine and the night in washing, cooking, and cleaning her house. Children were employed from earliest years, some so young that they were put to bed when they got home. The working day varied; for men it was often twelve hours, for women and children it was longer. At the Felling Pit at the beginning of the nineteenth century boys' hours were from eighteen to twenty. There was thus little daylight for father or children out of the mine. The race lived underground like the refugees in Les Misérables, who lived in

---

[26] H. O., 42. 161.

[27] Galloway (*Annals of Coal Mining*, 1st series, p. 305) says employment of women and girls underground in Tyne and Wear district ceased about 1780.

[28] Boyd, *op. cit.*, says women hewed in Yorkshire, and in most districts only "hurried" (p. 84).

the sewers of Paris. One miner described how he used to put his child in its cradle in the seam where he worked, to keep the rats off his dinner. Children who were going to work in the mines were often brought to the pit on their fathers' backs.[29]

If the treatment of the miners gave the new society the look of a civilisation in which human life seemed a good deal less important than the profits of capital, the same impression was made, not on the working classes only, by the behaviour of the shipowners on the Tyne and Wear. In 1815 there was a seamen's strike in the north-eastern ports, which was suppressed after a long struggle by the use of troops.[30] The cause of the strike was the conduct of the shipowners, who made a practice of undermanning their ships and refused, in spite of the appeals of the magistrates, to bind themselves to any fixed scale. Local opinion was largely on the side of the seamen, and the behaviour of the owners was stigmatised in severe language by the general commanding the troops, by several of the magistrates, including the Vicar of Bishops Wearmouth, and by a Home Office envoy who, going down to the scene of the dispute with the strongest bias against the men, gradually learned that the seamen who had upset the entire industry of the ports, forbidding any boat to leave without their sanction and taking over the discipline of the towns, had been driven to these measures by the masters' wanton disregard of life. "Ships from these ports," he wrote to Sidmouth, "have gone to sea shamefully deficient in strength to navigate them, and should ever the subject excite the attention of the legislature, hundreds of cases may be produced in which avarice has risked at sea a helpless insufficient crew in a crazy but highly insured ship." After a good deal of bickering between the Home Office and the Admiralty a twenty-gun ship was sent to Shields. The sentiments of the bluejackets were so strong that the officers doubted whether they would act against the men, and the officers themselves were scarcely less warm in their sympathy with the cause of the seamen or their admiration of their bearing and discipline. They tried to act as mediators, but found that the seamen would not accept any undertakings that did not formally bind the masters. The men's suspicions were soon justified. Cartwright, the Home Office envoy, relates

---

[29] According to census of 1841, there were 83,408 men over twenty, 32,475 under twenty, 1,185 women over twenty, and 1,165 under twenty (Engels, p. 241).

[30] For documents on the subject, see H. O., 42. 146.

in a letter to Sidmouth how he found himself at a public table among shipowners, and "heard a full discussion of the subject. They openly, to my deep disgust, avowed the base dissimulation with which they are acting, and that they intend to observe any terms they may *agree to* only till the present compact association and the consequent danger are dispersed."

General Riall describes a characteristic incident after the men had been overcome by military force. "At Sunderland, where a compromise had been made with the Ship Owners and an agreement entered into with the Seamen that a certain number were to be taken into each Ship according to her size or Tonnage, they have broken their faith, in a very shameful manner, the numbers were actually taken on board *eight* ships, but after the ships had got a certain distance from the Harbour the extra men they had promised to take were relanded." In this case, although the men's demand commended itself as fundamentally just to persons who were shocked by their way of presenting it, no influence could prevent the masters from taking complete advantage of the victory they owed to the intervention of the forces of the Crown, and magistrates continued to urge the Home Office in vain for measures to enforce some respect for human life on this formidable interest.

The new power of capital seemed all the more crushing and overwhelming because even the efforts of leading employers could not soften its incidence. Brotherton, when he was sent to the Reformed Parliament by the electors of Salford, put this truth about the agitation against the long hours of children. Parents had petitioned in their tens of thousands, and forty of the largest manufacturers in Manchester had signed a manifesto, but unless the law intervened, no force could shake a system that was defended, in some quarters as essential to manufactures, in others as essential to parents. John Fielden, according to Cobbett, worked up one-hundredth part of all the cotton imported into England, and he employed two thousand persons, but neither he nor any other employer believed it possible to abate the evils of the system under which they grew rich, without the help of Parliament and the successful coercion of the entire class of employers.[31] It happened more than once in the course

---

[31] In Fielden's mill the hours were at first ten a day. His father, competing with men using the same machinery and working for 77 to 84 hours in the week, raised the hours to 12 a day and 11 on Saturday. After 1819 (under Peel's Act) the hours for children were reduced to 72 (*Curse of the Factory System*, p. 34).

of agitations for better wages that the workmen were able to enlist the support and sympathy of a considerable body of masters, but sympathy and support were valueless, because Parliament would not ratify their wishes. Men might work astonishing miracles in acquiring mastery and guidance over the forces of fire and water, but the industrial system itself was so contrived as to make the public spirit, or the human sympathy, or the generous common-sense of the best employers, dependent on the selfishness or indifference or the blind greed of the worst. A good man who built a mill gave a hostage to the man who wanted to work the longest hours at the lowest wages. The history of the cotton industry, of the framework knitters, and of the ribbon weavers shows that there were many employers who understood that low wages were bad for industry and bad for the nation. With the economic notions then in power, the workmen had to convince either the most unenlightened employer or Parliament before they could obtain a remedy. Even Robert Owen's successful experiment in the economy of good wages and shorter hours made no impression on his competitors. The fierce struggle that is the subject of this book looks from one point of view like a class conflict of a most cruel and exhausting kind. So it was: but it was none the less a conflict in which there were employers as eager for the victory of the men as the men themselves. In the old days the workmen were dealing with a comparatively small circle of masters; they were now pitted against a system, and not only they, but every good employer and every good citizen as well. At Leicester on one occasion the men were supported by the Lord Lieutenant, Mayor, Aldermen, and the churches and chapels. The Industrial Revolution had delivered society from its primitive dependence on the forces of nature, but in return it had taken society prisoner.

The spectacle of this new power as a profane and brutal system that spared neither soul nor body, and denied to men and women the right to human treatment, was impressed upon the imagination with special force by its ruthless violation of all the ties and affections of the family. These ties were particularly strong in a community where the rich would not have expected to find them. All observers agreed that among the miners the women had great influence over their husbands, and that they were invariably consulted on all questions of strikes and combinations. "The females exercise or are destined early to exercise an unusual and unlimited influence over the miners: and nearly the whole of the arrangements and duties of upper ground life are by common consent deputed to them."[32] The idea of the family wage as the economic unit, though not of course explicitly formulated, governed men's thinking about the industrial system, and thus the factories seemed to offer special advantages to the poor by providing employment for their children. A manifesto from the Female Political Union of Newcastle, in 1839, put just the opposite view that it was a special grievance that men's wages were so low that the mother and her small children were driven to work at a labour that degraded soul and body.[33]

When the revolt against the barbarities began, it was a common retort that if this system was bad the parents were to blame, for they sent their children into the factory. This argument disregarded history. The system began with serf labour from the workhouses, and it was not until the weavers had been reduced to want that they took their children to the hated mill.[34] In many parishes the overseers refused relief unless the children went out to work.[35] A family could not live on an income of five or six shillings a week. Cobbett described how women took their children to the mill through the snow; the child was crying, but the mother too was crying.[36] It is true, again, that a

---

[32] Children's Employment Commission, Report of 1842.

[33] Dolléans, Le Chartisme, vol. i. p. 241.

[34] The first children were the sons of Irish weavers (Fielden, p. 12).

[35] See, e.g., the evidence of William Osburn, ex-overseer of Leeds, before Sadler's Committee as to the practice of the Leeds overseers; also of assistant overseer of Keighley (G. Sharpe).

[36] Oastler was asked by Sadler's Committee whether he knew instances in which parents lived entirely on the earnings of their children, and he replied: "Yes, I met with a case, a little while ago, of a man who lives a short distance from my house, and who said to me, 'I hope you will get this Ten Hours Bill passed; I have two children, one seven and the other thirteen, at work at the factories, and I have not had the least stroke for'—I think he said—'the last thirteen months.' He told me that they were earning seven or eight shillings a week, and he said, 'That little girl has to go a mile and a half very early, to her work, and she comes home at half-past eight, and all that I see of her is to call her up in the morning, and send her to bed, and it almost makes my heart break. We cannot get any work, and I know that I am living by the death of that child'; and he cried when he told me. In fact, they weep when they tell their tales, and the poor children weep to."—Quoted, Wing, Evils of the Factory System, p. 100.

great deal of the beating in the factories was done by the workpeople without orders, or even against orders, but that only emphasised the brutality of the system. Fathers beat their own
children to save them from a worse beating by some one else;
overseers and spinners beat children, sometimes no doubt from
sheer brutality, but often because they had to get so much work
out of them or go. In 1833 nearly two-thirds of the boys in
mills, and one-third of the girls, were directly employed by men
workers,[37] but the men workers did not prescribe the hours or
the volume of work to be done. The system imposed on children
more work and longer hours than human nature could bear, and
somebody had to wring it out of them. Everywhere this cruel
necessity hemmed in the life of the new society, and the new
system wore a more inexorable face just because it made workmen, or even parents, the agents of its iron rule. In some cases,
of course, not involuntary agents, for there have always been
parents ready to exploit their children, and the factory system
offered a powerful incentive to that spirit. One witness before a
Lords Committee boasted that he had broken his child's arm
for disobedience in the mill. A system such as this was bound
to find parents, and bound to make parents, callous to their children's sufferings, and no charge more bitter could be brought
against it.

That system further aggravated the horrors of industrial life
by setting up a class of small contractors for child labour. The
piecers were generally provided and paid by the wheelmen or
spinners out of the wages per lb. weight they received from the
millowner.[38] One of the witnesses, Mr. George Gould, before
Peel's Committee in 1816, said that spinning men and women
were allowed to employ children of their own selecting, and if
they could get a child to do their business for a shilling, or one
and six, "they would take that child before they would give
four, five, six, or seven shillings to an older one."[39] In the mines,
again, the women and children who dragged the tubs were sometimes engaged and employed by the hewers. Thus the avarice
of men and women of their own class was made another
scourge for the backs of the children. The vested interest thus

---

[37] Factory Commission, Supplementary Report, 1834, part i. p.
130.
[38] See Colonel Fletcher of Bolton's letter about the Factories,
H. O., 52. 3.
[39] Quoted Hutchins and Harrison, op. cit., p. 25.

established has been at all times a serious obstacle to reforms, and the industrial life of the nation has not yet been freed from it.

The miners were a better paid class than the weavers during the last part of the period discussed in this book, but if their earnings were higher, the nature of their work made a higher expenditure on food necessary. A pamphlet was published by the Northumberland miners in 1825, with the title *A Voice from the Coal Mines*. The writer takes a man with wife and three children and puts his gross earnings at £2 a fortnight. This, he says, is a high figure. Deductions for fines, rent, and candles will bring it down to thirty shillings, or fifteen shillings a week. How far will this go?

	s.	d.
Bread, 2½ stone at 2s. 6d. per stone	6	3
1 lb. of butcher's meat a day, 7d. per lb.	4	1
2 pecks of potatoes at 1s. a peck	2	0
Oatmeal and milk for seven breakfasts at 4½d. each morning	2	8
	15	0
The family need as well to produce comfort—		
2 oz. of tea at 6d. per oz.	1	0
2 lbs. sugar at 8d. per lb.	1	4
1 lb. salt butter	1	2
1 lb. cheese	0	9
Pepper, salt, mustard, vinegar	0	4
Soap, starch, blue, etc.	1	6
Tobacco, 1½ oz.	0	5¼
1 pint of ale a day	1	9
Clothing for five persons	3	0
£1	6	3¼

Is this too much? the writer asks, and he replies that many colliers would die of want if they did not take their children to work fourteen hours a day as soon as they could speak and walk.

The Oldham miners issued a handbill in 1818 addressed to the gentlemen of Oldham and Manchester.[40] "It is well known to the greatest part of you that when you come to the side of a Coal Pit for to look down, that sight will make many of you to

[40] H. O., 42. 179.

tremble; but was you to go down to the bottom of the Pit, and there see the dangers that Colliers are exposed to, you would never think the wages too much was they to get a Pound per day. . . . We think it very hard that we must be confined in the bowels of the Earth from 9 to 10 and from that to an 11 and 12 hours or more to the day, for 10 to 12, and from that to 14 shillings per week." One of the Factory Commissioners took evidence from miners in 1833, and the answers to his questions showed that in Lancashire men got 15s. a week when in full employment, but often they did not receive more than 10s. in the week, and out of that they had to pay for tools and candles. It was stated that colliers were short lived, and that if they lived to fifty they were unable to work and came upon the parish.[41]

The depreciation of human life was thus the leading fact about the new system for the working classes. The human material was used up rapidly; workmen were called old at forty;[42] the arrangements of society ensured an infinite supply; women and children were drawn in, and at the end the working class, which was now contributing not only the men but the entire family, seemed to be what it was at the beginning, a mere part of the machinery without share in the increased wealth or the increased power over life that machinery had brought. For the revolution that had raised the standard of comfort for the rich had depressed the standard of life for the poor;[43] it had given to the capitalist a new importance, while it had degraded the workpeople to be the mere muscles of industry. Men, women, and children were in the grasp of a great machine that threatened to destroy all sense of the dignity of human life. We have now to see what inspirations were to be found in the towns where they lived, or in the character and aspect of government, justice, law, and order, to keep that struggling sense alive.

---

41 The Commission of 1842 reported that in Lancashire, Derbyshire, and Yorkshire "each generation of this class of the population is commonly extinct soon after fifty."

42 Engels, op. cit., p. 160. Sadler said that spinners rarely lived beyond forty.

43 Compare Knight's letter to Sidmouth, July 17, 1817 (H. O., 42. 168): "MY LORD,—I have always been intimately acquainted with the circumstances of the labouring class in the vicinity of Manchester, and I can assure your Lordship that they have seen very few good days since the year 1792, compared with those they experienced before that period; notwithstanding the vast improvements which have during that time been made in their Manufactures."

CHAPTER III

THE NEW TOWN

The capital idea associated with towns and town life in history is the idea of shelter. Shelter first from the primitive dangers to mankind, nature, wild beasts, hostile tribes, robber barons. The town walls enclose a refuge where men and women can break or check the power of circumstances over their lives: a fortress where, relatively secure from want and violence, they can practise the arts of peace. As their wants multiply and their ambitions expand, their imagination is enriched, and the town comes to be the shelter not of life only, but of good life, protecting and fostering not only the food and homes of men and women, but light and knowledge, the humanity and culture that come from association and experiment, ideas of liberty and justice, the desire for development and self-expression. The town thus comes to symbolise the pride of man in his power, his initiative, his energy, his sympathy, the variety and the character of his needs. To the people of ancient Athens, or of Florence or Siena in the twelfth and thirteenth century, or of Norwich or York in the fifteenth century, their town was not a mere roof from the wind and the rain: it was a living personality, expressing and cherishing the instincts, tastes, beliefs, and corporate pride of the citizens, widely and richly pictured.

This city life had produced the art and literature of Greece and Italy, and in England a spirit of enterprise in representative government and public administration that influenced profoundly the form and development of our national institutions. The history of these towns, their brisk and eager life, their triumphs and their crimes, the active share that the citizens had taken in building, adorning, defending, and serving them, were reflected in their streets and halls and churches. The old English towns were often overcrowded, unsanitary, honeycombed with alleys and courts that never saw the sun or breathed the air, but the fancy, and emotion, and the skill and craftsmanship of different ages, had made them beautiful and interesting. They were the home of a race, with all the traditions and pieties and heirlooms of a home.

It was of immense moment to the citizens of such towns whether their towns were beautiful, well governed, and administered with justice and magnanimity: this mattered much more to them than half the wars that have filled so disproportionate a page in the writing of history. It made just as great a difference to the people living under the shadow of the new industry whether Bolton and Oldham and Bradford and Manchester and Gateshead were beautiful or ugly, nobly or ignobly built and ruled. It made an even greater difference than would appear at first sight, for two reasons: England was still a country with very little government from the centre, and almost all the local responsibilities, health, housing, education, police, that are now subject to strict inspection and control, were left to the unchecked discretion and pleasure of magistrates and borough rulers. Parliament and Government knew nothing of this side of life. They passed no laws and exercised no supervision or initiative. The new industry had produced problems that were general, but except in respect of criminal law the central Government still looked upon them as local, and disclaimed all concern. The character of its local government and the success of its town life were therefore of even more engrossing concern to that population than they are to us to-day with our modern centralisation.

The form and appearance of the town were also of vital importance. There is a great chapter in Victor Hugo's *Notre Dame de Paris* describing the rise of printing and the overthrow of architecture as the principal language of mankind. But we have to remember that the population in the new industrial districts was a population for which literature scarcely existed, that the boundaries of their lives were for many the boundaries of their imagination, and that the only things that spoke to their minds were the mill in which they worked and the town in which they lived. In their work they had none of the excitement or pleasure of handicraftsmen; they worked among ugly things, in ugly factories or ugly mines, for though an engine or a wheel may have a noble beauty and design, its beauty is obscured for those who are tending one small part of it and doing nothing else. Thus the monotonous strain of an occupation that gave no scope to the mind, and its unattractive setting, rendered them all the more dependent on their surroundings, making it more certain that they would derive from their buildings and their streets and their homes the spiritual influence that others would find in their work, and others again, by means of literature, in the imagination and experience of distant worlds and distant ages. The sights and sounds of his daily life affect every one, and they do not affect a person less because he receives few impressions from other sources.

Perhaps the best way to describe the new towns and their form of government would be to say that so far from breaking or checking the power of circumstances over men's lives, they symbolised the absolute dependence and helplessness of the mass of the people living in them. They were not so much towns as barracks: not the refuge of a civilisation but the barracks of an industry. This character was stamped on their form and life and government. The mediæval town had reflected the minds of centuries and the subtle associations of a living society with a history; these towns reflected the violent enterprise of an hour, the single passion that had thrown street on street in a frantic monotony of disorder. Nobody could read in these shapeless improvisations what Ruskin called "the manly language of a people inspired by resolute and common purpose," for they represented nothing but the avarice of the jerry-builder catering for the avarice of the capitalist.[1] It would be as reasonable to examine the form and structure of an Italian *ergastulum* in order to learn the wishes and the character of the slaves who worked in it. Nobody could find a spell of beauty or romance to supply the pieties of the old city, or to kindle a civic spirit in the great tide of human life that poured in from the villages that had lost their commons or the distant towns that had lost their trade. Their towns were as ugly as their industries, with an ugliness in both cases that was a symptom of work and life in which men and women could find no happiness or self-expression; the brand of a race disinherited of its share in the arts and the beauty of the world.

"The singers have sung and the builders have builded,
    The painters have fashioned their tales of delight;
For what and for whom hath the world's book been gilded,
    When all is for these but the blackness of night?"[2]

And these towns were precisely what they looked. They were settlements of great masses of people collected in a particular place because their fingers or their muscles were needed on the brink of a stream here or at the mouth of a furnace there. These

---

[1] "The population is crowded into one dense mass, in cottages separated by narrow, unpaved, and almost pestilential streets."—Kay, quoted by Wing, *Evils of the Factory System*, p. lxxi.
[2] William Morris, *The Message of the March Wind*.

people were not citizens of this or that town, but hands of this or that master. Often the houses where they lived, and the shops where they bought their food, were supplied by their employers.

The extreme type of this organisation was the mining village. The Society for Bettering the Condition of the Poor described with great enthusiasm the arrangements made by the Duke of Bridgewater for the management of his collieries near Manchester.[3] The colliers were all his tenants at will ("an encouragement to good conduct" as the Society puts it), and when they were paid their wage each month, the shopkeeper, also the Duke's tenant, brought their bills to the colliery agent, who paid the bill and handed the surplus to the collier. "Thus the collier always has credit for necessaries and reasonable comforts; and, at the same time, is not able to squander the mass of his gains, to the injury of himself and his family." A rather different view of this arrangement was put before the public in the course of the coal strike on the Tyne in 1765, when a correspondent wrote to Lloyd's Evening Post,[4] giving a picture of the colliery economy: "This Overseer, who by the by is seldom distinguished for the amiableness of his character, constantly keeps a shop contiguous to the Pit where he lays in every necessary both for the belly and the back, and obliges the poor men to buy whatever they want from him, stopping it out of their wages at a stipulated sum a week till the whole is discharged." Even Lauderdale, the most inflexible of doctrinaire economists, supported the extension of the early and not very effective Truck Acts to mines in 1817, declaring that he knew of cases of the grossest fraud, miners being compelled to pay 12s. for 6s. worth of flour. But even if this system was administered with absolute honesty and good faith, it remained true that this society was a society depending entirely on the industry, living under its shadow, immersed in its economy, with no life or interest outside. And, of course, the colliery owners were the masters of the situation: in the Northumberland strike of 1832 one clergyman owner evicted all his tenants during a raging cholera.

This was true of the mining village, and only less true of the textile town. The capitalist built the houses. We have accounts of the system from different points of view. Cooke Tay-

---

[3] Reports of Society (1798), vol. i. p. 170.
[4] September 25, 1765.

lor[5] writing of it with enthusiasm, Gaskell[6] with dislike, and Engels[7] with the fierce abhorrence that he felt for almost all the aspects of the factory system. Cooke Taylor thought it reintroduced the old patriarchal relations of society, that the workmen were better housed, and that the fear of losing his rents operated on the mind of the millowner as a motive for humane conduct in the mill. Gaskell thought the actual accommodation better than the housing of the poor elsewhere, but he argued that the arrangement reduced the workman to a slavery as complete as that of the West Indies. Moreover, it was combined with a system of truck; in some cases the masters sold meat and coal themselves above the market price, in others they built shops and taverns, and the workmen knew that they were expected to patronise their masters' tenants. Gaskell contended also that the masters were grasping and avaricious, that they drew revenues of 13½ per cent. from these houses, and that they used this arrangement to prolong the working day. In fact the masters had found the practice so advantageous that they adopted it in the neighbourhood of towns, and not only in the remote country: the population round Hyde, Newton, and Dukinfield, which was housed in the main in this way, increased from 3,000 to 26,000 in the first thirty years of the century. This kind of economy was seen at its best in some model establishments like those of the Gregs or the Ashtons or the Strutts, where the capitalist supplied church, school, and reading-room; at its worst in cases where the masters made their workmen pay rent for houses whether they lived in them or not, and evicted them without mercy in times of strike.[8]

The industrial towns were not, of course, all of them colonies established beside a factory or mine. Manchester, Leeds, Preston, Sheffield, and other towns were not the creation of the Industrial Revolution: they were towns of antiquity renowned already as centres of special industries or trades. Such towns were not thrown up by the Industrial Revolution, but they were

---

[5] *Tour of Manufacturing Districts* (1842), p. 159.
[6] *Manufacturing Population of England* (1833), p. 347 ff.
[7] *Condition of the Working Classes in* 1844, p. 184.
[8] Engels, p. 104; cf. *Life of Bright* (Trevelyan), p. 74. There was an interesting difference between the mining and the textile colony. In the mining colony the house rent was nominal, 3d. or 6d. a week; in the textile colony it was a more or less commercial rent, 3s. or 3s. 6d. a week. The mining village was in this respect like a great estate, and of course it was a good deal older than the textile town.

overwhelmed by it. An advertisement that appeared in a Macclesfield paper in 1825 gives us a picture of the reckless way in which the new industry satisfied its demand for labour without regard to the comfort of the new town: "To the Overseers of the Poor and to families desirous of settling in Macclesfield. Wanted between 4,000 and 5,000 persons between the ages of 7 and 21 years."[9] The *Annals of Agriculture* give a picture of the plight of one of these towns when this avalanche of population swept into it. The writer is describing Preston and its neighbourhood in 1791:[10] "Sudden and great call and temptation for hands from the country, of this county and others, and many distant parts; crowded of course in their lodgings; tempted, by extra gain, to long continued application at sedentary work, in air contaminated both by the exhalation and breathing of many people together, and also the effluvia of the material used, in confined places; and, though getting good wages at what they think easy work, yet (by the natural consequence of so many different manufactures, flourishing all over the county, and so suddenly increasing, provisions being dear, as you would see from my last) perhaps living but poorly in diet, these people are frequently visited, especially in autumn and beginning of winter, with low and nervous fevers; in short, putrid and gaol distempers, that often cuts off men, leaving families behind; and who by the high rent that all the above must cause on houses, gain settlements, come from where they will." Nassau Senior has drawn a picture of those parts of Manchester that were inundated by the Irish tide: "As I passed through the dwellings of the mill hands in Irish Town, Ancoats, and Little Ireland, I was only amazed that it is possible to maintain a reasonable state of health in such homes. These towns, for in extent and number of inhabitants they are towns, have been erected with the utmost disregard of everything except the immediate advantage of the speculating builder. A carpenter and builder unite to buy a series of building sites (*i.e.* they lease them for a number of years) and cover them with so-called houses. In one place we found a whole street following the course of a ditch, because in this way deeper cellars could be secured without the cost of digging, cellars not for storing wares or rubbish, but for dwellings of human beings. Not one house of this street escaped the cholera. In general the streets of these suburbs are unpaved, with a

9 *Annual Register*, 1826, p. 62.
10 *Annals of Agriculture*, 15. 564.

dungheap or ditch in the middle; the houses are built back to back, without ventilation or drainage, and whole families are limited to a corner of a cellar or a garret."[11] Chadwick summed up the conditions under which the working classes lived with an apt illustration: "Such is the absence of civic economy in some of our towns that their condition in respect of cleanliness is almost as bad as that of an encamped horde or an undisciplined soldiery."[12] It looks as if all the creative and organising enthusiasm and spirit of the age had gone into the making of machinery and those conquests over fire and water that had produced the new industry. Men were so engrossed in building mills that towns were left to build themselves.

These towns, too, were now losing their last glimpse of nature. Formerly the men and women who lived in the English town, like those who lived in Pisa or Verona, were never far from the open country: their town life was fringed with orchards and gardens. But as the Industrial Revolution advanced, a Manchester was growing up in which the workmen would find it harder and harder to escape out of the wide web of smoke and squalor that enveloped their daily lives. And as the towns grew, the spaces of common within their borders became more valuable, and they were appropriated by the powerful classes. The Duke of Norfolk of the day is chiefly known in history as the Whig noble who was dismissed from the Lord Lieutenancy for proposing the toast of "Our Sovereign the People." To the people of Sheffield he was better known for his deeds than for his oratory, for he was a principal promoter of the Enclosure Acts that turned seven thousand acres of commons into a gold mine for a few families.[13] Civilisation, in this and other guises, was rapidly painting the green spaces black on the industrial map. Manchester still had her Angel Meadows, but they were no longer meadows, and the only angel that came near them was the Angel of Death. Cooke Taylor declared that he would rather trust himself to the savages of New Zealand than to a race bred in such surroundings. For the workman, Manchester was a prison: he was excluded from all the amenities that other classes enjoyed. "The commons on which the labourers indulged in healthful sports are enclosed; policemen

---

[11] Quoted Engels, *op. cit.*, p. 63.
[12] Quoted Hutchins, *Public Health Agitation*, p. 64.
[13] See *Some Forgotten Facts in the History of Sheffield and District*, by Carolus Paulus.

guard the streets and keep the highways clear; high walls enclose demesnes, and even the iron palisades that surround ornamental grounds are jealously planked over to prevent the humble operative from enjoying the verdure of the foliage or the fragrance of the flowers."[14] "Have we not seen the commons of our fathers enclosed by insolent cupidity—our sports converted into crimes—our holidays into fast days? The green grass and the healthful hayfield are shut out from our path. The whistling of birds is not for us—our melody is the deafening noise of the engine. The merry fiddle and the humble dance will send us to the treadmill. We eat the worst food, drink the worst drink— our raiment, our houses, our everything, bear signs of poverty, and we are gravely told that this must be our lot."[15] Dr. Hawkins had remarked to the Factory Commission the effect of this on the health of Manchester. "It is impossible not to notice the total absence of public gardens, parks, and walks at Manchester: it is scarcely in the power of the factory workman to taste the breath of nature or to look upon its verdure, and this defect is a strong impediment to convalescence from disease, which is usually tedious and difficult at Manchester."[16] Meanwhile the same process that swept the colour from the town swept the colour too from the sky. In the middle of the eighteenth century the smoke was so thick in Arnold Bennett's Five Towns on a Saturday afternoon that people had to grope their way in the streets of Burslem.[17] It is true that some observers had found an extraordinary poetry in this new atmosphere, and one critic of the day, anticipating the triumphs of the art of Muirhead Bone, wrote in rhapsody of the black streams and the chimney tops,[18] but this was an acquired taste, and it was human nature to prefer the lost rainbow to all the gorgeous canopy of mill or furnace.

Life in such a town brought no alleviation of the tyranny of

---

[14] Cooke Taylor, op. cit., p. 129.

[15] Pioneer or Trade Union Magazine, October 19, 1833.

[16] Second Report, 1833. Aston in his Picture of Manchester (1810), which does not err on the side of depreciation, observes about the streets of Manchester that attention had been "too minutely directed to the value of land to sacrifice much to public convenience or the conservation of health" (p. 220).

[17] See Wedgwood, Staffordshire Pottery and its History, p. 65. Bradford kept out factories at first on this account. See James, History of the Worsted Manufacture, p. 592.

[18] Smart, Econ. Annals, 1801–20, p. 709.

the industrial system; it only made it more real and sombre to the mind. There was no change of scene or colour, no delight of form or design to break its brooding atmosphere. Town, street, buildings, sky, all had become part of the same unrelieved picture. The men and women who left the mill and passed along the streets to their homes did not become less but more conscious of that system as a universal burden, for the town was so constructed and so governed as to enforce rather than modify, to reiterate rather than soften the impressions of an alien and unaccommodating power. The town was as little their own as the mill. For the working classes had no more control over their own affairs outside than inside the factory. The weaver of Burnley or the spinner of Rochdale had less to remind him that he counted in the life of a society than his grandfather who had helped to administer the little affairs of the village and to regulate the use of its common pastures.

Mr. and Mrs. Webb have traced the history of town government during this period, and they have shown that it took many different forms. Their general conclusion is that the Report of the Municipal Commissioners of 1834, from which most people derive their impressions of municipal administration before the reforms of the following year, misstated the quantity and quality of the vices of the old boroughs. But in all cases, whether the town was well governed or ill governed, whatever the faction or group that held the control and appointed the Borough-reeve or the Constables and the numerous minor officials, the working-class population had nothing to do with it except to obey its decrees. Manchester was an unincorporated borough, and as late as 1838 Cobden complained that this community of 200,000 people was governed from Rolleston Hall in Staffordshire. At Rolleston Hall lived the Lord of the Manor, whose steward nominated the jury of the Court-leet who held all the real power. The chief officials were a Borough-reeve and two Constables chosen annually from the most respectable of the inhabitants, by a jury impanelled by the steward of the manor, at the latter of the Court-leets which were held by the Lord of the Manor every year at Easter and Michaelmas. The Borough-reeve was always an ex-Constable. The Deputy Constable had a salary of £350 a year in addition to fees, and he became, when a man of energy like Nadin, the real ruler of Manchester. The power of this little gang was challenged in 1817 by what Mr. and Mrs. Webb call a turbulent democracy, but that democracy making its voice heard at vestry meetings, and qualifying in large

numbers for membership of the body known as Police Commissioners, was not a democracy of working men but of shopkeepers and publicans. (Professor Chapman[19] suggests that
Manchester as an unincorporated borough was free from the
restrictions that hampered immigrants elsewhere, and that it was
partly due to this that it became the centre of the new industry.)
Bolton, Bury, Rochdale, and many of the smaller towns in Lancashire and Cheshire were governed in the same way. The
Court-leet, under the presidency of the agent of the Lord of
the Manor, would meet yearly and appoint a Borough-reeve or
similar officer, Constables, Ale-tasters, Pig-ringers, Bellmen, and
other officials. If a town had a charter its government was in
form different, but the working classes had, as a rule, no more
to do with the choice or the control of the Mayors and Aldermen than they had with the choice and control of Borough-
reeves and Constables. In Preston, for example, there was a
popular franchise for the House of Commons, every male over
twenty-one with a six months' residence being an elector, but
the municipal dignitaries who governed the town itself elected
each other.[20] Leeds, again, was governed down to 1818 by a
"little group of friends and relations who served in turn as
Mayor, Aldermen, and Churchwardens, and appointed, without.
cavil, their own nominees as Overseers and Surveyors of Highways."[21] In that year the rule of this little Tory oligarchy was
disputed by the excluded Whigs, who used the vestry meetings
for that purpose and obtained from the magistracy the control
of Poor Relief and Highway Administration. When the new
working class was collected in old towns, it found itself governed by a close corporation and a municipal magistracy, and
when it was living in one of the vast tracts from which everything that is associated with the country had suddenly been
swept away except feudal forms, it was committed to the care
of a Court-leet formed from the classes that were always described at the time as "most respectable."

Whatever the form of government here or there, there was a
general agreement about the needs of the working classes. The
town which at one time in English history had provided artists,
players, minstrels, great pageants and guild festivals, represented

---

19 *Cotton Industry*, p. 154.
20 See Baines's *Lancashire*, ii. p. 491. Preston sent Henry Hunt to
the unreformed House of Commons.
21 Webb, *Manor and Borough*, 421 f.

now the meanest and barest standards of life. Scarcely a year passed without some improvement in the arts of manufacture and production, but for the great armies of men, women, and children harnessed to the thunder and lightning of the new science, the art of living had been degraded to its rudest forms. These towns illustrated, indeed, a remark made by Windham when defending a bad cause, in the debate on bull-baiting, that men of his own class were apt to think of the common people as people whose only business it was to eat, sleep, and work. The working classes were regarded as persons incapable of profiting by leisure, and fit only for the long discipline of factory hours.[22] There were conspicuous exceptions to this general spirit, and exceptions among employers. No man fought harder for a shorter working day and a more humane life for the factory workers of Lancashire than John Fielden,[23] the great cotton spinner of Todmorden, and the crusade against the cruelties of the woollen factories was launched by John Wood, the worsted manufacturer of Bradford. Rathbone Greg, one of the family of that name, wrote in favour of reducing hours. Some employers provided schools and libraries for their workpeople, and the Strutts of Derbyshire supplied not only schools and library, but a swimming-bath with an instructor, and a dancing-room. But, generally speaking, the employing class, though perhaps they would not have said of all the labours of mine and mill, with Bishop Berkeley addressing the Irish peasants, "Labor ipse voluptas," would certainly have thought that any voluptas that the poor could enjoy would do them more harm than any labour their masters could impose on them. It was a favourite argument for long hours in the mill that the hours spent elsewhere would be spent in drinking, and the favourite argument for low wages was based on the same general view of the working classes. The employing class were not of course peculiar. It was a commonplace in the speeches in Parliament, though many members must have known very little of the industrial districts, and Pitt summed up the artisan population of the northern towns as

---

22 "All experience proves that in the lower orders the deterioration of morals increases with the quantity of unemployed time of which they have the command" (An Inquiry into the Principle and Tendency of the Bill for imposing certain restrictions on Cotton Factories, 1818, quoted by Hutchins and Harrison, op. cit., p. 28).

23 The factory workpeople of Lancashire put up a statue to Fielden in gratitude for the Ten Hours Bill.

"ignorant and profligate."[24] The working men of Manchester were fond of music, and Cooke Taylor, who visited the public houses, found that there was a marked difference between the manners of the workmen in houses where music was allowed and those where it was forbidden. "The operatives of Manchester have shown their taste and capability for higher enjoyments than smoking and drinking. I have gone into some of the concert-rooms attached to favoured public-houses which they frequent, and I have never been in a more orderly and better-behaved company. The music was well selected, the songs perfectly unobjectionable; the conversation, in the intervals between the pieces, not only decorous, but to some degree refined, and the quantity of liquor consumed by each individual very trifling. But I have also been in houses where music was prohibited, and the scenes which I witnessed will not bear description."[25] Yet Cooke Taylor found that it was the practice of the magistrates, as a rule, to refuse licences to public-houses where concerts were held. It was generally agreed that drunkenness was particularly common in Lancashire, and in 1819 Norris, the Stipendiary Magistrate of Manchester, wrote to the Home Office to recommend that an Act of Parliament should be passed to make it compulsory on employers to pay their workpeople singly and at the factory. It was the general practice to pay a lump sum to one of the workpeople, who took it to the public-house where there were regular pay-tables.[26] In this way the children had to go to the public-house to be paid, and of course they were expected to drink. Thirteen years later Detroisier, a witness before the Factory Commission, pointed to the same practice as an important cause of early drinking: the piecers had to go to the public-house for their wages.[27]

It was not surprising, as Detroisier said, that the working classes who were offered little else took their pleasures in vicious

---

[24] House of Commons, May 16, 1794.

[25] *Tour in Manufacturing Districts*, p. 131.

[26] H. O., 42. 184. Miners were often paid in the same way. See *Report of Society for Bettering the Condition of the Poor*, vol. i. p. 227.

[27] The authorities were not always agreed on the disadvantages of drinking. In 1819 the reformers started a temperance crusade as a way of starving the revenue. The Manchester churchwardens spent £80 in placarding the town with an appeal to the citizens to show their attachment to King, Church, and Constitution by drinking the good old English drinks (Prentice's *Manchester*, p. 151).

and brutal amusements. These included bull-baiting and cock-fighting, practices that were still legal down to 1833. There was a regular trade connected with the latter sport, men appearing as cock-feeders and cock-heel makers in the Directories of the time.[28] It was stated in the House of Commons that bull-baiting was a favourite sport in Lancashire, Staffordshire, and Shropshire, but that it was unknown in Yorkshire and Northumberland. Attempts were made in 1800 and 1802 to put down these practices, but without success. It is not always easy to trace the line that divides a noble from a barbarous pleasure in the treatment of animals, or to ascertain the exact ratio that prowess must bear to suffering if a sport that involves the infliction of pain is to rank as a sport that gentlemen ought to enjoy. In the debates in Parliament in 1800 and 1802 a good many speakers, and some, at any rate, of the promoters of the Bill, were preoccupied with the effects of bull-baiting in making workmen disorderly and idle. It was unfortunate for the Bill that it was in the hands of Sir Richard Hill, a typical representative of the school that rarely supports a good proposal except for bad reasons. So far as the question of cruelty was concerned, there were three lines of argument. It was possible to distinguish bull-baiting from stag-hunting and fox-hunting, or to approve of both or to condemn both. Windham, for example, who opposed legislation strongly, argued that bull-baiting was no more cruel than hunting, and that though he was not a sportsman himself, he was not prepared to forbid the sports of his friends. He would, however, introduce such a Bill himself if Parliament interfered with the pleasures of the poor. Canning extolled the sports of all classes, declaring of bull-baiting that "the amusement was a most excellent one; it inspired courage, and produced a nobleness of sentiment and elevation of mind."[29] On the other side, speakers like Sheridan contended that the poor were capable of enjoying other amusements, that there was nothing to prevent them from playing cricket, and that though the magistrates were far too ready to suppress innocent diversions, this particular cruelty was generally recognised as a scandal. Sheffield had apparently at one time a cruel amusement of its own[30] that disappeared under the pressure of public opinion. Cocks were

---

[28] Leader, *Sheffield in the Eighteenth Century*, p. 44.
[29] Canning modified his views two years later and decided not to vote either way. See *Windham's Papers*, ii. 189.
[30] Leader, *Sheffield in the Eighteenth Century*, p. 46.

tied to a stake and then used as targets by men and boys who
pelted them with large billets of wood. Mackenzie,[31] describing the Northumberland pitmen, mentioned that they dressed
in gaudy colours on holidays, with variegated patterns, and that
their amusements were cock-fighting, bowling, foot-races, hand-
ball, quoits, cards, and when possible hunting or fowling.
Yorkshire was pre-eminently the county for horse races. The
"Lancashire way of fighting" was the common description of a
particularly violent kind of single combat, of which Baines gives
an account in his *History of Lancashire*.[32] "At almost every Assizes at Lancaster several individuals are tried for murder or man-
slaughter, arising out of battles, when, to the astonishment of
strangers, evidence is given of parties mutually agreeing to fight
'up and down,' which includes the right of kicking (or purring,
as it is called) on every part of the body, in all possible situations, and of squeezing the throat or 'throttling' to the very verge
of death. At races, fairs, and on other public occasions, contests
of this nature are witnessed by crowds of persons who take part
on each side, with as much interest as is excited by the regular
boxing matches of the south. That death often occurs in such
battles will not be thought extraordinary, especially when it is
considered that clogs or heavy wooden-soled shoes, with iron
plates and studded with large nails, are commonly worn in the
districts where this barbarous custom prevails."

Bamford gives an account of a fight of his father's that lasted
two full hours, "up and down fighting," at the Boar's Head at
Middleton.[33] It was characteristic of the upper-class treatment
of such difficulties that the method adopted for putting down
this amusement was the revival by some of the judges, in a country where every civilising influence was withheld, of the old
punishment of burning in the hand.[34]

Just at the close of our period Lord Shaftesbury was travelling
by one of the new railways through the Midlands, and he put

[31] Mackenzie, *View of the County of Northumberland*, 1825, p.
208 f.

[32] Vol. i. p. 537.

[33] A witness, John Taylor, before the Select Committee on Accidents in Mines in 1835, said that he had known the mining population in Cornwall for thirty-six years, and that great changes had been
made by the influence of Methodism: "there is not now the fighting
which was formerly prevalent."

[34] Baines's *Lancashire*, ii. p. 537. This punishment was abolished
in 1822.

into his diary this significant and interesting reflection: "These towns always affect me—the mass of human kind whom nothing restrains but force or habit, uninfluenced because unreached by any moral or religious discipline, presents a standing miracle."[35] The idea of the town as a focus for civilisation, a centre where the emancipating and enlightening influences of the time can act rapidly and with effect, the school of social arts, the nursery of social enterprise, the witness to the beauty and order and freedom that men can bring into their lives, had vanished from all minds. Englishmen thought of their great towns not with hope, or pride, or ambition, but with a haunting fear, reminding themselves not of the light that might be diffused, but of the darkness that overspread them. The real difficulty was that most of the upper classes, though they were afraid of the darkness, were still more afraid of the light. Place wrote in 1832, the Whigs being then in office: "Ministers and men in power, with nearly the whole body of those who are rich, dread the consequences of teaching the people more than they dread the effect of their ignorance."[36] If this was true in 1832, it was still truer during the generation that preceded the passing of Reform; if it was true of a Government that contained Grey and Brougham, it was certainly much truer of the Sidmouths and Liverpools and even of Pitt and Canning. The Government so described by Place was the first to give a sixpence of public money to education.

The state of the manufacturing districts in this respect was one of the chief scandals of Europe. In 1818 about one in four of the children of the poor were receiving education of some kind,[37] and Lancashire was one of the most backward counties. But the mere statement of this figure would give an exaggerated impression of the education of the working classes.[38] In

---

[35] Hodder, *Life and Work of Lord Shaftesbury*, vol. i. p. 257.

[36] Graham Wallas, *Life of Place*, p. 338.

[37] Spencer Walpole, *op. cit.*, i. 212.

[38] Cf. evidence before Select Committee on Accidents in Mines, 1835, 1198. The Factory Commission Report of 1834 contains a table giving returns from factories of the workers in Lancashire mills: 17 per cent. could not read and 62 per cent. could not write. In Yorkshire the figures were 15 and 52, in Cheshire 10 and 53. Aberdeen was the most backward county in Scotland, and there the figures were 7 and 54. In Lanarkshire and Renfrewshire, the two largest factory counties, the figures were 4 and 46 and 3 and 46 respectively. Dr. Mitchell's Report, p. 46.

1842 a careful review of the state of the industrial districts was made for the Report of the Commission on Children's Employment, and the results were remarkable. The Commissioners found "that neither in the new Colliery and Mining towns which have suddenly collected together large bodies of the people in new localities, nor in the towns which have suddenly sprung up under the successful pursuit of some new branch of Trade and Manufacture, is any provision made for Education by the establishment of Schools with properly qualified teachers, nor for affording the means of moral and religious instruction and training, nor for supplying the spiritual wants of the people; nor in general is there any provision whatever for the extension of educational and religious institutions corresponding with the extension of the population." In Derbyshire, where there were a few free and national schools, colliers' children were formally excluded by the rules. At this time Leonard Horner reported that in an area of thirty-two square miles comprising Oldham and Ashton, with a population of 105,000, there was not a single public day school for poor children.[39] In 1839, 1840, and 1841, 40 per cent. of the men and 65 per cent. of the women married or witnessing marriages in Lancashire and Cheshire could not sign their names.[40] Where schools existed, the education given was of the poorest quality. Schoolmasters were often men or women who had been disabled by accidents in the factory, or had failed to earn a livelihood in any other occupation. "The refuse of other callings," they were described later; sometimes they could not write themselves.

In this respect England was far behind the rest of the civilised world; "Prussia is before us; Switzerland is before us; France is before us. There is no record of any people on earth so highly civilised, so abounding in arts and comforts, and so grossly generally ignorant as the English."[41] Most of the Governments of Europe interested themselves in education during the eighteenth century: Prussia, Austria, and the Catholic and Protestant States of Germany. Turgot, Condorcet, and Talleyrand devised elaborate schemes for France, and these schemes were carried out in part by Napoleon. In England the importance of public education had been preached by thinkers so diverse as Blackstone, Adam Smith, Eden, Malthus, and Bentham. Yet in Eng-

---

[39] Factory Inspector's Report for 1842, p. 21.
[40] Porter, *Progress of the Nation*, 1851, p. 700.
[41] Dean Alford in 1839.

land no Minister ever showed a trace of the imagination or the zeal that had inspired the Fredericks in Prussia, Maria Theresa in the Empire, Turgot or Condorcet or Napoleon in France, or Florida Blanca in Spain. England almost alone in Europe was quite content to leave the education of the poor to the charity-schools and the Sunday-schools.

There were two statesmen who tried to bring England into the daylight. One was Whitbread, the other Brougham. In 1807 Whitbread introduced a Bill for the general provision of elementary schools throughout England, but the House of Lords rejected it at the instance of the Lord Chancellor (Eldon) and the Archbishop of Canterbury (Manners-Sutton), the only support for it coming from Lord Holland who introduced it, and from Lord Stanhope. The general hostility of the governing classes was shown in the adverse reports of the magistrates among whom the Bill was circulated. The Bill in its original form made it compulsory on all parishes to provide education out of the rates, but Sturges Bourne persuaded the House of Commons to make this provision optional. The vestries were to report to the magistrate, and the magistrates to sanction a rate. All children of the poor were to receive two years' schooling free.

There were two powerful currents of hostile opinion. One was represented in the speeches of Windham and Giddy. Windham, after the death of Fox, was the best scholar in the House of Commons, and Giddy[42] was President of the Royal Society and a great patron of scientific enterprise. Windham declared himself a sceptic as to the value of the "diffusion of knowledge," and defended his view by a significant illustration: "It was said, look at the state of the savages when compared to ours. A savage among savages was very well, and the difference was only perceived when he came to be introduced into civilised society." He also quoted Dr. Johnson as saying that it was not right to teach reading beyond a certain extent in society. "The danger was, that if the teachers of good and the propagators of bad principles were to be candidates for the control of mankind, the latter would be likely to be too successful."[43] Giddy developed this argument three months later: "However specious in theory the project might be, of giving education to the labouring classes of the poor, it would in effect be found to be prejudicial to their morals and happiness; it would teach them to despise their

---

[42] 1767–1839.
[43] *Windham's Speeches*, vol. iii. p. 17. (April 24, 1807).

lot in life, instead of making them good servants in agriculture, and other laborious employments to which their rank in society had destined them; instead of teaching them subordination, it would render them factious and refractory, as was evident in the manufacturing counties; it would enable them to read seditious pamphlets, vicious books, and publications against Christianity; it would render them insolent to their superiors; and in a few years the result would be that the legislature would find it necessary to direct the strong arm of power towards them, and to furnish the executive magistrates with much more vigorous laws than were now in force."[44]

The other contrary current was represented in the speech of the Archbishop of Canterbury, who objected to any system that put the control of education elsewhere than in the hands of the bishop of the diocese.

Such daily education as was given was given in schools founded by one of two rival societies. One society, founded in 1808 and patronised by the rich Whigs and Quakers, adopted Joseph Lancaster's ideas of popular education with general religious instruction; the other representing the interests of the Established Church and adopting the ideas of Dr. Bell, was founded in 1811.[45] The one movement blossomed into the British and Foreign Schools Society; the other into the National Society for Promoting the Education of the Poor in the Principles of the Church of England. Whitbread's successor in the leadership of the cause of popular education was Brougham, whose exertions in this cause were perhaps the happiest chapter in his chequered career. In 1820 he introduced a Bill, based on the reports of a Committee which he had persuaded Parliament to appoint four years earlier, empowering Quarter Sessions to found schools on the representations of two magistrates, the local clergyman, or five resident householders. The schoolmaster was to be appointed, not by the magistrates as in Whitbread's Bill, but by the vestry; the clergyman was to have the right to examine and dismiss him. Further, the Bishop could act as Visi-

---

[44] *Hansard*, ix. p. 798nn.

[45] Even Pitt, who had been content to leave the country entirely destitute of education, wrote to Bishop Tomline in 1802 that he was strongly persuaded that Mr. Lancaster's project, if allowed to operate to any great extent, was likely to produce great mischief, and that it was very important to find some safe and effectual substitute (Rose, *Pitt and Napoleon*, p. 110).

tor or appoint the Dean or Archdeacon as Visitor, and the Visitor could remove the master. The Bill passed its second reading, but Brougham then withdrew it. According to the *Annual Register* there was violent opposition alike from the Church and the Nonconformists; according to a statement made by Brougham fourteen years later, it was the hostility of the Nonconformists that decided him to abandon the Bill. But though Brougham did not fare any better than Whitbread in this part of his scheme, his efforts had one permanent important result. In 1816 he obtained the appointment of a Commission to enquire into the abuses of Charitable Endowments, and this inquiry was the parent of the Charity Commission.

More significant than the dislike of education was the spirit of those who favoured it. Hannah More allowed no writing for the poor because she did not want to make fanatics; one of the Manchester parsons[46] told the Factory Commission in 1833 that writing was not taught in any of the Church Sunday-schools, and there was great objection to teaching the poor to write among many persons who contributed liberally to the support of Sunday-schools. Mrs. Trimmer, regarded in many quarters as dangerously advanced, kept her ambitions within reason; she put it that the lower sort of children might be so far civilised as not to be disgusting.

Detroisier, the secretary of the National Political Union, who had begun life in the mill and had afterwards become a lecturer and a social worker, the founder of Mechanics' Institutions in Hulme and Salford, cited the remark of a large employer, when asking him to recommend a porter, as characteristic of very many of his class: "I don't want one of your intellectuals; I want a man that will work and take his glass of ale: I'll think for him."[47] This is an excellent description of the upper-class mind. Some would concede to Hannah More that property would be safer if the poor were taught to read the Bible, but they were determined that the upper classes should do their thinking for them.

The objection to an educated working class was part of the general philosophy of the governing world. For the first time there existed a vast proletariate, with no property but its labour, and therefore in the eyes of its rulers bound by no ties to the

---

[46] First Report, Factory Commission, Evidence of Huntingdon, Rector of St. John's. Tufnell, p. 49.

[47] First Report of Factory Commission, 1833, E, p. 18.

society in which it lived except by the ties that discipline could create. The upper classes would have said of this proletariate what Ireton, speaking in the Council of the Parliamentary Army in 1647, had said of tenants, labourers, tradesmen, and all persons outside the men of landed property and the members of trading corporations, that "they had no interest in the country except the interest of breathing." The working classes were therefore regarded as people to be kept out of mischief, rather than as people with faculties and characters to be encouraged and developed. They were to have just so much instruction as would make them more useful workpeople; to be trained, in Hannah More's phrase, "in habits of industry and piety." Thus not only the towns they lived in, the hours they worked, the wages they received, but also the schools in which some of their children were taught their letters, stamped them as a subject population, existing merely for the service and profit of other classes.

CHAPTER IV

JUSTICE

In the speech that marked the beginning of the long duel with France, Pitt made the proud declaration that "it was the boast of the law of England that it afforded equal security and protection to the high and the low, the rich and the poor." This statement, when placed beside the cold facts of contemporary English life, looks like sheer hypocrisy. When other politicians repeated it after Pitt had dragooned the country by Treason and Sedition Acts, it looked more like hypocrisy than ever. But the men who said this were not consciously misrepresenting the truth: they had a definite picture of England in their mind.

Within a certain charmed circle England remained, even in the darkest hours of superstition and coercion, a remarkably free society. We have only to think of the speeches of Fox and Sheridan, or the poems of Byron and Shelley, to recall the latitude allowed to criticism in certain ranks; within those ranks rebellion and free thinking enjoyed a licence that seemed astonishing to those who tried to say and write what they thought under a Continental government. For the power of the aristocracy had prevented the growth of a system which in other countries gave the official special advantages in respect of justice over the private citizen. Hence at the beginning of the nineteenth century the upper-class Englishman was the freest man in Europe. So clearly was the immunity of this society recognised, that the blasphemy laws were never set in motion against any member of the upper class, though the Saints were making them a terror to the poor. Canning and his fellow-writers on the Anti-Jacobin could take what liberties they pleased with the Liturgy or the Bible. Of course free criticism was not encouraged. Miss Edgeworth wrote *The Absentee* as a play, wishing to strike the conscience of Irish society in London, but Sheridan warned her that it would never pass the Censor. But men of the privileged classes could say and write things that would have carried a rebel into jail under any other government in Europe.

This was a very important fact, and it had momentous consequences in English history. It was the result of the Whig Revolution, which put an end to the state of things that had grown up under the Stuarts with courts that were the servile instruments of the Crown. An Englishman, since the beginning of the eighteenth century, had been tried by judges who were not the mere creatures of the Court, but men holding an office from which they could not be removed except by an address from both Houses of Parliament. In the country, justice was administered by a country gentleman, not some alien official like an intendant, but a squire living among the people over whose affairs he had jurisdiction, and therefore alive to all the influences of local association and atmosphere. This was what the upper-class Englishman meant by the "equity of our laws," why they talked of English justice with an enthusiasm that bewilders readers of Fielding or Goldsmith, or those who follow the labours of Romilly and Bentham, and why Pitt, whose long career opened with such promise of reform and improvement, never put a finger on the worst abuses of that system. The caprice of the Crown had been abolished: the supremacy of the Law had been established, and in a class that regarded the defence of the rights of property as the main business of society, the spirit and the working of English institutions all tended to protect the normal Englishman from the encroachments and the extortions of the State. Trial by jury and independent judges, these were the securities of English justice; the normal Englishman was thought to be the Englishman with property, and a system that provided for him was equitable and adequate.

Having established this broad principle that justice should be in the hands of representative and independent men, who held the large general views of their society, and would not serve the insidious aims of a Court, the upper classes paid little attention to the abuses that disgraced the actual administration of the law. As the new population increased and new problems arose, the machinery of the law-courts became obsolete and defective. Instead of reforming the system, the governing class contented itself with adding new felonies and making the penal law more savage. By the end of the century, with the panic of the Revolution, a new danger came into their minds. There was now no quarrel between the aristocracy and the Crown, and whereas a generation or two before English gentlemen thanked heaven that they did not live under the justice of a despotism, they now prayed to God that they might never live under the justice of an anarchy. The days of the Stuarts seemed remote compared with the misfortunes that had overtaken property across the Channel. Consequently the majority of the upper classes came to look upon judges and magistrates not as persons trying to do justice between man and man, but as the most effective part of the system of repression. Pitt gave the keynote in the remarkable speech that he made on the trial of Muir,[1] when in whitewashing the notorious Braxfield he declared that "the judges would have been highly culpable if, vested as they were with discretionary powers, they had not employed them for the present punishment of such daring delinquents and the suppression of doctrines so dangerous to the country."[2] From this time judges and magistrates, with few exceptions, regarded themselves as the policemen of the existing order and the predominant ideas. The rebels among the aristocracy were safe from them, as a rule, for tradition was too strong, and the men themselves too formidable.[3] There was some check on the power of the magistrates in London in the independence of the London juries displayed in the acquittal of some famous prisoners such as Thomas Hardy. In the new industrial districts the magistrates had a comparatively free hand and there the fear of industrial disorder was much stronger.

One of the kindest, and one of the most enlightened men of the time, a Spitalfields manufacturer, speaking of the poor crowded together there, and the good effects of Sunday-schools, remarked: "I believe no instance is to be found where so multitudinous a poor congregate together in so small a space with so little inconvenience to their neighbours."[4] The upper classes could rarely escape from this way of looking at the working classes, but whereas Mr. Hale talked of inconvenience, the north-country magistrate would have used a sharper word. The law put unlimited powers into their hands, and in using those powers they did not think of the working classes as men and women to whom they owed justice, but as a body of revels dangerous to society. In the letters from magistrates to the Home Office, and from the Home Office to magistrates, the law is treated

---

[1] Muir was a young Scottish reformer who was tried for sedition and sentenced to fourteen years' transportation. Braxfield, characterised by Cockburn as a coarse and dexterous ruffian, is drawn in Stevenson's *Weir of Hermiston*. He was the Jeffreys of Scotland. Every member of the jury (packed by the presiding judge) had belonged to an association which had expelled Muir for his political opinions. Those opinions differed scarcely at all from Pitt's earlier opinions.—Erskine May, ii, 293.

[2] House of Commons, March 10, 1794.

[3] Pitt once thought of trying to send Fox to the Tower, but he decided that it would be too great a risk.

[4] *Report on Mendicity*, 1815; see *Ann. Reg.*, 1815, p. 599.

as an instrument not of justice but of repression. There is consequently no aspect of their lives in which the working classes appear so conspicuously as a helot population. For to the inequalities of the law inseparable from the inequalities of circumstances, and aggravated by all the gross anomalies of the legal system of the time, there was added the inequality that was deliberately set up when the courts became the recognised instrument of a class supremacy. Moreover, the workman was rarely tried by his peers. He was generally sent to prison by a magistrate. Lord Holland dwelt on this as a growing evil.

A great part of the new population was subject to county magistrates. This was true even of Manchester with her population of 200,000 people,[5] and many of the Lancashire and Yorkshire towns were in the same case. For many years it was the custom in the Duchy of Lancaster to exclude manufacturers from the Bench,[6] and at first sight it might seem that landowners and parsons would be able to deal justly with the workmen, who were not their own servants but the servants of a class that many of them disliked and despised. The Home Office records show, however, that there were overruling prejudices in their minds scarcely less fatal to justice than the motive of direct and evident self-interest. The country gentlemen were apt to give the manufacturers a wide berth until they became millionaires, but they had their own quarrel with the class that the manufacturers oppressed. If the employers regarded the discontent of the workmen as a menace to profits, the squires and parsons regarded it as a menace to property and order. There were some respects, indeed, in which the manufacturers understood the new population better than did the territorial class. Philips, a leading Manchester manufacturer, though one of the least enlightened of his class on the subject of factory legislation, protested strongly in Parliament against the use of spies, a favourite method among several of the county magistrates of securing the ends of justice. On the Combination Laws the magistrates were sometimes more hostile than the masters, and even went so far as to put those laws into force against workmen acting in concert with their masters. It would certainly have been difficult to find any set of manufacturers more destitute of sympathy with the working classes than the active justices who looked after the

---

[5] After 1813 Manchester had one stipendiary magistrate.
[6] Webb, *Parish and County*, p. 383n. See Debate, House of Commons, May 12, 1813.

working men of Manchester. For the rest the new power was in most places well represented on the Bench. Colonel Fletcher of Bolton was a coalowner, and he took care that his brother magistrates put his workmen in prison when they struck for an advance of wages.[7] The factory visitors reported in 1828 that the Factory Acts were a dead letter at Wigan, because all the magistrates there were manufacturers and therefore disqualified for trying breaches of the Act.[8] Consequently they all broke it at their pleasure. In other parts of the country, manufacturers were often on the Bench, and there were frequent complaints to the Home Office of the abuse by employers of their powers. In 1820 the High Constable of Bradford in Wiltshire brought serious charges of this kind against the employers in his neighbourhood,[9] and Lord Bute in 1826 said that the case of Glamorganshire was serious:[10] in the hundred of Caerphilly and Merthyr Tydfil the only magistrates were two ironmasters employing four or five thousand workmen apiece, who were constantly trying their workmen for offences against themselves.[11] These men were responsible for carrying out the Truck Acts or the Acts prohibiting the payment of wages in kind. A Monmouthshire coalowner, who was a magistrate, wrote to the Home Office in 1830 during a strike that was partly a strike against the illegal truck system: "The steps I shall propose to take will be to have the men apprehended who have left their employ and to have them sent to the treadmill."[12]

The Combination Laws, though they drew an important distinction between masters and men, did on paper profess to restrain the masters from combining. In fact they were never interpreted by the magistrates as applying to the masters at all. The masters combined freely, and in no single instance were they punished. Their immunity was indeed so well established that they never thought it necessary to put the thinnest disguise on their combinations against their men. In 1823 four of the chief employers in Knaresborough and the neighbourhood, employing some fifteen hundred linen weavers, concerted a large reduction in wages, following on three reductions in eight years.

[7] H. O., 42. 179.
[8] H. O., 52. 5.
[9] H. O., 44. 1.
[10] H. O., 52. 4.
[11] H. O., 52. 4.
[12] H. O., 52. 9.

The men struck, but after twenty-eight weeks they had to yield. The masters, who combined openly for this purpose, published an abstract of the Combination Law to prevent people from subscribing for the support of the men.[13] The employers knew very well that they ran no risks. Gravener Henson, in 1811, tried to prosecute some masters at Nottingham who had published their resolutions to reduce wages. He went to the magistrates, who said they had not sufficient evidence. He produced the newspaper, and invited them to summon the printer and hear his evidence. They advised him to go no further. He made a fresh application, and in form the magistrates assented, but when he asked for a warrant the Town Clerk refused to grant it, because he could not prove the parish in which they had met.[14] No formal difficulties like these ever stood in the way of a magistrate if the offenders were workpeople and not masters.

A still more graphic and striking illustration of the justice with which the magistrates treated the claims of the working classes is provided in the history of the struggles of miners and ironworkers against the fraudulent truck system. Parliament did not concede much to the working classes, but the concessions, such as they were, lost all their value from the refusal of the magistrates to carry out legislation that was obnoxious to the masters. Down to the end of our period colliers and ironworkers were engaged in a series of strikes to compel the masters to do what the law ordered them to do; these strikes were conducted with bitter feeling on both sides, and the maintenance of order became a serious difficulty; the soldiers were called in, life was lost, and this confusion and misery were caused, not by demands from the men for better wages or conditions, but by the plain and open violation of the law on the part of the masters. The fact that the law was not carried out is established, not from the controversial manifestoes of the men, but from the frank admissions of the magistrates, who, for the most part, seem to have taken it for granted, that if the masters would not obey the law, nothing could be done to enforce obedience. When the trouble became serious they met, not to put the Truck Acts into operation against the masters, but the Vagrancy Acts against the men. As they could not persuade the masters to obey the law, they sent the men to prison for trying to make them do so.

---

[13] Committee on Artisans and Machinery, p. 541.
[14] Committee on Artisans and Machinery, p. 280 f.

There was a Truck Act on the Statute Book as early as 1726,[15] the first applying to the woollen industry. From 1749[16] there are various Truck Acts applying to other industries, including the iron, but not the coal and steel industries. In the coal and iron works of the Midlands and Wales the masters paid to a large extent by means of their "Tommy-shops," and the abuses were particularly flagrant. This system was a perpetual cause of ill-feeling in the life of the district; it poisoned the relations of masters and men, and it vitiated all the calculations of the wages paid, so that the men felt that in every quarrel the employers were deceiving the public by their statements of the "ample pay and constant work"[17] enjoyed by their misguided men. This was the feeling of others beside workmen. In the course of a dispute in 1816, in which colliers and ironworkers were resisting a reduction of wages, the solicitor to the Bench at Merthyr wrote to the papers to say that the colliers had 15s. a week and the firemen 21s. to 25s. a week.[18] But a magistrate from a neighbouring hundred wrote to the Home Office: "Nothing could be more untrue than the letter in the *Courier*, signed Wm. Meyrick, with respect to wages per week, as the mode is to pay them by weight or measure, and that only monthly, which gives the Iron Masters an opportunity of imposing on the people by obliging them to go to their Shops."[19] In the following year a number of Staffordshire magistrates, not themselves employers, impressed by the scandals of this system, obtained special legislation from Parliament, two Acts[20] being passed forbidding the payment of wages in the steel and coal industries otherwise than in money. Three years later the law was stiffened, an Act being passed in 1820 forbidding employers to make any stipulation as to the expenditure of wages.[21] This law was to be renewed from year to year. But the laws remained idle, and in 1821 the whole district was blazing again.

The quarrel began with a reduction of wages in the Wellington district; the masters agreed among themselves on a reduction of 6d. a day, and after some rioting, in the course of which the

---

[15] 12 George I. c. 34.
[16] 22 George II. c. 27.
[17] H. O., 42. 154.
[18] *Ann. Reg.*, 1816, Chronicle 167.
[19] H. O., 42. 159.
[20] 1817: 57 George III. c. 115; 57 George III. c. 122.
[21] 1 George IV. c. 93.

yeomanry were called in and two workmen were killed, a compromise was reached and wages were reduced by 4d. a day.[22] Next year there was a new movement among the masters, beginning at Tipton, and this time the employers decided to recoup themselves for the fall in the price of iron, not only by reducing wages, but by raising prices in their "Tommy-shops." Of this, wrote a correspondent, whose letter was sent to the Home Office,[23] "the men have now availed themselves as a plausible and (I may safely add) a real cause of complaint. By this practice the Coal and Iron masters compel their workmen to accept of two-thirds of their wages in goods, such as Sugar, Soap, Candles, Meat, Bacon, Flour, etc., instead of money, at an unreasonable large profit. This appears the real cause of complaint more than the reduction of wages, and is really very hard upon them, and as the masters contrive to evade the Act of Parliament the Men seem to have no relief but ceasing to work."

Faced with the prospect of a serious strike and a great deal of misery, the magistrates gave their attention to the subject with remarkable results. In the first place, the two parson magistrates of Bilston wrote to the Home Office enlarging on the merits and popularity of the truck system, which Parliament had pronounced illegal.[24] The magistrates of the district then proceeded to issue a hand-bill[25] stating that after a meeting of the principal coal and iron masters they were convinced that the men were receiving from 2s. 6d. to 3s. a day, "with the Advantages of three Pints of Pit Drink, and Firing for their Families, and can, at the present Moment, generally have full employment"; that the practice of paying otherwise than in money was rare, and that they intended to put into force the Vagrant Act against "all Persons going about from Door to Door or placing themselves in Streets, Highways, or Passages, to beg or gather Alms." The men refused the protection of the law for their legal rights, adopted violent measures for checking the supply of labour, "cutting the ropes and ducking and half drowning" blacklegs. In the course of an affair between a mob of colliers waiting for some returning blacklegs and the soldiers, a collier was shot and killed.[26]

---

[22] H. O., 40. 16
[23] H. O., 40. 17.
[24] H. O., 40. 17.
[25] H. O., 40. 17.
[26] H. O., 40. 17.

In his district there was one magistrate who thought that laws ought to be put in force even if the powerful classes disliked them. He was a parson in Wolverhampton named Haden. He wrote an interesting letter describing his experience in administering the law:—[27]

> . . . On some of the Coal Masters still persisting in the oppressive practice of paying their Workmen in *Truck* or *Tommy-Tickets* so called, I issued four Summonses and heard them this Morning at our Public Office. It was curious to see what artifices they made use of, to prevent my fixing upon the most proper person to pay the just demands of the Complainants. One gave me for Answer that "he only brings the money to pay the workmen." He then brought forward one Walter Davis (no doubt the Butty Collier) who said that "he was not a Butty Collier, but merely a *Dogger* or overlooker, to see that the men do their work." Various other evasive answers were given; but I at last told them that if they did not immediately pay them *in Cash*, I would make an order and enforce it. I procured a Tommy Ticket from one of the Complainants, which I have the honour to inclose, that you may see their plan. No name is affixed as to the Master, Issuer, or Shopkeeper: but the Interpretation of it is—that *Jones* is to receive 8s. in Truck from E. P. N.—a *Shopkeeper whose Name is North, in league with the Master*!! When I added that if the Men were not instantly paid their *full* Wages in Money without any abatement, *I would lay that Ticket before the Higher Powers*, they seemed alarmed and paid them instantly. The Court was crowded with Colliers, all of whom appeared much pleased with my decisions. I mention this merely to show you by what means 'they would become peaceable and fully satisfied.
>
> This information I hope and trust will convince you and His Majesty's Government, as to the indispensable necessity of *continuing* the 1 G. 4. cap. 93. You perhaps will coincide with me in opinion that the following clause would answer every purpose, namely, *That no Tommy Ticket, or Truck, shall be allowed to be given or set off as and for Workmen's Wages; one Justice of the peace to Summon, and the Adjudication of two or more Justices to*

---

[27] H. O., 40. 17.

be final, and no Appeal.—I have the honor to be, sir, your
most obedient humble Servant,

A. B. HADEN.

The right Honorable ROBERT PEEL,
    etc. etc. etc.

TICKET.

Due to   JONES.

Eight Shillings —— Pence.

8/-   From E. P. N.

1820. 17.

A fierce struggle was carried on, at the same time, over the
same question, in Monmouth and on the Welsh borders, and
the men succeeded in obtaining a declaration from the ironmasters that they would drop their tommy-shops and pay in cash.[28]
This promise was apparently kept, at any rate for a time, but of
course it did not cover the collieries not worked by ironmasters.
In 1823 a magistrate, who had interested himself in the men's
grievances from the first, wrote to the Home Office:[29] "The
workmen in the collieries of this neighbourhood are at present
in a state of great irritation and discontent owing to that abuse
which has been the real though sometimes latent cause of all
the disturbances which have taken place amongst them, namely
the pernicious practice of paying workmen in shop goods instead
of money, which now prevails here to a degree unknown since
the riots of 1816, and which has been resorted to by the Master
Colliers (who for the most part are not proprietors) since the
conversation in the House of Commons on the renewal of the
late Act obtained at the insistence of the Staffordshire magistrates. . . . The rapid rise in the prices of provisions since and
the unrestrained manner in which the men are compelled for
the most part to receive their wages in goods instead of in money
at prices 20, 30, and 40 per cent. higher than in the markets
and open shops have of late been laying the sure foundations
of future disturbances."

Nearly ten years later, when there were disturbances in the

---

[28] H. O., 52. 3.
[29] H. O., 44. 13.

Dowlais and others works, the officer sent down to restore order reported that the truck system survived, and that many workmen were compelled to pay 15 or 20 per cent. above the market price for their provisions.[30] In the same year (1832) the masters met at Abergavenny and undertook to abolish the truck system, which "some of them were reluctantly obliged to acknowledge was one of the original causes of the agitation in the mining district."[31] In the colliers' strike in Staffordshire in 1831 the potters held a great meeting at Hanley and decided to help the miners, "in the defense of their just rights."[32] Among the miners' grievances recited in their resolution an important place was given to the continuance of the illegal truck system. It is not surprising that the system was still in force in remote places in 1842,[33] seeing that it flourished in districts where there were powerful landlords, like Lord Bute and the Duke of Beaufort, taking an active part in the administration of justice and public affairs, although it was admittedly the cause of continual disorder.

The lives and liberties of a class that was unable to secure from the magistrates a semblance of the protection that Parliament had designed for it, were not likely to count for very much in the eyes of the authorities that administered the law. It is not too much to say, in the light of the Home Office papers, that none of the personal rights attaching to Englishmen possessed any reality for the working classes. The magistrates and their clerks recognised no limit to their power over the freedom and the movements of working men. The Vagrancy Laws seemed to supersede the entire charter of an Englishman's liberties. They were used to put into prison any man or woman of the working class who seemed to the magistrates an inconvenient or disturbing character. They offered the easiest and most expeditious way of proceeding against any one who tried to collect money for the families of locked-out workmen,[34] or to disseminate literature that the magistrates thought undesirable. Lloyd, the clerk of the magistrates at Stockport, one of the most energetic officers of the law in the north of England, believed that he could throw into prison as rogues and vagabonds the spinners who

---

[30] H. O., 40. 30.
[31] H. O., 40. 30.
[32] H. O., 52. 15.
[33] Mines' Report, 1842.
[34] Cf. H. O., 42. 118, December 13.

were on strike parading the streets of that town.[35] The Home Office, however, endorsed the letter "There must be proof of Poverty and of refusal to work."

A parson magistrate wrote to the Home Office in 1817 to say that he had seized two men who were distributing Cobbett's pamphlets and had them well flogged at the whipping-post under the Vagrancy Laws.[36] A man caught taking a peep-show round the country, containing among other curiosities a coloured print of Peterloo, who fell into the hands of the Vicar of Chudleigh, got off more lightly, being sent to the House of Correction as a vagrant till the Sessions.[37] In their eagerness to pounce on sedition, the magistrates sometimes made an awkward slip. In 1819 a man was arrested on as grave a charge as could well be incurred: that of selling the works of Tom Paine himself. He was thrown into prison, and there he would have remained had not a respectable gentleman written to the Home Office to point out that a very unfortunate mistake had been made, enclosing at the same time a copy of the work that had brought a highly religious man into a very disagreeable position. The pamphlet is preserved with the Home Office papers.[38] The magistrate had seen the incriminating name of Paine and looked no further, but the pamphlet is in fact a publication of the Religious Tract Society, composed by Mrs. Trimmer herself, containing a repulsive version of Paine's habits of life and manner of death, set off with an equally repulsive picture, with the object of enhancing the dignity of the Christian religion.[39] It is difficult to see how any workman could have eluded the wide net cast by one Nottinghamshire magistrate, who, finding it impossible to formulate any charge against two men whose influence he thought bad and unsettling, wrote to the Home Office suggesting that he might demand sureties for their good behaviour:[40] they were

---

[35] H. O., 42. 179.
[36] H. O., 42. 159.
[37] H. O., 42. 199.
[38] H. O., 42. 199.
[39] There was a considerable literature of this kind on the subject of Paine's death. One pamphlet bears this title, "Radicals and True Patriots compared, or Living Evidence from New York of Paine's character and last hours contrasted with those of the patriotic Duke of Kent and the late great and good King George the Third, compiled from the narrative of a late resident at New York and other authentic sources. By a Clergyman, late of Oxford."
[40] H. O., 42. 155.

poor men, and their only friends were poor men: consequently they would be unable to produce sureties and could be shut up in jail for the winter.[41]

Until Peel's advent the Home Office appear to have done nothing or next to nothing to discourage illegalities on the part of the magistrates, and the law-officers on one occasion set an example in proposing to violate the principles of what Bacon calls "clear and round dealing" between men. This was in 1802, when there were disturbances in the south-west over the introduction of gig-mills.[42] A number of shearmen waited, by invitation, on a manufacturer named Jones to discuss the situation; the meeting broke up without result, and the delegates, seven in number, told the manufacturer that the shearmen throughout the country were united in their opposition to the new machinery. The account of these proceedings was sent to the Home Office, and it bears the following remarkable endorsement:—

> "We are of opinion that the Conduct of the Individuals who came to Mr. Jones's House will support an Indictment for a Conspiracy, and we should recommend an Indictment to be prepared and sent down to the Assizes for Wiltshire charging these seven men with such Conspiracy, and that Mr. Hobhouse and the other persons present with Mr. Jones should attend at the Assizes to go before the Grand Jury with the Bill.
>
> Sp. Perceval.
> Thos. Manners Sutton."[43]

This tempting invitation was declined by the employers, but the methods of justice revealed in the Home Office papers were in keeping with this proposal. As Lord Pembroke put it in writ-

---

[41] The Settlement Laws were sometimes convenient for this purpose. In 1819 a working man took part in starting a reform society at Wigan, and alarmed the magistrates by publishing a pamphlet calling on Britons to prove to the world that they were countrymen of Boadicea. Fortunately the town clerk found that the man had previously been removed from Wigan under the Settlement Laws, so the parish officers procured a warrant and locked him up for a month. H. O., 42. 189.

[42] Gig-mills were machines for raising the nap on the surface of cloth, which was afterwards shorn. This raising had previously been done by hand with teazles.

[43] H. O., 42. 65.

ing to the Home Office, the working classes were "unfortunately
true to each other,"[44] and the magistrates had consequently to
resort to craft to surprise them into disclosures. One method was
to arrest a number of men, and then try to make them compromise each other. During this affair in the south-west a Wiltshire
magistrate wrote that he had held out every temptation to ac-
complices without effect, and that six shearmen had been sent
to prison the previous week under the Combination Laws, two
of them for refusing to give evidence. "I am bringing forward as
many Cases as I can under the Combination Act, and by forcing
some to give Evidence against others, I hope to provoke some
quarrels amongst them, and by that means to be able to bring
some of their Deeds to light."[45]

The law, set in force by every kind of trickery, including the
use of unscrupulous characters as spies, was administered as a
rule by men who regarded the working classes as a population
amenable to no influence but that of terror. An example of the
value put on a man's freedom was given by Mr. Justice Park,
who, as the Attorney-General for the County-palatine of Lancaster, had played an important part in the punishment of the
disturbances of 1812. Park, when a judge in 1818, sentenced a
labourer at the Salisbury Assizes to eighteen months' imprisonment for stealing a sack of oats. The man, on receiving sentence,
asked the judge how he could recover the wages that were due
to him. Park responded by converting his sentence into one of
transportation for seven years.[46] The view of the ruling classes
was well illustrated in the case of a child of ten who was sentenced to death in 1800 for secreting notes at the Chelmsford
Post Office.[47] The judge, Baron Hotham, wrote to Lord Auckland: "All the circumstances attending the transaction mani-
fested art and contrivance beyond his years, and I therefore
refused the application of His Counsel to respite the Judgment
on the ground of his tender years, being satisfied that he knew
perfectly what he was doing. But still, he is an absolute Child,
Now only between ten and Eleven, and wearing a bib, or what
your old Nurse (my friend) will know better by the name of a
Pinafore. The Scene was dreadful, on passing sentence, and to
pacify the feelings of a most crowded Court, who all expressed

[44] H. O., 42. 66.
[45] H. O., 42. 66.
[46] *Taunton Courier* in H. O., 42. 180.
[47] H. O., 42. 49.

their horror of such a Child being hanged, by their looks and manners, after stating the necessity of the prosecution and the infinite danger of its going abroad into the world that a Child might commit such a crime with impunity, when it was clear that he knew what he was doing, I hinted something slightly of its still being in the power of the Crown to interpose in every Case that was open to Clemency." The sentence was commuted, and the boy was sent out to Grenada for fourteen years, apparently by a private arrangement with a member of the Grand Jury who had estates there. The transportation of children was, of course, a common occurrence. The list of prisoners sent up from London and Middlesex in 1817 included two boys aged ten and thirteen under sentence of death,[48] and the list from the Chester Assizes the next year includes a sentence of death on a boy of fourteen for stealing a silver watch and two bank notes.[49] Two boys aged ten and twelve were sentenced to transportation for seven years, at the Manchester Quarter Sessions in 1813, for stealing linen from a warehouse.[50] A boy of fourteen was hung at Newport in 1814 for stealing. A woman whose husband had been transported for felony committed the same felony in the hope of joining him in exile, but the judge thought it necessary to make an example and hanged her instead.[51]

We have a grave picture of the justice shown to the poor, drawn by a lawyer who was as nervous as anybody else of industrial disorder. In 1828 Brougham made a speech on the State of the Law, which is invaluable as a record of legal procedure and habit in those days. In that speech he argued before a House of Commons that might be ignorant on many subjects, but was certainly not ignorant about magistrates and magistrates' ways, that magistrates committed a great many persons who ought to be discharged, from motives of vainglory and from motives that were even worse. He was referring to Peel's Bill for extending the payments of expenses of witnesses and prosecutors out of the county rates. "It is not to be doubted that it has greatly increased the number of commitments, and has been the cause of many persons being brought to trial who ought to have been discharged by the Magistrates. The habit of committing,

---

[48] H. O., 42. 158.
[49] At the same Assizes a cooper from Newport was transported for life for stealing a handkerchief, value sixpence. H. O., 42. 180.
[50] Meinertzhagen, *From Ploughshare to Parliament*, p. 186.
[51] Spencer Walpole, i. 196, quoting Police Com. of 1818, p. 175.

from this and other causes, has grievously increased everywhere of late, and especially of boys. Eighteen hundred and odd, many of them mere children, have been committed in the Warwick district, during the last seven years. Nor is this a trifling evil. . . . Many are the inducements, independent of any legislative encouragement, to these commitments. The Justice thinks he gains credit by them. He has the glory of being commemorated at the Assizes before the Lord Judge and the Sheriff, and the Grand Jury, and all who read the Crown Callendar. On that solemn occasion he has the gratification of hearing it fly from mouth to mouth—'He is a monstrous good magistrate: no man commits so many persons.' Then there is the lesser glory acquired among neighbours, into whose pockets they are the means of putting money, by making them prosecutors and witnesses in petty criminal cases; and thus converting (as Sir Eardley Wilmot says) their journey of duty into a jaunt of pleasure to the Assizes. The reputation of activity is very seducing to a Magistrate; but I have known it curiously combined with things more solid than empty praise."[52]

It was certainly unfortunate for the class that filled the prisons as they filled most of the undesirable situations in life, that the prosecution of offenders at this time was so lucrative a business. Nadin, the notorious Deputy Constable of Manchester, found that he had hit on a career as enriching as the most enterprising career in commerce or industry. Originally a master spinner, he attracted the notice of the Society for the Prosecution of Felons by his skill as a thief taker, and through their influence he became Deputy Constable of Manchester. A Manchester correspondent wrote to the Home Office in 1816, urging that a very necessary reform in police legal procedure was the abolition of the system by which responsibility for initiating prosecutions rested with officials who drew a profit from them. He alleged that in Manchester the Clerk and the Deputy Constable made every little offence a felony for the sake of the perquisites, and that Nadin had already made £20,000 out of his position.[53] In 1818 another correspondent wrote setting out the rewards that the Deputy Constable received for obtaining a conviction.[54] For most serious offences the reward was £40, together with the Tyburn ticket (the right of exemption from service in parish

52 *Speeches*, ii. p. 376.
53 H. O., 42. 153.
54 H. O., 42. 174.

offices). On one occasion Nadin had sold the Tyburn ticket for £300.[55] Nadin's unpopularity may have coloured the general opinion of his character, and an official who is much more afraid of letting a guilty man escape than of putting innocent men in prison, who thinks that justice and terrorism are much the same thing, may appear to owe to avarice the zeal that needed no such bribe. But nobody ever questioned the belief that when Nadin retired he took a fortune with him from an office on which he had entered a poor man, and the sort of men he employed can be judged by the admission that one of his police constables at Peterloo made under cross-examination, that "he had been in the habit of inveigling persons into the uttering of forged notes for the purpose of convicting them, and that he had succeeded in hanging one man in this way."[56]

In 1818 Bennet[57] brought in a Bill to abolish the scandal of blood money, or the system referred to by Nadin's critic, under which the successful prosecutor was entitled to a reward of £40 in the case of conviction on any one of several charges. The debate that followed[58] shows that police conspiracies for the sake of this reward were not uncommon. Bennet, who had been Chairman of a Committee on the state of the police in the metropolis, said "he was convinced he was not exaggerating when he said, that it had been a long-established practice in this country for individuals, day after day, and year after year, to stimulate others to the commission of crime, for the purpose of putting money into their pockets by their conviction."

Romilly, who supported Bennet strongly, "commented on the rapacity of police officers, not only in London, but also in other great towns, and stated, that in Birmingham a case had lately occurred wherein police officers had earned £120 by the conviction of three boys." Alderman Wood said that police officers went so far as to employ counsel in order to secure a conviction; and that anybody who had experience of the courts could see how eager they were to have a man committed for a capital offence. Mackintosh also spoke of the scandalous scenes that the country had often witnessed, and contended that false accusation had lately become a most flourishing trade. Copley, afterwards Lord Lyndhurst, objected to this statement as too

---

[55] See also Philips's Speech, House of Commons, March 5, 1818.
[56] Ann. Reg., 1820, p. 860.
[57] See Vol. II, p. 20.
[58] See Parl. Debates, March 2, April 13, and May 4, 1818.

sweeping, saying that in his experience on the Midland circuit he had never known an instance to justify it, to which Romilly replied that he did not know what proof Copley thought necessary to establish the fact of an abuse, but that for himself he thought the conviction of five innocent men, which had happened not long since, a sufficient argument for reform. The law-officers carried an amendment, empowering the judge to give a reward at his discretion, and the Bill passed in this form, the fixed statutory rewards being abolished. At the same time, prosecutors were allowed their expenses.

There have always been Englishmen who could break through the prejudices of their class, and the time we are discussing was no exception. In Parliament men like Sir William Meredith,[59] Bennet, Romilly, and Whitbread were always protesting against the carelessness of human life and human liberty that had become habitual in the use of their power by Ministers and magistrates; in the Derbyshire trials of 1817, Joseph Strutt made great efforts on behalf of the prisoners, and there must have been on other Benches some men of the humanity and independence of Capel Lofft of Suffolk. But the general temper was reflected in the minds of Sidmouth or Parson Hay or Fletcher of Bolton. Ministers and magistrates were careless about their methods and their punishments, because the world of the ruling class did not seem more separate to the poor than the world of the poor seemed to the ruling class. To the rich the mass of the people seemed ripe for rebellion. In 1801, Ainsworth, a big manufacturer of Bolton, wrote to Peel that if the French invaded and the soldiers were withdrawn, the people would rise.[60] Bury was also said to be ready for revolution, and two years later, when a French invasion seemed possible, the Mayor of Leicester wrote to the Home Office: "I think that if whilst the Enemy remains in force the people of this Town were to suffer from the want of Bread, a fourth of the population would join the French Standard if they had an opportunity."[61] The mutual

---

[59] Meredith, a Rockingham Whig, and formerly a Jacobite (died 1790, left Parliament 1777), was Romilly's predecessor. See his speech on the brutalities of the Penal Law in 1777 (May 13). He first moved (November 27, 1770) for an inquiry into the Penal Code, and it is interesting to note that his motion was seconded by Fox, who was then a Tory. Trevelyan, *Early Life of C. J. Fox*, p. 405.

[60] H. O., 42, 61.

[61] H. O., 42. 73.

distrust of the upper classes and the workmen was not less acute than the mutual distrust of two hostile races, and the industrial towns had the moral atmosphere of a society kept uneasily in order by a system of martial law. This state of things was at its worst long after the war was over and all danger of invasion had ceased.

The principal argument put forward by the magistrates in opposition to a Bill, introduced by Bennet in 1817 and again in 1819, to deprive the justices of their absolute power over licences, was the argument that magistrates used that power for purposes of their own, and that by this control over the publican they were able to make public-houses an important source of information about the intentions and temper of the working classes. One magistrate wrote that those who had not lived in the Midlands had no idea of the difficulties of the magistrates there: "A strong combination of the ill-disposed, which includes, I am sorry to say, nearly the whole class of working manufacturers."[62] The magistrates who sent spies into the taverns and into little trade unions and workmen's societies and chapels, who tried to bribe men in prison to betray their comrades, who treated strikers as vagrants and children wearing bibs as dangerous characters, were not administering justice with even hand to a society of fellow-citizens; they were trying to terrorise an underworld; they were watching for the first stir and movement of its myriad hands.

---

[62] H. O., 42. 187.

CHAPTER V

ORDER

The impression created by the general behaviour of the magistrates was strengthened and dramatised by the force on which the ruling class relied for their purpose of keeping order. The modern police system dates, as everybody knows, from the day when Peel abolished the old London watchmen and created the organisation that advertises its author by its nickname. A century ago most of the great towns had the administrative equipment of villages. In most places the ultimate source of authority was a Justice of the Peace, not always accessible, and a small number of constables. Deficiencies of organisation were supplemented by the private incentives already described, and the men who acted under the constables in the big towns were often the greatest rascals of the place.[1] On paper the whole population might be called out in the form of the *posse comitatus*, or a town might be put under watch and ward and all its male inhabitants thereby requisitioned for police work, but neither of these courses was simple, and measures that can be adopted in extraordinary emergencies cannot be made part of the normal life of a society. Least of all could they be adopted for such problems as the problems that had now arisen. The whole theory of police conscription belonged indeed to an earlier regime; and though these antique methods were still tried on occasion, the results were not satisfactory. Manchester, Salford, Blackburn, Stockport, Barnsley, Nottingham, and Carlisle were put under watch and ward at the time of the Luddite disturbances. There were difficulties in the West Riding of Yorkshire, and the Clerk of the Peace at Wakefield reported that to apply the Watch and Ward Act would be to put arms into the hands of the most powerfully disaffected.[2] A West Riding magistrate attempted eight years later to mobilise the *posse comitatus* at Dewsbury.[3] Some blanketeers had been summoned before him for preventing others from working. A disorderly mob collected

---

[1] Readers of Godwin's powerful novel, *The Adventures of Caleb Williams*, will recollect the character of Gines, who alternated between the professions of thieving and thief-taking.
[2] H. O., 42. 122.
[3] H. O., 52. 1.

and threatened to rescue the prisoners. In this emergency he gave immediate orders for the *posse comitatus* to be called out (there being no special constables or military at hand), when to his surprise he found he could not muster more than fifty persons in a market town containing nearly eight thousand souls. There was a general fear among shopkeepers of losing custom. Some towns had special arrangements; Manchester, for example, had obtained an Act of Parliament establishing a body of Police Commissioners, though they were only becoming efficient towards the end of our period.[4] But, for the most part, these towns kept order by a handful of constables acting under the directions of magistrates, few in number and often living at a distance. A correspondent wrote to the Home Office in 1819 describing the district that comprised Oldham, Middleton, and Ashton, and extended to Yorkshire, as being entirely without magistrates.[5] It is not surprising that there was a continual demand from these places for a proper police force and system. The Bishop of Durham, for example, wrote in 1815 after the strike already described, representing the urgent need for an efficient police force for the ports of Sunderland and North and South Shields.[6] Similar representations were made to the Home Office from Nottingham, Newcastle, Wakefield; and in 1812 General Maitland reported that the Manchester magistrates were inclined to bring up the question of a permanent police establishment, and that he had told them that there would be considerable objections to such a proposal. A beginning was made towards the end of our period in Cheshire, but throughout the commotions of the time the north and the Midlands depended, so

---

[4] The police force in 1816 consisted of 4 beadles, 200 special constables, and 53 night watchmen with rattles (Aston, *Manchester*, p. 27 ff.).

[5] H. O., 42. 193. Cf. H. O., 42. 163. Two magistrates from Rochdale complained that they were the only acting magistrates among a population of 100,000.

Cf. also H. O., 42. 165, 1817. Memorial from Potteries for stipendiary (refused). District 40 miles in circumference, with more than 50,000 inhabitants; no acting magistrate within these five parishes (Stoke-upon-Trent, Burslem, Wolstanton, Trentham, Norton in the Moors), average distance of magistrate, 9 miles, which meant a journey of 40 miles first to obtain warrant and back, then to attend hearing.

[6] H. O., 42. 146.

far as a civilian constabulary was concerned, on such casual and ineffective provision as we have described.

How, then, was order preserved? For the answer to that question we must turn to the history of the British Army. Down to the Revolutionary War, England had a very small standing army, and it was the custom to quarter such troops as were kept in England in alehouses, barracks being used only in garrison towns and fortresses. The military needs of England governed the distribution of the British troops, and the traditional jealousy of a standing army showed itself in the arrangements for their housing. Blackstone had declared that "the soldiers should live inter-mixed with the people; no separate camp, no barracks, no inland fortresses should be allowed." During the French War, Pitt effected a revolution, abolishing the old habit of quartering soldiers, and spreading barracks over England. Now this revolution was not a military measure at all. It was, as Mr. Fortescue has shown, purely a measure of police. Its origin is disclosed in the Home Office papers. In the summer of 1792, Dundas sent a Colonel De Lancey on a tour of inspection in the north of England to find out what he could about the disposition of the troops, and "how far they were to be depended upon in any emergency."[7] De Lancey reported that it was "a dangerous measure to keep troops in the manufacturing Towns in their present dispersed state, and unless Barracks could be established for them where they could be kept under the eyes of their officers it would be prudent to Quarter them in the towns and villages in the vicinity, from whence in case of emergency they would act with much more effect." This report led to the policy of covering the manufacturing districts with barracks. The policy was not adopted without some discussion in Parliament, though Pitt succeeded in screening most of his plans until they had been carried out.[8] In the course of these debates the political character of these measures was frankly acknowledged by Sir George Yonge (Secretary at War) and by Pitt himself. Pitt put the motive quite clearly: "The circumstances of the country, coupled with the general state of affairs, rendered it advisable to provide barracks in other parts of the kingdom. A spirit had appeared in some of the manufacturing towns which made it necessary that troops should be kept near them." The critics of this policy

[7] H. O., 42. 20.
[8] See Fortescue, *History of British Army*, iv. 903, and the complaints of the Opposition, April 1796.

included Fox, who addressed himself to this point: "If there were places where the existing police was insufficient, let means be tried to remedy the defect, but let it not be pleaded as a reason for keeping up a military force; for of all sorts of police, a military police was the most repugnant to the spirit and the letter of our Government, and ought to be the last that ever Parliament should adopt."[9] There was another debate in 1796,[10] when Windham, defending the building of barracks as a means of isolating the soldiers, said Government should act on "the maxim of the French comedian: 'If I cannot make him dumb I will make you deaf.'" To which Fox replied that the number of persons who were totally deaf being unfortunately limited, it would be difficult to recruit an entire army of the desirable kind, but that perhaps foreign mercenaries who could hear, but would not understand, would answer the purpose Dundas had in view.[11]

The policy of building barracks was thus pushed forward briskly; at the beginning of the French War the Government had barrack accommodation for some 21,000 troops in forty-three garrison towns; by 1815 a hundred and fifty-five barracks had been built to contain 17,000 cavalry and 138,000 infantry.[12] Troops were distributed all over the country, and the north and Midlands and the manufacturing region in the southwest came to resemble a country under military occupation.[13] The officers commanding in the different districts reported on the temper and circumstances of their districts, just as if they were in a hostile or lately conquered country; soldiers were moved about in accordance with fluctuations in wages or employment, and the daily life of the large towns was watched anxiously and suspiciously by magistrates and generals. But the

---

[9] Parl. Debates, House of Commons, February 22, 1793.

[10] Parl. Debates, House of Commons, April 8, 1796.

[11] Fox's bitter jest came true when a German legion was employed for keeping order while English militiamen were flogged in the streets of Ely. See *Cobbett's Trial for Seditious Libel in* 1808.

[12] Halévy, *Histoire du Peuple Anglais au XIXe Siècle*, p. 68.

[13] Barracks for small bodies of cavalry were built at Birmingham, Nottingham, Northampton, Sheffield, Manchester, Coventry, York. Infantry were collected at Newcastle, Sunderland, Tynemouth, Carlisle, Chester, Liverpool. See Adolphus, *Brit. Empire*, vol. ii. p. 293. The Fourth Report of the Commissioners of Military Inquiry contains a list of the barracks which it was proposed to keep permanently, and a list of those that were to be given up at the end of the war.

problem was more complex than the ordinary problem of military occupation, for soldiers and inhabitants were of the same race, and much of the correspondence of the period relates to rumours that the soldiers were in danger of contamination. Colonel Vyse, commanding in the eastern counties, did not dare to make Norwich his headquarters in 1792 on account of its revolutionary tone,[14] and De Lancey thought the Greys should be moved from Manchester because they had been to a Presbyterian chapel where they might have learned sedition.[15] A Plymouth correspondent reported to the Home Office in 1795 that soldiers had been abettors of food riots in Devonshire,[16] and in 1816 a Home Office informant stated that he had been present in a public-house at Rowley when a soldier had said to his friends that he had received a letter from his father (who was unemployed and starving with his family in the same case) "charging him if any Riot took place in this country for want of work not to hurt none of them, but if compelled to fire either to fire over their heads, or to shoot the Tyger that gave the order, and to persuade all his comrades to do the same."[17] The Oxfordshire Blues were thanked by the mob for their sympathy with the rioters at Nottingham in 1800,[18] and Maitland reported in 1812 that serious attempts had been made to seduce his troops in Yorkshire.[19]

The same difficulty arose with the militia in a more acute form, for the militia were raised by compulsory ballot from the general body of the nation. In the food riots of 1795 the militiamen more than once took open part with the mob. This happened twice in Sussex in the month of April:[20] in one case the militia seized and sold flour at reduced prices at Seaford, and order was restored by bringing in the Lancashire Fencibles from Brighton. A sergeant of the Fencibles was killed. A court-martial was held and two militiamen were shot, and three received three hundred lashes apiece. Two were also hung for stealing flour, after a trial at the Lewes Assizes. At Chichester

---

14 H. O., 42. 22.
15 H. O., 42. 25.
16 H. O., 42. 34.
17 H. O., 42. 153.
18 H. O., 42. 51.
19 H. O., 42. 125.
20 See *Ipswich Journal*, April 25, 1795; and also *Annual Register* 1795, Chronicle, p. 23 f.

the militiamen broke open the prison and set at liberty a number of labourers who had been sent to jail for forcing a farmer to bring his corn to market. About the same time Sir John Carter wrote from Portsmouth that men belonging to the Gloucester regiment of militia had compelled the butchers to lower the price of meat.[21] In the affair at Cartwright's Mill in 1812 one Cumberland militiaman refused to fire. "The monster is in custody," wrote a correspondent of the Home Office, though he ended his letter with the admission: "I allow the poor are starving."[22] It is not surprising, in the light of these and similar incidents, that the ruling class distrusted the militia as a police force for use against great popular outbursts of discontent or hunger. As early as 1793, correspondents were writing to the Home Office to urge that the militia of Northumberland and Durham should be withdrawn as quickly as possible from their respective counties, and that others who had no local attachments should be substituted for them.[23] Similarly in 1812, Parson Hay wrote from Manchester to urge that if militiamen had to be employed they should be militia regiments from the south of England. Throughout that year there was great uneasiness about the militia. In Cheshire it was thought to be wiser not to call them out, and in many places where the force was called out some sifting was done first. Colonel Clay, reporting on Lancashire riots that same year, said about a riot in which three men were killed and twenty wounded, that the Cumberland militia behaved well; this staggered the mob, who had the idea that they would not act.[24] At Wakefield one of the reasons given for claiming more military protection was the intimate connection between the local militia and the insurgents.[25] In 1817 Lord Anglesey wrote to the Home Office that the local militia were useless, and he added, "And indeed it is very revolting to the feelings of any man to be called upon to attack his neighbours, and possibly his kinsfolk."[26]

These anxieties about the militia had an important consequence: they account for the military error that Pitt made in organising the volunteers at the beginning of the French War on

[21] H. O., 42. 34.
[22] H. O., 42. 122.
[23] H. O., 42. 24.
[24] H. O., 42. 122.
[25] H. O., 42. 122.
[26] H. O., 42. 160.

a separate basis. The volunteers under his system became a third force, naturally more attractive than the regular army or the militia. Mr. Fortescue has shown that the army took ten or twelve years to recover from this capital mistake. It was already difficult to get recruits for the army, militia service was unpopular, and Pitt seemed to go out of his way to set up a rival service and to grant exemption from the militia to any one who chose to become a volunteer. Politicians like Fox, and soldiers like Craufurd, pointed out from the first that this policy seemed designed to make it impossible to raise an army. If Pitt had been looking across the Channel merely, his method would have been as mad as it seemed to his critics at the time, and as it has seemed to military historians ever since. But he was looking across the Trent to the "ignorant and profligate" populations that filled the mining and factory districts. He was thinking less of the maintenance of the army for foreign service than of the protection of the existing system at home. The experiment broke down because the volunteers proved as untrustworthy as the militia. Pitt meant them to be a select force, but they developed into a force representing the general population. In most of the towns in the north, Sheffield, Manchester, Bolton, Bury, Stafford, Birmingham, the authorities reported at one time or another that the volunteers would not act, or even that they would act with the rioters, in case of food riots or strikes.[27] One force, however, answered all expectations. Aristotle and Bacon both remarked the suitability of cavalry to oligarchy, and when the volunteers were disbanded in 1813, the yeomanry were retained. They provided the authorities with their one efficient and trustworthy police force. During the industrial disturbances they were the principal auxiliaries to the regular army. It was their function to repress the less serious outbreaks, and to keep order in other cases until regular troops could be summoned. Their value was appreciated by the employers, and in 1816 Sir Mark Sykes, writing to the Home Office about a seamen's strike, reported that it was said that the local militia could not be relied on, that a corps of yeomanry could be raised without difficulty at Holderness, and that it would be worth more than all the

---

[27] H. O., 42. 51, 42 52, 42. 55, 42. 61. Fitzwilliam's letter about the Sheffield volunteers (H. O., 42. 51) betrays great sympathy with men called upon "to disperse an Assemblage of People composed probably of their particular friends and messmates, perhaps even of their own Wives and Children, calling out for Bread."

regiments of local militia in the West Riding.[28] In the same
year a Captain Littlewood pressed for the creation of a similar
force for use in Huddersfield, remarking that the better classes
should associate together in this way.[29] They became the most
unpopular set of men in England, and the hatred that is scat-
tered in sparks over Cobbett's pages reflects the feelings of the
great mass of Englishmen. When Castlereagh organised his local
militia, he found it necessary to put into an Act of Parliament
a provision that Friendly Societies were to be forbidden to expel
members on the ground that they had joined this force. A letter
to the Home Office[30] mentions that a man was thrown from
his horse near Oldham, that some labourers near hurried to the
scene in answer to cries for help, and that on coming up and
seeing a well-dressed man lying on the ground, they said to one
another that he was probably a cavalryman, and one and all
refused to help.

This incident followed closely upon Peterloo. The story of
that day is well known, and its full history belongs rather to
the reform movement than to the subject of this book, but the
main facts may well be recalled because they illustrate the argument of these chapters with peculiar force. The Lancashire
reformers decided to hold a great meeting in St. Peter's Fields,
on the outskirts of Manchester. The magistrates were uneasy
about the meeting, for popular discontent, inflamed by the recent
Corn Law, was acute: meetings had been held in various northern towns: an attempt had been made to organise a boycott of
exciseable goods, drilling had been going on, and several persons
had found their way into prison, where it was hoped that they
would learn that in the circumstances of contemporary society
to speak the truth or anything like it was sedition. But though
the magistrates disliked the meeting, they decided only a few
hours before it began that it could not be regarded as illegal.
When the vast throng assembled, there was nothing in its appearance to shake the opinion of the magistrates. The meeting
was in its Sunday clothes, bands were playing "God Save the
King," and one out of every three persons was a woman. The
chief orator of the day, Henry Hunt, a brave, vain, and sincere
man, had a taste for language that sounded violent and dangerous to the authorities, but even he could scarcely lead a revolu-

---

[28] H. O., 42. 155.
[29] H. O., 42. 155.
[30] H. O., 42. 194.

tion with so decorous an army. Bamford, the leader of the three thousand from Middleton, has described the scene when his contingent started; how he addressed them, saying that sticks were only to be carried by the old and infirm, that the procession was to march in military order, that the reformers were determined, by taking the most elaborate precautions against disturbance or confusion, to give the lie to their enemies who said the working classes were a rabble.[31] The Middleton Reformers, reinforced by another three thousand from Rochdale, set out on their slow march towards Manchester; a band was playing, the men were in their Sunday shirts, children were in the ranks, women and girls at their head. As they went their army was swollen by new contingents, and when they passed through the Irish weavers' quarter they were received with an enthusiasm more demonstrative than the enthusiasm of Englishmen, expressing itself in a language that few of them could understand. When all the contingents had poured into the Fields, the meeting numbered 80,000 persons, assembled to demand universal suffrage, vote by ballot, annual Parliaments, and the repeal of the Corn Laws. The town they met in, though almost the largest in England, was unrepresented in a Parliament that gave two seats to Old Sarum. Of the eighty thousand, the vast mass were voteless men and women, whom Parliament had handed over to their employers by the Combination Laws, while it had taxed their food for the benefit of the landowners by a most drastic Corn Law. The classes that controlled Parliament and their lives were represented by the magistrates, who were landlords or parsons, and by the yeomanry, who were largely manufacturers. Between those classes must be shared the responsibility for the sudden and unprovoked charge on a defenceless and unresisting crowd, for if the magistrates gave the orders, the yeomanry supplied the zeal. Hunt had scarcely

---

[31] A fact with which the magistrates made great play in their efforts to show that the meeting at Peterloo was revolutionary and dangerous was that one of the contingents carried a flag with a bloody dagger painted red. During the trials the story of the making of the dagger was told, and it shows that the colour that alarmed the magistrates was due to the Sabbatarian scruples of one of the reformers. A man named William Burns had undertaken to decorate the Bury flag: he meant to paint a yellow fleur-de-lys, but he could not find any yellow paint. Next day was Sunday, and he did not like to work on Sunday, so he painted the flag with the only paint he had in the house, which happened to be red. *Henry Hunt's Trial*, p. 259.

begun his speech, when the yeomanry cavalry advanced brandishing their swords. Hunt told the reformers to cheer, which they did; the yeomanry then rode into the crowd, which gave way for them, and arrested Hunt. But this was not enough for the yeomanry, who said, "Have at their flags," and began striking wildly all round them. The magistrates then gave the order to charge. In ten minutes the field was deserted except for dead and wounded, and banners, hats, shawls, and bonnets: the strangest débris of any battlefield since the madness of Ajax. Eleven people died, two of them women, one a child, and over four hundred were wounded, one hundred and thirteen being women. Of the wounded more than a quarter were wounded by the sword. So bitter were the hatreds and suspicions of class, that wounded men and women did not dare to apply for parish relief, or even go to hospital for treatment, for fear it should be discovered that they had received their wounds at Peterloo. A correspondent wrote to the Home Office to say that the woman from Eccles who had been killed was a dangerous character, for she had been heard to curse the curate.[32] The magistrates, hussars, and yeomanry were thanked by the Government; Fitzwilliam was dismissed from his Lord Lieutenancy for protesting at a great Yorkshire meeting; Hunt and three of his colleagues were sent to prison, Hunt for two years and a half, the others for a year. And Hunt, whose arrest was the nominal excuse for the violent onslaught, had actually offered to surrender himself to the authorities the night before.[33]

The scene at Peterloo illustrates very vividly all the conditions of the time. The working people who met there were excluded from the rights of citizens: they were refused representation, education, liberty to combine in answer to the combinations of their masters. The law existed solely for their repression and punishment. They were nowhere recognised as belonging to society, except in the sense in which his wheels and engines belonged to the owner of a mill. Their leaders were intrepid and public-spirited men, but little more: they were not statesmen who could make a nation out of chaos: they were not generals who could use the power of numbers against the overwhelming powers of wealth, education, custom, discipline, and force: they were not even heroes who could embellish, by the

[32] H. O., 42. 194.
[33] Prentice, *Manchester*, p. 158.

greatness of their minds and lives, the great history of the cause of freedom. The magistrates knew so little of the world they governed that they thought that a meeting to which reformers had brought their wives and children was designed for some violent purpose. Magistrates and yeomanry cared so little for the lives of a subject class that they exposed this crowd of defenceless people to all the dangers of a cavalry charge with a levity that revolted every onlooker and won the middle classes of England to reform. For though the magistrates and yeomanry made every effort to disguise the facts, the eye-witnesses included a number of independent people, and among others the reporter of the *Times*. The truth by this means travelled through the country, and almost every large town held a meeting of protest. Prentice describes the consequent change of mind in the middle classes as the breaking up of a long frost.

We have tried to set out a very rough picture of the kind of civilisation that enveloped the new working class: to sketch in general outline its home, its surroundings, its employment and diversions, the government and justice and institutions it received from its rulers, the atmosphere and complexion of its life. If we think of the characteristics that speak a society able to take a pride in itself, to attach and develop the affections and sympathies of those who live under its shelter, nothing strikes us so forcibly in the circumstances of this world as its sharply limited outlook, its conception of order as discipline, of government as force, of a town as a garrison overawing the plotting poor, and its consequent dread of any stimulus to public spirit or disinterested and emancipating ideas among the general body of the inhabitants. The Cheshire magistrates in 1819 wanted to suppress the Sunday-schools.[34] The spirit of the times was embodied in the common expression "policing the poor." It would be an error and an injustice to forget the special influences and circumstances of the period. The shock of the French Revolution had brought with it a new way of looking at the mass of the nation. When Bacon wrote on the dangers to which kings are exposed, he had treated the danger of popular insurrection as very slight, "except it be where they have Great and Potent Heads, or where you meddle with the Point of Religion or their Customs or Means of life."[35] This was the light in which the rank and file of the nation appeared to the ruling class down

---

[34] Prentice, *Manchester*, p. 156.
[35] Essay on Empire.

to the day when France destroyed their peace of mind. In English history for two centuries rebellion had been the business of aristocrats, churchmen, yeomen, squires, Puritans, in fact of everybody but the poor. The poor had rioted when food ran out, but these were local demonstrations, essentially temporary in their character. We have only to recall the key in which Burke himself wrote before 1789 to appreciate the depth of the change in upper-class thinking that followed the French Revolution. "When popular discontents have been very prevalent," he wrote in 1770,[36] "it may well be affirmed and supported, that there has been generally something found amiss in the constitution or in the conduct of government. The people have no interest in disorder. When they do wrong it is their error and not their crime." And he went on to quote Sully: 'Pour la populace, ce n'est jamais par envie d'attaquer qu'elle se soulève, mais par impatience de souffrir." There was no presentiment here of "the swinish multitude."

After the French Revolution the tone was very different. The poorer classes no longer seemed a passive power: they were dreaded as a Leviathan that was fast learning his strength. Regarded before as naturally contented, they were now regarded as naturally discontented. The art of politics was not the art of keeping the attachment of people who cherished their customs, religion, and the general setting of their lives, by moderation, foresight, and forbearance: it was the art of preserving discipline among a vast population destitute of the traditions and restraints of a settled and conservative society, dissatisfied with its inevitable lot and ready for disorder and blind violence. For two revolutions had come together. The French Revolution had transformed the minds of the ruling classes, and the Industrial Revolution had convulsed the world of the working classes. Politicians like Sidmouth, and magistrates like Hay, who saw the poor struggling in the débris of that social upheaval, never imagined that their lot could be made any lighter. They thought that any one who attempted such a task would merely precipitate a French Revolution in England: a revolution that would destroy the classes to which they belonged themselves, but would destroy the poor as well. Discipline, uncompensated by reform and unqualified by concession, was the truest kindness to the working classes. They would have paraphrased Rousseau's

---

[36] *Works,* ii. p. 224. (Thoughts on the Cause of the Present Discontents).

aphorism about nature, and said that the secrets they tried to hide from the working man were so many evils from which they wished to guard him. We shall see in a later chapter how the men and women whose lives were cast amid these dense shadows discovered some of these secrets for themselves.

CHAPTER VI

THE ECONOMIC CONDITIONS

Nobody would say of the industries discussed in this book that they were declining during this period. Nobody would say that they were stagnant. The history of the early years of the Industrial Revolution is a history of vast and rapid expansion. This is true of different industries in different degrees, but it is true in greater or less degree of all industries.[1] The immense increase of trade, helped and stimulated by new invention, new communication, new transport, new control of the forces of nature, was a conspicuous fact of their times for economists, thinkers, legislators, and all public men.

There is another fact not less conspicuous to those who have explored even the surface of this society. The wage earners employed in these industries did not obtain any part of the new wealth. They received more money in wages when employment was good than when it was bad, but the expansion of industry did not in itself increase their share in the wealth of the nation. They were shut out from the surplus profits of an industry that earned the fortunes that created a new and powerful rich class, besides enabling England to maintain a long war with France and to pay Europe handsomely to fight by her side. Indeed, their case was worse than this. The vast mass of people working in these industries were not even receiving a maintenance from them. It is true of the cotton weavers, of the frame-work knitters, even of some of the miners, that they were supported partly by the parishes, partly by their children. The industries that were making the new wealth were not supporting their workpeople. If a traveller had moved among the employers, and had been shown the brimming life of mills, mines, canals, and docks, he would have said that England as an industrial nation was making an advance unprecedented in the history of trade. If he had moved among the working classes, learned what wages they were receiving, how they lived, he would have concluded that

---

[1] The percentage of increase in import of raw cotton between 1764 and 1794 was 615, between 1794 and 1824, 445; of wool between 1790 and 1820, 280; in production of iron between 1750 and 1788, 210, and between 1788 and 1820, 488. See Lloyd, *The Cutlery Trades*, p. 399.

the industries in which they were employed were either stagnant or declining.[2]

Immense fortunes were made in cotton, wool, iron, and coal, but on the workers in these industries there fell degradation and distress. Not all employers grew rich with the Peels, nor did all the workmen grow poor with the hand-loom weavers, but the general feature of the times was the rise of a class of rich employers and the creation of a large and miserable proletariate. This remarkable contrast might seem to demand an explanation: it might provoke misgivings about the justice and good government of society, and make people wonder whether there was not some flaw in the structure that was disfigured by such a basis of misery. These doubts and misgivings entered the mind of the working classes and produced in time, a more or less organised demand for an altered distribution of the burdens and the powers of government. The upper classes (of course there were individual exceptions) regarded these doubts and suspicions as outraging the laws of nature and the laws of God. The progress of the world, so some would argue, depended on the fortunes of the Arkwrights and the Peels, and those fortunes in their turn depended on the very privations and hardships that appeared to put such discordant questions to the optimism of civilisation. The existing order, others would argue, was the dispensation of Providence, and it was blasphemy to scrutinise its justice or to try to modify its exactions. The social history of the period is largely the revolt of the working classes against this body of prejudice or superstition or reason, whichever people like to term it. This is not to say that the working classes thought of their revolt in this form. They were struggling for a direct and immediate object, to maintain a standard of life against forces apparently overwhelming. In one case they would ask for the enforcement of old and fading regulations; in another for a legal minimum wage; in a third for the right to combine. From time to time the political movement and the economic movement run into each other. The working classes came to doubt whether a Parliament that was always coercing

---

[2] It has been observed by a qualified critic that the title Porter gave to his work *The Progress of the Nation*, was hardly justified, and that the fifty years that followed the outbreak of the Revolutionary War, if they marked a vast increase of wealth in England, reduced the working classes to deeper poverty. See Hirst's Introduction to 1912 edition.

the poor and never restraining the rich was really possessed of an Olympian wisdom and impartiality in determining the issues that were raised by conflicts between masters and men. The subject of sinecures and pensions became interesting to a class half of whose wages went in taxes to a State that provided none of the rudiments of a civilised and rational life.[3] The economic struggle of the time was in this sense a general conflict. It is a struggle between men and masters, and a struggle also between a subject class and the classes that possessed the State. The word struggle is perhaps misleading as a name for so unequal a contest. The working classes were beating against closed doors, and when at last partly by their help those doors are broken open, it is not the working classes that gain an entrance. A complete social history of the times would therefore embrace the history of the movement for Parliamentary Reform, as well as the history of the battle for a standard of life. In this book we are only able to consider the more important circumstances and consequences of the political situation as they affect the position of the working classes as combatants. This is the subject of the present chapter.

The spirit of reform in England, which had been eager and active in 1780 and had been a powerful force in the overthrow of two Governments, had been put to sleep for some years by Pitt's triumph over the Coalition and his record of economies and improvements in office. The French Revolution rekindled it into flame. Everywhere old societies revived or new societies sprang into life for discussing ideas of just and free government, the meaning of citizenship, the grounds of right and duty in the State. The ruling class, with the exception of a handful of Whigs led by Fox, took fright at once. The French Revolution at an early stage began to look very different from the Revolution of 1688, which they regarded as the model for the behaviour of nations in such circumstances. What was perhaps worse, the new societies, partly drawn from small shopkeepers, artisans, and working men, looked very different from the respectable agitators for reform in 1780, who met under the aegis of a sheriff or a Lord Lieutenant and as often as not had a nobleman on the platform. Then came the red horizon of September, the November Decree offering the help of France to any people desiring to regain its freedom, the execution of the King, the declaration of war, and a universal frenzy of indignation and

---

[3] See *Agricultural and Industrial Magazine* for 1833.

terror throughout England. Pitt suspended the Habeas Corpus in 1794, and for the next eight years ministers and magistrates were free from this encumbrance; he passed two Bills for suppressing public meetings, and he instituted a series of prosecutions, of which the most famous ended in the acquittal of Thomas Hardy and his comrades by a London jury. The first democratic movement had been crushed.

After Waterloo the story is resumed. Political reform now became a serious object to the working classes. During the first Jacobin terror it had been possible and easy for a magistrate to incite a working-class mob to harry a working-class reformer. But a great change had come over the working classes in the last twenty years. They had learnt much from Cobbett, more perhaps from suffering, and by 1817 there was a widespread desire for the franchise. That was the year of the futile march of the Blanketeers. Castlereagh and Sidmouth replied by suspending the Habeas Corpus for a year,[4] by approving the conduct of the magistrates at Peterloo and by passing the famous Six Acts. One of the Acts made any meeting that tended to excite hatred and contempt of the Government an unlawful assembly, thus preventing all criticism and also putting any speaker at a meeting at the mercy of any spy. The punishments for seditious libel were made more brutal, and the stamp duty of fourpence was made chargeable on any paper or pamphlet costing less than sixpence. Under this legislation discussion or criticism of ministers or their policy was a perilous adventure.

Thus the working classes suffered as citizens, if the word can be applied to a class so ruthlessly shut out in the cold, not only by the denial of political rights, but by the denial of all liberty of speech. They could not declare their opinion on taxation, the Corn Laws, the Combination Laws, or any political issue, except at great risk. Under the Tories a working-class meeting in Manchester became a Peterloo. Under the Whig Government that passed the Reform Bill four working men were sent to prison for a year for attending an open-air meeting there. In the same year when the Government, to please the Saints, ordered a solemn fast as a way of keeping out the cholera, the leaders of the National Union of the Working Classes were prosecuted for organising a procession in London, carrying a loaf of bread and a round of beef with the inscription: "The

---

[4] Cobbett, thinking he could be of little use to his countrymen in prison, fled to America.

True Cure for the Cholera." But they were tried by one of the London juries that Governments always dreaded, and were acquitted. Neither Whig nor Tory statesmen thought the working man had any business with politics.

The war thus injured the working people by inflaming the fears and hatreds of class in their rulers, and by throwing a great body of moderate opinion on to the side of repression. It injured them also by aggravating all the elements of disturbance that belonged to the new industrial system. It has been well put that "the handicraft or guild system is associated with the *town economy*, the domestic or commission system with the *national economy*, and the factory system with the *world economy*."[5] Industry that is supplying markets all over the world is subject to violent fluctuations, and during those years of ungoverned enterprise, men who could put together a little capital, or borrow it, might start a mill, in the hope of sharing in the profits of these vast speculations. The new capitalists were all competing with each other for this distant custom, and the workpeople found themselves at the mercy of a series of guesses about the demands of the wide world. England had passed through many speculating crazes, but the new gamblers were playing with new stakes. We may illustrate it in this way. On two occasions the mirage of trade with South America has led to a great catastrophe. The more famous catastrophe, the South Sea Bubble, was an affair of finance. The people ruined were the people who are ruined to-day by a disastrous adventure on the Stock Exchange. But if those who bought the Company's shares at a fancy price had spent their money instead in building factories, collecting workpeople from various parts of the country, and pouring out goods to ship them to South America, and then found there was no market for them, the disasters of the early eighteenth century would have resembled those that overwhelmed industrial England a century later. M'Culloch has given a memorable description of the craze that brought ruin to numbers of workpeople in 1808 and 1809, when the whole eastern coast of South America was thrown open to British trade by the alliance with Spain. "Speculation was then carried beyond the boundaries within which gambling is usually confined, and was pushed to an extent and into channels that could hardly have been deemed practicable. We are informed by Mr.

---

[5] Professor Unwin, *Industrial Organisation in the Sixteenth Century*, p. 10.

Mawe, an intelligent traveller resident at Rio Janeiro at the period in question, that more Manchester goods were sent out in the course of a few weeks than had been consumed in the twenty years preceding; and the quantity of English goods of all sorts poured into the city was so very great, that warehouses could not be provided sufficient to contain them, and that the most valuable merchandise was actually exposed for weeks on the beach to the weather and to every kind of depredation. But the folly and ignorance of those who had crowded into this speculation was still more strikingly evinced in the selection of the articles sent to South America. Elegant services of cut glass and china were offered to persons whose most splendid drinking vessels consisted of a horn or the shell of a cocoanut; tools were sent out having a hammer on one side and a hatchet on the other, as if the inhabitants had had nothing more to do than to break the first stone they met with and then cut the gold and diamonds from it; and some speculators actually went so far as to send out skates to Rio Janeiro."[6] This outburst, accompanied by other disasters, was followed by an epidemic of bankruptcies in 1811: the distress of Lancashire was such that Sir Robert Peel declared that English labourers had never known such misery, and the wages of Bolton weavers fell to five shillings a week.

Another feature of the new system was the dependence of industries on one another. This dependence is, of course, a necessary result of specialisation and division of labour. In an early community, living on its own resources, the standing danger is the danger of famine; in a society, living by means of an elaborate system of exchange on the resources of the world, the standing danger is the danger that one link in the long chain of industries which connect the finished article with the new material will break, and several industries be made idle. Further, if supply or demand fails in one industry, the purchasing power of that industry is diminished, and other industries, dependent on the purchasing power of that industry, suffer. This process goes on indefinitely. The demands of the new world were various, and therefore capricious, in comparison with the simple wants of a poor country. Thus recurrent breakdowns were part of the price paid for the highly civilised manner and equipment of life that Macaulay described with such enthusiasm. Great

---

[6] Quoted Smart, *Economic Annals*, p. 184. Exports of cotton goods went up from 9,846,000 in 1808 to 18,616,000 in 1809. *Ibid.*, p. 203.

industry follows certain cycles, or, as a French writer puts it, obeys a rhythm:[7] it develops in movements of rise and fall, and the transition brings unemployment and want.[8]

A war is, under any conditions, a disturbing force in a world so organised, and the French War, as it involved all Europe, was a specially demoralising force. The American War of 1775 to 1783 brought distress to cotton spinners and to the woollen trade at Norwich,[9] but the great war was a far heavier strain. The annual expenditure rose between 1792 and 1814 from something less than twenty millions to a hundred and six millions.[10] There were taxes on salt, soap, candles, leather, malt, sugar, tea, everything that the workman used. It has been estimated that the artisan at the beginning of the century found that the expense of living had increased fivefold since he began life.[11] But this, of course, was a small part of the burden it threw upon England, for the war had involved the whole civilised world, and every nation impoverished by its devastations. The poverty and misery it caused are incalculable, and it is no part of our task to try to estimate or describe them. But there were four respects in which the war intensified the perils and vicissitudes to which the working classes were exposed by the new system, and it is convenient to enumerate them, because they explain the special distress that marked particular years.

1. In November 1806 Napoleon tried to make a ring-fence round Europe to shut out British goods and another round England to shut out foreign goods.[12] The instrument of this policy was the Berlin Decree. England replied by the Orders in Council. The first, issued in January 1807, was a mild retaliation, the Government being anxious to avoid complications with the few Powers that were neutral, notably America, and merely struck at the coasting trade of France and her allies. Napoleon proceeded to order the confiscation of all British goods and colonial produce found in the Hanse towns. His blows at British trade were effective and our commerce was almost paralysed. The English Government accordingly decided to take more dras-

---

[7] Dolléans, Le Chartisme, i. p. 182.
[8] See Professor Smart's interesting discussion, Economic Annals, p. 606.
[9] See James, History of the Worsted Manufacture, p. 30.
[10] Porter (ed. 1851), p. 475.
[11] Smart, op. cit., p. 7, quoting H. Martineau.
[12] Smart, op. cit., p. 119.

tic measures,[13] and issued Orders in Council declaring the
dominions of His Majesty's enemies and of countries under their
control to be in a state of blockade. Lord Bathurst summed up
the situation thus: "France, by her Decrees, resolved to abolish
all trade with England. England said in return that France
should then have no trade but with England." The history of the
disastrous quarrel with the United States, in which we became
involved in spite of some attempts to qualify the system in her
favour, lies outside the scope of this book. All that it concerns
us to note is that this system of carrying on war by attacks on
trade brought great disorganisation and consequent suffering on
the manufacturing population. In 1809, Whitbread, in the
course of a speech against the Orders, mentioned that our imports of cotton wool had fallen by twenty-seven millions, and
that thirty-two cotton mills stood idle in Manchester. So acute
was the distress in 1812 that the assassination of Perceval, who
was the principal champion of the Orders, produced an outburst
of enthusiasm in the Midland counties that could scarcely have
been exceeded if the lunatic Bellingham had shot Napoleon
himself. Lord Holland alludes to this rejoicing in a characteristic passage in his *Memoirs*: "One of the leading manufacturers
of Birmingham, a strict Dissenter, who had come up to London
with petitions against the Orders in Council, lamented to me,
with a demure countenance and a subdued voice, the wickedness
of the times on which he had been cast, where, he said, as the
coaches arrived in various parts of the kingdom, the intelligence
of the murder of a fellow-creature had been received with more
exultation than horror, and even in some places greeted with
savage shouts of un-Christian joy. 'It is indeed disgusting; and
yet,' added he, with an arch, puritanical smile, 'it proves the sad
condition of the poor manufacturers, and it cannot be denied
that, in the present critical state of the question on the Orders
in Council, the finger of a benevolent Providence is visible in
this horrible event.' "[14]

2. During the war the Government were consumers on an
immense scale. They bought food to be shipped to the Penin-
sula, clothing from Yorkshire and Lancashire, and arms from
Sheffield and Birmingham. When peace came this expenditure
ceased; a customer who had been spending fifty millions went

---

[13] See Smart, *op. cit.*, p. 156.
[14] *Further Memoirs*, p. 131.

out of the market.[15] This vast expenditure, instead of setting in train a process that would produce and quicken a demand for commodities, had been spent in making people less able to consume them. Consequently the disappearance of this customer meant a violent and permanent shrinking in the market.

3. Matters were made worse by the condition of Europe. During the war, England, by reason of her security and her command of the sea, obtained more than her share of the trade of the world. This abnormal and temporary expansion caused an excessive investment in manufacturing plant. The English capitalist thought the demand would grow, and that peace would bring plenty, but when peace came, Europe was too poor to buy, and the special circumstances that had hampered her manufacturing enterprise no longer existed. Consequently the close of the war brought an immediate decline of trade to manufacturers who had counted on an expansion. Imports dropped by six and exports by seven millions. The price of copper fell from £180 to £80 a ton, and that of iron from £20 to £8. What this meant to the working classes can be seen from the case of the ironworkers and colliers of Shropshire and Staffordshire. In Shropshire twenty-four out of thirty-four blast furnaces ceased working and more than seven thousand ironworkers were thrown out of employment. Further, these furnaces had consumed eight thousand tons of coal a week, and as this coal was no longer wanted, the miners shared the fate of the ironworkers.

4. The close of the war was followed by the disbanding of the huge armies that England had been feeding and clothing and supplying with weapons and ammunition. Castlereagh stated in 1817 that no less than three hundred thousand soldiers and sailors had been discharged since the peace.[16] The ranks of labour were thus flooded at a time when wages were falling and the price of provisions was rising. The war then, in these several ways, added special complications to the struggle for a standard of life into which the working classes were thrown by the revolution in industry. With steady trade that struggle would have been bitter and severe, but the new system contained all the elements of violent vicissitude, and those elements again were aggravated by the war. Meanwhile the working classes,

---

[15] British expenditure fell from 106 millions in 1815 to 53 in 1818. Spencer Walpole, *History of England*, vol. i. p. 402, in quoting Porter, p. 483.

[16] Smart, *op. cit.*, p. 539.

who suffered as wage earners from all these disorganising forces, suffered as consumers from the political circumstances of the time, in particular from two causes, the course of the Currency and the Corn Laws. Each of these subjects, and especially the second, has a long history of angry contention, and contention of which the ashes are not yet cold. It is no part of our task to examine or to present all the considerations that have to be kept in mind in judging the policy of the Governments responsible for the several decisions that afflicted the consumer. We have only to note the effect of that policy on the working classes.

The Industrial Revolution, with its sudden expansion of commercial enterprise of all kinds, gave a great impetus to banking. Everybody wanted money, for canals here, for factories there, for all the operations of dealing and exchange, and banks sprang into life everywhere. Burke said that there were not twelve bankers out of London in 1750: in 1793 there were nearly four hundred.[17] Macleod says that shopkeepers, grocers, tailors, and drapers started up like mushrooms and turned bankers, and "issued their notes, inundating the country with their miserable rags." This process of issuing notes was carried to wild lengths, until in 1793 the Bank of England, alarmed by the drain of gold to the Continent, restricted its issue of notes. A panic followed, and of three hundred and fifty banks no fewer than one hundred stopped payment. Four years later there was a still more serious crisis. The fear of invasion caused a run on the country banks, and they applied to the Bank of England for relief. The Government meanwhile were making great demands on the bank for their payments abroad, and on a Saturday in February 1797 it was found that the bullion and coin in the bank had fallen to some £1,200,000. The Government summoned a Council for the Sunday, and an Order was issued suspending cash payments until Parliament could consider the situation. A Secret Committee of the House of Commons was appointed and on its advice an Act was passed forbidding the bank to pay its notes in specie, and this Act was to remain in force until six months after the signing of peace.[18] Thus a paper

---

[17] Meredith, *Economic History of England*, 318, quoting Macleod, *Theory and Practice of Banking*, i. 436.

[18] When the motion was adopted to appoint a Secret Committee the opposition moved a hostile amendment, to direct the Committee to inquire not only into the circumstances of the bank, but into the causes which had produced the Order in Council. See Debate on

currency was created that was not convertible into gold. Paper
money was not issued at first very much faster, and it maintained
its nominal value. But after 1803 the circulation of paper money
grew rapidly; we were sending gold instead of manufactures to
the Continent during the blockade, and in 1810, when the famous Bullion Committee was appointed, depreciation had gone
so far that £100 of paper money was only worth £86 10s. in
gold. This led, of course, to an immense inflation of prices. Mr.
Prothero thinks that from 1811 to 1813, when wheat was at one
time 126 shillings, one-fifth of the enormous price of agricultural produce was due to the disordered state of the currency.[19]
The depreciation of money and the fluctuation in the price of
gold (the premium in 1813 was over £29 per cent.; in 1815
with peace, between £13 and £14) produced high prices and
violent variations, each of them a catastrophe for the working
classes.[20]

In the history of the Corn Laws the important event for our
purposes is the Law of 1815. It is generally believed that the
Corn Laws before that date had no considerable influence.[21] Before the French War they were moderate, and during the war
it was a force more powerful than Parliament that ruled prices.
From 1808 to 1813 the home price never fell below 95s. 8d.

Sheridan's Amendment, February 28, 1797. They were defeated by
244 to 88.

[19] Prothero, *English Farming Past and Present*, p. 213.

[20] Spencer Walpole, *op. cit.*, vol. i. p. 403.

[21] The Act of 1773 admitted foreign wheat at 6d. a quarter as
soon as the home price had risen to 48s. a quarter, and though it
maintained the old bounty of 5s. a quarter on exported wheat, it made
both that bounty and the liberty to export cease when the home
price was 44s. In 1791 a less liberal Act was passed, prohibitive duties
were put on importation till the home price was 50s., and it was only
when the home price was 54s. that the duty fell to 6d. a quarter.
Exporting was forbidden when the home price was higher than 46s.,
and encouraged by a bounty when the price was below 44s. Then
came the French War and several bad harvests, the crops failing in
1795 and 1800, and the price of wheat reaching 122s. in 1796 and
155s. in 1801. In 1804, Parliament, alarmed by the violent fall to
50s., revised the Corn Laws once more; a duty of 24s. 3d. being
charged on imports when the price was below 63s., 2s. 6d. when the
price was between 63s. and 65s., and the duty of 6d. when it was
66s. Export was prohibited when the home price was 54s., and encouraged by a bounty when as low as 48s. See Lecky, *History of
England*, vii. 249, 261; and Smart, *op. cit.*, p. 372.

The war had raised freights to such an extent that importation was impracticable, and, as a rule, when there was scarcity in England there was scarcity over those parts of Europe whence supplies might have been drawn. There was indeed an important exception, for France and the Netherlands had good harvests in 1809 when the English harvest failed. It was the most bitter phase of our war with Napoleon, but he did not dare to try the patience of his farmers beyond a certain point, and he granted licences for exportation to England. In that extreme crisis we were partly fed by France.

But after 1815 the conditions were quite different. Three things happened to make it possible to import food with advantage. Charges for transport fell to their peace level, there was no war to disturb the production of corn in Northern Europe, and America, which was outside the influences of climate that dominated the sources from which England had previously taken her supplies, was beginning to send corn to Europe.[22]

This possibility, though it seemed satisfactory to the consumer, wore a different look to Parliament. Landlords and farmers had speculated on high prices, their manner of life was arranged accordingly: so were rents: and a great deal of land that did not repay cultivation if food was reasonably cheap had been brought under the plough. Dreading the effects of a violent fall in prices, and arguing that the way to steady prices and to secure adequate supplies was to be found in the encouragement of home resources, the Government passed a law designed to make perpetual the conditions created by Armageddon, and to do by import duties what had been done by restraint on exports due to the war. Imports were shut out by prohibitive duties until the home price was 80s. This figure was altered more than once, and in years of scarcity the Corn Laws were modified and relaxed, but it remains true that throughout the last seventeen years of our period they formed an important element in the misery of the time. Professor Nicholson says that "after 1815, and especially towards the end of the Corn Law period, the influence of the Corn Law was becoming real and serious; that is to say, the average was somewhat higher, and the extreme prices on occasions were greatly higher than would have been the case under free imports."[23] Fluctuations of prices fell, of course, with special severity on the poor, whose wages could not keep

---

22 Prothero, *op. cit.*, p. 271.
23 Nicholson, *History of the English Corn Laws*, p. 52.

pace with them. That wages lag behind prices was recognised
at the time by speakers like Huskisson.[24] Porter has given a good
example to show what high prices of corn meant to the working
classes. "If we contrast the weekly wage at the two periods of
1790 and 1800, of husbandry labourers and skilled artisans,
measuring them both by the quantity of wheat which they could
command, it will be seen that the former could in 1790 purchase 82 pints of wheat, and in 1800 could procure no more
than 53 pints, while for the skilled artisan the figures were 169
pints in 1790 and 83 pints in 1800." Professor Nicholson, who
quotes this passage,[25] gives his approval to Porter's conclusion:
"To talk of the prosperous state of the country under such a
condition of things involves a palpable contradiction. It would
be more correct to liken the situation of the community to that
of the inhabitants of a town subjected to a general conflagration
in which some became suddenly enriched by carrying off the
valuables, while the mass were involved in ruin and destitution."

Real wages thus fell rapidly in consequence of all the several
causes that raised prices, among which must be reckoned the
paper money and Corn Laws of the period. But there was another way in which high prices lowered wages. Porter observed
that pieceworkers tried to keep their families alive when bread
was dear by working longer hours, and thus they came to bid
against each other and actually beat down their nominal wages.
Professor Nicholson quotes[26] in support of this view the evidence of a bailiff before a House of Lords Committee in 1814,
from which it appeared that a landowner had been able to carry
out improvements more cheaply in the years of famine prices
because he contracted for some very large ditches at 6d. an ell,
though when food was cheaper he could not get the work done
for two or three times the price. This effect of the Corn Laws
was urged as an argument in their favour by a speaker in 1814,
who argued that high prices made labour cheap, for "when provisions were very cheap, artisans could earn in a few days what
was necessary to subsist them for many."[27]

We can illustrate the effect of an increase in prices on the
working classes from an interesting letter, written by Colonel
Fletcher of Bolton to the Home Office in 1822,[28] on the subject

[24] Smart, *op. cit.*, p. 413.
[25] Nicholson, *op. cit.*, p. 96.
[26] Nicholson, *op. cit.*, p. 53.
[27] *Hansard*, xxvii. p. 720.
[28] H. O., 40. 17.

of the prospects of trade in that town and district. Fletcher gave an analysis of the population, from which it appeared that of 100,000 persons, 90,000 were labourers. Of these 60,000 were weavers, 15,000 were bleachers, printers, dyers, masons, colliers, 10,000 were preparers and spinners, and 5,000 agricultural labourers. He put the wages of a family of five at 16s. 10d. in the case of weavers, and £1 4s. for other labourers. The cost of rent and fuel he put as half a crown a week. (In another letter he mentions incidentally that it was usual for people to sleep four in a bed in Bolton.) He put the effect of an advance in the price of provisions from 45s. to 65s. per quarter of wheat at 3s. 4d. per family. In the year of his letter wheat was lower than it had been for thirty years: next year it rose to 53s. 4d., in 1824 it was 63s. 11d., and in 1825, 68s. 6d.[29]

The war, the disturbance of the currency, the Corn Laws, brought great distress and misfortune to the people of England. But they also brought great riches to some of the people of England. There were financial houses founded on the profits of lending money to the Government to prosecute the war, there were landlords who were enriched by the Corn Laws, and if some manufacturers were ruined by the cyclones that swept over the markets of the world in years of crisis, many fortunes were made during this period. But of all the classes that bore the burdens of the war, and paid the penalty of their rulers' errors, no class was so destitute of compensations as the class that could only make its voice heard by food riots, and by the kind of demonstration that ended in a cavalry charge and half a dozen men or women sent to the gallows.

We have now to turn to the measures taken by the ruling class that affected the working classes not as citizens, or as taxpayers, or as consumers, or as producers for an irregular market, but as combatants in the struggle of a class against the new power.

---

[29] Prothero, *op. cit.*, p. 441.

CHAPTER VII

THE WAR ON TRADE UNIONS

The new industry, which had increased the need for Trade Unions, had increased their opportunities, for it massed men together in a common system, melted down individual grievances in a common discontent, made common deliberation and common action easier and simpler, and thus created conditions favourable to association on a larger scale. Employers again, with plant and machinery, were more vulnerable than the old masters who had little fixed capital and lost much less in strikes.[1] For the first time combination promised to become a weapon of real power in the hands of a class that had no other weapon when facing the superior forces of wealth, education, and influence with magistrates and the governing world. But if Trade Unionism found a new scope in the changed conditions of industrial life, it found a new spirit in the ruling classes. Combination had been punished, of course, before this time, both under conspiracy laws and under special laws against combination, of which, according to Whitbread, there were forty on the Statute Book in 1800. But before the famous legislation of 1799 and 1800, the State forbade combination, not as infringing the freedom of employers, but as infringing its own authority.[2] The theory was that the State regulated industry itself, and that combinations were unlawful as interfering with the province of the legislature. Hence, though a combination to reduce hours or raise wages was illegal, it was possible to combine against masters who refused to obey the law, and such combination was followed, not by punishment, but by discussion in Parliament of the merits of the regulation.

At the end of the century, under the influence of the ideas then in the ascendant, combination assumed a new aspect for the governing class. As a political danger, it seemed much more formidable since the French Revolution; as an economic danger, it seemed much more formidable to an age that had discovered that the employer was the best judge of all questions relating to the conditions of his industry.

The politicians who thought seriously about what they were

---

[1] Chapman, *Cotton Industry*, p. 184.
[2] Webb, *History of Trade Unionism*, p. 58.

doing in 1799, would have said that invention was rapidly producing a new world of trade, and that England's chances of making herself the mistress of this new world depended on the freedom and the daring of the great organisers. If their designs were successful, the workers would benefit; if, for any reason, they came to grief, the workers would suffer. The chief danger was mutiny and insubordination, and this was the danger from which the State ought to protect industry. Peace, order, and progress all turned on discipline; the rough artisans must not be allowed to act or to think for themselves, but must be made to accept the rule of their masters without question: they must take what wages their masters, who were the best judges of the circumstances of the trade, chose to give them. The State, that is to say, was to abdicate in favour of the employers. The employers' law was to be the public law. Workmen were to obey their master as they would obey the State, and the State was to enforce the master's commands as it would its own. This was the new policy behind the Combination Laws of 1799 and 1800. These two Acts, the second modifying the first, prohibiting all common action in defence of their common interests by workmen, remain the most unqualified surrender of the State to the discretion of a class in the history of England.

The word abdicate does not exaggerate the gravity or significance of the policy that the English ruling class adopted at this time. In English history there were great traditions of State regulation. The interest of the community in prices, wages, and the risks and consequences of the economic measures pursued by individuals, was affirmed and defended in a great number of statutes. There were statutes empowering magistrates to fix rates of wages, others empowering them to fix the price of bread. All kinds of regulations governed the conduct of the woollen trade, and there were elaborate laws laying down conditions of apprenticeship on which alone certain trades could be practised. During this period, as will appear in a later volume, the workmen more than once called on the State to act on this principle and to regulate the anarchy of the new competition, to protect human life in the avalanche of economic forces. The ruling class rejected this policy, but they did not merely leave the industrial world to itself. They put the masters into the place of the State.

The prestige of the new industry had enabled the manufacturers to talk to the State in the language that hitherto had been the prerogative of the landowner. "Our prosperity is yours. Our difficulties are yours. Prosperous manufacturers make a prosperous State. To check the conditions of our success is to impoverish the State. The conditions of success for the land-owner were enclosures and corn laws: for us they are cheap and docile labour, men and women forced to take such wages as we think well to give them. Prosperity and social peace point the same way. Insubordination is the enemy, yours and ours. Scratch a Trade Unionist and you will find a Jacobin; catch him talking in his sleep and you will overhear an atheist. Leave us to rule this new world. Withdraw your supervision and make laws giving us an absolute control." The ruling class were not all convinced. At one time or another this doctrine was combated by men like Whitbread, Sheridan, Holland, Burdett, and Fowell Buxton. But the answer of the generation that passed the Combination Laws, abolished apprentice laws and the regula-tion of wages, was simple and clear. A powerful class is often apt to say to itself, "L'Etat, c'est moi." The new capitalists were no exception. But few Governments have said so emphatically as the Governments of Pitt and Liverpool, "L'Etat, c'est lui."

The history and circumstances of this legislation require full description. In some respects it is the most important legislation of the period, and yet, as Mr. Justice Stephen remarks, "in the parliamentary history for 1799 and 1800 there is no account of any debate on these Acts, nor are they referred to in the *Annual Register* for these years."[3] Fortunately we are not left without record of these debates. They are reported in the *Par-liamentary Register*, the *Senator*, and the newspapers, and from these sources a tolerably full account of the proceedings can be collected. It appears that the two statesmen to whom these meas-ures were mainly due were Wilberforce and Pitt.

The immediate cause of this legislation was a petition from the master millwrights which reached the House of Commons on April 5, 1799, after the time fixed for receiving petitions.[4] In consideration of "the particular Circumstances" the House waived its rules, and allowed the petition to be read. The petition set forth "that a dangerous Combination has for some Time ex-isted amongst the Journeymen Millwrights, within the Metrop-olis, and the Limits of Twenty-five Miles round the same, for enforcing a general Increase of their Wages, preventing the

---

[3] *History of the Criminal Law*, vol. iii. p. 208.
[4] *House of Commons Journal*, April 5, 1799.

Employment of such Journeymen as refuse to join their Confederacy, and for other illegal Purposes, and frequent Conspiracies of this Sort have been set on Foot by the Journeymen, and the Masters have as often been obliged to submit, and that a Demand of a further Advance of Wages has recently been made, which not being complied with, the Men, within the Limits aforesaid, have refused to work; and a Compliance with such Demands of an Advance of Wages hath generally been followed by further Claims, with which it is impossible for the Masters to comply, without occasioning so considerable an Advance in the Price of Mill Work as most materially to affect the said Business, and the different Manufactories connected therewith; and that, in Support of the said Combination (notwithstanding they complain of the Insufficiency of their Wages) the Journeymen have established a general Fund, and raised Subscriptions, and so regular and connected is their System that their Demands are made sometimes by all the Journeymen, within the above Limits, at the same Time, and at other Times at some one particular Shop, and, in case of Non-compliance, the different Workshops (where their Demands are resisted) are wholly deserted by the Men, and other Journeymen are prohibited from applying for Work until the Master Millwrights are brought to Compliance, and the Journeymen, who have thus thrown themselves out of Employ, receive Support in the mean Time from their general Fund; and that the only Method of punishing such Delinquents, under the existing Laws, is by preferring an Indictment, at the Sessions or Assizes, after the Commission of the Offence, but, before that Time arrives, the Offenders frequently remove into different Parts of the Country, so that, even if their Places of Residence should be discovered, it would be a long Time before they could be brought to Trial, and the Expence of apprehending, and bringing them back, by *Habeas*, to the Place where the Offence was committed, is so heavy to the Masters, whose Businesses have been stopped by the Desertion of the Journeymen, that (aware of these Difficulties) the Journeymen carry on their Combinations with Boldness and Impunity; and that the last Obstruction given to the Business of the Petitioners, under which they are now suffering, and which rendered their Application to the Legislature necessary, did not take place until after the Time fixed by the House for receiving Petitions for Private Bills was elapsed: And therefore, praying, That Leave may be given to exhibit a Petition for Leave to bring in a Bill, for the better preventing of unlawful Combinations of

Workmen employed in the Millwright Business, and for regulating the Wages of such Workmen, in such manner as to the House shall seem meet."

The petition was referred to a committee composed of Sir John Anderson, the Lord Mayor and others, who reported on April 9 that its allegations were true, and asked for leave to bring in a Bill to prevent unlawful combinations of workmen in the millwright business, and to enable the magistrates to regulate their wages.[5] At this point Wilberforce rose to suggest that it would be better to have a general Combination Law. "These combinations he regarded as a general disease in our society; and for which he thought the remedy should be general; so as not only to cure the complaint for the present, but to preclude its return. He thought the worthy mover of this subject deserved praise for what he was doing, as far as the measure went; but if it was enlarged, and made general against combinations, he should be better satisfied with it, and then it would be a measure that might be of great service to society."[6] The Speaker told Mr. Wilberforce that a measure of the kind he proposed could not be founded on the present report, and the millwright business was accordingly proceeded with, and leave given to bring in a Bill. The Bill was read a first time on May 6,[7] and a second on May 10.[8] On May 10 came a first petition from the workmen, who asked to be heard by themselves or counsel, against the Bill. This petition was ordered to lie on the table till the report was received.[9] On May 20 came another petition from the workmen, and this was referred to the committee, who heard counsel for and against.[10] On June 6, when the report of the committee was considered, the question of the first petition from the workmen came up again. It was ordered that when the report was taken into further consideration, the petitioners should be heard, by themselves or counsel, against the Bill. "Then the House proceeded to take the said Report into further Consideration. And the House being informed that Counsel attended; a Motion was made, and the Question being put, That

---

[5] *House of Commons Journal*, April 9, 1799.

[6] *Parliamentary Register*, April 9, 1799. See also *Senator*, April 9, 1799; *Times*, April 10, 1799; *True Briton*, April 10, 1799.

[7] *House of Commons Journal*.

[8] *House of Commons Journal*.

[9] *House of Commons Journal*, May 10, 1799.

[10] *House of Commons Journal*, May 20 and 31.

the Counsel be now called in; It passed in the Negative."[11] On the third reading of the Bill on June 10, there was a debate in which Sir Francis Burdett and Benjamin Hobhouse alone opposed the Bill, whilst Sir John Anderson, Buxton, C. Smith, Hawkins Brown, H. Lascelles, Lord Sheffield, the Solicitor-General, Ellison, and Bragge supported it.[12]

Burdett "opposed the principle of the Bill. He thought the existing laws sufficient for every fair and reasonable purpose the framers of the Bill could have in view, and believed that there was seldom a combination of the kind complained of, without a great grievance to provoke it. He quoted Dr. Adam Smith in support of his opinions, and maintained that it was the wise policy of every well-regulated state to leave trade of every kind to find its own level."[13] Mr. Benjamin Hobhouse spoke in the same sense, and also alluded to the refusal of the House to hear the journeymen's counsel.[14] The supporters of the Bill agreed with the general principle of leaving trade and labour to find their own level, but denied that the principle applied to these particular circumstances; they were also "for the most part of opinion that this Bill should be followed up by one more general, in order to prevent all combinations."[15] The Bill passed the House of Commons, but was dropped in the Lords owing to the introduction of the more comprehensive measure.

On June 17 of the same year (1799), seven days after Burdett's speech and appeal to Adam Smith, Pitt asked and obtained leave to bring in the Workmen's Combination Bill.[16] "Mr. Chancellor Pitt said, it was his intention to endeavour to provide a remedy to an evil of very considerable magnitude; he meant that of unlawful combination among workmen in general—a practice which had become much too general, and was likely, if not checked, to produce very serious mischief. He could not state particularly the nature of the Bill which he intended to move for leave to bring in; but it would be modelled in some respects on that of the Bill for regulating the conduct of the

---

[11] *House of Commons Journal*, June 6, 1799.

[12] *Parliamentary Register*, June 10, 1799. See also *Senator*, June 10; *Times* and *True Briton*, June 11; and *London Chronicle*, June 8-11.

[13] *Times*, June 11, 1799.

[14] *London Chronicle*, June 8-11

[15] *Ibid*.

[16] *Parliamentary Register*, June 17; *Times* and *True Briton*, June 18; *London Chronicle*, June 15-18.

paper manufacturers. He wished to call the particular attention
of the House to this important matter."[17] As reported in the
Times,[18] Pitt referred specially to the combinations in the
northern parts of the kingdom.[19] When leave had been given to
bring in the Bill it was ordered, say the Journals of the House
of Commons,[20] "that Mr. Chancellor of the Exchequer, Mr.
Attorney-General, Mr. Solicitor-General, Mr. Rose, Mr. Long,
and Mr. Bragge do prepare, and bring in, the same." The Bill
was a close copy of the Papermakers Act referred to by Pitt,[21]
and the preparation had evidently been done beforehand, for
the very next day Mr. Rose[22] presented the Bill, and it was read
a first time. The Bill which had now started on its lightning
career through Parliament was certainly drastic enough to satisfy
Wilberforce and Pitt. It passed too rapidly to allow of the presentation of many petitions, but the calico printers of the London
district contrived to present one,[23] and Mr. Gurney appeared
as their counsel in the House of Lords.[24]

Under this Act[25] any workman who combined with any
other workman in order to get an increase of wages or a decrease of hours was liable to be brought up before any single
magistrate—it might be one of the employers for whom he was
working—and on conviction be sent forthwith to jail for three
months, or to hard labour in the House of Correction for two.
The same process and the same penalties would await him if he
should "by any Means whatsoever, directly or indirectly, decoy,
persuade, solicit, intimidate, influence or prevail, or attempt or
endeavour to prevail," on any worker to leave his work, or if
"being hired or employed" he refused to work with any other
person. Further if he himself attended any meeting for the purpose of shortening hours or raising wages, etc., or "directly or
indirectly" induced any workmen to attend such a meeting, or

---

[17] *Parliamentary Register*, June 17.

[18] *Times*, June 18.

[19] It seems probable that the Government were alarmed by the
newly formed Association of Weavers in the north.

[20] *House of Commons Journal*, June 17.

[21] 36 George III. c. 3 (1796); but the Papermakers Act had fixed
hours of work to ten or eleven a day.

[22] Rose was Secretary to the Treasury.

[23] *House of Lords Journal*, July 5, 1799.

[24] *House of Lords*, July 9. For long account of Mr. Gurney's
speech, see *True Briton*, July 10.

[25] 39 George III. c. 81.

contributed to such a meeting, or collected money for such a meeting, he made himself liable to the same penalties. The effect of these clauses was well described in the criticisms of the petitioners against the Act next year, "that the said Act appears to the Petitioners to have created new Crimes, of so indefinite a Nature, that no one Journeyman or Workman will be safe in holding any Conversation with another on the Subject of his Trade or Employment; and that the Petitioners and others are, by the said Act, deprived of a Trial by a Jury of their Country, and to be tried by One Justice of the Peace, who, for the most part, is engaged in Trade and whom, in all Cases, it is competent to the Masters to select."[26] Another petition pointed out that in the Act it was "declared illegal, directly or indirectly, to attempt to prevail upon any Journeyman or Workman to quit the Service in which he is employed; and that the said Act, by the use of such uncertain Terms, and others of the same Nature, has created new Crimes of boundless Extent . . . and that, in many Instances, the Crimes created by the said Act are such as will encourage wilful Perjury in Witnesses, from the great Difficulty of its being discovered, and will of course expose the Petitioners to numberless false Accusations at the Pleasure of any malicious Prosecutor. . . ." In fact, if the law were not repealed, "it will hereafter be dangerous for the Petitioners to converse with one another, or even with their own Families."[27] If a workman was convicted, his only remedy was to appeal to Quarter Sessions, but before he could do this he must enter into Recognisances "with Two sufficient sureties in the Penalty of Twenty Pounds." The removal of a conviction by *Certiorari* was expressly forbidden. By another clause it was enacted that any person, whether a workman or not, who contributed "for the Purpose of paying any Expences incurred or to be incurred by any Person acting contrary to the Provisions of this Act" was liable to a £10 fine, whilst the receiver might be fined £5. In reference to these clauses, the petitioners pointed out that when workmen had been convicted by a single justice who was probably engaged in trade, a master himself, "the Parties nevertheless are not even permitted to remove any Conviction by such Justice . . . by *Certiorari*, or any other Writ or Process whatsoever,

26 Petition from Liverpool, *House of Commons Journal*, June 13, 1800.
27 Petition from London and Westminster, *House of Commons Journal*, June 13, 1800.

into any of His Majesty's Courts of Records at Westminster; and
that, although a Right of Appeal is given by the said Act against
any Conviction by such Justice to the General or Quarter Sessions of the Peace, yet the Sureties and Recognisances required,
and the great Expence of such Appeal, puts that Remedy beyond the Reach of the Petitioners, and other Workmen, who
earn, by their daily Labour, barely sufficient to maintain themselves and Families; and the said Act expressly forbids, under
a severe Penalty, any Person from subscribing or contributing
any Sum or Sums of Money whatsoever, for the Purpose of
paying any Expences incurred, or to be incurred, by any Person
charged with having acted contrary to the Provisions of the said
Act."[28]

Other clauses dealt with the funds which workmen had
raised to forward or protect their interests. Any money contributed for any purposes forbidden by the Act which remained
undivided for three months after the passing of the Act, and any
contributions paid in after the Act, were to be forfeited, half
going to the King, and the other half to any one who liked to
sue for it. Further, any person who had charge of such money,
and was liable to be sued for it, was compelled to answer any
questions about it on oath, "and no Person shall demur to, or
refuse to answer such Information, by reason of any Penalty or
Forfeiture, to which such Person may be liable, in consequence
of any Discovery which may be sought thereby." In other words,
the man was obliged to incriminate himself. His only method of
escape was afforded by the next clause, which provided that if
the holder of such money at once paid it into court and gave all
information about investments, then he was to be discharged
free from all penalties. In reference to these clauses the workmen pointed out "that the said Act empowers Trustees, Treasur-
ers, Collectors, Receivers, and Agents, to give up, in Breach of
their Trust, all Monies in their Hands, Custody, or Power, and
indemnifies them, in so doing, before any Court of Law or
Equity shall have pronounced on the Legality or Illegality of the
Purposes for which such Funds shall have been entrusted to
them; and finally, the Petitioners crave the most serious Attention of the House to that Part of the said Act, whereby all
Persons who shall be charged with having offended against the
same, are compellable to answer, upon Oath, all Questions that

---

[28] Petition from Liverpool, *House of Commons Journal*, June 13,
1800.

shall be put to them, notwithstanding any Penalty or Forfeiture, as the Act itself expressly states, to which such Persons may be liable in consequence of any Discovery which may be sought thereby."[29] Another petition pointed out that it had "hitherto been a recognised and established Principle of the Law of this Land, that no one shall be compelled to incriminate himself. . . ."[30] Finally, a clause in the Act gave any justice power to grant a licence to an employer to employ unqualified workmen, all regulations to the contrary notwithstanding, if the qualified workmen refused to work "for reasonable Wages" or in any way impeded the course of business. This meant, as the petitioners pointed out, "that the same Magistrate, who has thus the uncontrolled Power over Offenders within the Act, will, in many Cases, be enabled to fix the Rate of Wages of Journeymen and Workmen, and, upon their Refusal to work for such Wages (however inadequate to their Labour), may license Masters to employ in their respective Trades all Persons indiscriminately, to the Detriment of those Trades, and to the utter Destruction of the Workmen who have served regular Apprenticeships therein."[31]

The parliamentary history of the Bill was brief and rapid. The Bill, as we have seen, was presented and read a first time, and on Pitt's motion[32] was sent to a committee of the whole House. A week elapsed before the committee reported, the delay being due to pressure of other business. On June 26 Mr. Bragge reported to the House, and by July 1 the Bill had passed all stages in the House of Commons, and twenty-four days after its introduction in the House of Commons it had received the Royal Assent.[33]

The only opposition that was offered to the Bill came from Mr. Benjamin Hobhouse in the Commons and Lord Holland in the Lords. Hobhouse restated the arguments against the principle of the Bill which he and Burdett had advanced against the Millwright Bill, and with regard to its details he laid stress on the monstrous injustice of making workmen liable to sum-

---

[29] Liverpool and Manchester Petitions, *House of Commons Journal*, June 13, 1800.

[30] Newcastle-on-Tyne Petition, *House of Commons Journal*, July 21, 1800.

[31] London and Westminster Petition, *House of Commons Journal*, June 13, 1800.

[32] *Senator*, June 19, 1799.

[33] *House of Commons Journal*, July 12, 1799.

mary conviction by a single magistrate for expressions of opinion
or even insinuations. He tried without success to amend the
Bill, and to secure that workmen should not be convicted except by two or more magistrates.[34] In the Lords Holland made
a powerful speech, arguing that the men were the weaker party
in all bargains between masters and men, and that the Bill
would make them weaker still; that the masters had infinite advantages in a dispute without this additional and unjust help
from the law. He accused the masters of taking advantage of the
general prejudice of the times against the poor, excited by the
Revolution, in order to pass a Bill that would make their workmen even more dependent. The Bill took away trial by jury,
and put the workmen at the mercy of the employers, who were
magistrates and could play into each other's hands. The opportunity of appeal was worthless, because no workman could find
£20, as the law required. It often happened that an increase of
wages was necessary on principles of justice and humanity, and
this Bill made it impossible for workmen to raise their wages.
He contended that it was most improper that so small a House
should pass a Bill of such importance. If the Bill was necessary
and proper, it was a Bill of great importance; if it was unnecessary, as he thought it, it was big with very dangerous consequences indeed. The supporters of the Bill did not attempt to
reply to him, and his proposed amendment was rejected without a division.[35]

It has been shown that, owing to Pitt's haste to pass a Bill for
suppressing Trade Unionism, working men had had no opportunity of making their views known to Parliament before the Bill
became law. Next year Parliament was flooded with petitions of
protest from all parts of the country: London, Liverpool, Manchester, Bristol, Plymouth, Bath, Lancaster, Leeds, Derby, Nottingham, and Newcastle-on-Tyne.[36]

The discussion was, consequently, reopened, and this time
the workmen's case was put with the unanswerable wit and eloquence of Sheridan himself. The amending Bill was introduced[37] by Colonel Gascoyne, a Tory M.P. for Liverpool, who

[34] *Parliamentary Register*, June 26, 1799.

[35] *Parliamentary Register*, July 9, 1799. This speech of Lord Holland's was printed at Manchester and Liverpool for distribution. Lady
Holland's *Journal*, ii. 102.

[36] *House of Commons Journal*, June 13, 19, 27, 30, July 21, 1800.

[37] *House of Commons Journal*, July 4, 1800.

joined forces for this purpose with his Whig fellow-member for that city, the famous cavalry officer, General Tarleton; but the proceedings resolved themselves in the main into a battle between Sheridan, on one side, and Pitt, with the Attorney-General and the Solicitor-General (Sir John Mitford, afterwards Lord Redesdale) and Sir William Grant on the other.[38] Sheridan said that "a more intolerable mass of injustice had never been entered on the Statute Book," and that this "foul and oppressive" Act ought to be repealed.[39] Pitt defended the Act, though he disclaimed the responsibility for introducing it, and said that its principle was good and ought to be strengthened. The House was not prepared to go so far as Sheridan, but there was a general concensus in favour of considering the petitions, and as he could not secure the repeal of the Act, Sheridan lent his energies to the task of removing some of its worst features. A committee was appointed, consisting of Pierrepont, Gascoyne, Tarleton, Dent, the Lord Mayor of London, and Sheridan, to prepare and bring in an amending Bill.[40] The Act of 1800[41] was an improvement on its predecessor in certain details. Thus "two magistrates" were substituted for one magistrate as the court with power to convict a workman, it was provided that a magistrate who was a master in the particular trade affected should not sit on the bench to try offences under the Act, and a certain vagueness was eliminated by substituting "wilfully and maliciously" for "directly and indirectly" in describing the offences to be punished. But the most important change was the addition of certain arbitration clauses which provided that in a dispute over wages or hours both parties could name an arbitrator; and if the two arbitrators could not agree, either party could require them to submit the points in dispute to a Justice of the Peace, whose decision would be final. On the third reading of the amending Bill[42] these clauses were attacked by the Attorney-General, who declared that this arrangement would have the tendency to fix wages, and that the men might "name an improper person that a master would be obliged to meet—this

---

[38] For account of debates see *Parliamentary Register*, June 30 and July 22, and the *Times*, July 1, and *Morning Post* and *True Briton*, July 23
[39] *Times*, July 1.
[40] *House of Commons Journal*, June 30, 1800.
[41] 39 and 40 George III. c. 106.
[42] July 22, 1800.

would be a sort of Solicitor-General in that trade, who would no doubt be paid and indemnified for his labour and genius."[43] Pitt upheld this criticism, to which Gascoyne and Sheridan replied by pointing out that the clause was taken almost verbatim from the Act passed in the same session for establishing arbitration in the cotton trade.[44] Pitt carried his motion for adjournment at the time,[45] but the clauses were ultimately adopted.[46] The final stages are unfortunately unreported. The Bill as drawn up by Sheridan and his colleagues on the committee contained a valuable clause to protect friendly and benevolent societies, but this clause disappeared.[47]

The greatest living master of controversial prose analysed the Combination Laws in a characteristic article in the *Political Register* that appeared the year before they were repealed.[48] In 1823 a spinner named Ryding was tried for an assault on a Preston manufacturer named Horrocks, who was also a member of Parliament. In the course of his trial it came out that Ryding had decided deliberately to wound Horrocks or his partner in order that he might be tried before a judge and jury, and thus bring before the world the injustice of the Combination Laws under which he and other spinners had suffered great priva-

---

[43] *Parliamentary Register*, July 22, 1800.
[44] 39 and 40 George III. c. 90.
[45] *Parliamentary Register*, July 22, 1800.
[46] For failure of these clauses see p. 137.
[47] That nothing in this Act extends "in any Manner to affect or render illegal any Clubs or Societies of Workmen now formed or hereafter to be formed, or the Funds of any Clubs or Societies subscribed or collected *bona fide* for the several beneficial Purposes of promoting the Knowledge of their respective Trades and Manufactures, and of providing Masters with Workmen, which latter Clubs or Societies are commonly called or known by the Name of 'Houses of Call,' and of purchasing Tools for Workmen, who may be incapable of purchasing the same themselves, or who shall have lost the same by Fire, or other inevitable Accident, and of granting the like Relief as is given by Friendly Societies established and enrolled under and by virtue of an Act passed in the 33rd year of His present Majesty, intituled 'An Act for the Encouragement and Relief of Friendly Societies,' to Workmen and their Wives and Families, who cannot receive such Relief from such last-mentioned Societies, by Reason of their not admitting any Persons to be Members thereof after a certain Age: anything in this or any other Act contained to the contrary thereof in anywise notwithstanding."
[48] *Political Register*, August 30, 1823.

tions, in consequence of their attempt to resist a reduction of wages. Cobbett wrote on the trial, putting his views in the favourite form of a public letter to Wilberforce, who had let drop the unfortunate phrase "free British labourers" in a speech on the West Indian slaves, and in the article he discussed the Combination Laws. After reciting their main purpose Cobbett goes on, "Well, Wilberforce; the combiners are to go to gaol or to the House of Correction, to the former for not more than three months, to the latter for not more than two months, for the first going off. *Two Justices of the Peace*, who are appointed and displaced at the pleasure of the Ministers, two of these men are to hear, determine and sentence without any *Trial by the Peers of the party*. It being very difficult to get proof of this combining for the raising of wages, there is a clause in the Act compelling the persons accused to give evidence against themselves or against their associates. If they refuse, these two Justices have the power to commit them to prison, there to remain, without bail or mainprize, until they submit to be examined or to give evidence before such justices.

"Now, you will observe, Wilberforce, that this punishment is inflicted in order to prevent workmen from uniting together, and by such union, to obtain an addition to their wages, or, as in the case of Ryding and Horrocks, to prevent their wages from being reduced. Every man's labour is his *property*. It is something which he has to sell or otherwise dispose of. The cotton spinners had their labour to sell; or at least they thought so. They were pretty free to sell it before this Combination Law of 1800. They had their labour to sell. The purchasers were powerful and rich, and wanted them to sell it at what the spinners deemed too low a price. In order to be a match for the rich purchasers, the sellers of the labour agree to assist one another, and thus to live as well as they can; till they can obtain what they deem a proper price. Now, what was there wrong in this? What was there either unjust or illegal? If men be attacked either in the market or in their shops; if butchers, bakers, farmers, millers be attacked with a view of forcing them to sell their commodities at a price lower than they demand, the assailants are deemed rioters, and are hanged! In 1812, a poor woman who seized, or rather, assisted to seize a man's potatoes in the market at Manchester, and, in compelling him to sell them at a lower price than that which he asked for them. this poor woman, who had, very likely, a starving family at home, *was hanged by the neck till she was dead!* Now, then, if it was a crime worthy of death to attempt to force potatoes from *a farmer*, is it a crime in the cotton spinner to attempt to prevent others from getting his labour from him at a price lower than he asks for it? It is impossible; statutes upon statutes may be passed, but it is impossible to make a man believe that he has fair play, if farmer's property is to be protected in this manner, and if it be a crime, to be punished by imprisonment, without Trial by Jury, to endeavour to protect the labourer's property.

"This Combination Act does, however, say that the '*masters shall not combine against the workmen.*' Oh! well then, how fair this Act is! And what then did Ryding mean, when he talked about the *partiality* of the law? What did he mean by saying that there was no law for the poor man; that there was no justice; that the masters could do what they pleased without being punished? Why, did he ever read this law? Does he know the contents of the fortieth of the *good old King, chapter* 106? Does not this law say that all contracts between masters and other persons for reducing the wages of men; does it not say, in short, that all such combinations of masters against workmen 'shall be, and the same are hereby declared to be, *illegal*, null, and void, to all intents and purposes whatsoever'? Does not the law say this; and does it not empower the two Justices to *send the masters to the common gaol and the House of Correction?* No, the devil a bit does it do such a thing! No such a thing does it do. However flagrant the combination; however oppressive; however cruel; though it may bring starvation upon thousands of persons; though it may tend (as in numerous cases it has tended) to produce breaches of the peace, insurrections and all their consequences; though such may be the nature and tendency of these combinations of the masters, the utmost punishment that the two Justices can inflict, is a *fine of twenty pounds*! But, and now mark the difference. Mark it, Wilberforce; note it down as a proof of the happiness of your '*free* British labourers': mark, that the masters cannot be called upon by the Justices to *give evidence against themselves and their associates.*"

The Combination Laws lasted for a quarter of a century, and during that time the workpeople were at the mercy of their masters. A great deal can be learnt about the effects and working of the Laws from the evidence taken by the Committee on Artisans and Machinery over which Hume presided in 1824. Francis Place collected enough facts to fill eight volumes. He showed that under cover of these laws magistrates had threatened workmen with imprisonment or service in the fleet as the alternative to accepting the wages their masters chose to offer them. "Could an accurate account be given of proceedings, of hearings before magistrates, trials at sessions and in the Court of King's Bench, the gross injustice, the foul invective, and terrible punishments inflicted would not, after a few years have passed away, be credited on any but the best evidence."[49] It is worth while to give a few illustrations from the evidence taken by the committee to which allusion has been made.

John Alexander, a journeyman bootmaker, described how Mr. Algar of Lombard Street halved his pay, and then when his six ot seven men refused to work for it, summoned them before the Lord Mayor for combination. They were imprisoned for fourteen days with hard labour. The Lord Mayor remarked that it was a hard case, and gave them the choice of this sentence or two months without hard labour.[50]

Joseph Sherwin, cotton weaver of Stockport, where the average wage was 8s. a week for fourteen hours a day, gave a case of a master in a steam-loom factory, in 1816, who reduced wages 3d. per loom for artificial light, i.e. a reduction of 6d. to most, to some few 9d.; the master forgot to return the reduction in summer, and when winter came again (1817) he wanted to make a fresh reduction; the workers objected and left work, twelve women and eleven men. They were taken before a magistrate, who sent them out into the yard to deliberate whether they would go to work or to prison; they refused to return at the reduced price, and were given a month's imprisonment, the women at Middlewich and the men at Chester.[51]

Another witness, William Salt, a cotton spinner, gave the following evidence:—

"Have you suffered prosecution under the Combination Laws?—Yes, in 1822.
"What were the circumstances of your case?—We had not the same wages as the other factories, and we gave notice.
"In what way?—Singly, by ourselves.
"All the men in the factory, or a limited number?—All of them.

---

[49] Place MSS. 27798-7.
[50] Report of the Select Committee on Artisans and Machinery, p. 133.
[51] Ibid., p. 418.

"In whose factory was this?—Mr. Marshall's, near Stockport.

"You gave notice verbally, stating that you could not continue to work, unless you had an advance of wages?—Unless we had an advance of wages, according to what others were giving; and on Saturday I left his employment; on the Tuesday he sent for me.

"Did the whole eighteen leave the employment?—Yes. I met with him 40 or 50 yards from the factory, and we had some conversation about the prices.

"Did the factory stop when you left?—No, but it stopped on Tuesday night, when master and me parted; I went my way home and he towards the factory.

"What followed?—As I was coming home, there was a large body of people on the road, my master and the constable were after me; and the constable, Mr. Pickford, struck me over the forehead, and took me off to gaol.

"Did you ask under what authority?—No; I asked not any thing.

"Did you not ask when they took you to gaol, by whose authority you were confined?—Yes; that my master had ordered Mr. Pickford to take me; on the next day I was taken up before Mr. Phillips, the magistrate; he never asked me any questions.

"Was any evidence given against you?—He examined my master, and he told him that we had combined together; no one was taken but me that night.

"Were any others brought before the magistrate at that time?—There was a warrant sent for five more.

"But were they before the magistrate at the same time with you?—Yes.

"Was any other evidence given?—The overlooker gave evidence against me.

"What was the determination of the magistrate?—I was not asked any question, I was taken back again, and there I remained to the next day, and then taken before the justice meeting; four justices were sitting there. And as soon as I entered into the room, one of the justices said, Which is Salt? I said, I am Salt; and he said I shall give you two months' imprisonment; and he said, I might think myself very lucky that I was not prosecuted under the Conspiracy Laws. This was on Wednesday; the other five were at the justice meeting, and stood upon my left. The question was asked, what must be done with them, and he said, Give them all alike.

"And were they all served alike?—Yes, two months' imprisonment."[52]

The number of prosecutions gives a very imperfect measure of the influence of the Combination Laws. In industrial warfare the threat was often as good, or better, from the point of view of the masters, than actual proceedings. It was a common practice for masters to take the preliminary steps and then to agree to withdraw if the men would publish a contrite submission in the local papers. Such an advertisement spread fear of the law as widely as the news that half a dozen workmen were in prison. An example of this form of a submission may be given from the columns of the Tyne *Mercury*:—[53]

"Whereas upwards of 80 Colliers and Workmen, of Poynton, Worth, and Norbury Collieries, in Cheshire, on the 24th September last, assembled together in a wood, and there resolved upon demanding from their employers an advance of wages according to written terms read to the meeting, and afterwards delivered to the underlookers of the said collieries. These terms being so extremely exorbitant, and the restrictions as to working so improper, that it was impossible they should be complied with; and all the said colliers left their work at once, and remained out of employment for nine weeks, to the great damage of the collieries, and to the extreme inconvenience of the public —for this unlawful and dangerous conspiracy a prosecution was commenced against the Secretary and Delegates of the conspirators, to answer which the undersigned were under recognisances to appear at the ensuing sessions at Chester, but have since applied to the masters (the prosecutors) to be forgiven, and to be permitted to return to their employment like the rest of the workmen, without any alteration in wages or restrictions demanded, which the masters have consented to comply with, upon condition of their signing a submission to be published at their expence, in the Chester, Manchester, and Derby papers, We, the undersigned, do therefore most humbly acknowledge the impropriety of our proceedings, and return our thanks for

---

[52] Report of the Select Committee on Artisans and Machinery, pp. 415–16.
[53] January 8, 1811.

the lenity we have experienced in the very serious prosecution that pended over us, being withdrawn."[54]

In another submission, eighteen crofters of Bolton, of whom one alone could write, not only apologise for joining a society that had turned out to be a combination for raising wages, and thank the master bleachers for withdrawing a prosecution, but recommend all other crofters to desert this illegal society at once. In this case the masters were represented as relenting because of "the numerous families" of the workmen.[55]

The Combination Laws forbade combination among masters as well as among men, but in this respect they were a dead letter. The masters were not obliged, like the men, to give evidence against each other, and Place pointed out to the Committee in 1824 that it was virtually impossible for workmen to prosecute employers.[56] Some of the masters were not aware that they came under the laws at all,[57] and the magistrates turned a blind eye on the most public and overt acts of employers. There was indeed no concealment of the truth that the masters acted habitually and openly as if the laws had placed no restraint on their freedom to combine for reducing wages.[58]

That the ruling class regarded the Combination Laws as directed solely to the purpose of preventing the men from combining is clear from two facts. In the first place, although the laws were seen by everybody to be absolutely inoperative so far as employers were concerned, there was no proposal to amend

---

[54] There are eleven signatures. Three write their names, eight men make a mark. For other cases cf. Shipwrights in 1801 (H. O., 42. 62) and Coventry ribbon weavers in 1821 (Artisans and Machinery, p. 604).

[55] *Manchester Mercury*, October 30, 1810.

[56] "Have you ever known a master prosecuted by the men for combination?—No: I believe it would be nearly impossible to prosecute a master to conviction. To prosecute at all, money must be raised; to raise money there must be a combination among the men, and then they may be prosecuted by the masters. If, as the law now stands, the men were to prosecute the masters, there would be a cross prosecution. The Combination Law compels the men to give evidence against one another, and thus the prosecution may almost always be effectual. No law compels the masters to give evidence against one another: thus it is almost impossible ever to convict a master." Artisans and Machinery, p. 47. For Gravener Henson's attempt see p. 66.

[57] See evidence of R. Taylor, *ibid.*, p. 53.

[58] See, for example, circular published by four hundred manufacturers in Sheffield, March 25, 1814, *ibid.*, p. 401.

them in order to make them effective. On the contrary, the only proposals made were proposals for making them more drastic in relation to men's combinations.[59] Adam Smith had given as one of his reasons for opposing combination laws the injustice of their incidence, it being so much easier for masters to combine in secret than for men. The ruling class acted as if the inequalities of circumstance were just the other way. In the second place, Sheridan and his friends had contrived, in spite of Pitt's opposition, to introduce some arbitration clause into the Act. These clauses were useless, because the masters were able to evade them,[60] but Parliament never tried to oblige the masters to accept them.

The repeal of the Combination Laws, which was brought about in 1824, is perhaps the most remarkable achievement in this period. It is certainly the greatest achievement in Place's remarkable life. Place (1771 to 1854),[61] for some years a journeyman breeches-maker, and afterwards a tailor, boasted with justice that on becoming a master he did not forget that he had been a journeyman, and from the year 1810, when he had been

---

[59] See, for example, application from Yorkshire magistrates, supported by Wilberforce, the member for the county, in 1802 (H. O., 42. 66). Efforts were made by the masters in 1814 and 1816 to obtain a more stringent Combination Act. Memorials were presented to Government by the master manufacturers of Lancashire. The master hosiers of Nottingham and the Glasgow manufacturers wished for a similar measure (H. O., 42. 139; 42. 149 and 150). Sidmouth was sympathetic. "I incline to think that more *rope* must be given, but I am satisfied that in the ensuing Session the Interference of Parliament will be indispensably necessary," he wrote in 1814 (H. O., 42. 141). In 1816, however, when he referred the memorial to the law officers, the latter "declared their opinions that the Laws were sufficient . . . and that they could advise no application to Parliament for an extension of the Laws or for the Indemnity and Protection of Prosecutors and Witnesses" (H. O., 42. 195).

[60] There was no provision to compel an arbitrator to act. One witness before the Committee on Artisans and Machinery of 1824 described how he had tried, with the goodwill of the magistrates, to initiate proceedings under these clauses, but the masters had checkmated him. The magistrates had looked with sympathy on an attempt to settle disputes without disturbance to the public peace. Evidence of Peter Gregory, p. 603; cf. Committee on Petitions of Ribbon Weavers, 1818, p. 11. For full discussion of the failure of these clauses see succeeding volume.

[61] The whole story is told by Mr. Graham Wallas, *Life of Place*, chap. viii.

enraged by a savage sentence passed on the compositors employed by the *Times*, he devoted his life to the destruction of these laws. Place was a friend and follower of Bentham, a disciple of Malthus about population, and an economist with strong *laissez-faire* convictions. On many questions his opinions were those of the ruling class. He disliked any legislative interference with wages, shrank from legislation that might hamper the capitalist, and believed that attempts to regulate industry would be a dangerous encroachment on the free direction of capital, and an unjust disturbance of the world of labour. But his school differed from the employers in regarding the world of trade as a world with its own laws, and they taught that to forbid the workmen to combine was just as much an infraction of those laws as to regulate hours and wages by an Act of Parliament. If men and masters were left to themselves, wages would follow a law as immutable as the law of gravity. It was wrong to impede the flow of these forces by preventing either the masters or the men from making the best terms that they could. Place further regarded the Combination Laws as a cause of bad feeling and irritation, and he was possessed by the wild notion that if they were abolished, Trade Unions would melt away. Fortunately his delusion about the future did not bewilder his vision of the best measures to be taken at the present, or hamper the skill, patience, and perseverance with which he carried through this great reform. The difficulties before him were very great; for the workmen were slow to support what they thought was a hopeless enterprise, and for years he worked at his object under discouragements that would have overwhelmed any one but a man of his fortitude and tenacity. He gradually produced the desired impression among the Trade Unions, and then in other quarters the sky cleared. For five years, from 1822, the Tory party were under the direction of three men, Canning, Huskisson and Peel, who had all in different degrees assimilated the main ideas of the economists, and whose policy it was to remove obstacles to trade and industry. In this spirit Huskisson wished to get rid of the laws that prohibited the emigration of artisans and the exportation of machinery, and the atmosphere was particularly favourable to an attempt to abolish the laws that oppressed workmen as trade unionists. Place's ally in Parliament was Joseph Hume (1777–1855), the indefatigable Radical critic, who added "retrenchment" to the watchword of his party, and preached individualism for nearly forty years in the House of Commons. Hume and Place between them succeeded in accomplishing an almost unnoticed revolution. The proceedings began with a motion made by Hume on February 12, 1824, for a committee to consider the laws relating to the emigration of artisans, the exportation of machinery, and combination among workmen. Hume stated in his speech that he had originally only intended to ask for the reconsideration of the laws on the first two of these subjects. Huskisson, who was then President of the Board of Trade, supported the motion strongly, and said that under the Combination Laws combinations had increased instead of diminished.

A committee was appointed, its most active members were all men friendly to repeal, and in the next three months the two Radicals had it all their own way. Representatives were sent from various towns to give evidence. At Stockport the Mayor called a public meeting which was attended, as Major Eckersley, the commanding officer at Manchester, put it, "by all the rabble of the town."[62] A committee of seven masters and three or five workmen was appointed to act together. Norris, stipendiary magistrate of Manchester, blamed the Mayor, who might have put into the heads of the workpeople what they otherwise would not have thought of. The Liverpool representatives were brought into the town in triumph on their return, the shipwrights taking a holiday for the purpose.[63] Hume was chairman, and he and Place stage-managed the proceedings with extraordinary skill and success. Place was a superb master of the art of manipulating politics, and he managed to secure, not only that the men's case should be put at its very best, but also that those masters who favoured repeal should give evidence before those who wanted to keep the Combination Laws. Malthus gave evidence for repeal, and said the Combination Laws had had a pernicious effect on wages. If the conspirators had waited to present a report of the usual kind, the report would probably not have been unanimous, but Hume skilfully substituted for a complete report a series of declaratory resolutions. These resolutions were submitted on the 21st of May. The rest followed fast. Indeed, there was just as much dispatch and just as little discussion in the operation of putting down the Combination Laws as there had been in setting them up. The session was almost over. The Bill repealing the laws got its second reading on June the 1st, and

---

[62] H. O., 40. 18.
[63] H. O., 40. 18.

was passed without any debate four days later.[64] So rapid and noiseless had been Place's triumph, that next year the Prime Minister (Liverpool) and the Lord Chancellor (Eldon) both declared that they were unaware of the nature of the Bill, and that if they had known what it was they would have opposed it.[65]

The Act was sweeping in its terms. "Journeymen, workmen, or other persons who shall enter into any combination to obtain an advance or to fix the rate of wages or to lessen or alter the hours or duration of the time of working or to decrease the quantity of work or to induce another to depart from his service before the end of the time or term for which he is hired or to quit or to return his work before the same shall be finished, or not being hired, to refuse to enter into work or employment, or to regulate the mode of carrying on any Manufacture, Trade, or Business or the management thereof, shall not therefore be subject or liable to any indictment or prosecution for conspiracy, or to any other criminal information or punishment whatever under the Common or the Statute Law."

The sleep of the upper classes did not last very long. The Trade Unions took advantage of their new freedom to claim a share in the prosperity of trade, as was natural seeing that most workmen had been ground down under these laws. It is interesting to notice that Major Eckersley, in command at Manchester, who was usually not at all inclined to see things from the workmen's point of view, wrote to General Byng, January 27, 1825,[66] to say that there were various spinners' strikes in progress, and that some manufacturers with large capital were calling for the re-enactment of the Combination Law. "Were I allowed an opinion on the subject, I should certainly say it might be well to pause for a while." The time has not been sufficient to see the effects. "It has, at any rate, the salutary one of making the masters bestir themselves and to look a little to their workpeople, which in most cases was before almost entirely neglected." The next

[64] Huskisson's speech in House of Commons, *Hansard*, March 25, 1825.

[65] Some weeks after the Bill had become law, the magistrates in a Lancashire town sentenced certain cotton weavers to imprisonment for acts that were no longer punishable (Webb, *Hist. of Trade Unionism*, p. 92). The Act is 5 George IV. c. 95. The Act, besides repealing the Combination Acts, exempted workmen's unions from prosecution for conspiracy.

[66] H. O., 40. 18.

winter resounded with the quarrels of masters and men. Hume
and Place, justly afraid for the consequences on the mind of
Parliament, made great efforts to restrain the workmen from re-
taliating on masters who had made themselves conspicuous by
oppression when under the shelter of the old Law.

The shipowners appealed to Huskisson, who was member for
Liverpool, as well as President of the Board of Trade, and he
came down to Parliament next session quite prepared to pass a
Bill drafted by the shipowners which would have meant the
death of Trade Unions.[67] He began by moving on March 29,
1825, for a Select Committee to inquire into the conduct of
the workmen and the effect of the recent Act. In the debate
that followed there was a general condemnation of the men, and
Peel declared that what was wanted was a Bill to put down all
combinations among masters and men alike. Like Huskisson,
he blamed Hume's committee of the previous year. Hume argued that the masters were at fault as well as the men, and
Gurney defended the committee of 1824: "The President as
Vice-President of the Board of Trade had attended all its sittings
and the conclusions had been unanimous." Grant, afterwards
Lord Glenelg and Colonial Secretary, who was at that time Vice-
Treasurer of the Board of Trade, said the workmen had abused
the kindness of Hume's committee. The House agreed to the
motion, and a committee carefully chosen by Huskisson was
duly appointed. The chairman was Wallace, the Master of the
Mint, and Huskisson, Peel, and the Attorney-General took part
in its proceedings. But it was impossible to exclude Hume, and
Hume, with Place at his elbow, managed to upset a good many
plans. The Trade Unions were thoroughly alarmed, and committees sprang up all over the country to agitate against a re-
enactment of the Combination Laws. The Easter holidays gave
Hume and Place an interval for organising their defence. Place
published an answer to Huskisson's speech and got up the workmen's case from agents and delegates. As a result of all these
preparations Hume was able in committee to destroy the original
scheme of the Government, which was to prepare a Bill forbidding the subscription of any funds to a trade or any other
association, unless some magistrate approved its objects and became its treasurer; and the committee reported in favour of a
Bill which recognised the right of collective bargaining, though
it defined the legitimate purposes and aim of association very

---

[67] Webb, *History of Trade Unionism*, p. 94.

narrowly, and put a great weapon in the hands of the employers, by using such vague terms as "molesting" and "obstructing" to describe forbidden methods. This Bill the Government adopted and carried. The chief champions of the men in the debates on the Bill were Hume, Burdett, and Denman. Hume said that if the magistrates were allowed to punish a man for such an indefinite offence as molesting, the Bill would be simply a Bill to keep down wages, and he tried to get rid of the word "molesting" and also to add a clause "that every master of workmen, and the father and son of such master, be rendered incapable of acting as a justice of the peace in cases of complaint under the Act." Denman tried to substitute the verdict of a jury for conviction before two magistrates. The *Place MSS.* give a most interesting account of the proceedings from Place's point of view. "Sir Francis Burdett and Mr. Hobhouse supported Mr. Hume, but he had to bear the vehement attacks of the whole ministerial bench—Huskisson, Peel, Wallace, Canning, the Attorney-General, etc. etc. No terms either as to truth or decency of language, to the utmost extent which ingenuity could use, so as not to be reprehended by the Speaker, were spared."[68] Hume and Denman's efforts at amendment were unavailing.

The new Act[69] was a disappointment to the shipping industry, and to the other powerful interests that had hoped to see the Combination Laws set up again. It differed widely from the Bill that the Government had meant to introduce. Place and Hume by their skill and pertinacity, the Trade Unions by giving the impression that they would resist the re-enactment of the old laws by violence, had defeated the intentions of the masters and the Government. In this sense the proceedings are a great moral triumph for Place and Hume. But the Trade Unions, though given recognition, were left without much elbow room. The section which exempted them from prosecution for conspiracy was omitted in the new Act, which recites the various offences that are punishable and then excludes from its operation persons meeting together to determine the conditions as to wages and hours which each or all shall demand. The collective bargain is recognised, but efforts to make it effective are still surrounded with danger.

How much the working classes lost in happiness, in physical energy, in moral power, in the inherited stamina of mind and

---

[68] Wallas, *Life of Place*, p. 236.
[69] 6 George IV. c. 129.

body, during the years when these overwhelming forces were pressing them down, it is impossible to estimate. They were years of great moment to the race, and English history would have been very different for many generations after the close of this period if the workers had been allowed to use the resources of organisation for the defence of a standard of life, and if the rulers of England had not tied their hands behind their backs at the time, more than any other, at which they needed all their strength. The Combination Laws gave the masters unlimited power to reduce wages and to make conditions more severe. They established the new industry on a basis of exploited labour, wages representing not the share of the working classes in the new wealth, however that share might be assessed, but the degree of misery to which men and women, forbidden to defend themselves, might be reduced in this or that place and this or that trade in the wild competition of the forces that used and ruled them. The industry in which fortunes were made most rapidly was the industry in which the mass of workers were degraded to the deepest poverty, just because the cotton weavers were not protected by any traditions of regulation, or by any special difficulties in their employment demanding special skill or special physical strength. The Parliament that passed the Combination Laws proclaimed a doctrine of serf labour and low wages. Every working man was either to accept the wages that his employer, with the law behind him, chose to give, or to become a vagrant. That was the ruling fact about the new industry. The working man was heavily handicapped already. He had against him the power of the new capital and the irregularities of trade that crippled his resources by periodical spells of unemployment. Into that scale Parliament threw the weight of the law. The working classes had in the last resort only one weapon, the weapon of violence,[70] and the class of workers that came out of the struggle best were those who could intimidate the magistrates.

For the mass of working men and working women thus treated, there was only one way of keeping body and soul together. The children were sent to the mill or the mine. The Combination Laws put the children as well as their parents at the disposal of the employers. In the view of the ruling class the child of the weaver or the miner had no claims on society:

---

[70] See Buddle's evidence before 1829 Lords Committee on Coal Trade, pp. 68 and 69.

there was no reason to educate him except that some rudiments of knowledge might make him more useful in industry, and there was every reason to keep such education as might awaken discontent out of his reach. He was born into a serf class. Thus the consideration of the policy of the ruling powers brings us to the subject of the children of the factory and mine, for the Combination Laws and the employment of children on a great scale are two aspects of the same system.[71]

[71] Cf. evidence of Gifford (p. 397) and Sherwin (p. 420) before Committee on Artisans and Machinery.

CHAPTER VIII

THE EMPLOYMENT OF CHILDREN (I)

THE MILL

Michelet has told a domestic and apocryphal story to illustrate the severity and the strain of the great duel between England and revolutionary France. "When the English manufacturers warned Pitt that owing to the high wages they had to pay their workmen, they were unable to pay their national taxes, Pitt returned a terrible answer: 'Take the children.' That saying weighs like a curse upon England." The story, as M. Mantoux points out, is a legend, and in so far as it represents the exploiting of children as a new and terrible inspiration from Pitt, it is unjust to him: we give a little later the sentence from a speech of Pitt's that suggested this rhetorical passage. But the story, though a legend, is a legend woven round the facts, for during the first phase of the Industrial Revolution the employment of children on a vast scale became the most important social feature of English life, and its consequences are not exaggerated in Michelet's outburst.

The idea that the children of the poor should work for their living is a good deal older than the Industrial Revolution. Locke, the philosopher, proposed as part of a scheme for the reform of the Poor Laws which he submitted to the Board of Trade in 1697, that a working school should be established in each parish, which the children of all applicants for parish relief should be obliged to attend from the ages of three to fourteen.[1] In some of the Houses of Industry during the eighteenth century infants were employed at this tender age. In their own homes too the children's working life began early, and Defoe was moved to admiration by the busy spectacle of the Yorkshire clothiers: "Within we saw the Houses full of lusty Fellows, some at the Dye-vat, some at the Loom, others dressing the Cloths; the Women and Children carding or spinning, all employed from the youngest to the oldest: scarce any Thing above four Years old, but its Hands were sufficient for its own Support."[2] Pitt in his famous Poor Law Bill proposed that children should be

---

[1] Quoted in *Annual Register*, 1817, p. 279 ff.
[2] Defoe, *Tour*, 3. 145.

set to work when they were five; and his speech on Whitbread's Minimum Wage Bill shows the kind of impression that the beginnings of the great system of child labour in factories made upon his mind. "Experience had already shown how much could be done by the industry of children, and the advantages of early employing them in such branches of manufacture as they are capable to execute."[3]

The child labour that was becoming so important a part of industrial life at the time of Pitt's speech was different from the child labour described by Defoe; for whereas in Defoe's day the labour of children was ancillary to the labour of their parents, under the early factory system the employment of masses of children was the foundation of industry.

The factory children of the Industrial Revolution fall into two classes: (1) apprentice children, (2) free-labour children, or children living at home with parents or guardians. The apprentice children were the first to be employed. The early spinning machinery, invented whilst the wonders of steam were still unknown, needed water power for its working: hence the first mills were placed on streams, and the necessary labour was provided by the importation of cartloads of pauper children from the workhouses in the big towns. London was an important source, for since the passing of Hanway's Act in 1767 the child population in the workhouses had enormously increased, and the parish authorities were anxious to find relief from the burden of their maintenance. Jonas Hanway (1712–86), after a strange career as a traveller, in the course of which he made a journey down the Volga and by the Caspian to Persia with a caravan of woollen goods, had settled in London and given himself up to philanthropy. He was one of the founders of the Magdalen Hospital, and introduced the umbrella. By the Act generally called by his name,[4] passed in consequence of his untiring exertions, all London parish children under six years of age were boarded out, not less than three miles away, at not less than 2s. 6d. a week. An additional bonus of 10s. per child a year was given to each successful nurse. Before this Act very few parish infants survived to trouble the authorities. Hanway himself estimated the annual death-rate as 60 to 70 per cent.

---

[3] *Parliamentary Register*, February 12, 1796.
[4] 7 George III. c. 39.

The Act, according to Howlett, caused "a deficiency of 2,100 burials a year."[5] To the parish authorities encumbered with great masses of unwanted children, the new cotton mills in Lancashire, Derby, and Notts were a godsend. It must be remembered that, as a committee in 1815 pointed out, in London relief was "seldom bestowed without the parish claiming the exclusive right of disposing, at their pleasure, of all the children of the person receiving relief."[6] The manufacturers were anxious to oblige, and in one case, a Lancashire millowner agreed with a London parish to take one idiot with every twenty sound children supplied.[7] The guardians had thus available a system of transportation for poor children, which was cheaper and more effective than the transportation system that had brought relief to the London prisons.

These children were consigned to their employers at the age of seven and upwards, till they were twenty-one. Next door to the mills prentice-houses were built, and in these two buildings their young lives were spent, at best in monotonous toil, at worst in a hell of human cruelty. If their master failed in business, their labours ceased and they were cast adrift on the world. A model mill at Styall near Manchester employed from seventy to eighty children procured from the Liverpool workhouse, living in a small prentice-house near the mill. Here, where kindness was the rule, and the children's education was supervised by members of the owner's family noted for its benevolence, the working hours were seventy-four a week or over twelve a day, Saturdays included.[8] The majority of mills worked fifteen hours. In many of them, work, like the stream, never stopped by day or night, and the children who had tended the machines by day crept into beds left vacant by the children who were to tend them through the night. For this system of double shifts, in spite of its unhealthiness, it could indeed be said that the day children's hours were shortened by the fact that there were other workers to replace them, and that the night children had the compensation of time to play by day.

A vivid picture of life in these prentice mills was given before

---

[5] See Eden, *The State of the Poor*, i. p. 338.

[6] Report of Committee on Parish Apprentices, 1815. See *Annual Register for 1815.*

[7] See Horner's Speech, *Hansard*, June 6, 1815.

[8] Factory Commission, Supplementary Report, 1834, part ii. p. 302 f.

the 1816 committee by a certain Mr. John Moss, governor of the workhouse at Preston.[9] For a year, from February 1814 to March 1815, he had been master of about one hundred and fifty parish apprentices at a cotton mill at Backbarrow in Lancashire. Most of these children came from London, a few from Liverpool. The London children came at ages ranging from seven to eleven, the Liverpool children came from eight to fifteen: all were bound till they were twenty-one. Their regular working hours, Saturdays included, were from 5 A.M. till 8 P.M., and, with the exception of half an hour at 7 A.M. for breakfast, and half an hour at 12 for dinner, they were working continuously the whole time. They were, however, allowed to eat something whilst working in the afternoon. There were no seats in the mill. When lost time had to be made up, the hours were from 5 A.M. till 9 or 10 P.M., and this sometimes lasted for three weeks on end. There were two mills, and if the water was insufficient for both, one was worked with day and night shifts. On Sundays, always some, and sometimes all, were employed from 6 A.M. till noon cleaning machinery. Those who were not so employed were supposed to go to church, three miles away. It is not surprising to read that church-going was unpopular, and that the children would absent themselves under pretence of being needed at the mill. At night Mr. Moss regularly inspected their beds "because there were always some of them missing, some sometimes might be run away, others sometimes I have found have been asleep in the mill." The children often lay down on the mill floor and went to sleep before their supper. The bedding was simple and unclean; a blanket to lie on and another blanket, with a horse cover, to throw over them. During his time sheets were introduced. Nobody from London ever came to look after the children, who, according to Mr. Moss, developed into depraved characters. Once before Mr. Moss's time, when the mill had stopped payment under its former proprietors, the children were taken from the mill in a cart and turned adrift near the sands on the Lancaster road.

The story of the Backbarrow mill is interesting, if only for the light it throws incidentally on the mental attitude of the powers to whom these prentice children were consigned. The evidence of Mr. Moss pained the proprietors of the mill. They

---

[9] Report on Children in Manufactories, 1816 (Peel's Committee), pp. 178–85.

did not attempt to deny the length of the hours, but they repudiated with righteous indignation the insinuation that the children were not healthy and happy, and the still baser insinuation that they had neglected the Sabbath and failed in their duties as Christians. They forwarded to the Committee the following remarkable papers:—[10]

1. "I do hereby certify that I have attended the apprentice house of Ainsworth, Catterall and Co. of Backbarrow, upwards of 6 years, and that during that time the children have been particularly healthy, and the numbers of deaths very few. I consider the treatment of the children very good in all respects.

JOHN REDHEAD, Surgeon."

CARTMEL, May 25, 1816.

2. "These are to certify that the children or apprentices, belonging to the cotton factory of Messrs. Ainsworth, Catterall and Co. at Backbarrow in the parish of Cartmel in the County of Lancaster, generally and regularly attend divine service in the chapel of Finsthwaite every Sunday when the weather will permit: that during the service they behave with great propriety: they appear neat and clean, and in all respects demean themselves in a decent and orderly manner.

Given under my hand this 25th day of May 1816.

HENRY SEATLE, Minister of Finsthwaite.

P.S.—I beg leave to state that out of 150 children, the number employed, there have been only six deaths in the seven last years: and three of these came to the place in a very sickly state and one was drowned by accident.

HENRY SEATLE."

3. "We the undersigned do hereby certify, That we attend every Sabbath-day at the apprentice house of Ainsworth, Catterall and Company and accompany the children to Finsthwaite Chapel for the morning's service; that in the afternoon we teach them to read in the Bible, New Testament, or Spelling Book, according to their ability, and

---

[10] Report on Children in Manufactories, 1816 (Peel's Committee), p. 210.

that every attention is paid to the strict observance of the Sabbath.

J. SLATER,
WILLIAM FENNIX.

The above certified also by me
THOMAS COWARD,
Governor of the Apprentice House at Backbarrow."

The proprietors also sent up the overlooker to discredit Mr. Moss's statements.[11] The hours of work indeed were not disputed, and under judicious pressure the witness admitted that the machinery was cleaned on Sunday. But the health and the morals of the children were excellent now: whatever faults there might have been were due to Mr. Moss and his wife: for he failed to maintain proper authority, and she was "too high for her situation, she did not look after them as she should do." His answer to the charge that the apprentices were turned adrift when the mill stopped about seven years before was interesting. The children were set at liberty, not forced to go. There were provisions in the house, if they did not stop too long: they were not in a miserable situation, though, "to be sure, they would not be well off: they would have to beg their way or something of that sort."

These cotton mills, crowded with overworked children, were hotbeds of what was called putrid fever, and it was an epidemic at Radcliffe in 1784 that first drew public attention to the condition of the apprentices. In consequence of the recommendation of Dr. Percival (1740–1804), a public-spirited Manchester doctor, the Manchester magistrates passed a resolution that in future they would refuse to sanction indentures of parish apprentices to cotton mills where they would be worked at night or more than ten hours by day. Similar resolutions were passed by other northern magistrates later.[12] But these resolutions, unfortunately, did not affect the magistrates of the districts which supplied most of the children. No outside person, whether parent or magistrate, had any right to enter a mill or a prenticehouse: the apprentices were, in fact, absolutely at the mercy of their employers. The law in theory gave them a remedy; by 20 Geo. II. c. 19 (1747) an apprentice could appeal to a magistrate

[11] Report on Children in Manufactories, 1816 (Peel's Committee), pp. 288–93.
[12] See Report on Parish Apprentices, 1815.

against his master's ill-treatment, and if the case were proved, could obtain his or her discharge; by 32 Geo. III. c. 57 (1792) a successful complaint of this nature might even entail a £10 fine; but the risk that a child who passed his life shut up in the prentice-house and the mill would find his way to a magistrate was not very serious, and, if he succeeded, it was as likely as not that the magistrate would turn out to be his own or a neighbouring employer. Gisborne tells us that cruel punishments were inflicted on those who found some means of complaint.[13]

The epidemics in cotton factories continued unchecked. A Board of Health, formed in Manchester in 1795, urged the necessity of regulations, and at last, in 1802, Sir Robert Peel, himself one of the chief offenders, brought in a Bill on the subject.

Peel's character is an interesting study. A man who has been enriched by some abuse is generally too much afraid of the charge of hypocrisy, and the anger of those who are not yet satisfied with the profits they have derived from such a source, to attempt to reform it. This is perhaps the reason why it is so hard to act on the insidious maxim of Phocylides, to acquire a competence and then to practise virtue. It is human to be morbidly conscious of one's own history, to dread the taunt of insincerity and cant, to shrink from calling for virtue when your neighbours know that your pockets are bursting with the revenues of vice. The first Sir Robert Peel showed, like his greater son, that whatever his faults, he could break free from the most compromising past, and face the most biting of all charges. His mills had been notorious for their scandals, and in 1784, and again in 1796, the magistrates had made complaints.[14] Under the shadow of this record Peel dared to turn reformer. With an intellectual honesty that is rare, he disowned the illusion with which most millowners satisfied their consciences, that the victims of this system were really gainers by it. "Having other pursuits," he wrote afterwards, "it was not often in my power to visit the factories, but whenever such visits were made, I was struck with the uniform appearance of bad health, and in many cases, stunted growth of the children; the hours of labour were regulated by the interest of the overseer, whose remuneration depending on the quantity of work done, he was often induced to make the poor children work excessive hours, and to stop

---

[13] Eden, op. cit., i. p. 422.
[14] See speech of the younger Peel, Hansard, February 19, 1818.

their complaints by trifling bribes."[15] The result of his attention was the 1802 Act.[16]

The original Bill was "for the better preservation of the Health and Morals of Apprentices and others employed in cotton mills and cotton manufactories"; in deference to Wilberforce's appeal the last words were changed to "cotton and other mills, and cotton and other manufactories," but in its final form, though this title remained, the regulations applied only to cotton and woollen mills. There were several debates on the Bill,[17] and unsuccessful efforts were made by Lord Belgrave, Burton, Wilberforce, the Attorney-General (Perceval), and Lord Stanley to include free-labour children in the scope of the measure, Lord Belgrave declaring with vehemence that "Wealth was pursued in this country, with an eagerness to which every other consideration was sacrificed, and with excesses calculated to call down the vengeance of Heaven, if the Legislature did not put a stop to them." Burton contended that the children living at home were even worse off than the apprentices. Sir Robert Peel, who thought that the Bill, as it stood, "would render the cotton trade as correct and moral as it was important,"[18] refused to extend its scope: on one occasion, indeed, he urged that if regulations were necessary for the free children, they should be made the subject of a different Bill, but later on he declared his conviction that any such regulations must be prejudicial to trade.

The Act prescribed that all cotton or woollen mills or factories where three or more apprentices or twenty or more other persons worked, must be kept clean and airy. Most of the provisions applied only to apprentices. These children were not to work more than twelve hours a day, exclusive of meal times, and these twelve hours must be taken between 6 A.M. and 9 P.M. Night work was prohibited after June 1803, except in the case of the bigger mills, which were given from six months to a year to prepare for the change. Part of the working day was to be given up to instruction in reading, writing, and arithmetic: each apprentice was to have one new suit of clothing every year, and boys and girls were to sleep in separate rooms and not more than two in a bed. The Act made provision for their religious duties: for an hour every Sunday they were to be "in-

---

[15] 1816 Committee, p. 132.
[16] 42 George III. c. 73.
[17] *Parliamentary Register*, April 6 and 14, May 4 and 18, 1802.
[18] *Parliamentary Register*, April 6, 1802.

structed and examined in the principles of the Christian religion, by some proper person provided by the master or mistress"; once a year the clergyman of the parish was to examine them, once a month, at least, they were to go to church, and in England they were to be confirmed, in Scotland they were to receive the sacrament, between the ages of fourteen and eighteen. The Justices of the Peace at their Quarter Sessions were to appoint two visitors, unconnected with the mills, one a magistrate, the other a clergyman, who should have full power to inspect the mills and enforce the Act.

It is interesting to notice the welcome given by the employers to this, the first Factory Act. From Manchester, Glasgow, Preston, Leeds, Keighley, Tutbury, and Holywell came protests from millowners, declaring the Act to be "prejudicial to the Cotton Trade" and also "impracticable."[19] A further light is thrown on these objections, and also on the treatment of the children, in some papers about the Act printed in the Reports of the Society for Bettering the Conditions of the Poor. One of these papers consists of Observations on the Act, drawn up by the proprietors of some mills at Burley, near Otley.[20] They point out that the cotton trade cannot go on unless about a sixth of the apprentices can be worked at night. "Free labourers cannot be obtained to perform the night work, but upon very disadvantageous terms to the manufacturers," besides, night work "is incontestably proved not to be injurious" to the health of the apprentices, so why should the legislature interfere? As for the clause about the education of the children in working hours, no doubt education is desirable, "and is what all humane masters would wish to see accomplished"; but to take an hour or two from the twelve working hours "would amount to a surrender of all the profits of the establishment." The severest strictures are reserved for the clause which gives the two visitors power to inspect the mill. The apprentices, especially those from London, come from low and vicious surroundings, and need very strict discipline to reform them and to keep them in the narrow path. "What effects will be produced in such establishments by the introduction of visitors (whom the children will regard as invested with a controlling power over their masters) it is easy to foresee. All sub-

---

[19] *House of Commons Journal*, February 11, 14, 22 and 25, 1803.
[20] Vol. iv., App. p. 9. The Society refuted the arguments of the proprietors.

ordination will be at an end, let the visitors conduct themselves with what discretion they may; the Mills and Factories will become a scene either of idleness and disorder, or of open rebellion; or the masters, harassed and tired out by the incessant complaints of their apprentices, and the perpetual interference of the visitors, will be obliged to give up their works; and some of them, after being involved in difficulties (resulting from the operation of the Act) may perhaps become bankrupts, or be obliged to remove to a foreign country, leaving their apprentices a grievous load upon the parish where they were employed." In their last sentence they demand either a repeal or a modification of the Act, as "indispensably necessary to the future success of a great number of persons embarked in the spinning and manufacturing of Cotton; who have not only contributed largely to the public revenue, but, after having rescued a great number of children from vice and misery, have at a heavy expense trained them up in the habits of industry and religion, and rendered them (before a load upon society) now some of its most useful members."

These gloomy anticipations were soon found to be baseless. The bark of the Act was worse than its bite; the magistrates and parsons appointed as visitors did not push matters to uncomfortable extremes, and in most places it was left to the employers to decide whether or to what extent they should obey the law. The instance of Backbarrow, quoted above, shows how this discretion was sometimes exercised.[21] An attempt to help the parish apprentice at the other end, by forbidding them to be sent more than forty miles from the indenturing parish, was made in 1811 by Mr. Wilbraham Bootle, who brought in a Bill to this effect,[22]

---

[21] Some returns relative to mills and factories pursuant to an Address of the House of Commons of March 8, 1810, are contained in H. O., 42. 104. In them the Middlesex Deputy Clerk of the Peace makes the pertinent remark: "If the Parliament intended this Act should have any Effect the Entry should have been enforced by a penalty, and it should have been someone's Business to see it enforced; as it is, it will ever remain a Dead Letter, and will soon be ranked amongst the Obsolete Acts."

[22] In 1807 a Bill for the better regulation of Parish Apprentices, introduced by Colonel Bathurst, had passed the House of Commons. Curwen, on its introduction, remarked that he had recently met a caravan in the north of England with sixty children crowded into it. The Duke of Norfolk obtained the rejection of the Bill in the House

but faced with determined opposition from the London parish
authorities, who were in no mind lightly to resign their liberty
to dispose of superfluous children, Mr. Bootle dropped the Bill
and obtained the appointment of a Committee instead.[23] This
committee, of which Romilly, Horner, and Whitbread were
members, reported on May 19, 1815.[24] "It would have been,"
they said, "obviously an impracticable task to have attempted to
ascertain the number of parish apprentices bound from various
parts of England, to a distance from their parents," hence
their inquiries were confined to parishes within the Bills of
Mortality,[25] where since 1767 (by 7 George III. c. 39, Hanway's Act) lists of parish apprentices had been kept. It is note-
worthy that Peel estimated the number of parish apprentices in
cotton mills to whom his 1802 Bill would apply as 20,000.[26]
The demand for parish children, owing to changes in the system
of manufacture, had fallen considerably since then. The committee found that in the ten years from 1802–11 inclusive, out
of 5,815 children in all from these parishes, 2,026 were bound
to persons in the country, and of these three-quarters were
bound to masters in the cotton trade. Inquiries were made
about the fate of these two thousand children, with results which
are startling, when we recollect that public attention had long

---

of Lords on the grounds that a clause which bound children to attend
the Established Church every Sunday unless they were of a different
persuasion, might induce some of them to say that they were of a
different persuasion "in order that they might obtain the day for the
purposes of play." See *Parliamentary Register*, June 30, July 13, July
16, and July 27.

[23] See Romilly on this in his *Diary* (*Life*, ii. 188 and 203).
Romilly had suggested the inclusion in the Bill of a clause postponing
the payment of premiums. "Instances (and not very few) have occurred in our tribunals, of wretches who have murdered their parish
apprentices, that they might get fresh premiums with new apprentices."

[24] The Report is printed in the *Annual Register* for that year.

[25] The Bills of Mortality were annual returns of births and deaths
within various parishes in London and Westminster, and some out-
parishes in Middlesex and Surrey.

[26] "Was it a small matter that twenty thousand children, who
hitherto had been abandoned to ignorance, were to be instructed?
That so many children, before neglected, naked, and given up to all
manner of profligacy should now be instructed in religion and morality, made good members of the Christian Church, and good subjects
of the Government?"—*Parliamentary Register*, May 18, 1802.

been drawn to these apprentices, and an Act passed on their behalf thirteen years before.

Now serving under indenture	644
Served their time, and now in the same employ	108
Served and settled elsewhere	99
Dead	80
Enlisted in the army or navy	86
Quitted their service, chiefly run away	166
Not bound to the person mentioned in the return kept by the company of parish clerks	58
Sent back to their friends	57
Transferred to tradesmen in different parts of the kingdom	246
Incapable of service	18
Not accounted for or mentioned	5
In parish workhouses	26
Not satisfactorily or intelligibly accounted for by persons to whom they were bound, or by the overseers where the masters have become bankrupts	433
	2,026

The committee passed severe strictures on the system of binding children to masters at a distance, and a few days after their report Mr. Wilbraham Bootle again presented a Bill to limit the radius within which they might be apprenticed to forty miles. This Bill passed the Commons, but met with opposition in the Lords, and was held over till next session. The following year (1816) it passed both Houses,[27] and the carts ceased to dump their living freights at the mill doors.

If we date the factory system as beginning in 1775,[28] we see that it took over forty years for the rulers of England to stop this wholesale cruelty. But the system was dying of itself, and another form of child labour had grown up. The change from water power to steam made it possible to build mills and factories in towns, and to employ the children of the neighbourhood instead of imported apprentices. In the early days of the factory

[27] 56 George III. c. 139. London children might not be apprenticed more than forty miles away, children from parishes over forty miles from London might be apprenticed at a greater distance, provided the justices specially authorised it.

[28] Cunningham, *op. cit.*, p. 346.

system the operatives refused to let their own children enter the mills, but economic pressure in time wore down this reluctance. The hand-loom weavers during the slow decay of their industry could only keep the wolf from their doors by means of their children's earnings.[29] "Formerly," said one of them, "when weaving was better, the weavers in general employed the children in their own houses; in consequence of that, they had an opportunity of bringing them up, and giving them good moral instruction; now, since the weavers' wages have been reduced so extremely low, they send them to the factories, and that is one great grievance to the feelings of a moral man, that he is not able to bring up his children under his own eye. . . ."[30] When a weaver's wages had sunk to 6s. 6d. a week, the earnings of his children in the factory became an integral part of the family income, and parish relief was refused if he had children whom he could send into the mill. Sometimes, too, an adult worker was only given work on condition that he brought children with him.[31] Thus grew up that disastrous system under which the children of the family were looked upon as breadwinners, and the prosperity of the English manufactures was based on this helpless misery. How, Robert Owen was asked, could the children be supported if they did not go to work till they were twelve? "I recollect the period well," he answered, "when there were not any manufactories in several parts of the country (I speak of England and Wales) and the children, as far as I recollect, of the poor, were then as well fed, as well clothed, and, as far as my memory serves me, looked as well as now, and few of them were employed regularly until they were twelve, thirteen, and fourteen years of age."[32] The usual, and so to speak, the official age, at which these free children began their mill life was six or seven, but Robert Owen stated that many were employed under that age, at four or five,[33] and in one instance he had heard of a baby of three working. "The way," he said, "in which many of these infants are first employed

---

[29] Cf. "Printed Addresses from an Old Weaver" in H. O., 42. 122 and 40. 1.

[30] Committee on Artisans and Machinery, 1824, p. 397.

[31] See Sadler's Committee, 1832, pp. 124–6.

[32] Before Peel's Committee, 1816.

[33] In the Baptist Sunday-school at Manchester there were two factory children of five years old and five of five and a half years. See Whitelegg's evidence before Peel's Committee, 1816.

is to pick up the waste cotton from the floor: to go under the machines, where bigger people cannot creep, and the smaller they are the more conveniently they can go under the machines."[34]

When once children had become wage earners, their working life differed little from that of the apprentices already described. They entered the mill gates at 5 or 6 A.M., they left them (at earliest) at 7 or 8 P.M., Saturdays included. All this time they were shut up in temperatures varying from 75 to 85. The only respite during the fourteen or fifteen hours' confinement was afforded by meal hours, at most half an hour for breakfast and an hour for dinner. But regular meal hours were privileges for adults only:[35] to the children for three or four days a week they meant merely a change of work; instead of tending a machine that was running, they cleaned a machine that was standing still, snatching and swallowing their food as best they could in the midst of dust and flue. Children soon lost all relish for meals eaten in the factory. The flue used to choke their lungs. When spitting failed to expel it, emetics were freely given.[36]

The work on which these children were engaged was often described as light and easy, in fact almost as an amusement, requiring attention but not exertion. Three-fourths of the children were "piecers"—that is, engaged in joining together or piecing the threads broken in the various roving and spinning machines. Others were employed in sweeping up the waste cotton, or removing and replacing bobbins.[37] Fielden (1784–1849), the enlightened and humane employer who represented Oldham with Cobbett, and shares the laurels that grace the memory of Shaftesbury and Sadler, made an interesting experiment to measure the physical strain that the children endured. Struck with some statements made by factory delegates about the miles a child walked a day in following the spinning machine, he submitted the statements to a practical test in his own factory, and found to his amazement that in twelve hours the distance covered was not less than twenty miles.[38] There were indeed

---

[34] *Ibid.*, p. 88.

[35] Baines, *History of Cotton Manufacture*, p. 462, quotes a mill where mechanics have half an hour for tea, but this is not allowed to children and other workers.

[36] See Mr. Price's evidence before Peel's Committee, 1816.

[37] See Baines, *op. cit.*, pp. 456 and 459.

[38] Fielden's *Curse of the Factory System*, p. 40.

short intervals of leisure, but no seats to sit on, sitting being contrary to rules. The view that the piecers' work was really light was expounded by Mr. Tufnell, one of the Factory Commissioners. Three-fourths of the children, he says, are engaged as piecers at mules, and whilst the mules are receding there is nothing to be done, and the piecers stand idle for about three-quarters of a minute. From this he deduces the conclusion that if a child is nominally working twelve hours a day, *"for nine hours he performs no actual labour,"* or if, as is generally the case, he attends two mules, then "his leisure is six hours instead of nine."[39]

The fourteen or fifteen hours' confinement for six days a week were the "regular" hours: in busy times hours were elastic and sometimes stretched to a length that seems almost incredible. Work from 3 A.M. to 10 P.M. was not unknown; in Mr. Varley's mill, all through the summer, they worked from 3.30 A.M. to 9.30 P.M.[40] At the mill, aptly called "Hell Bay," for two months at a time, they not only worked regularly from 5 A.M. to 9 P.M., but for two nights each week worked all through the night as well.[41] The more humane employers contented themselves when busy with a spell of sixteen hours (5 A.M. to 9 P.M.).

It was physically impossible to keep such a system working at all except by the driving power of terror. The overseers who gave evidence before Sadler's Committee did not deny that their methods were brutal. They said that they had either to exact the full quota of work, or to be dismissed, and in these circumstances pity was a luxury that men with families depending upon them could not allow themselves. The punishments for arriving late in the morning had to be made cruel enough to overcome the temptation to tired children to take more than three or four hours in bed. One witness before Sadler's Committee had known a child, who had reached home at eleven o'clock one night, get up at two o'clock next morning in panic and limp to the mill gate.[42] In some mills scarcely an hour passed in the long day without the sound of beating and cries of pain.[43] Fathers beat

---

[39] Quoted Baines, *op. cit.*, p. 459.
[40] Evidence of Richard Cotton before Sadler's Committee.
[41] Evidence of Alonzo Hargraves before Sadler's Committee.
[42] Evidence of A. Whitehead (a clothier) before Sadler's Committee.
[43] Evidence of M. Crabtree and Bennett (a slubber) before Sadler's Committee.

their own children to save them from a worse beating by other overseers. In the afternoon the strain grew so severe that the heavy iron stick known as the billy-roller was in constant use, and, even then, it happened not infrequently that a small child, as he dozed, tumbled into the machine beside him to be mangled for life, or, if he were fortunate, to find a longer Lethe than his stolen sleep. In one mill indeed, where the owner, a Mr. Gott, had forbidden the use of anything but a ferule, some of the slubbers tried to keep the children awake, when they worked from 5 in the morning to 9 at night, by encouraging them to sing hymns. As the evening wore on the pain and fatigue and tension on the mind became insupportable. Children would implore any one who came near to tell them how many hours there were still before them. A witness told Sadler's Committee that his child, a boy of six, would say to him, " 'Father, what o'clock is it?' I have said perhaps it is seven o'clock. 'Oh, is it two hours to nine o'clock? I cannot bear it.' "[44]

Oastler was once in the company of a West Indian slave-master and three Bradford spinners. The four fell to talking about their different labour systems, and when the slave-master heard what were the children's hours he was astounded. "Well," he observed, "I have always thought myself disgraced by being the owner of slaves, but we never in the West Indies thought it possible for any human being to be so cruel as to require a child of nine years old to work twelve and a half hours a day, and that, you acknowledge, is your regular practice."[45] The little factory slaves were the children of free men: some of brutal and callous parents, many of parents who took them to the mill with broken hearts, knowing the life that was before them, knowing also that unless they took them the parish would leave them to starve.

We have seen that as early as 1802 speakers in Parliament declared the condition of these children to be as bad as or worse than that of the apprentices. This was quite true, but it was not till 1815 that any steps were taken to reform it. It was Sir Robert Peel again, incited by Robert Owen, who took the first step in Parliament. In 1802 Peel had deprecated any interfer-

---

[44] Evidence of John Allett before Sadler's Committee.

[45] Oastler's evidence before Sadler's Committee. A doctor, J. R. Farre who gave evidence before Sadler's Committee, had formerly practised in Barbados, and he said the adult negro slave worked shorter hours than the factory child.

ence with the labour of children living at home. Yet here again he had the courage and honesty publicly to change his mind when Owen proved to him that he was in the wrong. He saw that the growth of factories in towns had created new conditions, and that to call the children employed there free agents was a bitter mockery. Peel began his efforts on behalf of the free children by introducing, in June 1815, a Bill, drawn up at Owen's instigation, to amend and extend the 1802 Act. According to this Bill, which applied to all cotton, woollen, flax and other mills, manufactories and buildings, no child, whether apprenticed or not, was to work under ten years old, and the factory hours for children were limited to twelve and a half a day, of which ten and a half only were to be spent in "laborious employment" and the remaining two in meals and education. As the inspection under the 1802 Act was admittedly inefficient, Peel proposed that proper persons should be appointed for the work at Quarter Sessions, and paid for their trouble. Peel did not wish the Bill to pass that session, but wished it to be printed and circulated during the recess. William Smith and Horner welcomed the proposal, but Philips, a big millowner, gave a foretaste of the stubborn opposition he was to offer later.[46] The Bill was put off for three months on the report stage, and next year (1816), instead of reintroducing it, Peel, to Owen's disgust, moved for a committee to consider the state of children in manufactories. This committee took the evidence of forty-three witnesses, not one of them a worker. The witnesses fall roughly into three groups, doctors, advocates of the children's cause, and employers or their agents. The first group, of doctors, all agreed with more or less emphasis that the existing conditions of work must be deleterious to the health of young children, one of them basing his objection to long hours on "the natural appetency of all young creatures to locomotive exercise and the open air."[47] The second group of advocates of the children were many of them merchants, and most of them had come into contact with the children through Sunday-schools. Some were men who from motives of sheer humanity devoted their lives and incomes to the effort to obtain legislation. They all testified to the misery and to the ill-health of the children. One

[46] Brotherton, M.P. for Salford, said in the House of Commons on May 9, 1836, that all the master spinners of Manchester except himself opposed the Bill (Wing, *Evils of the Factory System*, p. 397).

[47] Sir Gilbert Blane, p. 45.

of them, Theodore Price, a magistrate, declared, "I never will sign an indenture to a cotton mill so long as I live—that is, under the present existing laws." Some laid stress on the injury to morals as well as to health, disregard of the Sabbath and grosser crimes being mixed up in the indictment. The generation that was being reared in these conditions was vividly described by one witness: "Their conduct on a Sunday is such, that females as well as men, insult often their well-behaved superiors in the streets, and that to such a degree that well-behaved, discreet gentlemen, even if they meet the factory people, will, if possible, go on the other side of the street to avoid them."[48]

The third group of employers or employers' spokesmen with the exception of Robert Owen and Sir Robert Peel, ridiculed the idea that the children were overworked. They admitted that the regular factory hours varied from thirteen to fifteen a day: that is, from 6 A.M. to 7 P.M., or from 5 A.M. to 8 P.M., with sometimes half an hour, sometimes an hour for dinner, and other meals usually taken at work, but these hours, they said, agreed with the children wonderfully. Factory children, they urged, were healthier, more intelligent, more moral than others: looks, they pleaded, are deceptive: when long hours have to be worked, said the manager of Mr. Gott's mills, the children are less tired than the adults. For the children's sake they deprecated shorter hours, it would be exceedingly prejudicial to their morals to let them out earlier. "Nothing," said one of these philanthropists, who worked his children from 6 A.M. to 8 P.M., "is more favourable to morals than habits of early subordination, industry, and regularity."[49] They all agreed that legislative interference would spell ruin to the country and put money into foreigners' pockets. Some of these employers came from other trades, dreading inclusion in the Bill: amongst them was Josiah Wedgwood the younger, who had never heard of any evil effects of overwork in the potteries.

The unanimity of the employer witnesses was broken, as we have said, by Owen and Peel. Owen might be, in some respects, a man of splendid visions, but in this matter he was a man of practical experience, who had tested the effect of different hours on output. Peel underwent a searching cross-examination, in which his past misdeeds and his inconsistencies were mercilessly exposed. He suggested certain alterations in the 1815 Bill, made,

---

[48] Evidence of Mr. George Gould, fustian merchant.
[49] Evidence of Mr. G. A. Lee, cotton millowner.

no doubt, in deference to the millowners' cry of foreign competition. The age at which children might be employed was put at nine instead of ten, and the factory hours were lengthened to thirteen, of which one and a half were to be spent in meals and recreation. Here again his honesty prevented him from thinking such a proposal the best thing for the children. "At present," he said, "the hours allotted to the employment of children may be said to exceed their strength, but that being a peculiar business in which adults and children are employed promiscuously, we could not do justice to one without injury to the other, and therefore the time allowed for the working of those mills being thirteen hours, deducting one and a half hours for meals and recreation, will not place our foreign trade in any unfavourable situation, because no foreigners are known to work the same number of hours."

The evidence given before this committee was published, but, owing to Peel's illness, no measure was brought forward in Parliament till early in 1818. It was preceded by two significant petitions from the grown-up cotton factory operatives of Manchester and Bolton, for a shortening of their hours. The Manchester petitioners pointed out that they worked in the factories "from fourteen to fifteen hours, including the time allowed for dinner, every day of the week, except Saturday, when the working hours are somewhat reduced," that this work, performed in ill-ventilated, over-heated rooms, with dust and cotton flying about, had most injurious consequences to their health, and "that the Petitioners, in representing their unfortunate situation, beg leave to observe, that they also feel the unhappy condition of young children working in factories, who in many instances are connected with the Petitioners by the dearest ties of relationship." They ended by praying "that a law may be passed to restrict the time of actual labour in Cotton Factories to Ten hours and a half each day, so as to allow within the ordinary space of twelve hours, half an hour for breakfast and an hour for dinner."[50]

The petition from Manchester was presented by Sir Robert Peel, who declared that the sight of the miserable men who brought it up had moved him to tears. A few days later (Feb.

---

[50] *House of Commons Journal*, February 18, 1818; Cf. Chapman, *Cotton Industry*, p. 97. Cf. also H. O., 42. 179. Hollis, one of the spinners sent up to London with petitions, said many petitions were sent up after the end of the sessions.

19, 1818) he presented a Bill applying to cotton mills and factories only. This Bill, in which, as he afterwards explained, he had tried to reconcile the relief of the labouring class with the interests of the proprietors, was less drastic than the 1815 measure. It prohibited any children under nine from working. The factory hours, as in the 1815 Bill, were to be limited to twelve and a half, but now one hour was to be taken for dinner and half an hour for breakfast, so that the time for actual "laborious employment" was to be eleven hours. The important clause, that, instead of the magistrate and clergyman visitors of the 1802 Act, duly qualified persons should be appointed by Quarter Sessions and adequately paid for their trouble, was retained. This Bill passed safely through the House of Commons, in spite of a good deal of vehement opposition.[51] Most of the protagonists on either side spoke more than once. The Peels, William Smith, Burdett, and Wilberforce spoke for the Bill, and Philips and Finlay (both millowners), Lord Lascelles, Lord Stanley, and Sir James Graham spoke against it. The "established principle which gave the parent the labour of his child during his minority so long as he gave him adequate support" was invoked against the Bill. Philips grew so eloquent about the healthy delights of life in cotton mills, that the younger Peel retorted that cotton factories had better be erected by the State as health resorts. Philips also attacked the idea of interference with a candid avowal that "The low rate at which we had been able to sell our manufacture on the Continent, in consequence of the low rate of labour here, had depressed the continental manufacturers, and raised the English much more than any interference could do."[52] He also warned the House that the consequence of an attempt to regulate labour would be to "spread Luddism through the whole country."[53] Canning probably represented the majority of the House when he declared himself anxious to hear the question discussed. "If ever he came to the House without prejudice respecting any subject, it was with respect to this subject. The only prejudice he felt was the conviction resulting from all speculations on political economy, in favour of non-interference between man and man. But that degree, not of prejudice, but of disinclination, was, by mere

---

[51] For an excellent summary of the Debates, see Smart, *Economic Annals*, chap. xxx.

[52] *Hansard*, April 27, 1818.

[53] *Hansard*, February 23, 1818.

examination, he would not say changed, but become the ground of much desire to hear discussion upon the subject."[54] Sir Robert Peel stated that the master manufacturers who supported the Bill were more numerous than those who opposed it; and the Stockport petition for the Bill was signed by seventeen master manufacturers. Many of them, he added, wished the provisions to be extended to adults. It was clear that the adults would have welcomed shorter hours, even at the price of lower wages.[55]

Though the 1818 Bill passed the Commons, it was killed in the other House by Lauderdale, the inveterate opponent of all measures to protect the weak by State interference. Lauderdale (1759–1839), who had been a fierce opponent of Pitt, was now on the brink of the political change, which he formally made in 1821, but his economic ideas remained throughout fixed and unyielding. His *Inquiry into the Nature and Origin of Public Wealth* had given him a certain position as an economist which survived even his heavy and awkward humour. Sheridan once said about a good story: "Don't tell that to Lauderdale, for a joke in his mouth is no laughing matter." This was very true of the witticisms with which he enlivened his exposition of *laissez-faire* doctrine, and no man contrived to make political economy so terrible a muse for the poor. Lauderdale destroyed the Bill for the session by persuading the House of Lords to ask for further evidence. He professed himself able to produce medical witnesses to prove that factory children had excellent health, and that employment in cotton factories tended to promote growth. He kept his promise, and certainly undermined the position of those who had relied, in their advocacy of the Bill, not on common-sense but on medical evidence. Lord Liverpool said bluntly that all the medical staff of Manchester could not make him believe that children would not be overworked by fifteen hours a day, but these distinguished doctors would not commit themselves to such bold generalisations. At the invitation and under the auspices of some of the masters they had visited factories, or specially selected rooms in factories, and had seen that everything was satisfactory. They would only testify to what they had seen, and refused to be inveigled into any *a priori* opinions as to the length of time a child could work without injury to health. One well-known doctor even refused to commit himself to the statement that a child's health would be injured

---

[54] *Hansard*, April 17, 1818.
[55] See speeches of Peel and William Smith.

by standing for twenty-three out of the twenty-four hours. As a result of their evidence[56] Lauderdale could declare it proved that parents of weakly children eagerly sought for their admission into factories.

The master spinners of Manchester evidently thought that the agitation was safely over. A curious light is thrown on their attitude by Mr. Norris, the Manchester stipendiary. In September 1818 he wrote to the Home Office to say that the master spinners had been considering the question of hours, and had resolved "to restrict them to twelve working hours per day. This may prevent any further discussion on this point in Parliament."[57] The resolution however does not seem to have taken effect, and in January 1819 he wrote again: "Great and I think *not unfounded* apprehension of some mischief again occurring is entertained by the master spinners from the manner in which Mr. Gould is again moving amongst the operatives the question of time, etc. They believe that this was the main origin of the late turn out, and that if again agitated the same result is *sure* to follow; this is an *uniform* opinion amongst them."[58]

Next year (1819) Lauderdale was less successful. The friends of the Bill proposed another committee to take more evidence. Lauderdale, who the year before had been indignant at the suggestion that their lordships should "encroach upon that great principle of political economy, that labour ought to be left free" without investigating the subject, was now averse to further inquiry. Thanks, however, to the earnest advocacy of the Bishop of Chester (George Henry Law (1761–1845), afterwards Bishop of Bath and Wells), who, since the question had been discussed, had taken the trouble to visit the mills in his diocese, and declared the conditions destructive to children's lives; and thanks also to the support of Lord Liverpool and Lord Holland, Lord Kenyon succeeded in getting another committee appointed. To those who pinned their faith to medical evidence the results must have seemed bewildering, for the medical men who appeared before this Committee gave opinions diametrically opposed to those of their colleagues before the 1818 Committee. The most interesting evidence was that of some operatives, who told of the long hours, the heat, the food made nauseous by

---

[56] House of Lords Committee, 1818.
[57] H. O., 42. 180.
[58] H. O., 42. 183.

flue and dust, the use of the lash to enforce attention. One portrait of a master is perhaps worth quoting: the witness, John Farebrother, was explaining that his master made him, when he was overlooker, beat the children when he failed to extract a certain quantity of work from them: "Which master was that? . . . Mr. Luke Taylor; I have seen him with a horsewhip under his coat waiting at the top of the place, and when the children have come up, he has lashed them all the way into the mill if they were too late: and the children had half a mile to come, and be at the mill at five o'clock."[59] These operatives paid the penalty of their courageous revelations, and on their return to Lancashire had very great difficulty in getting employment again.[60]

The result of this inquiry was the passing through both Houses of the 1819 Cotton Factories Regulation Act.[61] This Act is often called Peel's Act, but it is perhaps unfair to his memory to give it this name, for it was Peel's Bill altered, with its best features eliminated. It was introduced by Kenyon in the Lords, and passed thence down to the Commons, where it was not debated. By this Act, which applied to cotton mills and factories only, no child under nine was to be employed, and for children between the ages of nine to sixteen the factory hours were to be limited to thirteen and a half, of which half an hour was to be spent on breakfast and one hour on dinner, leaving twelve, or the same number as that allowed by the 1802 Act, for actual work. Night work was also forbidden. It is worth noting that Peel had originally, in 1815, in his first speech, proposed ten hours as the period for actual work. The great blemish of the Act was that it left the old arrangements for inspection by a magistrate and a clergyman unchanged, thus destroying its whole efficacy. An amending Act allowing greater latitude for overtime was passed next year (1820), but, except for the purpose of relieving employers with specially sensitive consciences, this Act was unnecessary, for the 1819 measure was

59 House of Lords Committee, 1819.

60 See Committee on Artisans and Machinery, 1824, p. 412 f. "When they returned home they were flung out of employment, and so persecuted by the masters throughout the country that they had no employment for weeks and months after, and some of them were obliged to leave the country for America, in consequence of giving evidence."

61 George III. c. 66.

a dead letter.[62] In 1825 John Cam Hobhouse could state that only two convictions had ever taken place under the Act, although it was well known that in the best managed mills the children's actual working hours were twelve and a half, and in other mills fifteen or sixteen.

Hobhouse himself brought in a Bill in 1825 with the object of preventing evasions of the 1819 Act, by making the attendance of witnesses compulsory. This Bill, in its original form, also reduced the hours of actual work from twelve to eleven, as Peel had proposed in 1818. Hornby objected to this reduction as being equal to a diminution of the total annual production of two and a half million pounds. Hobhouse boldly retorted that it would be "better to give up the cotton trade altogether than to draw such a sum out of the blood, and bones, and sinews of these unfortunate children."[63] Peel the younger gave but a lukewarm support to Hobhouse's proposal, doubting the policy of limiting hours. Philips again argued that managers of cotton mills were the best judges of what regulations were necessary, and Hobhouse, in face of opposition, found it necessary to drop his proposal to shorten hours to eleven, and to confine himself to a reduction of hours on Saturday from twelve to nine. Altered in this fashion, Hobhouse's Bill was allowed to pass both Houses, Huskisson admitting that, though he disliked any interference with free labour, yet, as Parliament had decided on that policy in 1819, its action should be made effective. Peel the younger, much changed from the earlier Peel, who had declared it "disgusting"[64] to see children sent to school after thirteen or fifteen hours of bodily exertion, deprecated even the shortening of Saturday hours without a Commission. A good

---

[62] For Reports from Visitors in 1823 and 1824, see H. O., 52. 3 and 44. 14. The committee appointed for the hundred of Leyland reported to the Quarter Sessions at Preston "that they have not found any instance whatsoever in which the Acts . . . have been observed either as respects the employment of children being less than nine years of age, or as to whitewashing or ventilating the said manufactories." The visitors for the parish of Winwick profess that they are ashamed to send their report, knowing that it is "replete with equivocation and deceit," *i.e.* that they have been deceived. Colonel Fletcher of Bolton reports that the children under nine were hidden from the visitors' sight.

[63] *Hansard*, May 16, 1825.
[64] *Hansard*, April 27, 1818.

feature of Hobhouse's Act[65] was that it forbade proprietors of mills or their fathers or sons to hear complaints under the Act as magistrates.

It is significant that Parliament had again refused to go so far as the better masters themselves were willing to go. During the course of the debates a petition was received from several cotton employers in the Manchester district, urging Parliament to prescribe an eleven and a half hours' day, with eight and a half on Saturdays for all classes of operatives, and stating that "the Petitioners would cheerfully of themselves adopt the above regulation, provided there was a fair prospect of its becoming general."[66]

History repeated itself in 1831. Hobhouse, with the full concurrence of the big manufacturers, brought in another Bill, limiting the factory hours to thirteen, of which eleven and a half were to be actual work, and prohibiting night work to all persons under twenty-one. The provisions were to apply not only to cotton mills as before, but to all textile industries. This Bill met with a good deal of opposition in the Parliament elected to pass the Reform Bill. The Bill ultimately became an Act in a mutilated form, cotton mills only being included in its scope, and the old hours remaining unchanged. This Act ends the factory legislation of our period. Children were left entirely unprotected, except in the cotton industry, and in the cotton industry their masters might work children of nine for twelve hours a day exclusive of meal times. Such regulations, however, as were imposed were academic, for no effective machinery was provided to enforce them.

The struggle for the ten hours' day, led by Oastler and Sadler, falls outside our scope; but one of its incidents fitly closes this subject. During the agitation over the Reform Bill, Sadler was President of a Select Committee of the House of Commons appointed to examine into Factory Children's Labour. Before this committee there files a long procession of workers, men and women, girls and boys. Stunted, diseased, deformed, degraded, each with the tale of his wronged life, they pass across the stage, a living picture of man's cruelty to man, a pitiless indictment of those rulers who in their days of unabated power had abandoned the weak to the rapacity of the strong.

---

[65] 6 George IV. c. 63.
[66] *House of Commons Journal*, May 16, 1828.

CHAPTER IX

THE EMPLOYMENT OF CHILDREN (II)

MINES AND CHIMNEYS

When the opponents of factory legislation found it difficult to persuade reformers that the children working in their mills were happy and well, they tried another argument and asked why it was only children in the factories that deserved the protection of the State. There was some point in the challenge. It was perhaps due to the general habit of regarding the miners as a special and isolated world that the scandal of the employment of children underground attracted scarcely any notice at all. When the Northumberland miners put their grievances before the public in 1825[1] they made a special point of the long hours worked by boys, but Parliament seems to have ignored the subject. We have occasional glimpses of this side of the life of the pit in papers of the time, in references in the Reports of Committees on Accidents, and in some information collected by a Factory Commissioner in 1833. But the earliest systematic presentation of the facts was made in 1842 in its First Report by the Commission on the Employment of Children and Young Persons which was appointed in consequence of Lord Shaftesbury's efforts.

At that time boys were employed everywhere, girls in certain districts, Lancashire, Cheshire, the West Riding and South Wales, besides Scotland. In some of the districts where girls were employed, they were apparently employed as often as boys. Children were employed as trappers, that is to open and shut the doors that guided the draught of air through the mine; as fillers, that is to fill the skips and carriages when the men had hewn the coal; and as pushers, or hurriers, that is to push the trucks along from the workers to the foot of the shaft. But in some mines these trucks were drawn instead of being pushed. "A girdle is put round the naked waist, to which a chain from the carriage is hooked and passed between the legs, and the boys crawl on their hands and knees, drawing the carriage after them."[2] In the early years of the century this arrangement was

---

[1] See *A Voice from the Coal Mines.*

[2] Children's Employment Commission, First Report, Mines, 1842, p. 67. "There are very few under six or seven who are employed to

very common, and women and girls were so employed. By 1842 it was more usual to have small iron railways, and the carriages were pushed along them. The trapping was done everywhere by children, generally from five to eight years of age.[3] A girl of eight years old described her day: "I'm a trapper in the Gamber Pit. I have to trap without a light, and I'm scared. I go at four and sometimes half-past three in the morning and come out at five and half-past. I never go to sleep. Sometimes I sing when I've light, but not in the dark: I dare not sing then."[4] One of the sub-commissioners remarked: "I can never forget the first unfortunate creature (of this class) that I met with: it was a boy of about eight years old, who looked at me as I passed through with an expression of countenance the most abject and idiotic—like a thing, a creeping thing peculiar to the place."[5] The trappers generally sat in a little hole, made at the side of the door, holding a string in their hand, for twelve hours. As a rule they were in the dark, but sometimes a good-natured collier would give them a bit of candle. In the West Riding the work of hurrying or pushing the corves was often done by girls at the time of the Report: "Chained, belted, harnessed like dogs in a go-cart, black, saturated with wet, and more than half naked—crawling upon their hands and feet, and dragging their heavy loads behind them—they present an appearance indescribably disgusting and unnatural."[6]

The hours varied in different parts of England.[7] The Commission put them at twelve in Staffordshire, Shropshire, War-

---

draw weights with a girdle round the body, and those only where the roof of the pit is so low for short distances as to prevent horses of the smallest size, or asses, from being employed."—Evidence of a medical gentleman about Shropshire, *ibid.*, p. 10.

[3] A witness or viewer before the 1835 Select Committee on Accidents in Mines declared that the mines would be "unworkable to profit" if adults were employed as trappers.

[4] Children's Employment Commission, First Report, Mines, 1842, p. 71.

[5] *Ibid.*, p. 77.

[6] Children's Employment Commission, First Report, Appendix; Part ii., 1842, p. 75.

[7] The Commission found considerable discrepancy between the statements of hours from employers and employed, *e.g.* in the south part of the West Riding the coalowners stated the working hours at six or seven a day, the managers, agents, etc., at ten or eleven, the colliers at eleven, and the children at twelve. The trappers, of course, were the first to come and the last to go.

wickshire, and Leicestershire, and at from thirteen to sixteen in Derbyshire. In the north of Lancashire they varied from eight to twelve, whereas in Oldham they were sometimes fourteen or fifteen. In North Durham and Northumberland they were sometimes as long as in Derbyshire. Night work was common in Warwickshire, and the usual practice in Lancashire, Cheshire, Cumberland, and North Wales. It was not uncommon in Northumberland and North Durham, and cases had occurred of boys working for forty-eight hours on end. The conditions and treatment varied. The children who suffered most were the apprentices from the workhouses: "these lads are made to go where other men will not let their own children go. If they will not do it, they take them to the magistrates, who commit them to prison."[8] There were more apprentices in Staffordshire than anywhere else, but there were a good many in the West Riding and in Lancashire. Derbyshire was singled out as the worst county by the Commission. This was partly due to the system of letting the mines to "butties" or small contractors, partly to the nature of the mines. In mines with thick seams it was usual to make good roadways, but in less profitable mines the roads were only just large enough to enable small children to get the corves along them. "In many mines which are at present worked, the main gates are only from twenty-four inches to thirty inches high, and in some parts of these mines the passages do not exceed eighteen inches in height."[9] In this respect Derbyshire and the West Riding were among the worst counties. It was reported that there was much more cruelty in the Halifax pits than in those at Leeds and Bradford. A sub-commissioner met a boy crying and bleeding from a wound in the cheek, and his master explained "that the child was one of the slow ones, who would only move when he saw blood, and that by throwing a piece of coal at him for that purpose he had accomplished his object, and that he often adopted the like means."[10] The witnesses, examined by a Factory Commissioner at Worsley near Manchester in 1833, said that "purring," which was Lancashire for kicking, was a common way of punishing boys and girls in the mines there. The Commissioners of 1842 found that the coalowners took very little interest in the children employed in their mines after their daily work was over, and it is certainly not difficult

[8] First Report, p. 41.
[9] Children's Employment Commission, First Report, p. 45.
[10] Ibid., p. 130.

to believe this, seeing that when Lord Melbourne was Prime Minister, and delighting England by his graceful friendship with the young Queen, the children were working in his mines from 6 o'clock in the morning to 8 o'clock at night. In Lord Balcarres's pits at Aspall Moor the children worked from 5 A.M. to 6 P.M., and some of them were workhouse apprentices. The conditions seemed scandalous enough to the Commission in 1842, but in some respects, at any rate, the children were worse off twenty years earlier.[11] Thus one witness said that when he began to work, at eight years old, as doorkeeper in Felling Pit in 1798, he used to be eighteen or twenty hours down the pit without coming up. Another witness, an underviewer, said that thirty-five years back the boys used to work from 2 A.M. to 8 or 9 P.M. Another witness described the life of a pit-boy fifty years earlier. The boys began at six to eight years old, as trappers, and were paid fivepence a day. From twelve or fourteen to seventeen or eighteen they worked as putters or drivers, being harnessed two together to drag their heavy loads. Their hours were from 2 A.M. to 8 or 10 P.M. every day except Saturday. In busy times they never saw the daylight from Sunday to Saturday afternoon.

The Commissioners reported in 1842, speaking of the worst practices in the West Riding, that the proprietors disclaimed all responsibility and concern. It is difficult to imagine that the proprietors anywhere else were more sensitive. They included men of great power and influence, men like Lord Londonderry, Lord Durham, Lord Melbourne, Lord Granville. These noblemen did not wash their hands of the business that made their wealth, for they took an active part in putting down strikes and crushing Trade Unions.[12] They differed on many questions, but on those questions they were in agreement. Lord Melbourne made it pretty clear in 1832 that he would have liked to re-enact the old Combination Law, in order to deal with the Miners' Unions.[13] But not one of them seems ever to have opened his mouth on the subject of the slave children in their mines, or

---

[11] George Stephenson told the Select Committee on Accidents in 1835 that children were formerly employed at a younger age, and used to be carried on their fathers' backs to the mines. He was not aware that it hurt their health.

[12] Lord Granville gave his manager in his Staffordshire pits orders to discharge any men belonging to the Union (Select Committee on Accidents in Mines, 1835, Wm. Forrester's evidence).

[13] See Speech in House of Lords, June 29, 1832.

supposed that they were under the slightest obligations to the society that gave them their wealth and power.[14]

The factories and the mines were responsible for the greatest sum of infant misery, but there is an instance of the refusal of protection to children which is, in a sense, more surprising. Throughout this period efforts were being made to rescue the little children whose business it was to climb the chimneys in large houses, and yet the period closes without the passing of a single measure to protect them beyond the Act of 1788, which was very modest on paper, and absolutely ineffective in practice. In this case there were no powerful interests concerned; even the most vivid imagination could not discover any danger from foreign competition, and the miserable little boys were not shut up in some remote factory, but were crawling about in the arteries of the great houses occupied by the legislators themselves. It is worth while to tell in some detail the story of the chimney-sweepers' apprentices.

The use of children for sweeping chimneys was a practice peculiar to the British Isles. It came into vogue in English towns early in the eighteenth century, but did not spread to Scotland till about 1788.[15] On the Continent it was unknown. As chimneys developed from wide funnels into narrow and complicated flues their cleaning became a more difficult matter; and the discovery of human brushes that could crawl along any flue, however sharp the angles and however winding the passage, encouraged builders to further feats of complexity. This change in chimneys, which reflected a change in domestic habits, is well described by a correspondent in the *Annual Register* of 1787.[16] This gentleman went to live in an old mansion near Exeter in 1777. "But as in most of the old houses in England," he says, "the chimneys, which were perhaps originally built for the purpose of burning wood, though they had been contracted in front, since coal fires came into general use, to the modern size, yet they were still above, out of sight, extravagantly large. This method of building chimneys may perhaps have answered well enough while it was the custom to sit with the doors and win-

---

[14] The coalowners, in their manifesto during the strike of 1832, said that they paid trappers tenpence a day for work that merely required attention. See Coalowners' Manifesto, *Newcastle Chronicle*, March 17.

[15] Evidence before Lords Committee, 1818, p. 88; and Report, *House of Lords Journals*, May 18, 1818.

[16] P. 85.

dows open; but when the customs and manners of the people began to be more polished and refined, when building and architecture were improved, and they began to conceive the idea of making their chambers close, warm, and comfortable, these chimneys were found to smoke abominably, for want of a sufficient supply of air." He explains how he contrived to contract the chimney, leaving only a space of twelve by fourteen or sixteen inches for a boy to go up and down.

There are no exact records of the number of chimney-sweeps, masters, journeymen, and apprentices. Two hundred masters is the number estimated for London in 1797, 1804, and 1817.[17] In all these estimates, twenty only are stated to be in easy circumstances, and hence able to treat their apprentices well. In the estimates of 1804 and 1817, five hundred is given as the total number of apprentices in London, of whom eighty to a hundred were bound to the twenty prosperous masters. A witness in 1817 calculated that in England, exclusive of London, there were about five hundred climbing boys,[18] so that the whole number may be roughly put at four hundred masters and one thousand boys.

The boys were, as a rule, children whom nobody wanted. Many were paupers apprenticed to their masters by parish authorities, who were too glad to get rid of the burden of their maintenance to trouble about their fate. Others were sold by inhuman parents for two or three guineas: the smaller the child, the better the price: and the parents would take them round and dispose of them to the highest bidder. A few were kidnapped or enticed away. In one instance of this kind, which created a good deal of commotion, the little victim of four was sold by a beggar woman for as much as eight guineas.[19]

"Is not £8 a large price?" a master chimney-sweep, who had been offered a boy for that sum, was asked in 1818. "Oh yes, very large."—"Why was so large a price asked for that boy?"—"Because this is a free country."—"Was he a small boy?"—"Yes, very small of his age."[20] Some were the children of master chimney-sweeps. When girls were employed, as was sometimes the case (e.g. two girls of the name of Morgan swept the chim-

[17] See Reports of Society on the Poor, i. p. 110; and House of Commons Report on Chimney Sweeps, 1817, p. 7.
[18] Mr. Wm. Tooke, before 1817 Committee, Evidence, p. 33.
[19] 1817 Report, Evidence, p. 34.
[20] House of Lords 1818 Report, p. 40.

neys of Windsor Castle[21]), they were usually the children of the sweeps. The age at which the children began their career in climbing varied: some were apprenticed as young as four or five, most were from six to eight.

They started with a period of extreme misery, mental and physical, until they became inured to their trade. Their terror of the pitch-dark and often suffocating passage had to be overcome by the pressure of a greater terror below. In order to induce them to climb up, the more humane masters would threaten to beat them, or perhaps only promise them plum-pudding at the top; the less humane would set straw on fire below or thrust pins into their feet. A careful master would send an experienced child up behind to show the newcomer how to place his feet and to catch him if he fell. Sometimes the seasoned boy would bring up pins to prevent halts in mid-chimney. When the "repugnance" of ascending the chimney, as it was euphemistically called, had been overcome, there followed many months of acute physical suffering from the sores on elbows and knees. Gradually these parts would grow insensible. "Some boys' flesh," said a master in 1817, "is far worse than others, and it takes more time to harden them." He estimated that it took six months, as a rule, for the parts affected to grow "cartilaginous."[22] The more humane masters would work them leniently during this time, but "you must keep them a little at it even during the sores, or they will never learn their business." When their extremities were hardened and their fears subdued, they settled down to their grimy lives. The best masters made a practice of washing them once a week; the less careful would leave them unwashed from year's end to year's end. A witness in 1788 stated that he had known many boys serve four or five years without being once washed.[23] Some masters used to take them to the New River on Sunday mornings in the summer, but leave them coated with soot all the winter.[24] They slept almost invariably, with the soot, in a cellar: sometimes on bags of soot, with another bag to cover them: sometimes on straw, and occasionally on a mattress. Part of the apprentices' duty was to advertise their masters by "crying the streets," a practice deprecated by the more prosperous sweeps, who did not need this advertisement. "There is nearly

---

[21] 1817 Report, Evidence, p. 29.
[22] Ibid., p. 19.
[23] House of Commons Journal, May 1, 1788.
[24] 1817 Report, Evidence, p. 9.

as much reason," wrote the Bishop of Durham in 1799, "for sending round the bricklayer's lad, with his hod of mortar and a few bricks, screaming his master into that employment which neither his situation or character would otherwise give him any pretension to, as the loading with his bag and implements of trade, a little child already suffering by dirt, hunger, cold, and the want of domestic comfort; and sending him to disturb the streets by his cries, till some unknown person calls him in, and employs him in his trade."[25]

As may easily be imagined, the occupation of a chimney-sweep was both dangerous and unhealthy. A disease known as chimney-sweep's cancer was common, and unless it was treated with the knife at an early stage it was fatal. Apart from the dangers of suffocation in narrow or horizontal flues, the boys ran the risk of being burnt either when they were sent up, as was a common custom, to extinguish a chimney on fire, or when they lost their way in a maze of flues and found themselves in a lighted one. Most boys in the trade were stunted in growth, blear-eyed from the soot, and "knapped-kneed" from climbing when their bones were soft and from dragging heavy loads. "The knees and ancle-joints mostly become deformed, in the first instance, from the position they are obliged to put them in, in order to support themselves, not only while climbing up the chimney, but more particularly so in that of coming down, when they rest solely on the lower extremities, the arms being used for scraping and sweeping down the soot in the meantime: this in addition to that of carrying heavy loads confirms the complaint."[26]

The first attempt to improve the condition of these climbing boys by Act of Parliament was made in 1788, and the credit for it must go to Mr. David Porter, benevolent master chimney-sweep of Little Welbeck Street. Mr. Porter had first interested that many-sided philanthropist, Mr. Jonas Hanway, in the subject. Mr. Hanway died before anything was done, and Mr. Porter next induced "a Committee of very respectable Gentlemen" to inquire into the state of the boys. This Committee and Mr. Porter presented petitions to Parliament in April 1788 for legislation, and stated "that, if the Petitioners were to enumerate such Hardships and Cruelties as have come to their Knowledge in the Course of their Enquiries upon this Subject, it would almost exceed Belief, and is better suppressed than made public in

---

25 Reports of Society on the Poor, ii. p. 111.
26 Evidence of Mr. R. Wright, surgeon, 1817 Report, p. 24.

a Country renowned for its Humanity."[27] The dangers of legislative interference with freedom of contract had not yet sunk
deep into the Parliamentary mind, and a Bill, introduced by
Mr. Robert Burton, was passed that same session without any
difficulty. According to a witness in 1817,[28] it was maimed in
the Lords by the omission of clauses for licensing masters, regis-
tering apprentices, and prohibiting calling the streets.[29] This
Act (28 Geo. III. c. 48) talked in its preamble of the "various
complicated Miseries, to which Boys employed in climbing and
cleansing of Chimneys are liable, beyond any other Employment
whatsoever in which Boys of tender Years are engaged . . . ,"
and it sought to mitigate them by ordering that no boy should
be apprenticed before he was eight years old, that no master
should have more than six apprentices, each of whom must
have his master's name and address on a brass plate stuck in
front of his leathern cap, and that no boy should be let out for
hire or "call the streets" after midday, and before seven in winter
or five in summer. A schedule to the Act gave the form of indenture which a master must sign, by which he pledged himself,
amongst other things, to cause the apprentice "to be thoroughly
washed and cleansed from Soot and Dirt at least once a Week,"
to send him to church on the Sabbath day, not to make him
climb any chimney actually on fire, "not make use of any violent
or improper Means to force him to climb or go up any such
Chimney"; and, lastly—an ominous clause—"in all Things [to]
treat his (or her) said Apprentice with as much Humanity and
Care as the Nature of the Employment of a Chimney Sweeper
will admit of."

This Act was a dead letter. No machinery had been provided
to carry it out; the masters who had been cruel before did not
change their habits because they had placed a signature on a
piece of parchment, and the traffic in tiny children went on
unchecked. The happy owners of the smallest-sized living
brushes used to let them out to other masters for special jobs,
and handbills advertising "small boys for small flues" were
common. To save appearances before the magistrates, indeed,
the parents would state the age as eight years, or else the boys
would be employed without regular indentures, till they reached

[27] *House of Commons Journal*, April 22, 1788.
[28] Mr. Wm. Tooke, 1817 Report, p. 7.
[29] Lord Thurlow was credited with erasing this last clause. Evidence before Lords Committee, 1818, p. 177.

a more mature age. One master sweep, Thomas Allen by name, who gave evidence before a Committee in 1817, had been articled in a public house in 1795 at the age of three and a half.[30] In one case that has been handed down to us the Act proved of real use. In the absence of his mother, the father of a boy of five sold him for three guineas to Henry Doe, a master sweep. When the mother returned she was frantic at the fate of her child, and, with the help of a kind-hearted solicitor, informed against the master and got back her boy.[31] Most of the boys had, of course, nobody who was interested in them except the very persons who consigned them to their lot. It must be remembered also, in excuse for the master sweeps, that, if all the chimneys were to be swept by boys, tiny children were indispensable. Incredible though it may sound, some flues which children swept were only seven inches square. For such chimneys not only a tiny child but a naked tiny child was necessary.

"If the Chimneys happen to be too small," said a witness in 1788, "they call the Boys down, strip them, and beat them, and force them up again, by which means they become crippled."[32] In 1817 things had not changed much. "I have seen them," said a master sweep, "make them strip themselves naked and threaten to beat them; I have been obliged myself to go up a chimney naked, but I do not like to see my children do so."[33]

In the small flues the children had to keep their arms straight up above their heads; "if they slip their arms they get jammed."[34] If their shirt was crumpled, they might be stuck fast, unable to move.

A master sweep in 1788 estimated that a chimney should be twelve inches square for a boy of seven to go up with ease.[35] In 1818 chimneys seven inches square which boys swept were still being built.[36] A graphic description of the attempted sweeping of one of these small chimneys, which was about a brick and a half square, was given by its owner in 1817.[37]

The chimney went nearly straight up from a copper: a young

---

[30] 1817 Report, Evidence, p. 46.
[31] Ibid., pp. 35–36.
[32] House of Commons Journal, May 1, 1788.
[33] 1817 Report, Evidence, p. 23.
[34] 1818 Lords Report, Wm. Cooper's evidence.
[35] House of Commons Journal, May 1, 1788.
[36] See Bennet's Speech, House of Commons, February 18, 1818.
[37] 1817 Report, Evidence, p. 32.

boy was brought in to sweep it: "There was a hole made in the side for the boy to go up, and the boy was repeatedly driven in at the hole, but the mortar and soot fell in such great lumps upon his head, and with such force, that if he had not had a cap upon his head it would have been broken. Upon seeing the boy writhing in order to get into the chimney, and being satisfied he could not conveniently get up, although the man who was his master being without feeling seemed to say it was mere idleness in the boy, and that he would force the boy up, I would not suffer it, and the chimney was not swept."

The Act of 1788, as we have said, was a dead letter. Occasionally individuals interested themselves in the boys: Sir Thomas Bernard related with enthusiasm how on a surprise Sunday visit to Mr. Porter's establishment he found the apprentices fresh from church eating boiled mutton and rice pudding;[38] and at Kingston-upon-Thames, in 1798, a lady in the neighbourhood, "distinguished as much by her benevolence as her rank," presented the boys with clothes so that they might attend Sunday-school.[39] It may be noticed that Sabbatical observances had an hygienic as well as a religious importance for these soot-caked children. Attendance at church ensured a weekly wash. Some London master sweeps, at the instigation of Mr. Porter, and under the guidance of the Society for Bettering the Condition of the Poor, instituted a Friendly Society in 1800,[40] in order amongst other things to enforce the regulations of 1788, but only the better-class masters joined, and nothing came of it. In 1803 a Society for Superseding Climbing Boys was formed with Mr. Wm. Tooke as a leading spirit, and this Society took the excellent practical step of offering a reward for a sweeping machine. They also, in 1804, promoted a Bill which passed the Commons, by which all sweeps within ten miles of the Royal Exchange had to be licensed and registered, the apprentices were not to be hired or lent out by their masters, and none but apprentices were to be used as climbing boys. No record has survived of any debate on this mild Bill, but its provisions proved too much for the Lords, who, after recommitting it three times, rejected it on July 19, in a House composed of one Archbishop, five Bishops, three Dukes, five Earls, one Viscount, and ten Barons.

---

[38] Reports on the Poor, i. p. 112.
[39] Ibid., ii. p. 108.
[40] Ibid., ii. p. 316.

For the next thirteen years the London Society for Superseding Climbing Boys set itself the uphill task of overcoming prejudice by proving that machinery could be employed with success instead of boys. The machine that was most satisfactory was one invented by a Mr. Smart in 1803. Mr. Smart himself estimated after fourteen years' experience that 99 per cent. of existing chimneys could with care be swept by his machine. The Society furnished likely men with this machine, and endeavoured to create a demand for its services. A similar society was formed in Sheffield in 1807.[41]

Some interesting experiments by a Society formed at Leeds for superseding the use of boys gave the following results.[42] The machine was applied to 1,411 different chimneys of all kinds. Two men sent with machines to the larger houses succeeded in 89½ per cent. A man sent to both big and small houses succeeded in 95 per cent. A man "more exclusively employed in the Small Houses, in Cottages, Workshops, and Farm Houses where less attention is paid to external or internal appearances in the Chimnies," succeeded in every case.

It was, in fact, in big mansions and public offices that the difficult chimneys were found, and it was precisely in these chimneys with their horizontal reaches that there was danger of suffocation for the human brush. The child would make his way up to the top of the chimney, and then descend slowly, sweeping the soot down as he went. When he reached the bend where the flue turned at right angles, he would find great masses of soot into which he might slide as into a death trap. If he lost his head and got jammed, his fate was sealed, unless his cries could bring help in time. Opposition to the use of machines came chiefly from the more prosperous master sweeps and from the servants in big houses. The Sheffield Society already mentioned, after ten years of vain attempts to improve the lot of the apprentices by voluntary effort, petitioned Parliament in 1817 for the prohibition of climbing boys. Master sweeps, they pointed out, would never use machinery in place of boys so long as boys were allowed to climb, for this reason, that a man had to work a machine himself with a boy as an assistant only, whereas, under the existing system, a man could have as many apprentices as he liked (the law being a dead letter) and could send them out in all directions, "satisfied if they do but bring back every

---

[41] See Report in *Annual Register*, 1809, p. 827.
[42] *House of Lords Journal*, May 8, 1818.

day a certain sum of Money, and a certain quantity of Soot, he may all the time be indulging himself at his Ease."[43]

Another reason for the hostility of the master sweeps was the fear that others might take their business or "mystery" from them. This fear was sharpened by the fact that the different societies for superseding climbing boys, finding it impossible to enlist the help of the regular sweeps, had often been forced to employ outsiders to work their machines. Many masters in London took machines with the object of showing how unsatisfactory they were, and by purposely creating dirt created also a prejudice.

The experts, in fact, constantly assured the housekeepers and servants that machinery was useless, and would not only leave their chimneys dirty, but cover the room with soot. If required they were ready to demonstrate this. A striking illustration of this temper was shown in the case of the House of Commons, where the Speaker directed that machinery should be tried. The master sweep who came to apply the machine pretended that he could manage only nineteen out of sixty-one chimneys. Here the matter might have ended but for the intervention of the housekeeper,[44] who determined to have them swept under his own superintendence. The result was that sixty out of sixty-one were swept by the machine, and the sixty-first merely required some slight alteration to make it amenable to machinery.[45]

The story of the attempts made in 1817, 1818, and 1819 to prohibit the use of climbing boys is sad and strange reading. The hero is Henry Grey Bennet,[46] the Radical M.P., who attacked the Game Laws and the barbarities of the Penal Code, the friend and correspondent of Creevey; the villain is Lauderdale. The proceedings began hopefully with the presentation of several petitions in favour of abolishing climbing boys, and the appointment of a Committee in 1817, which took the evidence of philanthropists, doctors, and master sweeps, most of whom had been apprentices themselves. The Committee's Report was of a sensational kind, and its authors did not, like the respectable

---

[43] *House of Commons Journal*, 1817, June 5.

[44] The housekeeper was Mr. John Bellamy, famous for the stories of his pork pies.

[45] *Hansard*, House of Lords, March 15, 1819, Lord Auckland's speech.

[46] The Hon. H. G. Bennet, 1777–1836, second son of fourth Earl of Tankerville, M.P. for Shrewsbury, 1806 and from 1811 to 1826.

gentlemen of 1788, think it necessary to spare the feelings of "a Country renowned for its Humanity." The evidence in favour of prohibition was overwhelming. A Bill was brought in by Bennet with Wilberforce's help, enacting that in future no boy should be bound till he was fourteen, and that no apprentice should henceforth climb chimneys. An exception was made for existing apprentices over fourteen years old. But the session was too far advanced for the Bill to make further progress. Next year (1818) Bennet brought in a Bill on February 9th, similar to that of the last session, except that the prohibition of the use of climbing boys was not to be enforced till May 1819. Bennet could quote five fatal accidents to climbing boys in the course of the previous year, two of them "attended with circumstances of peculiarly aggravated cruelty," as a further argument for the Bill, if any were needed.[47] He pointed out, in reply to Lord Milton's plea for delay, that the only chimneys that could not be swept except by boys, "belonged to those who could well afford to alter them if they pleased," and denounced with feeling the policy of "sacrificing the children of the poor in order to preserve the chimneys of the rich." The Bill passed the Commons, but the Lords, who owned so many of these tortuous chimneys, thought proceedings had been too much hurried and appointed a Committee to take evidence. The minutes of evidence are very full and particularly interesting. The master chimney-sweeps who opposed the Bill had marshalled many witnesses, but it is doubtful whether their testimony would always have precisely the desired effect. Some of them were enthusiastic, for example, in their approval of the use of children to extinguish chimneys on fire, a practice prohibited by the Act of 1788, but still universal.

"Have you ever known an Instance of a Boy sent up a Flue on Fire?" was asked of one master sweep, who answered, "Yes, and rejoiced I have been many a Time, when such a Job has

---

[47] *Hansard*, February 18, 1818. Just four months before a boy of twelve had been suffocated in a banker's chimney in Somers Town. He had been sent by his master, in an exhausted condition, up a flue so hot that potatoes were baking in the oven. He reached the top and was heard "sobbing and crying very much" as he came down. He was finally taken out with his skin scorched, about four feet from the oven. It is fair to the baker to say that when he came home and found the boy up the chimney, he broke away part of the flue in hopes of saving his life, but it was too late. See Evidence of Clerk and Middlesex Coroner before 1818 Lords Committee.

come to my Master, to get Sixpence for myself, or a Shilling; an active Child will not let the Fire rest on him; we pin the Bosom of the Shirt over, secure it in every Way, so that the Fire cannot get at him; we wet the Brush and then when one Boy is tired, we send up another, and if he keeps in Motion, the Fire will not lodge; if he is sluggish, he will be likely to be burnt."[48] "A Boy need never be burnt up a Chimney on Fire," said another, "if he is a good Boy for Work."[49] One of the witnesses against the Bill was Mr. David Porter, who had done so much to promote the Act of 1788. He had left the trade fifteen years before and had turned builder. He displayed a strange ignorance of abuses more recent than 1788, and declared that he had never seen a flue up which it was dangerous to send a boy of eight. By a strange irony of fate he himself had built the chimney in Cumberland Street, where one of the five fatal accidents of the previous year had taken place. "The Chimney," he said, "is horizontal, and the Boy should have had another Boy to take the Soot as he travelled on, and then the accident would not have happened."[50] As it was, the boy was suffocated.

The Lords Committee reported that there was not yet enough evidence to justify the Bill, and advised delay till the Surveyor-General should have furnished the report that he had been asked to make. The Bill was accordingly dropped. The Surveyor-General's report on the practicability of superseding climbing boys was published on February 1, 1819. It was based on a number of careful experiments made under the supervision of "an active and intelligent clerk" in the Board of Works, of the name of Davis. Davis divided the London flues into four classes according to their complexities. The first three classes, which embraced 990 out of 1000, could all be swept either by a machine or, where that failed, by ball and brush; the fourth class of very complicated flues, or ten out of 1000, could be partly swept by ball and brush, but there were left some "which have several bends and are frequently horizontal." Opponents always pointed to the existence of these flues as an unanswerable objection to the abolition of the use of climbing boys. Mr. Davis took a very different view. "In these cases," he reported, "it is alike necessary to let in registers or doors, whether they are swept by Boys or Machines, there being no other security for the

---

48 Lords Committee, 1818, Evidence, p. 135.
49 Ibid., p. 220.
50 Ibid., p. 112.

safety of the Boys than this measure, which when done, actually presents the means of sweeping by a common machine."

Next year (1819) Bennet introduced his third Bill. His case was now fortified by the experiments detailed in the Surveyor-General's report. Unfortunately, the Surveyor-General himself had inserted a sentence into his covering report to the effect that total abolition was at present impracticable, an opinion entirely at variance with Davis's report, unless the Surveyor-General merely meant that time must be allowed to make the necessary alterations. The Bill of 1819 resembled Bennet's earlier Bills, except that the time limit prohibition was now extended to May 1821.

Opposition to the measure in the House of Commons had stiffened, and there were considerable debates.[51] The arguments against the Bill followed the usual lines: first, the abuses did not exist, or were exaggerated; secondly, if they existed, they were necessary; thirdly, if they were abolished, greater evils would follow. Sir J. Yorke and Denman were the chief speakers against the Bill, Denman in face of all the facts refusing to "conceive that the people of this country were so attached to cruel treatment, merely because it was cruel, as to continue to sweep with children, when it would be better to sweep with machinery."[52] Amongst others Brougham spoke for the Bill, justifying interference in the present case on the ground that "little less than crime was attempted to be practised." Wilberforce retorted on Denman's argument with the crushing illustration of the slave trade, where interest and humanity might have been supposed to prompt the owner to look after his human cargo. Perhaps the most original argument produced against legislation was that of Mr. Ommaney, who asserted that "The boys generally employed in this profession were not the children of poor persons, but the children of rich men, begotten in an improper manner." In spite of opposition the Bill passed safely through the Commons, but, like its predecessor, was wrecked in the Lords, though Lord Auckland, Lord Grosvenor, and Lord Harrowby made efforts to save it. Lauderdale attacked it with vehemence, using what Lord Harrowby described as the resources of Joe Miller, for lack of valid arguments. Even the fact that fire insurance offices had not petitioned against the Bill was adduced as a proof that the Bill would increase the risk of fire, and there-

---

51 *Hansard*, February 12, 17, and 22, 1819.
52 *Hansard*, February 17, 1819.

fore the profits of these offices. He argued that reforms of this kind should be left "entirely to the moral feelings of perhaps the most moral people on the face of the earth";[53] and also, it might have been retorted, the only people who practised this particular species of cruelty.

The Bill was thrown out at the Committee stage by 37 to 20. Bennet, baffled but still undaunted, proceeded on May 19 of the same year (1819) to introduce a new Bill, not to prohibit climbing, for he saw that this was hopeless, but to improve conditions. In this reform he had on his side the principal master sweeps who had protested against prohibition. By this Bill no boy was to be apprenticed till he was ten, no girl was to be employed, no apprentices were to be let out for hire, and nobody in the employment of chimney-sweeps was to call the streets. This Bill passed the Commons without opposition, but again the House of Lords refused all help to the little grimy victims of their chimneys. It was in vain that Auckland pointed out that the Bill simply laid down practical rules approved by the trade. The scare of fire could not be produced now. Instead, the Lord Chancellor (Eldon), with a lawyer's subtleties, mocked at the wording of the Bill: it was absurd to talk of a "female girl or woman."[54] How could crying the streets be prohibited? Might not the doors be knocked, and so a greater nuisance ensue? Lauderdale, who in one stage of his opposition to reform had announced himself willing to support prohibition, if satisfactory machinery were invented, now took up a broader ground of objection.

"If the legislature attempted to lay down a moral code for the people, there was always a danger that every feeling of benevolence would be extirpated."[55] Their Lordships were so much alarmed by this prospect that they promptly threw out the Bill by 32 votes to 12, and the old evils went on unchecked except by private benevolence till after the period with which we deal.[56]

---

[53] *Hansard*, House of Lords, March 8, 1819.

[54] *Hansard*, House of Lords, May 24, 1819. The actual words, as Lord Lansdowne pointed out, were "female child, girl, or woman."

[55] *Hansard*, May 24, 1819.

[56] The later history of the chimney-sweep's boy may be given briefly. In 1834 an Act was passed (4 and 5 William iv. c. 35) which forbade the binding of any boy under ten, and the employment of children under fourteen unless apprenticed or on trial. Boys were to have a two months' trial before being apprenticed, to be examined

The history of the chimney-sweeper's boy is in some ways the most remarkable phenomenon of this period. It seems incredible that Parliament should have refused to reform so inhuman a system when virtually the only difficulty was the taste for elaborate chimneys in grand houses. An architect, who appeared as a witness before the Lords Committee in 1818, admitted that the horizontal flues were only needed because the owners of mansions wanted greater comfort and luxury, and it was frequently objected to the proposal to have a register door that it would disfigure "a handsome apartment." In this case Lauderdale and his friends were in fact obstructing the development of machinery, and behaving precisely as they accused the workmen of behaving in regard to factory improvements, the interests at stake being not the bread of thousands of poor men and women, but the display and pomp of a handful of very rich families.

It requires an effort as we think of the children in the mill, punished with the punishment of Sisyphus for the pleasures of a life they had never tasted, and of the children in the mines, keeping their blind vigil before the sun had risen, and keeping their blind vigil after the sun had set, to remember that this was an age in which childhood and all the promise and mystery of childhood were taking a new place in the affections of the cultivated classes. Rousseau's spell had less power in England than on the Continent, but even in England Emile had given a great stimulus to the study of the play and development of children's minds. Charles and Mary Lamb were publishing *Poetry for Children* and the *Tales from Shakespeare* which are still in common use, and the Edgeworths, the Aikins, and the Taylors, who were all writing at this time, were to rule the imaginations of children for many generations after their own, with a sway as absolute as the sway of Scott or Mayne Reid over the imaginations of boys. The greatest portrait painter of the age was describing the charm

---

by a magistrate at the end of that time, and not to be bound unless willing. This was the Act in force at the time Dickens wrote *Oliver Twist*, published in Bentley's *Miscellany*, 1837–39. Blake's poems on the chimney-sweeps had been published in 1789 and 1794. In 1840 an Act was passed (3 and 4 Vict. c. 85) by which nobody under twenty-one was to be allowed to climb chimneys and no child under sixteen was to be apprenticed to a chimney-sweep. This Act was amended in 1864 (27 and 28 Vict. c. 37), when a chimney-sweep was forbidden to employ any child under ten except on his own premises. Bennet, the best friend of the climbing boys in Parliament, only lived to see the first of these Acts passed; he died in 1836.

and grace and laughter of happy and careless childhood. But so deep and distant was the underworld where children were stolen from the sunshine as soon as they could creep beneath an engine or watch a trap-door in a mine, that the sleep of those rulers who admired Sir Joshua's portraits of innocence, and took pride in their sensibility and tenderness, was never broken or haunted by an echo of the

> "Voces, vagitus et ingens
> Infantumque animae flentes in limine primo,
> Quos dulcis vitae exsortes et ab ubere raptos
> Abstulit atra dies."

CHAPTER X

THE MIND OF THE RICH

In this chapter we shall try to understand the temper and the reasoning of the society that passed the Combination Laws, tolerated the horrors inflicted upon children, and accepted the standing misery of the poor as a recognised and indispensable condition of national welfare. How did such men and women interpret society and its duties, economic relationships and economic laws, religion and its message of brotherhood and pity?

We do not mean, of course, that men and women go through life asking themselves at every turn, how they justify their own special good fortune in the social system under which they live, any more than the poor man or the unfortunate man goes through life thinking from morning till night of his grievances against that system and of nothing else. Most people take the gifts that life sends them without asking of life that it shall provide a soothing philosophy as well. To the average successful employer, or to the gentleman living on an inherited property, or to the younger member of a noble family living on an ancient sinecure, the reflection that nine out of ten of their countrymen were finding life a much more difficult and painful business was not always knocking with a disturbing summons at heart and conscience. They had not made the world, and the power that had made it was wiser than such wild men as Paine or Cobbett, or the workmen who cheered a mountebank like Hunt, broke up good and expensive machines, and were so stupid as to think that strikes and quarrels with their employers could mend anybody's fortunes. Life was full of strange phenomena, and the Bible, with its shrewd outlook, had prepared the world for the poverty of the poor. Men and women who reasoned like this were not particularly heartless or cruel. They took the world as they found it. This is the attitude of all people to some of the facts, and of some people to all of the facts, that meet them day by day. One of the most powerful and passionate leaders of the crusade against the long hours of the factories has told us how he lived for many years in the mills, and that John Wood's appeal came to him as a revelation. The story of Richard Oastler is a sufficient warning against the temptation to see the facts of an age apart from their atmosphere.

But if the established order is its own justification to many minds, it remains true that the turn which social history takes in any age results in part from the ideas and opinions that are in the ascendant. To understand the resignation, we might almost call it satisfaction, with which this generation accepted a state of things that seems to the modern mind to mark so definite a catastrophe of civilisation, we must examine the intellectual currents of the period. There was no lack of speculation or discussion. The House of Commons listened at one time to Burke, at another to Ricardo. Adam Smith and Malthus were becoming as familiar in parliamentary debates as Cicero or Virgil. Bentham and James Mill inspired Joseph Hume. In the House of Lords there was King who used Political Economy to threaten the rich, and Lauderdale who used it to punish the poor. Brougham, with an energy like that of steam that could be harnessed to almost any task, was never tired of explaining everything to everybody. There were other prophets and critics who were less successful in reaching the upper classes—Godwin, Paine, Hodgskin, Thompson, Ogilvie: economists who ploughed an unpromising furrow at the time, though some of them were to reap a rich harvest later. For the moment their message seemed wicked and ludicrous enough, but Owen, scandalously as he appeared to misconceive the blessings of the new industrial system, once had a debate all to himself in a House of Commons a little shocked by its own boldness.[1]

There was then no lack of discussion, and the age that established the new industry on the basis of exploited labour would have resented the suggestion that it was acting blindly or carelessly. And with justice, for the general economic view that grew up in this period, reconciling the intelligence to this inhuman spectacle, lived and flourished long after the generation of Peterloo had gone to its grave. In some senses, the accepted explanation of economic society was not less important in its consequences than the laws that Sidmouth and his friends passed in defence of that society. That explanation was a conclusion from a number of principles, so combined and arranged as to present a solid obstacle to all plans of social reform. It is worth while to glance at the stages by which the fatalist view of the condition of the working classes came to dominate politicians, and to see how, by taking this truth from one economist and that from another, the educated classes built up an edifice of gloomy error

---

[1] *Hansard*, xli. 1189; House of Commons, December 1819.

which earned for their political economy its just title of the dismal science. We do not propose, of course, to describe all the economic doctrines that influenced or failed to influence the governing classes during this period; that would be a theme not for a chapter but for several volumes. We are concerned only with the way in which the political economy they learned led these classes to regard the main problems discussed in this book; from this point of view we may trace the development of economic fatalism through four stages.

1. Adam Smith, releasing economics from the old mercantilist superstitions, set the whole world in a new light, displaying trade as an elaborate and varied life of mutual service, a system in which men and nations were not all engaged in snatching advantages from each other, but unconsciously helping and developing each other. He examined all the restrictions and regulations by which nations had tried to increase their prosperity at the expense of the rest of mankind, and governments had tried to direct the operations of traders and capitalists, and argued that they had done harm rather than good to the peoples who thought they were benefiting by them, because they interfered with "the obvious and simple system of natural liberty." The upper classes took that phrase from Adam Smith, and applied it to the relations of capital and labour, but it was rarely and only after a long interval that they applied it to anything else. There is a well-known story that Pitt, present at a dinner where Adam Smith was also a guest, insisted on standing till Adam Smith was seated, declaring "we are all your pupils." The description was not true, even of Pitt, but it was truer of Pitt than of most people, for he carried the Commercial Treaty with France, and was only prevented by a factious Opposition from carrying a Commercial Treaty with Ireland. Pitt had, at any rate, risked his popularity for the sake of Adam Smith's principles. For the upper class in general Adam Smith's teaching had a narrower theatre. The doctrine that trade was mutual service, that the activities of individuals enriched the community, under "the obvious and simple system of natural liberty," undermined the basis of the legal regulation of commerce and industry. Politicians who had been brought up in a society which had on its Statute Book innumerable laws designed to prevent the exploitation of the public by monopolists, or to limit, in the defence of order and peace, the access to particular trades and careers, or to protect private accumulations and interests, or to maintain a

standard of life, found in the new philosophy a summons to disentangle industrial life from all this web of prudence. All this machinery disappeared. The Assize of Bread in London was one of the latest survivals, and it was abolished in 1815. The regulation of wages had often been in the past the weapon of the employers, but at the end of the eighteenth century a situation had arisen in which the labourers looked to it for help. The politicians who rejected their appeal did not pretend to reject it on the ground that, as the rich were more powerful than the poor, such a law would always be administered in their favour.[2] Pitt rejected it in the name of the new political economy, arguing that "trade, industry, and barter would always find their own level, and be impeded by regulations which violated their natural operation and deranged their proper effect." This meant that it was bad for trade to attempt to interfere with wages, and therefore bad for all the interests affected. In 1813, when the statutes prescribing the regulation of wages were formally repealed, Sidmouth said that their existence had only just been discovered, and that it did not require such enlightened minds as those he was addressing to understand how pernicious such regulations must be. On all such questions the ruling class borrowed readily from Adam Smith the general notion that perfect freedom was the best stimulus to production, and that all the apparent or temporary disadvantages resulting from uncontrolled competition would sooner or later be eliminated by the natural operations of economic forces. This was almost the only lesson they learnt from him.

2. The second stage is represented by the doctrine of the employers' enlightened selfishness. The first discovery, that the State could not really protect the workman, was followed by another, even more interesting, that the employer could not really injure him. The workmen were in the hands of a power that was obliged by the law of its being to secure them all the comfort and freedom of which they were capable. This doctrine was pushed to its extreme by a thinker who might have been expected to revolt against this mechanical analysis of society; for

---

[2] Adam Smith had put it that "Whenever the legislature attempts to regulate the differences between masters and their workmen, its counsellors are always the masters. When the regulation, therefore, is in favour of the workmen, it is always just and equitable; but it is sometimes otherwise when in favour of the masters."—*Wealth of Nations*, bk. i. chap. x.

it is nowhere laid down with more unquestioning confidence than in Burke's *Thoughts and Details on Scarcity* (1795):—

"But in the case of the farmer and the labourer, their interests are always the same, and it is absolutely impossible that their free contracts can be onerous to either party. It is the interest of the farmer, that his work should be done with effect and celerity: and that cannot be, unless the labourer is well fed, and otherwise found with such necessaries of animal life, according to his habitudes, as may keep the body in full force, and the mind gay and cheerful. For of all the instruments of his trade, the labour of man (what the ancient writers have called the *instrumentum vocale*) is that on which he is most to rely for the repayment of his capital. The other two, the *semivocale*, in the ancient classification, that is, the working stock of cattle, and the *instrumentum mutum*, such as carts, ploughs, spades, and so forth, though not all inconsiderable in themselves, are very much inferior in utility or in expense; or, without a given portion of the first, are nothing at all. For, in all things whatever, the mind is the most valuable and the most important; and in this scale the whole of agriculture is in a natural and just order; the beast is as an informing principle to the plough and cart; the labourer is as reason to the beast; and the farmer is as a thinking and presiding principle to the labourer. An attempt to break this chain of subordination in any part is equally absurd; but the absurdity is the most mischievous in practical operation, where it is the most easy, that is, where it is the most subject to an erroneous judgment.

"It is plainly more the farmer's interest that his men should thrive, than that his horses should be well fed, sleek, plump, and fit for use, or than that his waggon and ploughs should be strong, in good repair, and fit for service.

"On the other hand, if the farmer cease to profit of the labourer, and that his capital is not continually manured and fructified, it is impossible that he should continue that abundant nutriment, and clothing, and lodging proper for the protection of the instruments he employs.

It is therefore the first and fundamental interest of the labourer, that the farmer should have a full incoming profit on the product of his labour. The proposition is self-evident, and nothing but the malignity, perverseness, and illgoverned passions of mankind, and particularly the envy they bear to each other's prosperity, could prevent their seeing and acknowledging it, with thankfulness to the benign and wise Disposer of all

things, who obliges men, whether they will or not, in pursuing
their own selfish interests, to connect the general good with their
own individual success.

"But who are to judge what that profit and advantage ought
to be? Certainly no authority on earth. It is a matter of convention dictated by the reciprocal conveniences of the parties, and
indeed by their reciprocal necessities. But if the farmer is ex-
cessively avaricious? Why, so much the better—the more he desires to increase his gains, the more interested is he in the good
condition of those upon whose labour his gains must principally
depend."[3]

Similarly Burdett, whose political views were very different
from Burke's, in replying to Curwen, who was in favour of a
minimum wage for agriculture (1818), dismissed all discussion
of the rate of wages with the assertion that "no one gave less
to labour than it was the interest of the labourer to receive." This
belief that the more selfish the employer, the more certain he
was to treat his employees well, was carried by some of the new
economists to extravagant lengths.[4] It was against this opinion,
held with religious tenacity, that factory legislation made its
slow way, and the opposition to Peel's Bill for reducing the actual working day of children between nine and sixteen to eleven
hours was led by Lauderdale: "The employer was the person
most likely to be acquainted with the different degrees of
strength possessed by his workmen, and most likely to avoid over-
working them with a view to his own advantage." "The workmen" who were comforted with this aphorism were children of
nine and ten.[5]

3. This doctrine was supplemented by another that turned
the key more effectually still on the labourers' position. This
third stage is associated with the name of Malthus. At the end
of the century the belief took root among the governing class
that the recompense of labour was fixed by natural laws, and
that no human efforts could really alter it. Any struggle against

---

[3] *Burke's Works*, ed. of 1826, vol. vii. p. 383 ff.

[4] Cf. Report of House of Commons Committee on Poor Laws,
1817: "By following the dictates of their own interests, landowners
and farmers become, in the natural order of things, the best trustees
and guardians for the public."

[5] It is important to point out that not all economists took this view,
and M'Culloch himself was a strong supporter of factory legislation
for children. See letter to Shaftesbury, *Life of Shaftesbury*, i. p. 157.

this decree of nature would cause trouble and disorganisation, and in that way would inflict injury on the labourers themselves, but it could not increase their share in the national wealth. That share must always remain somewhere about the level of subsistence. This belief was introduced by the Physiocrats, who had their eyes on the peasant of eighteenth-century France. As Turgot put it, "In every sort of occupation it must come to pass that the wages of the artisan are limited to that which is necessary to procure him his subsistence. *Il ne gagne que sa vie.*" If this doctrine were true the only changes in real wages would be those consequent on changes of diet; if labourers took to living on cheaper food their wages would go down, if on dearer they would go up. It was the appreciation of this fact that set Malthus in opposition to Eden and all the other food reformers who wanted to simplify the labourer's meagre diet still further. Now, during the last phase of the ancient régime, this Physiocrat idea became naturalised in England. Both Malthus and Ricardo contributed to this result. Malthus, who started in revolt against the optimism which believed in the beneficence of nature, laid down a principle of population which, by explaining poverty, robbed it of its horrors for the rich. Population, he argued, tends to multiply faster than subsistence. Poverty is therefore inevitable, and unless mankind deliberately sets itself to check the increase of the race, vice and misery are the only means by which population and food can be adjusted to each other. This is, of course, a very general sketch of his teaching, and if we were discussing Malthus himself we should be obliged to qualify this summary by noting a number of important considerations that enter into his argument. We are concerned not with what Malthus taught the world, but with what the upper classes learnt from him.[6] For them his teaching was simple and soothing enough. The doctrine that poverty was inevitable and incurable put a soft pillow under the conscience of the ruling class. But his teaching offered still greater consolations to the anxieties of the benevolent, for it seemed to show that poverty was the medicine of nature, and that the attempts of Governments to relieve it were like the interference of unintelligent spectators with the skilful treatment of the doctor. The relief of poverty meant the increase of poverty,

---

[6] It must be remembered that it was the first edition of Malthus that really counted: the qualifications introduced into his second got no hearing. See Dr. J. Bonar on this, *Malthus and his Work.*

for if the conditions of the poor were improved, population would quicken its pace still further. Melbourne, who thought that to apply economic principles to the Corn Laws would be "the wildest and maddest scheme that has ever entered the imagination of man to conceive," thought that it was just as wild and mad to question the finality of those principles in sentencing the poor to eternal misery. For some years the influence of Malthus was supreme and fatal. Shelley, in the preface to his *Prometheus Unbound*, says that he had rather be damned with Plato and Lord Bacon than go to heaven with Paley and Malthus. It was a strange heaven that Malthus, as he was interpreted by the rich, offered to the poor.

4. A critic who splashed without ceremony into this argument might have accepted the main doctrine that food cannot be made to go round, without accepting the existing distribution of food as just or inevitable. But he was confronted with an explanation of that distribution which was as scientific as the explanation of poverty. As Professor Marshall has shown, the course of economic opinion has been profoundly affected by the fact that at the beginning of the nineteenth century the mathematical and physical groups of science were in the ascendant, and thus at a moment of critical importance in the development of economic speculation, all reasoning inclined to the deductive and abstract method. Both sides in politics gave their countenance to these economics of possession. Bentham, who laid the foundation of a philosophy that was fatal to the political pretensions of the aristocracy, and invented a formula that challenged the whole theory of a serf class on which his generation worked, was at the same time a warm defender of unlimited competition. Ricardo's brilliant and rather labyrinthine deductive reasoning has led later students to the most diverse conclusions. No thinker has been so variously interpreted, and Socialism and Individualism alike have built on his foundations. But of the character of his immediate influence there can be no doubt. The most important effect of his teaching in this particular sphere was to create the impression that every human motive other than the unfailing principle of self-interest might be eliminated from the world of industry and commerce; that the forces of supply and demand settled everything; that the laws governing profits and wages were mechanical and fixed. The share of labour was thus decided just like the price of an article, by the sheer power of competition. And this share gravitated towards the minimum of subsistence. The natural price of labour, he argued, depended

on the price of the food, necessaries, and conveniences required
for the support of the labourer and his family. "The market
price of labour is the price which is really fixed for it from the
natural operation of the proportion of the supply to the demand:
labour is dear when it is scarce and cheap when it is plentiful.
However much the market price of labour may deviate from its
natural price, it has, like commodities, a tendency to conform
to it." To do justice to Ricardo's theory of wages, it would be
necessary to take into account many important qualifications that
enter into his analysis, and we do not pretend that these sentences exhaust his contribution. But we are not discussing
Ricardo's economics, we are discussing Ricardo's economics as
they were interpreted by the powerful classes. Ricardo's ideas as
they were assimilated, helped to give a scientific basis to the
existing distribution: he did not himself lay down an iron law,
but his doctrine has commonly been treated as the doctrine of
an iron law. Science seemed to put its seal on the irremediable
poverty of the poor.

Neither Malthus nor Ricardo really taught the dogmatic despair which was generally received as the lesson of their phi-
losophies. Neither of them really thought existing society ideal
and their own principles entirely at home in it. Ricardo was a
political reformer, and he and Malthus both helped Hume to get
rid of the Combination Laws. Malthus declared more than once
that it was most desirable that the labouring classes should be
well paid. But their ideas, when adopted by other minds, hardened into a rigid and inexorable theory from which both of them
would have shrunk: a theory that was a stubborn barrier to all
social agitation. In that theory, tersely expressed in the phrase
that wages depended on "the ratio of population to capital," it
was laid down that the fund which was employed in the remuneration of labour could not at any given time be greater or
less than it was. The total of that amount was regulated by
circumstances: it represented the exact balance of certain economic forces. No human effort could increase its volume, but
human effort could vary its distribution. Human effort, that is
to say, could only interfere between the recipients, and such
interference would be unjust.[7] "The market rate of wages," as
M'Culloch put it, "is exclusively dependent on the proportion
which the capital of the country or the means of employing
labour bears to the number of labourers." The assumptions of

---

[7] See Dr. Bonar, op. cit., p. 278.

this sterilising theory were denied both by Malthus and by Ricardo at one time or another, but their language had been hammered into this theory. That theory became supreme in economics, and the whole movement for trade-union organisation had to fight its way against this solid superstition. For fifty years it was in power, until its most distinguished adherent, John Stuart Mill, disowned it in 1869.

The particular circumstances in which political economy first became a coherent study, an attempt to explain all phenomena in an organic sense, had a far-reaching effect on the development of English politics. From one point of view the quarrel between the Philosophic Radicals and the aristocracy is fierce and bitter. The aristocracy enjoyed certain vested interests which the Radicals attacked: the corn laws, sinecures, political patronage and power. In this arena the battle went on with great spirit and fury. All these questions concerned the poor intimately. It was of great moment to them that food should not be taxed, that public money should not be wasted, that government should be efficient, that other classes than the rich should be admitted to a share in power. But if we look at the supreme anxieties of the possessing classes at this time, the fear of social revolution, the dread of an attack on the existing economic order, we find that the Radicals and the aristocracy were at one. The Radicals wanted to equalise the conditions of life in so far as they could be made equal by the destruction of positive and formal privilege: they wanted to remove the causes that disturbed the normal balance of markets, and the proper working of supply and demand. The aristocracy opposed all these reforms, for they believed in inequalities of every kind, and they were reluctant to concede any of the immense advantages which law or tradition gave to their class. But when they were confronted with revolutionaries who asked for some kind of social readjustment, who thought that society did not distribute happiness in ideal or necessary proportions, who doubted whether cheap government and free competition could guarantee to the poor and the weak all the liberty and wealth of which they were capable, Radical and aristocrat stood together. The aristocrat believed in the unqualified right of private property, the Radical believed in the unqualified virtue of free competition. The aristocrat traced everything back to private property: the Radical to private capital. Thus, as against one kind of State activity

they were united. The Radical said that if the law ought not
to intervene to protect the rich, neither ought it, on the other
hand, to intervene to protect the poor. Hume, in spite of Adam
Smith, condemned legislation to forbid paying wages in truck as
an outrage on Free Trade, and Place said of the Ten Hours
Bill, "All legislative interference must be pernicious. Men must
be left to themselves to make their own bargains; the law must
compel the observance of compacts, the fulfilment of contracts.
There it should end. So long as the supply of labour exceeds
the demand for labour, the labourer will undersell his fellows,
and produce poverty, misery, vice, and crime."[8] Thus the only
party that was really able to help the labourers in their struggles
against the social power of the rich was the prisoner of its own
abstractions.

The origin of this association of Radicalism with the doctrine
of *laissez-faire* is to be found in the circumstances of the early
nineteenth century. In England, unlike France, the privileged
class was the governing class, and the Statute Book was crowded
with laws made to protect their privileges. To increase the power
of Government meant to increase the power of this class. The
early Radicals were face to face with two great social facts: the
first, the infinite harm done by bad laws; the second, the infinite
possibilities of human progress as seen in the light of the new
power of capital, the power which was changing the face of England and throwing up cities under their eyes. The temptation to
men living largely in an atmosphere of study, to trace all evils to
bad laws, and all good to the unchecked working of that new
power, was irresistible. Such an atmosphere was like sun and
rain to the wages fund theory, and thus a doctrine founded on
a misunderstanding of Ricardo and Malthus, which was the most
powerful sanction of the existing social order, became a property
of Radicalism. The Revolution of 1832 was more justly estimated by Grey than by Wellington. The political privileges of
the aristocracy were under the ban of the Radicals, but the
estates of the aristocracy were under their protection.

---

8 Wallas, *Place*, p. 174. It is important to remember that Place
preached the deliberate restriction of the family. He was prepared,
when once this principle had been adopted by the working classes,
for land nationalisation. Whereas politicians argued from Malthus
that the poor must be left to their fate, Place argued from Malthus
that the poor, when once they had learnt this truth, were masters of
their fate. Bentham and Mill agreed with Place, but did not preach
the doctrine in public.

The case for this political economy was put before the working classes in 1831 by a society which united Whigs and Radicals. The chairman of this "Society for the Diffusion of Useful Knowledge" was Brougham; the vice-chairman, Lord John Russell; the treasurer, William Tooke; and the committee included, besides Lord Ashley, Whigs like Althorp and Denman, Radicals like John Cam Hobhouse and James Mill.[9] Peacock immortalised this side of Brougham's career in *Crotchet Castle*, where he nick-named this society "The Steam Intellect Society," and in *Gryll Grange*, where he said that he would rather hear the cook lecture on Bubble and Squeak than hear one of the Pantipragmatics lecture on the difference between a halibut and a herring. This society published two books, one *The Results of Machinery*, the other *The Rights of Industry*, generally supposed to have been written by Brougham, in which the working of economic law is explained to the labourers. The books are written in an animated and graphic style, and the arguments are illustrated by entertaining examples that anybody can understand. Capital, or accumulation of former labour, is necessary because man "wants the gnawing teeth, the tearing claws, the sharp bills, the solid mandibles, that enable quadrupeds, and birds, and insects to secure their food, and to provide shelter in so many ingenious ways, each leading us to admire and reverence the directing Providence which presides over such manifold contrivances." A classical example of unprofitable labour is found in the people in France in the thirteenth century, who tried to get rid of a plague of rats by carrying on a process against them in the ecclesiastical courts. The dependence of wages upon supply and demand was explained by means of a curious illustration. "During a time of wild financial speculation in Paris, created by what is called the Mississippi Bubble, a humpbacked man went daily into the street where the stock-jobbers were accustomed to assemble, and earned money by allowing them to sign their contracts upon the natural desk with which he was encumbered. The humpback was doubtless a shrewd fellow, and saw the difficulty under which the stock-jobbers laboured. He supplied what they appeared to want; and a demand was instantly created for his hump. He was well paid, says the story. That was because the supply was smaller than

---

[9] Some working-class leaders wanted at one time to organise a rival propaganda. See *The Voice of the People*, May 28, 1831.

the demand. If other men with humps had been attracted by the demand, or if persons had come to the street with portable desks more convenient than the hump, the reward of his service would naturally have become less."

The burden of the book is the great danger of making capital timid, and the supreme interest that labour has in the protection of the rights of property. No remedy is tolerable that tends to flutter or disturb capital. If any labourer thinks his share in the national wealth is inadequate, he is warned that capital can enrich or impoverish a country, according as it pleases to stay or depart, and that, though the workman is entitled to unite with other workmen to make as good a bargain as he can, he must remember that the irritations that come from combinations for raising wages are the chief menace to the security of property. Labourers should save enough to make themselves independent of the vicissitudes of the markets. "When there is too much labour in the market and wages are too low, do not combine to raise the wages; do not combine with vain hope of compelling the employer to pay more for labour than there are funds for the maintenance of labour; but go out of the market. Leave the relations between wages and labour to equalise themselves. You can never be permanently kept down in wages by the profits of capital: for if the profits of capital are too high, the competition of other capital immediately comes in to set the matter right."

It is easy to see how this kind of reasoning produced the prevalent view of the capitalist as beneficent whatever the wages he paid or the conditions he imposed. If somebody thought that workpeople should have a little of the daylight for their own lives, the employer had only to say that all the profits of his industry depended on his last half-hour, and the kindest people saw that it was cruel to give the workmen a little leisure at the risk of their livelihood. Employers passed easily into the position of landowners. When the landowner looked in the glass he saw a public benefactor, who incidentally received sums of money in the form of rent; when the employer looked in the glass he saw a public benefactor, who incidentally received sums of money in the form of profits. There were good landlords and bad landlords, good employers and bad employers, but the dominant conceptions of the time made it an act of public virtue in itself to own land or to employ labour.[10] The employers, who

10 Nine Stockport hatters were sentenced to two years' imprisonment in 1816 for conspiracy. The judge (Sir Wm. Garrow), in sum-

expected the State to coerce their workmen into accepting their
conditions, had really persuaded themselves that they were the
guardian angels of society. The three Estates of the Realm were
now Crown, Landlord, and Industrial Employers.

Under all these influences there grew up a political economy
which bred an equable, or at any rate a resigned, temperament
towards many of the miseries of the world, and towards all the
suffering that was a consequence of the system by which the
life of society was explained. Political economy became, as Sydney Smith put it, a school of metaphysics. For the revolt against
this theory we have to look not to any political party, but to
Owen, Fielden, Sadler, Shaftesbury, Carlyle, Dickens, the So-
cialists and the Chartists.

If twenty persons of different temperaments have the same
philosophy put before them, they will produce twenty philoso-
phies. Each of them will choose some aspect that for one reason
or another makes a special appeal to his nature, or his experience, or his habits of mind. The most remarkable and significant
thing about the political economy that grew up from Adam
Smith, is the curiously one-sided and inconsistent way in which
it adapted his teaching. "The obvious and simple system of natural liberty" was a captivating formula. It came with a shock to
established prejudices and ways of looking at life, but once the
shock was over, the principle seemed clear and satisfying. What,
in point of fact, did Sidmouth's "enlightened minds" do with
it? They borrowed from it ideas that served as weapons for employers, and neglected every truth that seemed to threaten their
own interests. The prejudices from which they escaped into the
new light were the prejudices of other people. When they had
to choose between Adam Smith and their own prejudices, it was
not their prejudices that they sacrificed. This was not conscious
hypocrisy, but the kind of recognition of truth that stops short
at taking risks. The landlords and manufacturers behaved like
men who, when a wonderful flying machine is shown to them,
accept the assurance that it will fly well and safely, call those
who doubt it unenlightened, hurry everybody into it, and will

---

ming up remarked, "In this happy country where the law puts the
meanest subject on a level with the highest personages of the realm,
all are alike protected, and there can be no need to associate." . . . "A
person who like Mr. Jackson has employed from 100 to 130 hands,
common gratitude would teach us to look upon as a benefactor to
the community." (H. O., 42. 153.)

do everything to prove their confidence except get into it themselves. Adam Smith preached Free Trade and Individualism,
but for every line he wrote against the regulation of wages, he
wrote pages against import duties and Protection. Yet the landlords who deprived the working classes of the protection of the
State in the name of Adam Smith, saw nothing unenlightened
in protecting their rents by Corn Laws. The most flagrant violation of the obvious and simple system of natural liberty was not
the regulation of wages for the Spitalfields weavers, but the
Corn Law of 1815. That law was discussed amid the most violent storms of indignation from one end of the country to the
other, and nobody could pretend that it was passed by an over-
sight. The landlords of the House of Lords were reminded of
the teaching of Adam Smith by Grenville, and King, and half a
score of peers who entered a powerful protest on its Journals.
"Because we think that the great practical rule, of leaving all
commerce unfettered, applies more peculiarly, and on still
stronger grounds of justice as well as of policy, to the Corn
Trade than to any other. Irresistible indeed must be that necessity which could in our judgment authorise the Legislature to
tamper with the sustenance of the people, and to impede the
free purchase and sale of that article on which depends the
existence of so large a portion of the community." One of the
supporters of the Bill pointed to the heavy duties on woollen
goods (100 per cent.), cotton goods (85½ per cent.), glass (114
per cent.), brass and copper goods (59 per cent.), earthenware
(79 per cent.), dressed leather (142 per cent.); and even after
the important reforms of Wallace and Huskisson in 1823, from
which the beginnings of the liberation of trade are generally
dated, it remained true that English manufactures were heavily
protected. This discrepancy did not escape the working classes,
and more than once in their manifestoes to the public they challenged the validity of the doctrines of free competition which
landlords and manufacturers refused to accept when their own
interests were at stake. List, the great prophet of Protection, argued that it would have been the right policy for England in
1815 to make a clean sweep of protective laws and duties, and
that if this course had been taken her position as a manufacturing country would have been impregnable. As it was, the ex-
clusion of foreign corn from the English market had the same
effect as Napoleon's continental system; it drove the other nations of Europe to take up manufactures and to retaliate on
England with protective duties.

It would, however, give an exaggerated impression of the consistency of the ruling class, if we were to say that they talked like Adam Smith when the workers wanted something, and like an older Adam when they wanted something themselves. In dealing with the working classes, too, they discriminated. The Combination Laws of 1799 and 1800 were a flagrant violation not only of Adam Smith's general principles, but of his positive and direct teaching on that very subject.[11] Pitt was silent about his master, and it was Lord Holland in the other House who preached from the *Wealth of Nations*, and reminded his enlightened audience of Adam Smith's denunciations of the injustice that punished men for combining, while it was notorious that masters could combine with impunity. When Malthus gave evidence against the Combination Laws in 1824, he used Pitt's favourite phrase.[12] Moreover, down to 1824 it was still a crime to "seduce" an artisan to emigrate, and there were constant prosecutions under these statutes at a time when any master could try his fortunes in a foreign country, and any investor could subscribe to a foreign loan. Free labour had not Adam Smith's meaning: it meant the freedom of the employer to take what labour he wanted, at the price he chose and under the conditions he thought proper.

As economic opinion developed, the teaching of Adam Smith grew fainter and fainter. Thus it became a commonplace among magistrates and politicians that low wages were a great and necessary encouragement to industry, enabling England to keep her manufacturing supremacy, without which supremacy the workman would have no employment. This grew into a mechanical formula, and men repeated it in their sleep

"like a knitter drowsed,
Whose fingers play in skilled unmindfulness."

This argument was produced whatever the circumstances or industry under discussion, for example by the shipowners of the Tyne as a reason for giving low wages on the boats plying between Newcastle and London, though, as a local parson pointed

---

[11] *Wealth of Nations*, bk. i. chap. viii.
[12] "What effect have those laws had on wages?—They have had a partial effect; a pernicious effect, I think. Tending to depress them?—They have no doubt operated against the general principle of wages finding their natural level."—Select Committee on Artisans and Machinery, p. 601.

out, the trade was an absolute monopoly. Low wages were also regarded as a valuable stimulus to the workmen. Arthur Young was enthusiastic about high prices for the same reason: "The master manufacturers of Manchester wish that prices might always be high enough to enforce a general industry."[13] A good example of this spirit is seen in the criticisms of the Shearmen's Union contained in the Report of the Committee on the Woollen Trade (1806) drawn up by Wilberforce: "The least of the evils to be apprehended (though an evil in itself abundantly sufficient to accomplish the ruin, not only of any particular branch of Trade, but even of the whole commercial greatness of our country) is, the progressive rise of Wages which among all classes of Workmen must be the inevitable, though gradual result of such a Society's operations; . . . an evil, the fatal though more distant, and in each particular increase, more doubtful consequence of which it cannot be expected that the Workmen themselves should foresee so plainly, or feel so forcibly, as not to incur them, under the powerful temptation of a strong and immediate interest."

This belief in the value of low wages as an encouragement to industry received no sanction from Adam Smith, nor did the other favourite notion that the manufacturing capitalist could do no wrong. Adam Smith favoured high wages, combating the teaching of Petty and others of the earlier economists; he argued that workmen, so far from wasting away their energies in dissipation, were inclined rather to injure themselves by overexertion; that liberal wages, so far from turning them into drunkards and loafers, were a great incentive to industry; and that masters, so far from being the infallible agents of progress and humanity, often tried to reduce wages to the injury of society. He was in favour of Truck Acts. Again, though he acknowledged the great services of the Physiocrats, and would have dedicated the *Wealth of Nations* to Quesnai, if Quesnai had lived, he threw overboard their teaching about the subsistence wage. It is indeed no exaggeration to say that his views about labour, which were entirely disregarded by the upper classes of the day, stand out in such marked contrast to his predecessors as to represent an important part of his contribution to political economy.

The upper classes treated his teaching about the encouragement of industry by the right distribution of taxes in the same spirit. Adam Smith argued that in levying taxation, it was im-

---

[13] *Northern Tour*, p. 193.

portant to consider what taxes could be imposed without putting
a burden on industry. From this point of view he found an ideal
tax in a tax on ground rents. He recommended the taxation of
ground rents for two reasons: the first that such a tax discouraged no industry, the second that ground rents owed their value
altogether to good government, and it was therefore reasonable
that they "should be taxed peculiarly" for the support of government. During the Industrial Revolution the value of ground rents
was advancing at a rapid pace, and any pupil of Adam Smith
would have put a tax on the immense wealth created in the new
industrial towns and taken off the heavy burdens on food, clothing, and the materials of industry. It was calculated in 1833 that
a labourer earning £22 10s. was paying in taxes £11 7s. 7d.
a year.[14] At the same time the men who were growing fabu-
lously rich on the process that crowded the poor in dens and
cellars—Cooke Taylor spoke of rents increasing in Lancashire
3000 per cent.—contributed nothing of this great unearned revenue to the expenses of the State. Adam Smith's teaching that
ground rents ought to be taxed before the necessaries of life,
received just as much attention as his arguments against Protection.

We have not space to discuss the economic and political systems that the unfashionable thinkers of the time built on the
basis of Adam Smith's philosophy. They had very little influence
on the ruling class, and it was not until Dr. Menger made his
careful study of the origins of German Socialism that the importance of this early English school was appreciated.[15] But they
are of great interest in connection with the subject of this chapter, because they show how widely different an interpretation
was put on the new facts of English life and the new teaching,
by persons who were outside the special atmosphere that produced the Wages Fund Theory and the general law of beneficent fatalism. These thinkers all found in the new light an argument, not for accepting existing arrangements as a consequence
of nature, but for trying to alter them as a perversion of its
salutary principles. We may take one illustration. In his exposition of Political Economy to working men, Brougham made
great play with the difference between the conduct and career
of the Duke of Bridgewater, who spent his money in great re-

---

[14] See The Village Labourer, Vol. i, p. 169.
[15] See Professor Foxwell's Introduction to *The Right to the Whole
Produce of Labour*, by Dr. Anton Menger. (Macmillan, 1899.)

productive works like canals, and increased employment, and the Duke of Buckingham who ran through a fortune and died in a wretched inn "lord of useless thousands." The contrast would have served the revolutionary thinkers very well. Godwin, for example, would have seen in it an illustration of the importance of his doctrine of distribution, that he who had the best use for things should possess them. Charles Hall would have seen in it an argument for restraining the accumulation of unearned income in the hands of individuals. William Thompson would have said that it demonstrated the injustice and the mischief of a system of distribution that enabled the landlord and the capitalist to secure the surplus value of industry. Thomas Hodgskin, who was never tired of reminding society of Adam Smith's "natural system," would have used it as a text to preach his favourite doctrine that "the law of nature is that industry shall be rewarded by wealth, and idleness be punished by destitution; the law of the land is to give wealth to idleness and fleece industry till it be destitute."[16] But for the upper classes the moral was very different. They argued that if the poor were restless and discontented, combining and thereby threatening and reducing profits, rich men would be tempted to behave like the Duke of Buckingham; if, on the other hand, they appreciated the advantages of subordination, discipline, contentment, and resignation, rich men would be encouraged to imitate the public spirit of the Duke of Bridgewater.[17]

A recent writer has pointed out that in considering the pro-

---

[16] A placard that alarmed the magistrates was posted in Manchester in 1819. A number of people had issued a declaration that they intended to support the Constitution. They called themselves the Police Association. The Reformers' placard was a reply: "The oppressors have got possession of a great part of the property of the nation through the operation of Corn Bills and Combination Acts, which are directly calculated to make provisions dear and wages low." The placard set out the rival principles of the Police Association and the Reformers in parallel columns:—

Principles of Police Association.	Principles of Reformers.
The Poor to work 12, 13, or 14 hours a day, and almost starve to enrich others; and themselves to work none, live luxuriously, and heap up riches.	The People to work about 6 hours per day and live well: the idle alone to starve. H. O., 42. 189.

[17] During the debates on the Corn Laws in 1815 one speaker said that if they were not passed, he would shake the dust of England off his feet and spend his rents in a foreign country.

cedure adopted by the upper class when it set to work on the enclosures, we must remember that the eighteenth century politician looked upon England as a society of freeholders, and that they treated all public questions as if the majority of people were comparatively independent, whereas, of course, they were in fact powerless and helpless, needing the protection of the law and of Parliament.[18] This same kind of illusion blinded the generation that left the workmen to their fate in the Industrial Revolution. When Mackintosh talked of property as the cement of society, he meant that property was the common interest, that Government existed to protect the rights of property, and that if Government protected property the claims of every class were satisfied, and no class needed anything more. There were different ways of protecting property, and the difference between Tories and Whigs was the difference between antiquated and enlightened ways of protecting it. The great merit of the Reform Bill, in the eyes of many of its supporters, was that it called in the middle classes to take their share in guarding property. It was obvious, of course, that nine out of ten persons in England did not possess property, and it might therefore appear that the defence of property was only the interest of a minority. But Mackintosh would have answered that, in the first place, the security of property was the condition of making capital comfortable and at home, and, secondly, that any man by industry and self-control could acquire property: and therefore a society that protected property and all its rights was really protecting everybody. This view, though it seems to us strangely at variance with the facts of the time, received a certain colour from the large number of persons who passed from the wage-earning class into the master class. No atmosphere is so favourable to individualism as the atmosphere of a society in which genius and industry carry the exceptional man from one rank to another. Of those who tried to suppress combination some looked on Trade Unions as a menace to order, but others on them as encouraging a false ideal and a false view of society.

The employers in the northern towns were in many cases men who had risen from small beginnings, taking advantage of the openings afforded by the Industrial Revolution for the investment of savings and the application of personal pains and capacity, and the small man who has succeeded in this way is apt to think his own success a convincing illustration of the

---

[18] See Kennedy, *English Taxation*, 1640–1799, p. 91.

admirable order and arrangement of the world. Who shall say that the path to riches is barred to merit? Cannot anybody who has, in Bishop Berkeley's phrase, his four quarters and his five senses, do the same? The ideas of a working-class agitation are essentially corporate ideas, the demand for a better standard for a race of men and women: the ideas of the successful small employer are essentially individualist ideas, the demand that genius and industry shall be free. On the one view a man's loyalty is due to his fellows: the wage earner thinks of wage earners as a class: he belongs primarily to a society of men with common wrongs and common hardships, seeking a common remedy. On the other, a man's first duty is the duty of self-development: the employer thinks of society as a collection of individuals pursuing their own ends: he mistrusts the spirit of co-operation, and he thinks that in a world where to his knowledge, industry and concentration may win the highest rewards, every man gets ultimately what he is worth. The ideal working man on the first view tries to raise the status of his class; the ideal working man on the second view tries to change his own status and to become an employer.

On this view of life it seemed specially important to avoid discouraging private industry and effort by removing the pressure of want. Society ought to do nothing for its members that the prudent would do for himself, otherwise the motive to prudence would disappear, and men instead of acquiring property by self-denial would live on the public funds. Perhaps the most notable illustration of this spirit is the speech in which Brougham defended the new Poor Law in the House of Lords: a speech in which social imagination touches its lowest temperature. Applying this canon of the prudent man, Brougham argued that the only evils against which society should protect people were those the prudent man could not foresee; he could foresee old age, illness, unemployment: against these he should make provision. On the other hand, society might help him in the case of accidents and violent diseases. It is difficult, when one reads this speech, to remember that the prudent man who happened to be a hand-loom weaver in Lancashire (one of the largest classes of workpeople in the country) was earning a good deal less than ten shillings a week. It is perhaps still stranger to remember that no small proportion of the class that thought all this the wisdom of Solon were living on the public funds.

The idea of the State as an association for mutual aid had

almost vanished from the mind of a generation that believed
that the degradation of the working classes had begun with the
Speenhamland system, and would cease with the austerity of the
new Poor Law. Paine, who had presented a programme of old
age pensions, maternity benefits, and free and compulsory education, seemed a crude and mischievous politician to statesmen
who thought that the great secret that the State had to learn
was to leave mankind to the steam engine and the railways.
The doctrine that Brougham preached to the poor from the
House of Lords was once preached to the rich in another aristocratic chamber. Tacitus has described how a descendant of Cicero's great rival, Hortensius, came to the Senate to ask for a further grant of public money, on the ground that he had been
encouraged by Augustus to raise a family, in order to keep alive
the race of an ancestor whose gifts unhappily had only been
equalled by his extravagance. The Senate listened with sympathy, but Tiberius made one of his unfeeling speeches, re-
proaching Hortalus for interrupting the public business and for
putting the Senate and the emperor in an uncomfortable position. He went on to state the general objection to public doles
to private persons: "Otherwise industry will languish and idleness be encouraged, if a man has nothing to fear, nothing to
hope from himself, and every one in utter recklessness, will
expect relief from others, thus becoming useless to himself and
a burden to me."[19]

Tiberius was in advance of his age, and Tacitus tells us that
all except the sycophants listened in a pained silence, or declared their feelings by subdued murmurs. Brougham would not
have applied this formula to those who were released by the
generosity of the State from the duty of earning their living.
It had been so applied in the manifestoes of workmen, and the
favourite literature of the Reform movement consisted of pamphlets and statistics about pensions and sinecures. Brougham
and his friends applied it in all good faith to a race of men
and women to whom the State had presented itself, in Cobbett's
famous phrase, with a bowl of carrion soup in one hand and a
halter in the other. They thought that if society looked after the
capitalist, the capitalist would look after the workman, and that
if society took care of the interests of property, the deserving

---

[19] "Languescet alioqui industria, intendetur socordia, si nullus ex se
metus aut spes, et securi omnes aliena subsidia exspectabunt, sibi
ignavi, nobis graves" (*Annals*, ii. 38).

poor would become rich. We have now to see how this view, developed from this strange blending of optimism and pessimism in the interpretation of the social phenomena of the time, was modified or affected by the inspirations of religion and philanthropy.

CHAPTER XI

THE CONSCIENCE OF THE RICH

Those writers who like to dwell on the remarkable success of the Church of Rome in dealing with its enthusiasts, find the chief illustration of the corresponding failure of the Church of England in the history of the Evangelical movement. That movement would have embarrassed any Church, and it is not surprising that the sleepy and good-natured Establishment of the eighteenth century, with its languid and polite piety, its sensible and conventional sermons, and its free pagan life, dreaded and resented this outburst of passionate preaching in the fields and the streets. But the Methodist movement was, after all, so far as the discipline of the Church was concerned, a storm in a teacup in comparison with the great earthquakes that threw up the Dominican and the Franciscan Orders. Unfortunately for the Church of England, the Methodist revival found her more closely entangled than at any other time in the system and ideas of class domination. Macaulay has given a vivid picture of the tinker or coal-heaver who, on finding salvation, determined to devote his life to the teaching of religion, and, learning that there was no place for him in the Establishment, left a Church with whose beliefs and government he had no quarrel, to found a little Bethel or a little Ebenezer. But even if the bishop had been ready to welcome him as a fellow-preacher, the squire would certainly have thought that if this ludicrous fellow was to be allowed to open his mouth anywhere, it was less of an outrage that he should preach his crude and violent religion of terror and rapture outside the Church, than from a pulpit where he might molest the ears of the gentry. The history of the Papacy is the history of an Empire. The history of the English Church in the eighteenth century is one aspect of the history of a class. Consequently the Church of Rome kept the Franciscans, and the Church of England lost the Methodists.

But though the Methodist movement finally broke away from the Church, it was not without influence in the governing class. For a short time the new preaching became a fashion, and Lady Huntingdon brought Whitefield to her drawing-room to try his spell on the Duchess of Marlborough, Lady Suffolk (George the Second's mistress, whose sensitive ear caught a personal allusion in his sermon), Chesterfield, and Bolingbroke. Bolingbroke

told Whitefield that he had done great justice to the divine at-
tributes in his discourse. Lord Dartmouth threw himself into the
movement, and Cowper has commemorated his conversion in
Truth:—

> "We boast some rich ones whom the Gospel sways,
> And one who wears a coronet and prays."

Lady Huntingdon herself was an intrepid missionary. She had
an interview with the Archbishop of Canterbury and his wife, in
the hope of persuading them to renounce their excessive hos-
pitality, and in particular their famous Sunday parties. The
Archbishop showed neither penitence nor patience, and his wife
is said to have allowed her irritation to carry her beyond the
bounds of good breeding. Lady Huntingdon then tried George
the Third, who intervened with success. She afterwards became
a kind of archbishop herself when the quarrel broke out between the followers of Wesley and the followers of Whitefield,
for she was the great lady of the Calvinist movement, giving
money and guidance without stint, and Whitefield spoke of her
in the spirit of Mr. Collins's references to Lady Catherine de
Bourgh.

But the Evangelical revival had, of course, a great influence
within the Church as well, and many people who would have
repudiated the name of Methodist accepted its teaching. Wilberforce and his friends in the House of Commons represented
a powerful body of Evangelical opinion, so powerful indeed
that they were able to prevent Pitt from yielding to Pretyman,
when the French Revolution had frightened the Church from
its earlier tolerance, and the Government was tempted to make
war on the Nonconformists. This group of politicians is famous
for its part in educating England on the iniquities of the Slave
Trade, and for the development of a philanthropy that became
fashionable. What was the character and inspiration of this philanthropy? It is necessary to examine that influence on the upper
classes if we are to understand the toleration of abuses and
cruelties at a time when a considerable section of the ruling
world was seriously concerned about the responsibilities of
wealth and leisure. Hannah More is indeed as essential an element in the economy of the time as Ricardo or Malthus, Pitt or
Castlereagh The resignation of the upper-class world to the tor-
ture of children in a boyhood such as Mr. Bennett describes in
the early life of Darius Clayhanger, the frank renunciation of
all hope of a decent or civilised life on this side of the grave for

the majority of the people in the new towns, are not to be attributed solely to the atmosphere of capitalists and landlords, engrossed in their achievements or their gains, or to a blinding theory of wealth, or to the incapacity of a race bewildered by new and stupendous problems. We must take into account the way in which men and women capable of self-devotion and sympathy were brought, through the associations of religion and the inspirations of the Evangelical Revival, to regard the world around them.

The devout Christian, confronted with the spectacle of wrong and injustice, may draw either of two contrary conclusions. In the eyes of his religion the miner or weaver is just as important as the landlord or the cotton lord. Clearly then, one will argue, it is the duty of a Christian State to prevent any class, however obscure and trivial its place in the world may seem to be, from sinking into degrading conditions of life. Every soul is immortal, and the consequences of ill-treatment and neglect in the brief day of its life on earth will be unending. If, therefore, society is so organised as to impose such conditions on any class, the Christian will demand the reform of its institutions. For such minds Christianity provides a standard by which to judge government, the industrial and economic order, the life of society, the way in which it distributes wealth and opportunities. This was the general standpoint of such a man as Shaftesbury. But some minds drew a different moral from the equality that Christianity teaches. Every human soul is a reality, but the important thing about a human soul is its final destiny, and that destiny does not depend on the circumstances of this life. The world has been created on a plan of apparent injustice by a Providence that combined infinite power with infinite compassion. The arrangements that seem so capricious are really the work of that Power. But the same Power has given to the men and women who seem to live in such bitter and degrading surroundings, an escape from its cares by the exercise of their spiritual faculties. It is those faculties that make all men equal. Here they stand, in Marcus Aurelius's phrase, for a brief space between the two eternities, and no misery or poverty can prevent a soul from winning happiness in the world to come. Thus whereas one man looking out on the chaos of the world calls for reform, the other calls for contemplation: one says, Who could tolerate such injustice? the other says, Who would not rejoice that there is another world? One says, Give these people the conditions of a decent life; the other says, Teach them to read the Bible. Thus whereas religion might make men revolt against the economic teaching described in the last chapter, and men like Sadler or Oastler or Fowell Buxton were all influenced in this way, it might add another sanction of its own to the sanctions of that science. The economist besought the reformer not to quarrel with nature; the Christian might warn him not to quarrel with the dispensations of God.[1] For such minds Christianity was not a standard by which to judge the institutions of society, but a reason for accepting them.

During this time there were two movements that influenced the upper classes. One was the humanitarian movement that belonged to the general stream of liberal ideas due to the French Revolution. This was represented in one form or another by men like Fox, Grey, Meredith, Romilly, Bennet, Holland, Whitbread, Sheridan, Martin. These men were not revolutionary: they made a definite attack on particular abuses; they were sincere and above all they were absolutely fearless. They took up the cause of men whom they hated and dreaded, when those men were the victims of oppression. They saw that abuses could not be suppressed without reform, and they were not afraid of attacking vested interests, either in industry or in government. The other movement was the Evangelical movement. This movement produced great examples of personal self-devotion, the most notable being John Howard and Mrs. Fry. But it produced also a particular spirit in social politics which had great influence on the general conduct of the upper-class world. It is represented by Wilberforce in Parliament and by Hannah More in literature. It is obvious that much of the sympathy and goodwill that are to be found in every society must have been attracted to this movement, and the character of that influence, as guiding and affecting men's ways of looking at the social abuses of the time, is therefore of great importance. To understand what that influence was on politics, we must turn to the writings of its two great representatives, Hannah More and Wilberforce.

Hannah More's writings fill several volumes, but those who want to enter into the social atmosphere in which she and her friends lived, will find perhaps the best revelation in a book called *The Mendip Annals*, or *A Narrative of the Charitable Labours of Hannah and Martha More* in the Mendip villages.

---

[1] Despayre put this view:
"Is not His deed, what-ever thing is donne
In heaven and earth?"—*Faerie Queene*, i. canto ix. 42.

In the year 1789 Wilberforce was taken to see the famous Cheddar cliffs, but the beauties of nature were quite overshadowed in his mind by the poverty and squalor that he encountered in the neighbourhood. On his return he urged the sisters More to attempt the moral reclamation of the district, and they took up the task with great fervour and determination. They started Sunday-schools and Women's Benefit Clubs in several villages. These they managed despotically, and they used to pay periodical visits to see that their teachers and pupils had not lapsed from virtue and Bible reading, and to address the villages in a series of charges. The *Mendip Annals* gives us, sometimes in the language of Hannah, sometimes in that of Martha More, the impression that these surroundings made on these two women during a relationship lasting for more than ten years.

The condition of these villages was such that one of them was popularly known as Botany Bay or Little Hell. In one place Hannah More mentions that the wages are a shilling a day; in another that two hundred people are crammed into nineteen hovels. Of another parish she writes: "I will only add that we have one large parish of miners so poor that there is not one creature in it that can give a cup of broth if it would save a life. Of course, they have nothing human to look to but us. The Clergyman, a poor saint, told me, when we set up our schools there twenty-five years ago, that eighteen had perished that winter of a putrid fever, and he could not raise a sixpence to save a life." Nowhere perhaps was there a better illustration of the great process described in this volume, the exploitation, that is, of the mass of a race by the classes holding economic and political power. Now the sisters More were benevolent women who put themselves to great trouble and discomfort out of pity for these villages, and yet from beginning to end of the *Mendip Annals* there is not a single reflection on the persons or system responsible for these conditions. It never seems to have crossed the minds of these philanthropists that it was desirable that men and women should have decent wages, or decent homes, or that there was something wrong with the arrangements of a society that left the mass of people in this plight. This is their comment on the overcrowded glassworkers in the nineteen hovels: "Both sexes and all ages herding together: voluptuous beyond belief. The work of a glass-house is an irregular thing, uncertain, whether by day or by night: not only infringing upon man's rest, but constantly intruding upon the privileges of the Sabbath. The wages high, the eating and drinking luxurious—the body scarcely covered, but fed with dainties of a shameful description. The high buildings of the glass-houses ranged before the doors of these cottages—the great furnaces roaring—the swearing, eating and drinking of these half-dressed, black-looking beings gave it a most infernal and horrible appearance. One, if not two, joints of the finest meat were roasting in each of these little hot kitchens, pots of ale standing about, and plenty of early delicate-looking vegetables." Thus the guilty in this scheme of civilisation are not the persons who neglect to provide the decencies of life and housing and education for the men and women by whose labour they become rich, but the voluptuous glass-workers who feed their bodies on shameful dainties and enjoy delicate-looking vegetables and joints of the finest meat. The employers and gentry are sometimes blamed, it is true, in these pages, but they are only blamed for their want of sympathy with the efforts of the More sisters to teach religion. They are nowhere blamed for ill-treating their dependants, or told that they have any duties to them except the duty of encouraging them to listen to Hannah More on the importance of obedience, and on the claims to their gratitude of a Providence that had lavished such attention upon them.

In the summer of 1792 there was a colliers' strike to raise wages in Somerset. We learn from letters among the Home Office papers[2] that the men were trying to raise their wages from ten to twelve shillings a week; that they marched in great force through the county; that they were joined by two thousand colliers from Gloucester, and that though determined and united they were perfectly orderly. Their quiet behaviour was attested by the captain of dragoons whose duty it was to watch their movements. To these events, which were of great social significance and moment to the villages which the More sisters had taken under their wing, Hannah More makes one allusion: "The late strike among the colliers for increase of wages had drawn away some of our great boys who were obliged, though against their will, to join the common concern. This day to our no small joy we found them returned."

Martha More refers in another passage in the Journal to an invitation that came to the sisters from the church-warden and overseer of Blagdon, asking for a Sunday-school for their parish. This desire was due to their sense of the great wickedness of the parish which had been brought home to the village by the

---

[2] See H. O., 42. 21.

fact that a woman had just been "condemned to death for attempting to begin a riot and purloining some butter from a man who offered it for sale at a price they thought unreasonable." It would seem to most people that much as the village might need a Sunday-school, the judges who were responsible for this piece of barbarity needed one a great deal more, but the philanthropic sisters, both of whom refer to the case, have no complaint to make of the sentence. The More sisters took the parish in hand, with the gratifying result that they were able to report a few months later that many of the pupils "understood tolerably well the first twenty chapters of Genesis."

The period covered by this Journal was marked by two famines; they are naturally both discussed by Hannah More in her charges, and her comments on them are characteristic: "In suffering by the scarcity you have but shared in the common lot, with the pleasure of knowing the advantage you have had over many villages in your having suffered no scarcity of religious instruction." It mattered little that wheat was at 134 shillings a quarter, so long as the labourers who were living on a shilling a day had the story of Cain and Abel at their fingers' ends. But the subject of the famine was explored in a more comprehensive spirit in a charge that Hannah More gave to the women of Shipham in 1801: "It is with real concern that I am obliged to touch upon the subject which made part of my address to you last year. You will guess I allude to the continuation of the scarcity. Yet, let me remind you that probably that very scarcity has been permitted by an all-wise and gracious Providence to unite all ranks of people together, to show the poor how immediately they are dependent upon the rich, and to show both rich and poor that they are all dependent on Himself. It has also enabled you to see more clearly the advantages you derive from the government and constitution of this country—to observe the benefits flowing from the distinction of rank and fortune, which has enabled the high so liberally to assist the low: for I leave you to judge what would have been the state of the poor of this country in this long, distressing scarcity had it not been for your superiors. I wish you to understand also that you are not the only sufferers. You have indeed borne your share, and a very heavy one it has been in the late difficulties; but it has fallen in some degree on all ranks, nor would the gentry have been able to afford such large supplies to the distresses of the poor, had they not denied themselves, for your sakes, many indulgences to which their fortune at other times entitles them. We trust the poor in general, especially those that are well instructed, have received what has been done for them as a matter of favour, not of right—if so, the same kindness will, I doubt not, always be extended to them, whenever it shall please God so to afflict the land." The lesson was well learnt, and the villages in which the sisters laboured were conspicuous for their loyalty to Church and King. In one case it seems to have been learnt almost too well, with painful results described tactfully by Martha More: "An affecting circumstance took place about this time. Last year, when the common people showed their excess of loyalty by burning the effigy of Tom Paine, poor Robert Reeves and two or three more of our hopeful people, intending to show their zeal and attachment to their King and country, were tempted to join the people of Axbridge in this bonfire. The sad consequence which too usually attends such a public testimony of loyalty ensued—they were overtaken with liquor, and intoxication followed. Remorse and shame instantly took place. The following Sunday some could not appear at the school, and those who did hung their heads. The greatest apparent repentance succeeded—much praying and reading. In a few weeks all but Robert became a little reconciled to themselves: his sorrow was deeper and of long continuance. It preyed dreadfully upon his mind for many months, and despair seemed at length to take possession of him. H. had some conversations with him, and read some suitable passages from *The Rise and Progress*. At length the Almighty was pleased to shine into his heart and give him comfort, and he now, like Philip's eunuch, goes on his way rejoicing."

One of Hannah More's Cheap Repository Tracts told the story of a Lancashire colliery girl who was taken down the pit, when nine years old, to act as drawer with her brother, who was two years younger: "She cheerfully followed him (her father) down into the coal-pit, burying herself in the bowels of the earth, and there at a tender age, without excusing herself on account of her sex, she joined in the same work with the miners, a race of men rough indeed, but highly useful to the community." The father was killed by an accident down the pit in the sight of his children. The girl continued to work in the pit for fourteen years, at wages of 2s. a day, sometimes earning 3s. 6d. in twenty-four hours by taking a "double turn," and supporting her mother and two brothers for some years. Then her health broke down, "and her head was also troubled by some of those strange and unpleasant imaginations which are known by persons conversant with the diseases of the poor, to be no unusual consequence of bad food, and great bodily fatigue, joined with excessive grief." She applied for employment as a servant, but there was a prejudice against her because she had been a collier, and her application failed. Fortunately, by that comforting dispensation by which afflictions are turned into blessings, her bearing and patience attracted notice, inquiries were made at the colliery, and she received such a glowing character that she was taken into employment. "This story may teach the poor that they can seldom be in any condition of life so low as to prevent their rising to some degree of independence if they choose to exert themselves, and that there can be no situation whatever so mean as to forbid the practice of many noble virtues."

Wilberforce, who devoted his life and gifts to a humane cause, is the best representative of this religion, and a study of his speeches and writings shows that the tendency to regard Christianity in politics as only one of the sanctions of the existing order was no accident, but an essential part of its spirit. He was, as we have seen, largely responsible for the degradation of industrial life due to the savage measures taken by the upper classes to prevent working men from protecting their standard of living by defensive organisation. If any one event can be singled out as having led more than any other to that degradation, it is the enactment of the Combination Laws of 1799 and 1800 in which Wilberforce took a leading part. It is particularly interesting, therefore, to turn to the pages of his *Practical View of the System of Christianity*,[3] a work that attained an immense popularity, in which he has something to say on the relation of religion to the economic circumstances of society. There he explains that Christianity makes the inequalities of the social scale less galling to the lower orders, that it teaches them to be diligent, humble, patient, that it reminds them "that their more lowly path has been allotted to them by the hand of God; that it is their part faithfully to discharge its duties, and contentedly to bear its inconveniences; that the present state of things is very short; that the objects about which worldly men conflict so eagerly are not worth the contest; that the peace of mind, which Religion offers indiscriminately to all ranks, affords more true satisfaction than all the expensive pleasures which are beyond the poor man's reach; that in this view the poor have the advantage; that, if their superiors enjoy more abundant comforts, they are also exposed to many temptations from which the

---

[3] P. 314. The book was first published in 1798.

inferior classes are happily exempted; that, "having food and raiment, they should be therewith content," since their situation in life, with all its evils, is better than they have deserved at the hand of God; and finally, that all human distinctions will soon be done away, and the true followers of Christ will all, as children of the same Father, be alike admitted to the possession of the same heavenly inheritance. Such are the blessed effects of Christianity on the temporal well-being of political communities." Wilberforce, writing to Pitt about this book, described the chapter which contains this passage as the "basis of all politics."

It was perhaps not unnatural that a religion that seemed to reconcile men and women to the hardships of life by promising them a happiness that (far from being prejudiced) was actually enhanced by their disadvantages in this world, came to be thought of by the upper classes, when the French Revolution broke into their peace of mind, as designed for this very purpose. One distinguished churchman, indeed, deprecated the introduction of Christianity into such discussions on the ground that the poor were really much better off than the rich even without allowing for religion "which smooths all inequalities because it unfolds a prospect which makes all earthly distinctions nothing." His "Reasons for Contentment addressed to the Labouring Part of the British Public" is not among the best known of Paley's writings, though Paley himself, according to Leslie Stephen, ranked it first, but it is one of the most interesting documents ever published. In this paper, which appeared in 1793, Paley showed to his own satisfaction that there was scarcely any respect in which the poor were not more fortunate than the rich. Their apparent disadvantages were unreal. "Some of the necessities which poverty (if the condition of the labouring part of mankind must be so called) imposes, are not hardships but pleasures. Frugality itself is a pleasure. It is an exercise of attention and contrivance, which, whenever it is successful, produces satisfaction. The very care and forecast that are necessary to keep expenses and earnings upon a level form, when not embarrassed by too great difficulties, an agreeable engagement of the thoughts. This is lost amidst abundance. There is no pleasure in taking out of a large unmeasured fund. They who do that, and only that, are the mere conveyers of money from one hand to another.

"A yet more serious advantage which persons in inferior stations possess, is the ease with which they provide for their children. All the provision which a poor man's child requires is contained in two words, 'industry and innocence.' With these qualities, though without a shilling to set him forwards, he goes into the world prepared to become a useful, virtuous, and happy man. Nor will he fail to meet with a maintenance adequate to the habits with which he has been brought up, and to the expectations which he has formed; a degree of success sufficient for a person of any condition whatever. . . . With health of body, innocency of mind, and habits of industry, a poor man's child has nothing to be afraid of; nor his father or mother anything to be afraid of for him." The apparent advantages of the rich were equally unreal. The owner of a great estate does not eat or drink more than the owner of a small one, and he enjoys the pleasures of eating and drinking much less than the poor man. "The rich who addict themselves to indulgence lose their relish. Their desires are dead. Their sensibilities are worn and tired. Hence they lead a languid, satiated existence. Hardly anything can amuse, or rouse, or gratify them. Whereas the poor man, if something extraordinary fall in his way, comes to the repast with appetite; is pleased and refreshed; derives from his usual course of moderation and temperance a quickness of perception and delight, which the unrestrained voluptuary knows nothing of. Habits of all kinds are much the same. Whatever is habitual becomes smooth, and indifferent, and nothing more. The luxurious receive no greater pleasures from their dainties, than the peasant does from his homely fare. But here is the difference. The peasant, whenever he goes abroad, finds a feast, whereas the epicure must be sumptuously entertained to escape disgust." Such was the transcendental reasoning with which the great philosopher of the Church combated the spiritual sorcery of the French Revolution and the sacramental phrases of the Rights of Man.

The view that the poor were mistaken in supposing that they were worse off than the rich under the British Constitution, was developed by Hannah More in a series of political tracts that had an immense vogue. She published a great number of dialogues and jingles to illustrate the theme that the most modest attempt to reform or relax the ferocious laws that held society together would inflict great suffering upon the poor. Did not one and the same system guarantee the property of rich and poor alike? But though her trumpery pieces had a huge circulation there were many who thought it a mistake to rely solely on this common-sense reasoning for securing the permanent tranquillity and contentment of the poor. Among these was

Arthur Young, who published a paper in 1798 with the title, "An Inquiry into the State of Mind amongst the Lower Classes," to plead for the building of more churches. "A stranger would think our churches were built, as indeed they are, only for the rich. Under such an arrangement where are the lower classes to hear the Word of God, that Gospel which in our Saviour's time was preached more particularly to the poor? Where are they to learn the doctrines of that truly excellent religion which exhorts to content and to submission to the higher powers?" Arthur Young went on to suggest the building of a great number of churches in the form of theatres, with benches and thick mats for the poor, and galleries and boxes for the higher classes. His plea for the "truly excellent religion," though put in this persuasive form, had no immediate effect, but twenty years later, after the troubles of 1817, Parliament voted a million of public money for the construction of churches to preach submission to the higher powers. In the debates in the House of Lords, in May 1818, Lord Liverpool laid stress on the social importance of guiding by this means the opinions of those who were beginning to receive education.

But the French Revolution had another effect on the upper classes, for it seemed to many a warning against irreligion and the frivolous life. The red skies of Paris sobered the English Sunday and filled the English churches. The *Annual Register* for 1798[4] remarks, "It was a wonder to the lower orders, throughout all parts of England, to see the avenues to the churches filled with carriages. This novel appearance prompted the simple country-people to inquire what was the matter?" In the merry days of Archbishop Cornwallis, the Church, to the horror of George the Third, had set the fashion in Sunday parties. After the Revolution these dissipations ceased, and Sunday became much stricter. Wilberforce, in whose mind the most tremendous problems that the nation had ever faced did not overshadow the danger that the reassembling of Parliament on a Monday might cause many members to travel to London on a Sunday, persuaded Perceval, who spent a good part of his time in tracing parallels between Napoleon and the Antichrist of the Book of Revelation, to alter the day of meeting to Tuesday. "House nobly put off by Perceval," he records in his diary. A still more striking reform was the change from Easter Monday to Tuesday for the opening of the Newmarket Races. In the old

---

[4] P. 229.

times the villages on the route used to turn out on Easter Sunday to admire the procession of rich revellers, and their gay colours and equipment. The Duke of York, in answer to remonstrances, said that it was true he travelled to the races on a Sunday, but he always had a Bible and a Prayer Book in his carriage. The general uneasiness and alarm thus led to a more decorous observance of Sunday by the rich; for the poor the religious propaganda of the day meant something more serious than a change of fashion: it meant very real punishment and discipline. Before the Terror, Wilberforce had begun to concert measures for the stricter regulation of Sunday and the enforcement of the drastic laws that recommended Christian observances to the respect and affection of the poor.

Some particulars of this movement are given in a very interesting appendix to Mr. and Mrs. Webb's *History of Liquor Licensing in England*. In 1790 Wilberforce organised a national convention of Justices of the Peace, to arrange a simultaneous attack on loose living and free thinking, and during the following years a vigorous campaign was conducted by magistrates in different parts of the country, directed alike against keepers of brothels, profaners of the Sabbath, and obscure little printers and booksellers who passed a copy of Paine's *Age of Reason* across the counter. Some, inspired by Wilberforce's spirit, regarded the time spent by the poor on amusement as time stolen from the service of God; others regarded it as time stolen from the service of their employers. The Home Office papers contain an account of the measures taken in September 1802 for the apprehension and punishment of large numbers of persons, mainly Irish, who played Hurley in the Tothill Fields and "wickedly profaned the Lord's Day by exercising unlawful Sports and Pastimes."[5] About the same time Lord Pelham, who was then Home Secretary, was urged by the chairman of the Whitechapel magistrates to use his influence to secure the withholding of a licence from the Royalty Theatre, because "the allurements held out by the Performances at that Theatre to Workmen and Servants of the numerous Manufacturers in that Neighbourhood may induce them to live in habits of dissipation and profligacy, become idle and disorderly, and in consequence may be tempted to rob their Employers."[6] The writer enclosed a copy of a letter that the Duke of Portland had written in 1798

---

[5] H. O., 42. 66.
[6] *Ibid.*

at the request of "many of the most respectable and opulent Merchants." A still more serious abuse of Sunday was brought to the notice of the Home Office by a parson at Bolton in Yorkshire, who reported that seditious meetings were held on that day: it was dreadful "that the leisure allowed on this sacred day should be prostituted to such mischievous purposes."[7]

It is not surprising that this campaign against the liberties of the poor awakened a violent hatred in Cobbett. There was a good deal of the Puritan in Cobbett himself, as every one knows who has read his Advice to Young Men.[8] If Wilberforce could have reconciled it to his conscience to read anything that Cobbett wrote, he would have read a great deal of this book with satisfaction. Yet no man of his time was hated with such consistent and uninterrupted fury by Cobbett as was Wilberforce. When Cobbett was driven from the country by the suspension of the Habeas Corpus in 1817, he set out the advantages of America in a passage in which escape from Wilberforce marked the climax of happiness and good fortune: "And, then, to see a free country for once, and to see every labourer with plenty to eat and drink! Think of *that*! And never to see the hang-dog face of a tax gatherer. Think of *that*! No Alien Acts here. No long-sworded and whiskered Captains. No Judges escorted from town to town and sitting under the guard of dragoons. No packed juries of tenants. No Crosses. No Bolton Fletchers. No hangings and rippings up. No Castleses and Olivers. No Stewarts and Perries. No Cannings, Liverpools, Castlereaghs, Eldons, Ellenboroughs, or Sidmouths. No Bankers. No Squeaking

---

[7] H. O., 42. 60. The general point of view of the employing class was put in the Leeds paper quoted by Mr. and Mrs. Webb: "As this is the season when country feasts, wakes, etc., usually begin, a correspondent earnestly recommends it to the ministers and officers in every parish to prevent them from being held on the Lord's Day. Indeed, it would be much better to suppress these feasts entirely, for, as the Rev. Mr. Zouch justly remarks in his excellent pamphlet on the police, it is found by long experience that, when the common people are drawn together upon any public occasion, a variety of mischiefs are certain to ensue; allured by unlawful pastimes, or even by vulgar amusements only, they wantonly waste their time and money to their own great loss and that of their employers. Nay, a whole neighbourhood becomes unhinged for many days, quarrels are too often promoted, and the young and inexperienced are initiated into every species of immorality."—*Leeds Intelligencer*, June 20, 1786.

[8] Note the great resemblance between this book and Wesley's sermon on Redeeming the Time, *Works*, vol. vii. p. 67.

Wynnes. No Wilberforces. Think of *that!* No Wilberforces!"[9]
This is only one of many outbursts of Cobbett's feelings about
Wilberforce and the Saints. Cobbett, in fact, advised the middle
classes to live the sort of life in respect of enslaving pleasure
that Wilberforce wanted the law to force on the poor, but the
point of view of the two men was quite different. Wilberforce
thought that if the poor were amusing themselves they were
neglecting God and would lose eternal happiness. Cobbett
thought that the middle classes were losing their independence.

It is in the gradual discovery of the true spirit of this anti-
Jacobin propaganda that the explanation is to be found of some
of the most glaring of Cobbett's apparent inconsistencies. Cobbett
did not start with any quick sense for freedom. His feelings
towards Priestley and Paine in the Jacobin days were those of
any Philistine of his time; he regarded people with the "reformers' mind" with the same impatience as Major Thomas in
the *Madras House*,[10] and they found rude and even coarse expression in his American writings. In 1796 he wrote a scurrilous
life of Paine, giving vent to his chagrin on Paine's escape from
a French prison in these lines:—

"Tom Paine for the Devil is surely a match,
  In hanging Old England he cheated Jack Catch,
  In France (the first time such a thing had been seen)
  He cheated the watchful and sharp guillotine,
  And at last, to the sorrow of all the beholders,
  He marched out of life with his head on his shoulders."

In 1819 he made a dramatic, or rather a melodramatic, atone-
ment by bringing Paine's bones back to England, an act that
provoked Byron's bitter epigram:—

"In digging up your bones, Tom Paine,
  Will Cobbett has done well:
  You visit him on earth again,
  He'll visit you in Hell."[11]

But the inconsistency in Cobbett's behaviour was only apparent.

---

[9] *Political Register*, October 3, 1818.

[10] "It makes a man unhappy and discontented, not with himself
but with other people, mark you, so it makes him conceited and puts
him out of condition both ways. Don't you get to imagine you can
make this country better by tidying it up."

[11] E. I. Carlyle, *William Cobbett*, p. 212.

Never a theorist nor an idealist, he had a powerful and candid mind that dealt not with splendid abstractions but with the realities of society as he saw them. In 1796 he thought in America that the England which he observed at a flattering distance was a country without corruption or injustice where all classes lived in happy comradeship, and that Priestley and Paine and the rest were the bad sleepers of the State, always unsettling its peace and comfort. By 1819 he had found out his mistake. The first attempts to smother independent thinking had not seemed to menace the poor, but he had now learnt that the attack on Paine and the freedom of writing and printing were closely related to the general oppression and intimidation of the mass of Paine's countrymen. Once this was clear to him he fought for Paine's memory by methods that some of Paine's followers probably disliked more than they would have disliked his earlier invective.

But it was not only Cobbett who was embittered against Wilberforce. Bennet and Place regarded him with similar feelings, and even Romilly, the gentlest in judging his fellowmen, could not always restrain his tongue when Wilberforce was defending some particularly gross outrage on the poor.

Wilberforce showed great independence on occasions, doing violence both to his party sympathies and his private feelings on one memorable night when he voted for the impeachment of Pitt's closest ally, Melville. A vote that moved Pitt to tears must have cost Pitt's friend a heavy price. But his strong leaning to authority prevented him from displaying this independence on behalf of the victims of Ministers or magistrates. An interesting article was published in the *Scotsman*[12] contrasting him in this respect with Whitbread, whose presence in Parliament "was a guarantee against a host of abuses," whereas in the case of Wilberforce, "What jobs of oppression did he ever bring to light? What dealer in injustice or corruption was ever held in awe by his name or exertions?" Hazlitt, in his biting sketch, said of Wilberforce's philanthropy that it was not so ill-bred as to quarrel with his loyalty or banish him from the first circles. This is less than just to Wilberforce. It was not the desire for Sidmouth's good opinion that made him defend injustice: it was this prepossession, which grew stronger with time, in favour of the claims of authority.

[12] Quoted in *Manchester Observer* of March 7, 1818. See H. O., 42. 175.

For two years a handful of men, the chief being Sheridan, Burdett, and Courtenay, were beating against the conservatism of officials and the indifference of politicians in the effort to obtain some inquiry into the scandals of the Cold Bath Fields jail. In the end they succeeded: a Commission was appointed, and in December 1800 it presented a report that convinced the most incredulous of the reality of the alleged abuses. A special feature of this prison was the extraordinary treatment of persons who were not convicted of any crime. In one case a young girl had been kept in prison in order to be called as a witness against a man accused of attempting to rape her. There was no intention of bringing any charge against the girl herself. When the trial came on she was too ill to give evidence. It was discovered that she had been kept on bread and water for a month, and that though she was the wronged party in the case that was to be tried, she had been treated with a cruelty that would have been indefensible, if it had been inflicted on a convicted and sentenced prisoner. The Grand Jury and the Traverse Jury of the County of Middlesex both made presentments calling attention to the grave abuses of this prison, in which the fate of persons, who were neither charged nor convicted, depended entirely on their ability to pay for the necessaries of life. It happened that a large number of the suspected revolutionaries who were swept into prison when the Habeas Corpus was suspended, were lodged in the Cold Baths Fields prison, and it was probably due to this that some interest was taken in the state of the prison, and that the House of Commons was ultimately brought to take note of the fact that unconvicted persons were regularly kept without food for seventeen or eighteen hours at a time. One of the strongest speeches against an inquiry was made by Wilberforce, who met the complaint that innocent persons were being used brutally, with the happy remark that "It ought never to be forgotten that men who expose themselves to suspicion must often incur the disadvantages of guilt."[13] In an illuminating

---

[13] Contrast with Wilberforce's tone that of the Emperor Julian's "Letter to a Priest"; "And I will assert, even though it be paradoxical to say so, that it would be a pious act to share our clothes and food even with the wicked. For it is to the humanity in a man that we give, and not to his moral character. Hence I think that even those who are shut up in prison have a right to the same sort of care; since this kind of philanthropy will not hinder justice. For when many have been shut up in prison to await trial, of whom some will be found guilty, while others will prove to be innocent, it would be harsh

passage he remarked that "the minutes of the sittings of the Magistrates, to which he had alluded, would serve to show what had been the conduct of some of the prisoners, and the necessity there was to watch them with care. It appeared in these minutes that it was stated by the chaplain that two of the persons confined in this place, Burkes and Scott, had behaved so ill at church, had so openly expressed their contempt of the worship, that he proposed that their attendance should in future be dispensed with."[14]

Wilberforce's point of view was quite different from that of Romilly or Bennet or Sheridan. When it was proposed to suspend the Habeas Corpus, or to give arbitrary powers over the lives of the working classes to magistrates, they asked themselves whether such measures would not lead to the gross oppression of poor and defenceless people. Each of them had known such cases and brought them to light. Wilberforce asked himself a totally different question. He asked himself whether the Christian religion and the social order would not suffer if men whose principles and outlook he held in horror were allowed to write and speak as they liked. His answer to this question led him to support authority under all circumstances. Before the French Revolution he had been afraid of liberty of speech: after it he thought discipline the supreme need of the poor. In that cause inhumanity might become a duty. Wilberforce and some of his friends prosecuted a small bookseller for selling Paine's *Age of Reason.* The wretched culprit was found starving in a garret,

---

indeed if out of regard for the guiltless we should not bestow some pity on the guilty also, or again, if on account of the guilty we should behave ruthlessly and inhumanly to those also who have done no wrong."—*Works* of the Emperor Julian, with translation by Dr. W. C. Wright, vol. ii. p. 303.

[14] *Parliamentary Register*, December 21, 1798. Aris, the governor of this prison, who was held up to admiration by Wilberforce, was afterwards exposed and punished. A story was told of him that recalls an incident in the history of those political prisoners at Monte Fusco, whose sufferings are described by Mr. Trevelyan in *Garibaldi and the Thousand.* The jailer of the prison at Monte Fusco shot a nightingale because he thought its song was a consolation to the prisoners. One of Aris's prisoners, spending fifteen months in absolutely solitary confinement, was comforted by a robin that came in one cold day and made friends with him. Aris came into the prison one morning, saw the robin, and killed it. See Burdett's speech in debate on Habeas Corpus, February 17, 1818.

his children ill with small-pox, and Erskine, the prosecuting counsel, made a strong appeal for mercy. But Wilberforce boasts in his Diary that he and his fellow Christians stood firm, and insisted on the ruin of the man and his home. During the debates of 1817 on the suspension of the Habeas Corpus, Burdett put a pointed question to him.[15] He showed that persons were thrown into prison without trial, that they were kept for years in solitary confinement, and that they were forbidden any communication with the outside world. He reminded Wilberforce of the saying of Christ, "I was sick and in prison, and ye visited me not," and he asked what a Christian was to think of those who not only did not visit the prisoner themselves, but would not allow others to visit him. Wilberforce replied that religion had taught him to value the blessings which the country enjoyed, and to hand them down to posterity unimpaired.

When Bennet and other public-spirited men had exposed the infamous story of Oliver, the spy and *agent provocateur* who brought men to the gallows, Wilberforce said that his confidence in Sidmouth was unshaken, and that he was satisfied that there was no serious risk of injustice or oppression. His position was well put in two sentences of his speech: "He could readily conceive how the lower orders, that valuable portion of the community whose labour was so essential to the social system under which we live, might be tempted by the delusive and wicked principles instilled into their minds, to direct their strength to the destruction of the government, and to the overthrow of every civil and religious establishment."[16] That was the real danger. As for the danger of the abuse of those powers, did anybody think it existed, or that the public press did not provide all necessary security? Romilly reminded him that this speech was made after it had been proved that a large number of innocent people had gone to prison, when the use of spies had for the first time been admitted, and that though Wilberforce and men of his class might be in no danger, obscure weavers might spend months in prison without Parliament ever hearing of it.[17] It is not surprising after studying these speeches to find Wilber-

---

[15] *Hansard*, June 27, 1817.

[16] *Hansard*, June 23, 1817.

[17] Romilly quoted the case of a man who had been kept in prison for seven years. The victim was a youth of seventeen, who was shut up in 1795. See Burdett's speech, *Hansard*, February 26, 1817.

force, two years later, coming forward to express his approval of Peterloo.[18]

Wilberforce's humanitarian contemporaries thought that a Christianity which held that it would be wrong to consider Owen's schemes because he did not recognise the Christian religion, and yet condoned and supported all the cruelties and injustices of power, was hypocrisy. Here were men devoting themselves with great courage and public spirit to exposing abuses and pleading the case of a class unrepresented in Parliament and viewed with suspicion by magistrates, and at every step they found Wilberforce resisting them, and throwing the cloak of his character for independence and moral singleness of purpose over every species of oppression. Their view that he was a hypocrite was not unnatural, but it was unjust. Wilberforce acted consistently on his own principles. His great mission in life was to make men moral, as he understood morality. The thought of weavers and printers languishing in prison under Combination Laws, or the laws against freedom of speech and writing, which filled men of the world like Fox, Sheridan, Bennet, or Holland with rage and indignation, left Wilberforce cold. What tortured him was the thought that a man who read Paine and talked like a Jacobin, who grudged the rich their wealth, and the aristocracy their power, might still be at large, spreading the irreligious spirit of discontent. There was no hypocrisy in this; it was the way in which Wilberforce interpreted his religion. In questions where this disturbing element did not enter, where the demand was not that working men should be treated as persons with rights and liberties, but that suffering unnecessary from the point of view of discipline should cease, Wilberforce was a humane man. He did not prosecute the cause of the factory children or the chimney-sweeper children with the zeal that he devoted to reforming manners or the zeal that has made his name immortal in the history of the Slave Trade, but he supported others when they tried to reform these abuses, just as he supported the attempts to reform the Game Laws. He looked upon the cause of the factory children as similar in kind to the cause of the slaves. Economists might argue that the cruelties of the factory were essential to British industry, but he could not regard them as essential to the British constitution and its civil and religious establishments.

---

[18] Place wrote against his name in his report of the debate, "an ugly epitome of the devil" (Wallas, *Place*, p. 147).

Religious philanthropy taught two main lessons. The first was the duty of private benevolence. The rich and comfortable ought to visit the poor, to teach them the Bible, to take an interest in their welfare, to give them advice, alms, and soup, to found societies like the Society for Bettering the Condition of the Poor. Many persons carried out these tasks with great devotion, some, like John Howard and Mrs. Fry, with heroism. It was in this way, rather than by seeking to modify the arrangements of society, that the comfortable should discharge their obligations to the unfortunate. That a great deal of misery was alleviated by these ministrations is undoubted. The second lesson was the lesson of subordination and discipline. The rich and the poor were equal in the sight of God, but the effective recognition of equality was to come in another world. In this world the poor were not to presume on that principle: they were to learn patience and gratitude. The Evangelical religion made a special feature of gratitude. Wilberforce used to carry about, for use in meditation and prayer, a list of the advantages for which he owed gratitude to Providence, such as his rank in life, his parents, his home, and in particular his good fortune in being born in the country and the age that combined the greatest measure of temporal comforts and of spiritual privileges. A small weakly man, he would have been exposed at birth if he had been born in the days of his painted ancestors, whereas in eighteenth-century England he had found very little inconvenience from his poor physique. As Brougham's ideal was the prudent man, Wilberforce's was the grateful man.[19] Unfortunately the poor learned gratitude slowly, and hence it was necessary to make sharp laws for keeping them in order. The day would come when all classes would pursue the virtues that respectively became them, according to the revelation of the Gospel. For the present the poor must be taught their duties by Combination Laws, and the rich must be taught their responsibilities by the Bible. Thus the philanthropy of the rich, like the political economy of the day, helped to reconcile the conscience of the upper classes to a servile standard for the poor. For resignation was the message of religion as it was the message of nature.

---

[19] The concentration on this aspect of life, by a strange irony, brought the Evangelical very near to the Gods of Epicurus: "Comprehende igitur animo, et propone ante oculos, deum nihil aliud in omni æternitate, nisi, Mihi pulchre est, et, Ego beatus sum, cogitantem" (Cicero, *De Natura Deorum*, lib. i. cap. 41).

CHAPTER XII

THE DEFENCES OF THE POOR (I)

THE SPIRIT OF UNION

In his vivid picture of Latin society under the Empire, Dr. Dill
has described the "colleges" in which the obscure workman, shut
out from the brilliant world of power and fashion and pleasure,
contrived to satisfy his desire for comradeship, for the warmth
of sympathy in life, and the promise of memory after death.
The English workman under the new industrial system found
himself receiving government, justice, discipline, the ordering
of most of his comfortless life, from magistrates and masters, in
a world not less separate and cold. Like the cloth worker of
Brescia or the boatman of Lyons in the second century, the
Gateshead miner or the Bradford weaver was conscious of tastes
and faculties and needs for which no provision was made in the
scheme of his life, as that scheme was drawn by his superiors.
The man who has no share in the government of his parish or
mill needs some scope for his political capacities; the man who
spends his life "making the twenty-fourth part of a pin" needs
some sphere for his imagination; the man whose only provision
against accident or illness or the loss of his livelihood is the
reluctant succour of the poor law, needs some protection against
fortune; the man who lives under the unbridled power of employer and magistrate needs some protection against that power,
some pledge of help and friendship in the hour of struggle and
tribulation. These necessaries of his larger life the English workman sought during the Industrial Revolution in organisations
that he created and developed under the fierce discouragement
of his rulers. These institutions took the place in his life of the
sodalicia that had consoled the loneliness of the Latin poor.

For it was in those years that the institutions that are now so
pronounced a feature of artisan civilisation first became positive
forces in the life of the working classes. To trace the history of
Trade Unions, Friendly Societies, Co-operative Societies, Mechanics' Institutes, Sunday-schools, Methodist Chapels, and all
the various influences that helped to keep the soul alive in a
population living under conditions that degrade the mind, is
clearly beyond the scope of this work. To do justice to that
theme it would be necessary to describe the Reform movement
with its apostles and martyrs, Paine, Hardy, Thelwall, Watson

the Chartist, Muir, Gerrald, Place, Cobbett, and in the north in particular, men like Knight, Bamford, Prentice, Baines of Halifax, Taylor, Pilkington, and other brave men and good citizens whose names are only preserved in the criminal records of their country. Robert Owen, again, who taught a religion that borrowed too directly from the unsophisticated doctrine of Christianity to please the more cautious and experienced Christians of the House of Commons,[1] would occupy a place of his own as the prophet of co-operation in a wider and fuller sense than that term commonly bears. The Union Shop movement (1828–32) and one important phase in the Trade Union movement drew their inspiration and energy largely from his teaching.[2] In education of one kind or another there are the names of Raikes, Bell, Lancaster, Hannah More, Mrs. Trimmer, Birkbeck, Brougham, and Cobbett, a genius of a different temper from all the rest, whose papers and pamphlets were read with all the greater zest, as literature forbidden by a power that could punish disobedience with swift and arbitrary strokes. Sadler, Oastler, Fielden, Bennet, and Ashley, the leaders of the revolt against the sacrifice of infant life, have crossed these pages from time to time. Then there are the two men whose names Carlyle coupled together as an astonishing and alarming phenomenon to the idle rich, Ebenezer Elliott and Rowland Detroisier. One came from Yorkshire, the other from Lancashire. Elliott, a Sheffield ironworker who picked up some kind of education at a small Presbyterian school in Rotherham, is chiefly known as the Corn Law rhymer, but he covered a wide range, and he was the poet of Chartism as well as of Free Food. Detroisier, the son of a Manchester man and a Frenchwoman, who deserted him when a month old, was brought up by a benevolent fustian cutter and apprenticed to that trade. He learned to read and write at a Sunday-school. He had a chequered career, married early, and was often in want. His great strength of character showed itself in the use he made of his intervals of unemployment, for though almost destitute he turned his misfortunes to account by learning Latin, French, Physics, Mathematics. He embarked on more than one venture in commerce and industry,

---

[1] See Wilberforce's speech, Smart, *op. cit.*, p. 707 (1819).

[2] Though Chartism as a political movement ran counter to his doctrine, such notable Chartist leaders as Lovett and Hetherington, Cleave and Watson had all been his pupils (Dolléans, *op. cit.*, i. p. 197).

but he found his mission as a public lecturer, and he established some of the first Mechanics' Institutes in England, at Hulme and Salford. With human sympathies and democratic beliefs he combined Brougham's enthusiasm for education, giving popular addresses on such subjects as "The Benefits of General Knowledge, more especially the Sciences of Mineralogy, Geology, Botany, and Entomology." An address that he published on the importance of moral education to the working classes captivated enlightened London, and brought him into correspondence with Bentham. His eloquence on Reform platforms caused him to be chosen as secretary of the Political Union, and Prentice has described the effects of his speaking on an audience. He was a man of unbounded public spirit, a powerful force in the education of Lancashire.

But more important than Elliott or Detroisier was John Doherty, the chief working-class leader of the time. Doherty began life in a cotton mill near Larne, and migrated to Manchester in 1816 at the age of seventeen. He rapidly reached a position of influence among the cotton workers, and he took a prominent part in the agitation against the re-enactment of the Combination Laws in 1825. After leading the cotton spinners in their great but unsuccessful strike in 1829, he tried to turn the lesson of that failure to account, and to organise the forces of the working classes in the National Association for the Protection of Labour. *The Voice of the People*, which he edited, was the organ of that association, and afterwards, when apparently he had quarrelled with the executive committee, he edited *The Poor Man's Advocate*. At the time of the Committee on Combinations (1837) he was a bookseller in Manchester. Doherty's democratic convictions were genuine and ambitious. He wanted the working classes to organise their own education, in opposition to upper- and middle-class movements like the Society for the Diffusion of Useful Knowledge. Readers of the *Voice of the People* will be struck, too, by its modern spirit on the subject of the control of industry; for, in contrast to some other working-class leaders, he held that the development of machinery was inevitable, and in contrast to the economists of the day he held that if the new society was to have tolerable conditions of life, machinery must be brought under the direction of the working classes themselves. At a time when the working classes were tempted to adopt the materialist standards taught by the ruling class, Doherty was a powerful prophet of the creed that the aim and goal of human effort was not wealth but freedom.

Lastly, as our period closes, a battle began for a cheap Press. Birkbeck and Chadwick were agitating against the heavy tax on newspapers, and a whole army of working men defied the law and published journals without a stamp. In October 1830 Henry Hetherington began to publish the *Penny Papers for the People*. The battle was won in 1836, when the stamp was reduced from 4d. to 1d., but in the five years 500 persons had been sent to prison.[3]

Each of these influences had its share in modifying, in this or in that respect, the brutal results of a system that treated human life as one among several forces which drove the wheels of rapid wealth, and as nothing more. Each of them, in one way or another, taught either the rich or the poor that men, women, and children were not merely so much machine power in a world that had no use or care for anything but their fingers and their muscles. But the main burden of building up this side of life, of giving to classes that seemed to exist only for other people's ends a value and purpose of their own, of making wider and deeper the range and play of imagination and sympathy, of cherishing a spirit of association more daring and more ambitious than the spirit of the old *sodalicia*: this burden fell in the main on the nameless working classes themselves. They had to overcome all the obstacles that were put in their way by a class holding the power that law, custom, education, and wealth can bestow. Of all the documents in the Home Office papers, none illustrates better the difficulties of that struggle than a confiscated copy-book, seized by an active magistrate and sent to the Home Office in a time of panic as a dangerous piece of sedition, in which a working man, secretary of a little society of working-men Reformers, had been practising his elementary powers of writing and spelling.[4] Reform, education, combination wore a very different look to the rich and the poor. To the working classes they were ladders from a prison: to their rulers they were ladders whereby the proletariate might one day take the State by storm.

One form of association had been countenanced and even befriended by the ruling class. George Rose had passed more than one Act of Parliament to protect the funds of Benefit Clubs and

[3] See for description of the movement, Collet, *History of the Taxes on Knowledge*.

[4] H. O., 42. 157.

to regulate their management.[5] Benefit Clubs were, of course, no new feature of English life. Eden wrote an interesting chapter on them in his great work, pressing with an enlightenment unusual in his day for the recognition of the property of women. They increased rapidly at this time, and Rose stated in 1816 that there were 700,000 members of these societies in England. They were specially common in Lancashire and the new industrial districts;[6] in 1801 Lancashire had 820 registered societies, 200 more than any other county. These societies were very various in character. A few were connected with a mine or mill. Curwen told the House of Commons in 1816[7] that for thirty years he had made it a rule that every man employed at the Workington and Harrington collieries should contribute 6d. a week to a benefit fund, the employers paying a third of the sum subscribed. The fund was managed by a committee of workmen chosen by themselves. Curwen proposed a universal system of contributory insurance on this model as a substitute for the Poor Law. But the great majority of these societies were, of course, unconnected with the employers. They were indeed viewed with great suspicion by many magistrates as a disguise for combination of a less innocent kind. Colonel Fletcher of Bolton wrote, in 1817, that the weavers east of Manchester were about to strike, and that they had broken up a Friendly Society in order to provide themselves with strike pay.[8] In the same year the funds of a sick club were used for the maintenance of the Kidderminster weavers on strike.[9] Mr. Lloyd of Stockport, clerk to the magistrates, complained in 1818 that Friendly Societies were helping a man named Temple, whom he was prosecuting for conspiracy,[10] and he pressed for legislation to prevent this. An Act of Parliament[11] was passed the next year to strengthen the control of the magistrates, and also to make it necessary for the magistrates to satisfy themselves that any table of benefits that they sanctioned had been approved by two actuaries. A more important Act was passed in 1829[12] set-

---

[5] 33 George III. c. 54 (1793) and 35 George III. c. III (1795).
[6] Chapman, *op. cit.*, p. 182n.
[7] May 28, 1816.
[8] H. O., 42. 165.
[9] H. O., 42. 172.
[10] See p. 81.
[11] 59 George III. c. 128.
[12] 10 George IV. c. 56.

ting up an official corresponding to the modern Registrar of
Friendly Societies.

The suspicions of the magistrates were well founded, for a
witness told the Committee on Artisans and Machinery, in 1824,
the secret history of a Spinners' Union to which he had belonged
in 1810.[13] This Union extended on all sides of Manchester,
to Stockport and Macclesfield in the south, Stalybridge, Ashton,
and Hyde in the east, and Oldham, Bolton, and Preston in the
north. Business was conducted by a general congress of fifty
deputies. The meetings were carried on under the sanction of
Sick Club articles legally enrolled at Manchester, but the Society was governed by a set of private rules. This means of dis-
guising a Trade Union was in common use, according to the
Report of the Committee on Friendly Societies in 1825, and it
has been said that "most alliances to raise wages cloaked themselves under the rules of Friendly Societies. . . ."[14]

The great modern Friendly Societies, with a few exceptions,
trace their origin to this period, and to the districts that were
the home of the new industry. The Industrial Revolution transformed the old village club, with its easy-going finance and its
convivial life, into the great Orders that we know to-day.

The Co-operative movement also made its first start at this
time. In 1831 the dressers and dyers, in the course of a quarrel with their employers, set up an establishment of their own;
according to the *Voice of the People* it was a great success.
Doherty wanted other workpeople to copy this example. Mrs.
Webb has described, in her brilliant little sketch of that movement, the early adventures of this principle. In 1832 there were
some five hundred co-operative societies, predecessors of the
great Rochdale experiment of 1844, and though they came to
grief, they are significant as the first trial of strength in this
important and difficult form of association.

But, of course, the chief of the movements that developed
the mind and determined the history of the working classes was
the new Trade Union. Doherty thus described the main object
of the National Association for the Protection of Labour (the
combined Union of 1830), "to raise the working classes from
that state of moral degradation in which they were at present
sunk." During this time, as Professor Chapman has pointed out,
the Trade Union acquires a new significance, becoming less an

---

[13] Artisans and Machinery, p. 573.
[14] See Chapman, *op. cit.*, p. 181.

organisation for protecting the industry and more an organisation for fighting employers.[15] This is true, not only of spinners who worked in factories and colliers who worked in mines, but also, though more gradually, of weavers working in their homes. Not, of course, that these workpeople had yet settled or permanent unions of the kind that we know to-day in the great majority of industries, with highly organised schemes of government and a salaried staff. In this period these organisations were struggling into life, and struggling against the power of wealth and the power of law: against master, magistrate, and spy. Under the Combination Laws, as we have seen, men and women could not take a single step for the purpose of raising wages, or resisting a reduction of wages, or helping the victims of a lock-out, without risk of prosecution. Combinations of this kind were not always prosecuted. A man or woman trying to organise against the masters was like a person trying to get out of an unfamiliar room in the dark. His shins may escape nine times out of ten, but it is due to luck rather than to dexterity. Leadership or responsibility of any kind involved the gravest risks. Such a position brought no dignity or social repute: it invited the special hostility of magistrates and employers. Detroisier said that the employers' prejudice against intelligence and education was largely due to their animus against the leaders of their workmen, who were generally chosen for their superiority in these respects. These men were the natural victims, and at the first breath of trouble their houses were searched, their papers seized, and they themselves thrown into prison. Gravener Henson, the historian of frame-work knitting, was imprisoned when the Habeas Corpus was suspended, although his energy had been directed to restraining the workmen from violence, and he had recommended them to combine as an alternative to Luddite methods. But he had committed the crime of prosecuting employers for an offence under the Truck Acts.[16] Leaders were in a particularly dangerous position, because when a large number of workpeople were in prison, in peril of their lives, there was a considerable risk that one of them might succumb to the temptation of ingratiating himself with the authorities, and saving his neck, or

---

[15] Mr. and Mrs. Webb have given, in the opening pages of *Industrial Democracy*, an account of some of the early Trade Clubs, with their rule regulating the distribution of liquor, and forbidding obscene or seditious language.

[16] H. O., 42. 166.

lightening his punishment, by making charges against public men who were known to be obnoxious to the Government or the magistrates. Thus a man, under sentence of death for frame-breaking at Loughborough, tried to extricate his life by promising important disclosures incriminating Gravener Henson, and to whet the appetite of the magistrate he declared that Henson was equal to anything that ever Robespierre committed. At the very moment that this painful piece of perfidy was acting inside the prison walls, Henson was himself on his way to London to petition, at no small risk to himself, for mercy for the poor wretch who was trying to sell his advocate's life for his own.[17]

The story of William Temple is a good illustration of the difficulties and dangers to which a man who took any step for defending himself and his fellows was exposed. We can put together the main facts from two sources: Temple told his story to the Committee on Artisans and Machinery, and Lloyd, a chief actor, tells it in the Home Office papers.[18]

Temple was a spinner near Stockport. An old soldier, he had been in the ranks of the dishevelled army that dragged itself to Corunna with Sir John Moore. After the war he returned to civil life, resuming his employment as a spinner. He was soon to know that peace had only brought him a change of warfare. He and twenty of his fellows gave notice to their employer, a manufacturer named Smith, of Heaton Norris, near Stockport, but in the parish of Manchester, that they intended to quit his employment unless he raised their wages by a penny a hundred hanks. Other factories were giving three halfpence or twopence more than Smith for a hundred hanks. Smith refused, and they left his employment. Smith then sent the names of the twenty-one to all other manufacturers in the neighbourhood, asking them not to give them employment, with the result that six of the men who had already obtained work were turned off. Temple and his friends consulted a lawyer, instituted proceedings against Smith, and raised subscriptions. Mr. Lloyd of Stockport, clerk to the magistrates, replied by arresting Temple and fourteen others for conspiracy. The factory was in Lancashire, and on this ground the men could be prosecuted in Lancashire. But Lloyd reflected with great satisfaction, that as Temple and four others had appealed for subscriptions at Stockport

---

[17] H. O., 42. 163.
[18] Committee on Artisans and Machinery, p. 414 f.; H. O., 42. 179, 42. 180, 42. 184, 42. 186.

in Cheshire, they were liable in that county also. In Lancashire the charge was "assembling together and refusing to work for Mr. Smith": in Cheshire, "conspiracy to raise wages and control their masters." Temple got bail for the Lancashire charge, on which a true bill had been found in August, the trial being fixed for the Assizes of the following spring. He then hurried off to Chester, and at the Assizes at the end of August he traversed his case till the ensuing Assizes. He was ordered to find £200 bail himself, and two sureties in £100 each. This he could not do until December 14, so from August to December he spent in prison. On coming out of prison, he had still three months before his next trial was to come on, and he thought he could use the time for raising funds for the defence, so he published a broadsheet appealing to every mechanic, every friend of liberty, and every lover of justice to snatch him and his friends from "the savage grasp of an overbearing and hard-hearted employer." Lloyd of Stockport pounced on this, ordered Temple into custody, and called on him to find bail of two sureties in £50 each, to answer to a charge of libel at the next Chester Assizes. But Lloyd was evidently anxious to separate the case of the leaders from the cases of the others, and after some negotiations with Smith he arranged that the charges at Lancaster should be dropped, after an expression of regret and of submission from the culprits, and that the more serious offenders should be dealt with at Chester. There Temple and four others were tried in April, on a charge of "conspiring, confederating, combining, and agreeing for the price of their labour." Temple was sentenced to twelve months' imprisonment: Barnett got a similar sentence for calling a meeting, Swindells and Gooch three months for calling a meeting, and Bolton three months for meeting a person in the street and saying, "I wish you would come forward for these men, otherwise they will fall through." Thus Temple spent sixteen months in prison for the offence of leaving his employment and for asking for help to defend himself and his friends against Smith's proscription. Smith, on the other hand, was allowed to file a plea of justification. On coming out of prison, Temple was of course a marked man, and it was a year before he could get employment.

Temple's story before the Committee on Artisans and Machinery is instructive reading, but the Home Office papers are an invaluable supplement. For they show, in Lloyd's letters, that the magistrates made no pretence of acting impartially in these disputes. All that Smith had to do after writing to his fellow-manufacturers and setting the prosecution in motion, was to leave his workmen to Lloyd's tender mercies. The brilliant idea of prosecuting in two counties, which kept the wretched Temple flying from one court to the other, and of course made the defence infinitely more difficult and expensive, was his, and he chuckles over it. When Temple issued his appeal, it was Lloyd who seized him and asked for bail, adding in his letter to the Home Office "which I don't think he will be able to provide." Refusal to accept employment on their masters' terms was in the eyes of the magistrates an offence against society, and to demand better wages, or even to resent a reduction of wages, was to demand revolution. The meshes of the law were infinite, its penalties brutal, and its powers in the hands of men for the most part without imagination or sympathy, strangers to all the experiences and the difficulties of the poor. In such an atmosphere a Trade Union was a school of heroism and public spirit.

There was one danger from which the trade unionists of the industrial districts were rarely free, the danger of the serpent in their councils. The arts by which Castles, Oliver, and Edwards won their reluctant fame were the arts by which many of their contemporaries earned their living. The use of spies was common in all times of popular excitement or upper-class panic, and in some districts in the north and Midlands they became part of the normal machinery of the law. Bills for spies are for many years a regular feature of the Home Office papers. Spies were employed by the Home Office itself, by some of the officers commanding in the industrial districts, and by several of the more active magistrates or their clerks, notably by Fletcher of Bolton, Lloyd of Stockport, Enfield at Nottingham, and Parsons Ethelston and Hay in Lancashire. It sometimes happened that one magistrate arrested another magistrate's spy by mistake, with embarrassing consequences. This system was in force in the industrial districts long before the Luddite disturbances, for Bolton Fletcher sent up a bill for £123 in 1805, his agents being used on that occasion to watch a Weavers' Combination.[19] As spies had to justify themselves and to encourage the authorities to continue their employment, their trade was rather that of the artist than of the detective. If they had relied for their living on their observations, they would soon have starved. What was needed was imagination, the more finished the better, but the rudest gifts of the kind commanded a market, for the wild-

[19] H. O., 42. 82.

est legends were swallowed by many of the magistrates. Though
in many cases men of the worst character, and some of them
ex-convicts, their uncorroborated statements were accepted as
valid evidence, and five men were transported in 1813 on the
unsupported evidence of a spy, and a spy with a particularly
scandalous past. Spies were well paid.[20] But there were obvious
drawbacks to the occupation. The authorities kept the spies up
their sleeves as long as possible, but if once they had to produce
a spy in court[21] and confront working men with one of their
own comrades in his true character, it became necessary to move
him and his family to another part of the country.[22] Sometimes it was possible to smuggle him into the army, but this
after career was often an embarrassment, and the Home Office
papers contain many pitiful appeals. A Sheffield spy wrote to
the Home Office in 1818 describing his difficulties.[23] He had
found employment in Wardour Street, but had been identified,
insulted, and spat upon. He then tried to get away to America,
but the friend who was to accompany him robbed him and
decamped. He enlisted in the Marines, but one of the men
there knew him, so he had to fly again. He got temporary work
on a canal in Gloucestershire, wandered through Wales into

[20] For an example of payment see, in H. O., 42. 83, one of Bolton
Fletcher's bills from July 8 to December 21, 1805:—

		£			£		
B.	Time	£9	5	0			
	Expenses	17	2	11			
					£26	7	11
C.					4	11	0
T.	Time	£4	12	0			
	Expenses	4	8	6			
					9	0	6
L. F.	Time	£18	8	0			
	Expenses	4	18	0			
					23	6	0
					£63	5	5

In 1816 the bill for the half-year had gone up to £226 (H. O., 42.
160).

[21] Mr. Coldham, Town Clerk of Nottingham in 1814, argued
that a spy should not be produced as a witness in court, then we
should have "the source of our information pure and uncontaminated"
(H. O., 42. 137).

[22] Cf. H. O., 40. 1.

[23] H. O., 42. 182.

Lancashire, and enlisted once more at Manchester, but this time
he was recognised not by the class he had hunted but by the
class that had used him, and he found himself in the Manchester New Bailey as a deserter. He hoped the Government
would arrange to start him in a colony. Another spy wrote to
say that nobody would work with him, and that though Colonel
Fletcher of Bolton was anxious to put him into the Manchester
police, Norris, the stipendiary magistrate, thought he was too
well known and that it would not do.[24] The Home Office seem
to have acted handsomely in some cases, for the orphan child of
a spy who had given evidence against Hardy and Horne Tooke
was given £30 a year.[25] Perhaps the most importunate spy
was Fleming, the hero of the trial of the Thirty-Eight.[26] Originally a cotton weaver, he had learned his new trade in a school
where the necessary accomplishments were easily acquired, for
he served in the yeomanry in Ireland during the Rebellion.[27]
Taking the name of Edwards, he joined the Manchester Society
for Constitutional Reform, and sent his employer, Parson Ethelston, such stories of its designs as kept that zealous justice in a
perpetual fever of excitement and expectation.[28] He had one
disagreeable experience early in 1817, when he and another
spy went into Yorkshire, with £10 in their pockets from Mr.
Ethelston, to discover depots of pikes. At Huddersfield they
began to talk with some Democrats from Sheffield, whereupon
"they were seized as a matter of course by the officers of Justice
and thrown into Prison, after a night's confinement they were
taken before a Justice of the Peace (Mr. Haigh) who, conceiv-
ing them to be Rogues and Vagabonds, would hear nothing in
their defence, but sent them out of the Town immediately."[29]
He had another disagreeable experience in Stockport in 1818,
being denounced as a spy and expelled from a weavers' meeting.
The weavers on this occasion passed a resolution that, as the
"notorious villain" had entered their meeting, they proposed to
ask the Chief Constable to attend as a protection against his
perjuries.[30] This exposure put him on the shelf for a time, and

---

[24] H. O., 44. 7.
[25] H. O., 42. 67.
[26] This trial is described in *The Skilled Labourer*, Chapter x.
[27] H. O., 40. 10.
[28] H. O., 42. 156.
[29] H. O., 42. 160.
[30] H. O., 42. 179.

Ethelston got £10 out of the Home Office for him as a kind of unemployment pay.[31] Next year he was back at work sending Ethelston the news that Cobbett's arrival in Lancashire was to give the signal for a general rising: by this time he had clearly taken the measure of his employer, and discovered that the larger and stranger the fly that was offered to that open mouth, the more eagerly would it be swallowed. Fleming deposed to an interview with Cobbett, in which Cobbett deplored the fact that the general rising had not taken place earlier, whilst Cobbett's companion declared that he would give no quarter, but would hang, burn, and destroy everything.[32]

There was no influence at the Home Office checking this abuse until Peel became Home Secretary. As Irish Secretary he extinguished a promising career in espionage, and had he gone to the Home Office earlier, Oliver would have found a colder welcome.[33] With local authorities as credulous as Ethelston, as arbitrary as Lloyd or Hay, with a Home Secretary like Sidmouth, to whom every poor man was a Jacobin, a detective system based on spies who had every inducement to spin legends and to promote crime gave the excitement of peril to the daily life of the workman, and taught him honour and loyalty in the face of the temptations, not only of greed, but also of fear. Every little combination for raising wages or helping comrades lived in something of the atmosphere of a Russian revolutionary society: the blow might never fall, but the sword was always there. The solemn oaths and ritual that terrified the Government had a real meaning when men and women were trusting their liberties and their lives to each other.

In spite of these difficulties and dangers such associations were common. Occasionally women combined as well as men. From two documents seized and sent to the Home Office in 1818 it is clear that in the strike of that year men and women received equal strike pay.[34] A parson magistrate at Loughborough was much alarmed in 1811 by the conduct of the women

---

[31] H. O., 42. 180. He had already received £100 for his baulked enterprise in the trial of the Thirty-Eight at Manchester (see H. O., 42. 132).

[32] It is interesting to notice that General Byng at this time wrote: "I think Cobbett *might be had* without much trouble. He is poor, and I remark very cautious in what he says" (H. O., 42. 199; cf. H. O., 42. 200).

[33] The story of Oliver is told in *The Skilled Labourer*, Chapter xii.

[34] H. O., 42. 179.

lace workers, who had shown "a Spirit of Combination to dictate to their Employers and to raise the price of their Wages." These daring women had held meetings and sent emissaries to the neighbouring towns to extend their organisation and to collect funds, whereupon the parson had issued a warning that all such proceedings were a breach of the law.[35]

These associations were not confined within boundaries of place or trade. It is evident from the letters of magistrates, and the still better evidence of letters intercepted in the post or seized in other ways, that even in these early days there was a great deal of mutual encouragement and aid between different districts and different industries. Several cases were reported to the Home Office in 1801. A parson wrote in alarm that Holcroft of Bolton was in correspondence with the weavers of Scotland over the Weavers Bill;[36] the Mayor of Leeds forwarded a letter from a Leeds correspondent to somebody at Trowbridge stating that two men were going from Leeds to Wiltshire as delegates;[37] and a Midhurst employer sent a letter seized in his mill, which showed that a combination of paper-makers, spreading to Manchester and Wells, was concerting a uniform demand for higher wages.[38] The dispute in the clothing industry next year revealed a similar spirit. The shearmen of Wiltshire professed to have all the shearmen of England, Scotland, and Ireland[39] behind them, and though this may have been an exaggeration, it is evident that Wiltshire and Yorkshire were acting in concert. The Wiltshire shearmen printed a ticket with the motto, "May Industry and Freedom unite us in friendship," and Cookson, a Leeds magistrate, wrote to say that the Leeds shearmen had the same ticket and were, he believed, responsible for the Wiltshire policy. Cookson added that meetings were being held in a lonely place near Birstall, and that his informer had been too much frightened by the temper of the meeting to stay for its proceedings. He was so much impressed himself with the danger that he had dissuaded two manufacturers from carrying out their intention of introducing gig-mills. "Every Class of Workmen make a common cause with that of the Cloth-workers, and every turnout for advance of Wages is supported by general contribu-

---

[35] H. O., 42. 118.
[36] H. O., 42. 62.
[37] H. O., 42. 62.
[38] H. O., 42. 118.
[39] H. O., 42. 65.

tion from almost every other Class."[40] From the books of the Shearmen's Society, which somehow got into the hands of the Committee on the Woollen Manufacture in 1806, it appeared that contributions were received in 1802 from "clothiers, colliers, bricklayers, wool-sorters, from the clothiers' community, joiners, sawyers, flax-dressers, shoemakers, turnpikemen, cabinet-makers," also from Manchester, from patten-ring-makers and paper-makers.[41] Mr. Cookson drew a picture of successful combination in another letter the same year, in which he pressed for the further strengthening of the Combination Law.[42] He contended that great evils would follow if "the working people were allowed to feel and make known the extent of their power," and he wanted to "repress if not extirpate the Combination system . . . Indeed the evils call aloud for a Cure, or would soon extend beyond computation,—perquisites, privileges, Time, Mode of Labour, Rate, who shall be employed, etc. etc., all are now dependent on the Fiat of our Workmen. . . . It is now a Confirmed thing that a Bricklayer, Mason, Carpenter, Wheelwright, etc., shall have 3s. per Week higher Wages in Leeds or in Manchester, than at Wakefield, York, Hull, Rochdale and adjacent Towns, it is in orders too that Bricklayers and Masons Labourers at Leeds shall have 2s. per Week extra—no Workman will or dare deviate from these Terms, no Matter from whence he comes, and there arrived here last week on their way to Manchester Two Delegates from Carlisle summoned by the Lancashire Cotton printers, to agree upon certain advances in their Wages, who made no secret of their Mission." During a strike at Knaresborough in 1805, a man was caught carrying a letter to the weavers of York, and given three months' imprisonment under the Combination Law.[43] There were combinations spread over great districts among calico printers, frame-work knitters, coachmakers, coal-miners. During the trial of calico printers for combination in 1816, it appeared that they received help from musical-instrument makers, brush-makers, bellows-makers, shoemakers.[44] In the spinners' strike of 1818 there were subscriptions for the men in the towns of the Potteries.[45]

---

[40] H. O., 42. 66.
[41] 1806 Report on Woollen Manufactures, p. 355.
[42] H. O., 42. 66.
[43] Committee on Artisans and Machinery, p. 540.
[44] H. O., 42. 158.
[45] H. O., 42. 179.

An example of an extended combination in an old trade is furnished by the letters and papers that were intercepted during a strike of bootmakers in 1802 and 1804.[46] There was correspondence between Unions in London, Wakefield, York, Bath, Portsmouth, Liverpool. The papers contain a definition of a "scab": "And what is a Scab?—He is to his *trade* what a traitor is to his *country*: though both may be useful to one party in troublesome times, when peace returns they are detested alike by all. When help is wanted he is the last to contribute assistance and the first to grasp a benefit he never laboured to procure. He cares but for himself, but he sees not beyond the extent of a day, and for a momentary and worthless approbation would betray friends, family and country. In short he is a traitor on a small scale. He first sells the Journeymen, and is himself afterwards sold in his turn by the Masters, till at last he is despised by both, and deserted by all. He is an enemy to himself, to the present age and to posterity."

A letter from the Liverpool Union, dated November 14, 1803, gives a picture of some of the difficulties of a Union in these days:—

> LOVING SHOPMAITES,—I hope you will Excuse our neglect in not wrighting before now to return you our gratefull thanks for your timley asistance in our last contest with our tyrant, hopeing you will retain the same regard wich you have shown in your last contribushion towards us at a time when we was so much nesseated at any time should any thing of the kind happen to you you lose no time to inform us of your sittuashion that we may shew ourselfs as much in your intrest and well faire as lyes in our power as we still and allways shall think our indeted to you for the suploys we received from you without wich we must a suffered verrey much as we did not receive the suploys from the other towns as we Expected, but since we have got partley through our distresses we hope you will not omitt wrighting to us as we shall be obliged to you for your asistance in all cases to conduct us as we are but indriffrientley sittuated for we have so maney disarters the cause on a count of contribushions but this we dispise for if a man will not contribute to the suport of his fellow shopmates he is better at a distance than preasant.

---

[46] H. O., 42. 77 and H. O., 42. 59.

Amongst disarters Wm. Hall our last president wo has gone to phillipps purposley to instruct his aprentises on acount of wich he is going to ogment them to 30 he is hired for som time at so much pr week to instruct 2 boys at one time and John Welch and Thomas Richards and all the others has reduced there wages 2 pence pr paire wich we you will make as publick through your meetings what villands we have had amongst us—I suppose you have heared of the death of Mr Taylor our last clark wich has put us much about or we should a rote before.

P.S.—at the request of Mr Richardson our Seckeretary I was to inform you of the conduct of Charles Duggeon wo with 2 others dubblin Boot men has gone to our tyrant phillipps a longue with the other scabbs—So I conclude hopeing this will find you in good health.

I *remain yours truley,*
in defence of the trade,

THOS. FREASON.   FYR. CAPPER
   Clark.

This letter from Liverpool brings home to the mind the difficulties that beset working-class organisation at this time. Communication between different sets of people in different parts of the country, knowing comparatively little of each other, presented hard problems to a class in which reading and writing were not common accomplishments. If there had been no Combination Laws, this would not have been too simple a matter. As it was, any letter or messenger might fall into the hands of a magistrate or spy,[47] and to print a manifesto was to give the employer all the evidence he wanted if he wished to prosecute. In the case of the weavers the difficulties were especially serious, for whereas the spinners in the factory or the colliers down the mine were in daily touch with each other, the weavers could not discuss grievances or policy without holding a meeting or publishing some document. Then there was the danger of fraud and embezzlement. The funds of a Trade Union or of a temporary strike combination were at the mercy of any unscrupulous leader, and yet these combinations flourished and strikes were supported, as we have seen, by subscriptions from persons

---

[47] Letters could often be seized by Government warrant at post offices, *e.g.* Post Office warrant, 1812 and 1817 (H. O., 42. 165 and H. O., 42. 163).

with very little money to spare, who knew nothing about the strike leaders. Mrs. Sidney Webb says justly,[48] "It is assuredly to the credit of the English working man that numerous associations, both for trade union and industrial purposes, should have existed continuously for half a century with no other security but the personal honour of members and the personal honesty of officials." Mr. Fortescue, discussing the militia riots of 1809, caused in part by the belief among the working classes that they were being swindled by their officers, makes the following generalisation: "No man likes to be cheated, and no men enjoy it less than those who spend their lives in endeavouring to get the better of their neighbours. No class is so suspicious as the waged class, and thus its feelings are easily worked upon by unscrupulous men."[49] It would be interesting to know whether any other class of English society has ever shown such readiness to trust its fellows as the men and women who subscribed to Trade Unions when they were illegal associations. One working man put as much confidence in the public spirit of the manufacturers as these trade unionists put in the public spirit of their secretaries, and the fate of Samuel Crompton, the inventor of the spinning mule, should be kept in mind by those who blame the working classes, because they were less ready to trust their rulers than their leaders.

---

[48] *The Co-operative Movement*, p. 52.
[49] *County Lieutenancies*, p. 246.

CHAPTER XIII

THE DEFENCES OF THE POOR (II)

THE SPIRIT OF RELIGION

It was in the new industrial districts that the Evangelical revival had the most rapid and lasting influence in building up a religious life outside the Established Church. A Table published in the *Annual Register* for 1824[1] gives the distribution of the members of the Methodist Connexions throughout England. The counties in which the Methodists were strongest were the following: Yorkshire, Lincolnshire, Cornwall, Derby, Durham, Stafford, Nottingham, Leicester, Cheshire, Lancashire. In Yorkshire one person out of 23, in Lancashire one out of 51 was a Methodist; in Surrey the proportion was one to 249, in Sussex one to 211, and in Middlesex one to 152. According to Baines's *Lancashire*[2] there were 292 churches in Lancashire in 1824, 85 Catholic chapels, and 346 Nonconformist chapels.

At the beginning of the Industrial Revolution the Established Church hardly counted in the spiritual life of the districts where mines and factories began to collect these vast populations. In most of the places that were turned from rural solitudes into mining camps or textile towns, the Church scarcely existed for the poor except as the most unrelenting of the forces of law and order. Not, of course, that humane and sympathetic parsons were unknown. We have referred to Hodgson of Jarrow, and his efforts on behalf of the miners; one of the great leaders of the movement for the ten hours' day was the Rev. G. S. Bull, Vicar of Bierley near Bradford; the Vicar of Hinckley preached a sermon in 1820, a report of which was sent to the Home Office as a seditious document,[3] and more than once the parson sided with the workers in a strike. In 1817 the Derbyshire magistrates asked for a warrant against the curate of Pentridge, who had addressed the people at the funeral of a man who had been hung for arson, and declared that the man had been murdered. This curate was also supposed to have given shelter to one of the Derby rioters or traitors. "Woolstonholme," wrote the au-

---

[1] *Annual Register* (1824), Chronicle, p. 180.
[2] Vol. ii. p. 739.
[3] H. O., 44. 8.

thorities, "is of the lowest order of clergymen, uneducated, of vulgar habits, and low connections."[4] But, generally speaking, the parson was first and last a gentleman, and often a magistrate. When Bloomfield became Bishop of Chester in 1824, he was horrified to find that many of his clergy proved their mettle in the society of gentlemen not only in the hunting field by day, but over the bottle at night. Men who had more zeal and an active sense of responsibility threw themselves into their duties as magistrates with an ardour and a thoroughness that made the discontented look upon them as the most unpitying of the justices.[5] In the riots that broke out during the miners' strike in 1822 against a reduction of wages and for the abolition of truck, the Vicar of Abergavenny put himself at the head of the yeomanry and the Greys. He wrote to the Home Office in great spirits about it, adding that all that remained was to apprehend the rioters, "and then I shall be able to return to my Clerical duties." He wrote later that the miners were returning to work slowly because of "sinister influences," and that he had put six of the most obstinate in prison.[6] Lancashire possessed the two richest rectories and the richest vicarage in England: one of these, Rochdale, was given to Parson Hay as a reward for his exertions as a magistrate.[7] Hay was formerly a lawyer, and had thus received a training which had added to his influence as a representative of Christianity on the Bench.

But there was a great tract of this new life into which the Church did not enter at all. In 1792 the Mayor of Liverpool wrote to the Home Office, urging the Government to build churches in the numerous villages that had sprung up with the great growth of manufactures, giving as his reason, not the advantage of spiritual exercises, but the danger of leaving these places to the Methodists. "For, Sir, in all these places are nothing but Methodist and other Meeting Houses, and as the people in the Country are in general disposed to go to some place of

---

[4] H. O., 42. 170.

[5] A correspondent, writing to the Home Office in 1817, noted the great increase of parson magistrates (H. O., 42. 160).

[6] H. O., 40. 17.

[7] See Prentice, *op. cit.*, p. 169. The Bishop of Durham suggested in 1815 that a living should be given to a parson in recognition of his father's activity as a magistrate in the disturbances at South Shields. "The kindest act of remuneration for the father's services would be obtaining, through the Regent, a Chancellor's living for the son" (H. O., 42. 146).

Worship on the Sunday, they go to these because there is none other; and thus the youth of the Country are training up under the instruction of a set of Men not only ignorant, but whom I think we have of late too much reason to imagine are inimical to our happy Constitution."[8] It is interesting to note that the grant of a million for building churches in 1818 was justified on this very ground.[9]

On this population, partly neglected, partly dragooned by the Church, there descended a religion that happened to supply almost everything that it wanted. The Church offered no function to the poor man: his place was on a rude bench or a mat, listening to sermons on the importance of the subordination of the lower classes to the grand family worshipping amid the spacious cushions of the squire's pew. The Chapel invited him to take a hand in the management of the affairs of his religious society: perhaps to help in choosing a minister, to feel that he had a share in its life, responsibility for its risks and undertakings, pride in its successes and reputation. As a mere exercise in self-government and social life, the Chapel occupied a central place in the affections and the thoughts of people who had very little to do with the government of anything else. The management of common enterprises, involving relations with others, bringing in their train friendships, quarrels, reconciliations, all the excitements that spring from the infinite surprises and subtleties of human character, brought too the exchange of ideas and prejudices, not only within a small circle, but outside: the diplomacy and agitation of controversy, the eager and combative discussion of rival doctrines. If there was too little vitality in the Church of the day, nobody could complain that the Chapels, contending for Wesley or Whitefield, were in any danger of falling asleep. Steele distinguished between the Roman Church which said it was infallible, and the English Church which only said it was always right. There was no paralysing hesitation in the Calvinists who excommunicated Wesley, and the famous prayer that Toplady launched at him, the prayer that "He in

---

[8] H. O., 42. 20.

[9] In 1816 a gentleman wrote from Preston with regard to the proposal to build these churches, that he hoped they would appoint energetic young clergymen who could keep in touch with families of labouring classes, and so "strengthen a Link in Society almost broken in some Districts, and which has by its want of support enabled the Dissenters to extend themselves as they have done" (H. O., 42. 151).

whose hands the hearts of all men are, may make even this opposer of grace a monument of His almighty power to save," would have done credit to the self-confidence of either Church, or to the ecclesiastics who wrestled in hot and angry conflict for three days before that cultivated man of the world, Æneas Sylvius, over the question whether the blood shed by Christ during the Passion had or had not lost the hypostatic power of the Logos. The men and women who were drawn into the brisk, alert, and ardent life of the new religion found plenty to occupy their minds and to stimulate faculties and interests that were otherwise left neglected.[10]

For the Methodist movement carried the self-governing tradition of the old Nonconformist Chapel, which had shared in some degree the cold and calm philosophy of the Church, into a wider world and touched that world with a living passion. The old Jewish civilisation became actual and vivid to the men and women who listened to the rhetoric of the new type of preacher. The Sunday-schools, that spread rapidly over the north of England and the industrial districts, were primarily institutions for interpreting this civilisation to children brought up in factories and mines. These schools were not, of course, peculiar to the Nonconformist societies. Readers of *Shirley* will remember the great Whit Monday scene, when Mr. Helstone and his marching Sunday-school, playing "Rule, Britannia!" put to flight "the unholy alliance" of Baptists, Independents, and Methodists, who stepped out to the less bracing tone of a dolorous canticle given out by a fat dissenter, a spirit merchant by trade, who was said to have drunk more water in that one afternoon than he had swallowed for a twelvemonth before. But the great motive force in the founding and developing of these institutions had been the periodic Revival. A Revival fed the imagination of the new population on the exciting history of a fierce and warlike race living under conditions very unlike those of Manchester or Leeds, leaving a literature rich in metaphor and image, which awakened amid the bare and colourless life of the new civilisation dreams and reveries and visions full of awe and splendour. It is significant that this religion spread most quickly, and in its most extreme form, among the workers living in the deepest

---

[10] Cf. amongst the papers found on Pilkington, one of the Habeas Corpus prisoners of 1817, a discussion of Manichæism, that " 'orrid doctrine" . . . "that the good and evil that was in the world was the effects of two hopposit principles in the deety" (H. O., 40. 9).

gloom, for the miners were particularly given to Methodism. Perhaps the very dangers of their employment prompted them to seek this special and miraculous sense of protection, just as the belief in the miraculous salvation of religion is particularly strong among the deep-sea fishermen of Brittany.[11] This religion did for the working class what Greek and Roman literature did for the ruling class: drawing aside the curtain from a remote and interesting world, seeming thus to make their own world more intelligible. For the miner or weaver, the Chapel with its summons to the emotions, its music and singing, took the place that theatres, picture galleries, operas, occupied in the lives of others.[12]

There was, however, a deeper element in the fitness and relevance of the new religion. It can perhaps be described best by recalling a passage from Professor Gilbert Murray's discussion of Greek religion: "Any one who turns from the great writers of classical Athens, say Sophocles or Aristotle, to those of the Christian era, must be conscious of a great difference in tone. There is a change in the whole relation of the writer to the world about him. The new quality is not specifically Christian: it is just as marked in the Gnostics and Mithras-worshippers as in the Gospels and the Apocalypse, in Julian and Plotinus as in Gregory and Jerome. It is hard to describe. It is a rise of asceticism, of mysticism, in a sense, of pessimism; a loss of self-confidence, of hope in this life and of faith in normal human effort; a despair of patient inquiry, a cry for infallible revelation; an indifference to the welfare of the State, a conversion of the soul to God. It is an atmosphere in which the aim of the good man is not so much to live justly, to help the society to which he belongs and enjoy the esteem of his fellow creatures; but rather, by means of a burning faith, by contempt for the world and its standards, by ecstasy, suffering and martyrdom, to be

---

[11] See *Les Pêcheurs d'Islande*.

[12] It is significant that Cooke Taylor found that Ashton was the metropolis of the followers of Joanna Southcote. He gave as one reason for the greater popularity of Nonconformity in the north than in the south, that "there is a spice of the wild man in the foresters of Rosendale and Pendle." His appreciation of the advantages that Nonconformity derived from the system of giving functions to laymen made him favourable to Dr. Arnold's plan for copying this in the Church of England (*Tour in the Manufacturing Districts*, pp. 230, 292, 294).

granted pardon for his unspeakable unworthiness, his immeas-
urable sins."[13]

Now the England of 1800 belonged to both of these ages,
for the ruling class lived in the atmosphere of Sophocles, and
the poor in the atmosphere of Epictetus or St. Paul. The governing class consisted of gentlemen who were not merely politicians
and sportsmen. No stories of their dissipations can obscure the
truth that they were essentially men of taste and refinement,
who enjoyed nothing more than talking about literature, the
meaning of words, the ideas of writers, or history, or pictures, or
travel. They were at least as happy in a library as they were in
the saddle or round the card table. They knew what they liked,
they were at ease about their taste, they could act as patrons of
art and letters with the security of persons trusting their own
judgment rather than the nervous capriciousness of persons following anybody's judgment in preference to their own. They
found the world interesting, satisfying, and complete. This
happy and well-rounded civilisation proved its power not only
at the time but the spell it has cast over later generations. If
we could forget the boys of six buried for fourteen hours out
of the twenty-four in Lord Melbourne's mines, or the Wiltshire
labourers suffering a lifelong exile from their homes for refusing
to keep body and soul together any longer on cold potatoes, we
might feel as those gentlemen felt—for some of them could put
this background from their minds as successfully as some of
Sophocles' contemporaries could overlook the truth about slavery
—that no age had better reason to be contented with its life and
conduct. This life found its religious expression in a calm, dis-
passionate optimism. The extreme theories of eternal punishment
were forbidden by good taste and an instinctive respect for the
normal. Violent contention over doctrine had no attraction for
a class that cared much more for literature than for metaphysics,
for light verses than for heavy argument. Their own age had
found the key to every problem, and the revelations of Locke
were worth all the revelations of religion. Thackeray said of
Sterne's sermons that they had not a single Christian sentiment.
The ruling class found more reason to complain when Crabbe
introduced heaven and hell into his discourses, and begged him
to leave those extravagances to Methodists and confine his teaching to the prudence and reasonableness of virtue during this
life. Religion was, in fact, part of the civil constitution of society. The English Church accepted that position. It knew its

---

[13] *Four Stages of Greek Religion*, p. 103.

place in the domestic establishments of the State, and it took its colour for good and for evil from the world of the ruling class. It had no persecuting spirit,[14] no patience with emotion, no curiosity about doctrine, no prejudice against "this wicked world." Above all, it did not obtrude any view of life that made men less able or less likely to enjoy it.

The working classes had no use for this religion. They did not find themselves in a world of congenial occupation, with leisure graced by art and literature, rounded off by the polite worship of reasonableness and moderation that chose to call itself Christianity. Life did not seem to them the simple flow of satisfactory and sensible consequences from satisfactory and sensible causes. For them, as a great scholar said of the age of Marcus Aurelius, "Le monde s'attristait." Many things existed or happened that called for an explanation or a protest. Moreover, while the ruling class looked with composure on a civilisation that they guided, elegant masters of their world, the working classes were conscious of an overwhelming burden in the mass and power of the forces that seemed to hold them captive, and to reduce their place in the scheme of the universe to one of mean and helpless insignificance. A religion that tended to be little more than a religion of manners, teaching its adherents to admire the framework of a world made and ordered by a Providence of good taste and discreet conduct, offered neither explanation nor consolation in the depths of the mine or the heat and rage of the furnace. Sophocles taught a religion for citizens, for men with power and responsibility, with some control over their lives, a religion that could make citizenship a sacred calling, and add a new sanction to the claims of patriotism. But the miner or weaver was not a citizen; he had no power; he seemed the slave of the sternest destiny, and the good working religion of the mean, the religion of normal life, bore no relation to his circumstances. What he wanted was a religion that recognised that the world did not explain itself, and that it was full of seeming paradox and injustice and tragedy, for men and women ground beneath a power to which no man could assign limits, looked to religion for rescue from bondage, for an assurance that their obscure lives had some significance and moment.[15] This release they found in the spirit that had comforted the

---

[14] Down to the French Revolution. From that time it became intolerant but not from a religious spirit.

[15] Readers of Mrs. Gaskell's *North and South* will recall Higgins's outburst after his daughter's death.

poor and the perplexed of the human race whenever the facts
of life seemed to throw too violent a discredit on the justice of
heaven. The Methodists told the miners what Seneca told the
unhappy rich in the Claudian Terror, or Epictetus had told an
age seeking for new reconciliations amid the ruins of the old
religions, or St. Augustine had told the distracted peoples of
Europe after the sack of Rome, that every man carried within
him his own fate, and that the sovereign happiness of all, the
happiness of faith and resignation, was not the prize of wealth
or power or learning or conquest, but of a state of mind and
heart that poor could attain as readily as rich; the slave as readily
as his master. "Even to the poor, the lame, the blind, if they have
the divine love, the universe is a great temple, full of mystery
and joy, and each passing day a festival," was the message of
Epictetus.[16] "Whom the Lord Loveth He chasteneth," was the
message of Wesley. "God has the love of a father for good men,
and from love of them He orders that they shall be afflicted
with toil, sorrow, and hardship, that they may find their true
strength. . . . It is not what man bears, but how he bears it
that matters,"[17] was the message of Seneca. And whereas the
ruling class could not imagine a heaven that would be any improvement on this world, the Methodists taught that heaven was
the Fifth Act of a great drama in which patient and pious en-
durance of afflictions in this life will receive their reward and
man's desire for justice its final satisfaction.

What was the effect of this religion on the mind of the working classes? Many magistrates wrote to the Home Office that it
helped to make them discontented and to strengthen the forces
of working-class organisation. Thus the Vicar of Sandal near
Wakefield, writing in 1819, asserted that the greater part of the
people called Methodists were united with the Radicals, that
under the pretence of religious worship they met in private
houses, some of them houses licensed under the Toleration Act,
and formed plans for advancing wages. The Vicar wanted an
amendment of the Toleration Act.[18] The Nottinghamshire magistrates were much alarmed by the popularity of ranters' meet-

---

16 Dill, *Roman Society*, p. 393.
17 "Patrium habet Deus adversus bonos viros animum, et illos
fortiter amat; et operibus, inquit, doloribus, ac damnis exagitentur, ut
verum colligant robur. . . . Non quid sed quemadmodum feras interest" (*De Providentia*, ii.).
18 H. O., 42. 200.

ings in 1817, and took the advice of the law-officers about forbidding them.[19] Other magistrates, particularly parsons, thought the Government ought to watch them. But magistrates were not discriminating when discussing obnoxious persons or movements, and the term Methodist served as well as the very different term Jacobin for a description of the disreputable. Hannah More complained that malevolent critics even applied the term to her respectable philanthropy. Those who read more closely will observe that whenever any particular person is mentioned as seditious, he generally turns out to be a Baptist or Presbyterian.[20] The Dissenters had always been more or less radical, and a parson magistrate had a quick sense for sedition in those quarters. One parson wrote in 1798 that he was surrounded by Dissenters, who, though they thought it prudent to conceal their sentiments, were not to be trusted. He added that it was a misfortune that his living was so small, as his influence suffered in consequence.[21] The energetic Dr. Booker, Vicar of Dudley, took a gloomy view of the prospects of those who could find no room in his church. They have to go without God, he wrote, "or go to some of those Sectarian places of Worship, which are so promptly open to receive them: places, I am grieved to say, whither Traitors and Murderers think they may resort as to a Sanctuary from their crimes, and blaspheme a God of Righteousness and Purity by their addresses to his throne." He adds, however, "All sects are not included in this censure. Some I believe to be pious, exemplary, and loyal."[22] Those persons who had the good fortune to secure seats in Dr. Booker's church could during the service contemplate the Arms of the Prince

<hr>

[19] H. O., 42. 166.

[20] E.g. in 1793 in Manchester, the Presbyterians were supposed to be corrupting the Scots Greys (H. O., 42. 25). There is a letter from Bishop Horsley to Pitt saying that Dr. Stennett, who had just died, had been in charge of the money called "The King's Gift," a fund of £2,000 distributed among the Dissenting teachers of the different denominations. The choice of a successor was important, as if put in the right hands the sum might be of much benefit to Government. He wished to recommend a Mr. Martin, a "Particular Baptist." The Particular Baptists were unlike the Presbyterians and Independents, and were quiet and orderly people: Mr. Martin had been a strenuous opponent of the application to Parliament for the repeal of the Test and Corporation Acts (*Chatham MSS.*, 146).

[21] H. O., 42. 42.

[22] H. O., 42. 174.

Regent emblazoned on one of the principal windows of the "fine Gothic Sanctuary."[23]

The other point of view was also put before the Home Office and Parliament. The celebrated Methodist leader Dr. Coke wrote to the Duke of Portland in 1801: "I was not a little alarmed two or three days ago in hearing that three Methodists were taken up on suspicion or proof of being engaged in this rebellion business. But on the strictest scrutiny and fullest satisfaction, I was happy enough to find that these three men had been expelled the late Mr. Wesley's Society about five years ago solely for their democratic sentiments."[24] Joseph Butterworth, the well-known Wesleyan philanthropist, wrote to the Home Office, at the time of the Luddite disturbances, to complain of the arrest of a Methodist preacher near Bolton, for preaching in an unlicensed house. He argued that it was a very foolish proceeding to disturb the religious societies. "I have had ample information that the lower orders who are not religiously inclined are in a very disaffected, discontented state, and are almost ripe for a general revolt."[25] Butterworth's impressions were confirmed by a statement made by Brougham in the House of Commons when criticising the Preservation of the Public Peace Bill.[26] Brougham stated that the Methodists had proved themselves "lovers of peace." A charitable association, to which he belonged, was engaged in relieving distress in the worst districts in the bad times. At one place where the association had offered help, they had been told that the distress was so extensive that the whole fund of the association would not suffice, that every one was out of work, and that there had been no disorder. This was attributed to "the happy prevalence of the Principles of Methodism." A similar testimony was given to the effect of Wesleyan teaching on the Cornish miners during the riots of that year,[27] and in 1819 a Mr. Marris of Ardwick sent up handbills to show that the Wesleyan Methodists were loyal "even in Manchester." He mentioned that certain Sunday-schools had been started, in opposition to the Methodists, by a man who

---

[23] H. O., 42. 172.

[24] H. O., 42. 61. Stephens, the Chartist orator, had originally been expelled from the Wesleyans for attacking the factory system (Dolléans, op. cit., i. p. 170).

[25] H. O., 42. 124.

[26] House of Commons, July 13, 1812.

[27] Political Register, April 25, 1812.

had been expelled from the Methodist society, "because he had imbibed the principles of French Jacobinism."[28]

In the condition of England during the second half of the period discussed in this book it was not easy for the upper classes to regard any movement for reform as other than a turbulent and destructive agitation. The rulers of the Wesleyan Conference were in the same case. In 1817 an appeal was made to the Methodists to support reform, and they were reminded of their success in thwarting Sidmouth's invasion of their liberties in 1800.[29] But the Methodist leaders replied by warning their congregations to keep away from Reform meetings.[30] In August 1819 one of the secretaries of the Wesleyan Missionary Society sent to the Home Office the text of an address adopted at a Conference of Methodist Ministers at Bristol. The Address after speaking of the great distress of the time went on to condemn the agitation for reform conducted by "unreasonable and wicked men" and urged Methodists to remember that they "belong to a Religious Society which has, from the beginning, explicitly recognised as high and essential parts of Christian duty to 'Fear God and honour the King; to submit to magistrates for conscience' sake, and not to speak evil of dignities'." This address was typical of the temper of the official leaders then and for long afterwards. Dr. Wearmouth says that "with the formation of political societies in the winter of 1816–17, Methodism as practised by the Wesleyans openly abandoned its neutrality. Until the middle of the century opposition to working class societies became a leading feature of Methodist activity among the Wesleyan preachers."[31] How far this hostility was carried we can see from the behaviour of the Wesleyan ministers in Manchester after Peterloo. That outrage had united Whig and radical leaders in indignant criticism of the Government. Lord Fitzwilliam was removed from the office of Lord Lieutenant of the West Riding because he presided over a great meeting of protest. But Sidmouth was upheld by the Manchester Wesleyan ministers and a local preacher was expelled because he signed the "Manchester Declaration" against the magistrates. It is curi-

---

28 H. O., 42. 198.
29 For history of that attempt, see G. M. Trevelyan, *Clio, and other Essays*, p. 114.
30 H. O., 42. 161, and H. O., 42. 164.
31 *Methodism and the Working Class Movements*, 1800–1850, p. 176.

ous to find that the Minister who took the chair at the meeting at which this expulsion was pronounced was the father of J. R. Stephens, notorious for his advocacy of physical force during the Chartist agitation.[32]

The hostility of the Methodist leaders provoked recriminations from the Reformers. Cobbett writing in 1824 described the Methodists as "the bitterest foes of freedom in England. Amongst the people of the north they have served as spies and blood-money men. . . . The friends of freedom have found fault, and justly found fault with the main body of the established clergy . . . but, hostile to freedom as the established clergy have been, their hostility has been nothing in point of virulence compared with that of these ruffian sectarians. . . . Books upon books they write. Tracts upon tracts. Villainous sermons upon villainous sermons they preach. Rail they do, like Cropper and Bott Smith, against the West Indian slave-holders; but not a word do you ever hear from them against the slave-holders in Lancashire and in Ireland. On the contrary, they are continually telling the people here that they ought to thank the Lord for the blessings they enjoy: that they ought to thank the Lord, not for a bellyful and a warm back, but for that abundant grace of which they are the bearers, and for which they charge them only one penny per week each."[33]

Cobbett splashed his accusations pretty freely when he disliked a class or a man, and as he expresses his regret in this same article that hooligans are no longer allowed to break up Methodist meetings, asking for what else rotten eggs were meant, his statement that the spies were Methodists could not be accepted without confirmation from other sources. There is no hint to that effect in any of the Home Office papers on the subject. But his general view of the attitude of the Methodists and their influence, if it breaks out with a rage and vehemence peculiarly his own, does not differ from the accounts of his contemporaries.[34]

This political campaign was not the only obstacle that Methodism offered to the working class movement for industrial and political reform. Methodism provided remedies for distress and injustice that made many of its devotees less likely to accept the remedies sought by that movement. The brutal inequalities of

[32] Op. cit., p. 182.
[33] Political Register, January 3, 1824.
[34] See, for example, the address quoted in chapter xv.

life, the wrongs inflicted by man on man, the hardships of poverty and destitution, the conditions that stirred Stendhal so deeply when he visited England in the early twenties,[35] all these were to the Methodist passing vexations, a trial of faith for the Christian who could sustain his spirit on the sublime mysteries of his religion. Among the Home Office papers bearing on the distress and discontent of 1819 the reader comes upon a copy of the *Leeds Independent* containing side by side announcements of a great Reform meeting on Hunslet Moor and of a Methodist meeting at Skipton assembled to pass the following resolution: "This meeting deeply deplores the moral and religious state of the world, but especially of the Pagans, the Mohammedans and the Jews."[36] The original Methodist movement broke up into several bodies as one set of devotees after another took fire over some particular doctrine or principle, and each new body tended to carry further this missionary spirit, the habit of forgetting the new Manchester in contemplation of the New Jerusalem. The early history of the Primitive Methodist Connexion reads like the history of the early Christians in its sense of isolation from the world and its expectation of an imminent Day of Judgment. Its ardent apostles would certainly have said with Tertullian *Nec ulla res magis aliena quam publica.*[37] George Eliot described in *Felix Holt* a Methodist congregation of "eager men and women, to whom the exceptional possession of religious truth was the condition that reconciled them to a meagre existence, and made them feel in secure alliance with the unseen but supreme ruler of a world in which their own visible part was small."

In such an atmosphere the ardent Methodist teacher believed that Christians should seek not the reform of their material conditions but the ecstatic vision, the perfect peace of expectation. The Trade Union movement taught that men and women should try to use their power to destroy the uncontrolled power

---

[35] Stendhal gave it as his opinion that the state of the English poor was more wretched than that of the poor in Italy. (*Letters from London* in his published correspondence.)

[36] H. O., 42. 188.

[37] See Petty's *History of the Primitive Methodist Connexion.* When public affairs are mentioned at their conferences it is to thank God that England is not the seat of war, or that she has escaped the horrors of the Irish rebellion. The rising of the labourers in Hampshire in 1830 is alluded to without any semblance of pity for their treatment and punishment (pp. 21, 342).

of wealth in a world made by man; the Methodist that they should learn resignation amid the painful chaos of a world so made to serve the inscrutable purposes of God. The trade unionist taught that men were not so helpless as they seemed, for combination could give them some influence over the conditions of their lives. The Methodist taught that men were not so helpless as they seemed for religion could make them independent of the conditions of their lives. In this sense the two movements were rivals bidding against each other for the minds and the hearts of the great industrial population. In the great movement of enthusiasm and hope that followed the passing of the Reform Bill of 1832 the building trades of Birmingham conceived the project of establishing a great Hall to be at once a meeting place, a school for adults and children, a retreat for the old and a benefit Club. *The Pioneer*, commenting on this scheme, remarked: "This, we believe, will be the first successful attempt on the part of the operatives of England to possess their own place of assembly. We say THEIR OWN; for the Mechanics' Institutes already established in this country are anything but such though we are willing to admit that in many instances they have been productive of good." How many chapels had been built by working-class pennies before 1833?

In these ways Methodism discouraged or hindered the working-class efforts for parliamentary reform and the relaxation of the Combination Laws. Yet Methodism was to prove an important training ground for democracy. It produced great social reformers like Sadler, Shaftesbury's predecessor as parliamentary leader of the movement for reducing the working day in the factories. For it gave to men who undertook a public cause the courage and tenacity that are inspired by a sense of a religious mission. Moreover it created democratic communities in a world where power was in the hands of a small class, and those communities, unlike the Trade Unions, were not molested by the authorities. The technique, the methods and the organisation of these different Methodist bodies, with their camp meetings, their classes, their circuits had a profound effect on the Trade Unions, and later, on the Labour movement. The early Methodists introduced the practice of teaching writing in their Sunday-schools. Bamford describes the men and women who attended the Methodist school at Middleton where he was taught, and it is easy to imagine how valuable men who had learnt to write were to the early trade unions. The Church, according to Bamford, never taught the teaching of writing in its Sunday-schools, and the Wesleyan Methodists dropped it, no doubt from a fear of the uses to which working men might put their skill. Bamford says that the result of this deplorable decision was seen in the census of 1841 in which Lancashire had a larger proportion of persons unable to write their names than several counties with fewer means of instruction.[38] The Methodist society gave opportunities to poor men to learn to speak in public, to organise common effort, and to take part in government and administration. So Methodism, if it preached Toryism in its official declarations and a pietism that thought only of the next world in many of its chapels, was in fact an admirable school for democrats, equipping working men for popular leadership. The results were seen in the early days of trade unionism. Hepburn, the heroic leader of the Northumberland Miners in the great struggle of 1830 and 1831, was a local preacher, and of the six Tolpuddle martyrs five were Methodists. Thus Methodism, unfavourable and even actively hostile in some of its aspects, helped to build up a democratic structure for society by the life and energy and spiritual awakening that it brought to the first victims of the Industrial Revolution.

---

[38] Bamford, *Passages in the Life of a Radical*, i. 100.

CHAPTER XIV

THE MIND OF THE POOR

When the French Revolution broke out there was no resemblance between the spirit of the working classes in the north and the Midlands, and the spirit of the Paris democrat, on fire with vivid and emancipating enthusiasms. The English working classes in the centres of the new industry were conservative, insular, Philistine. Manchester, like Birmingham, was predominantly Church and King; and nobody who reads Bamford's description of the treatment his father and his father's friends received at Middleton will make the mistake of supposing that the Reformers whom Pitt persecuted were dangerous to the State by reason of their popularity. The working classes, as a body, in the north and the Midlands were profoundly indifferent to ideas or causes. So long as they could drink, watch a cock-fight or bull-baiting or horse-race, and earn a reasonable living, they were as contented as the squires whose tastes, if rather more expensive, were in kind not dissimilar. No visions exalted or disturbed their souls, and the *sansculottes* of Bolton or Wigan were as ready as the parsons or the squires to put anybody who talked or looked like a French Jacobin into the nearest or the darkest horsepond.

By the end of our period a great change had come over the working classes. They had become what Pitt and Castlereagh tried so hard to prevent them from becoming, politicians. They talked about the affairs of the State: they discussed the basis of rights and duties, they took an ominous interest in taxes and sinecures, and it was not the phrases of 1789 but the cry of Church and King that awakened their execrations. All the efforts of civilisation seemed to have been made in vain when the one question that absorbed the minds of the factory workers as they poured from the mills was the question whether Cobbett's *Political Register* had come with the latest coach.

The working classes were brought to the revolutionary temper that broke out in 1816 and 1830, and found its most complete expression in the gospel of the Chartists,[1] through a number of

---

[1] The Chartist movement throws an important light on the previous half-century, as it represents the climax of the struggles of the working-class mind.

stages. They were not converted by a lightning flash or by the magic of a phrase or by some gradual and liberating philosophy. What came about during this period was the alienation of the working classes, due not to the positive influence of ideas or enthusiasms, but to the effect of experience on ways of thinking and looking at life. To say this is not to detract from the superb and essential services to the development of working-class thinking of such men as Paine, Cobbett, and Place, and the lesser lights of the Reform movements: it is merely to recognise the truth that their teaching only bore fruit when actual experience had made men ready to receive it. There was no general revolt against the established order in 1790. The normal working man accepted the government and institutions of the country with as little question as the normal aristocrat. But the Industrial Revolution obliged everybody whom it affected to think about the problems it raised, and when they addressed themselves to these problems the rich and the poor started from different standpoints: the rich from the abstractions of property, the poor from the facts of their own lives. As a result there developed two different systems of morality. For it makes a great difference whether experience is passed through the sieve of hypothesis and theory, or whether hypothesis and theory are passed through the sieve of experience. The upper-class explanations ceased to be satisfying to men and women who wanted to know why they were starving in the midst of great wealth. Cobbett and Paine were intelligible to them and became their guides, just because they regarded society as existing for human needs, and asked of each institution not whether it was essential to an elaborate theory of property, but how it served men and women.

In the earlier years of the period with which we deal the working classes were inarticulate and illiterate, without leaders or spokesmen, but we can learn a good deal about their temper and their outlook on the changing world around them from the threatening letters or placards of the time. These documents form a good part of the papers of the Home Office during the years of famine at the end of the eighteenth and the beginning of the nineteenth centuries. Popular bitterness is mainly directed against farmers and dealers. Thus a confused and abusive paper about high prices, circulated in Swansea in 1793, begins, "Resolutions of all the poor who live by their daily labour, both in the Town and Country and a sincere Caution to all the petty Merchants who has no dependancy but makes a Trade by imposing upon the poor. . . ."[2]

Frequently the threatening papers took the form of doggerel rhymes. One from the Portsmouth Dockyard in 1800 runs as follows:—

"Farmers, Bakers, Butchers likewise,
An example there is put before your eyes.
It is the pride of your heart to see the poor starving,
You that have got a plenty do not care a farthing.

. . . .
. . . .

These Big dons will do just as they please,
They would make the poor believe the moon is green cheese.
If the yard will all be true and stand to these Rules
We will soon let them know who is the biggest fools."[3]

Another paper stuck up within the Portsmouth garrison gate, with three halters beside it, began:—

"A caution
To the Farmer, Miller, and Baker.
Here's Three you see,
Each of you take your Choice.
The greatest Rogue
May have the greatest Hoist."[4]

But it was not only the farmers and dealers that were assailed in these philippics. The writer of a threatening letter sent up from Devonshire, commenting on the saying of some local woman, "that Barley Bread and Tatoes was good enough for us Poor," took a broader and deeper view when he said, "God sent Meat into the World for us Poor as well as Rich and not to be starved alive."[5] Some successful food riots at Nottingham in 1800 were described in enthusiastic terms by a sympathiser.[6] The price, he says, was lowered "by nothing but the courage of the people in Declaring against Oppression, but what scarred the Gentlemen the most was to see the Union of parties their being

---

[2] H. O., 42. 24.
[3] H. O., 42. 50.
[4] H. O., 42. 51.
[5] H. O., 42. 50.
[6] See intercepted letter from T. E. Golby (H. O., 42. 51).

no Scrats nor painites nor no such song as God save the King to be heard, and the conduct of the people on tuesday who Stood the fire from the Yeomanry with such an Undaunted Courage that astonished the Gentlemen. . . . P.S.—I am told that the Gentlemen said if the Farmer could not live when it was Lowered they would Sink his Rent. Thus has two Species of Vilains been Brought to Reason by the Courage of the Tradesmen and Inhabitants of Nottingham. . . ."

The ruling class thought that the poor had to bear misfortunes, but that these misfortunes were greatly alleviated by the charity of the rich. In the documents that reflect the spirit of the working classes no language is more bitter and violent in tone than the language that alludes to alms and soup. Perhaps the most interesting paper of this sort, with its allusion to the improving advice of "the soup-maker," is one which was posted in the market place at Hitchin in 1800:—

"Advice to all poor tradesmen and labourers. With one consent lay all work aside and meet together in a body and see what is to be done in this case; for your work, all you can do, will not support you and your family. Your vile oppressors, see how they use ye; what yoke of bondage you are brought under. Be not afraid of horse nor standing arms but come forth with courage and resolution. If you give way to those villains you (will) always be bound under these chains wherein your liberty and freedom is entirely lost. Nothing's to be done without you take this step. Some may pretend to smooth and calm you, for here's our Soupmaker may come with doctrine of fine speech, as 'keeping a clean house' and 'the wife to give a smile.' Send him to where he comes from, and when we want him we will send for him. If nothing better can be done than already is I'd wish every man to leave his family and let the D—d Heathen do as they will, for why should we starve in a land where there is plenty, never themore. As a well wisher,

God bless the King."[7]

Colonel Fletcher of Bolton was scandalised by the bad taste of the Bolton weavers who carried through the streets the effigy

[7] H. O., 42. 49. The punctuation has been inserted and the spelling altered.

of an old worn-out soldier calling for soup.[8] Discontent took a more aggressive form at Wigan, and the Charity Committee was interrupted in the midst of its deliberations by a volley of stones from the objects of its proposed benevolence.[9] Pitt could persuade the House of Commons of anything with the charming simplicity of his formula that wages and prices must be left to find their own level. It had not occurred to him or to his hearers that the term could have any other meaning than the meaning they gave to it; but during a food riot in Oxford one speaker incited the mob to take things into their own hands, using Pitt's own formula as his justification. The farmers, he argued, were relying on the protection of the volunteers to keep their corn in their barns, and wait for starvation prices. The intervention of the mob was needed to readjust the balance to bring back prices to their natural level.[10] When the House of Commons discussed low wages they were apt to think of them as mere symptoms or incidents of an economic system. During a strike in the Midlands, a letter sent to a notorious sweater of women drew attention to another side of the question. The employer was asked whether he did not think that wages of half a crown a week would necessarily drive women to prostitution.[11]

The first rebel note that was sounded in this population was this note of hunger: it is aimed at farmers, dealers, and other persons suspected of profiteering. A more general and serious discontent followed the discovery that Parliament had no ear for working-class wrongs. For it was to Parliament that the workmen looked, and looked, at first, with some confidence. They began by asking Parliament to use its powers and to put in force existing laws and regulations, designed, as they believed, for their protection—laws regulating wages and the conditions of apprentices. This policy had, of course, no flavour of revolution about it, and the men who proposed it had no quarrel with society and no sympathy with the discontents of Reformers. But the policy was rejected by Parliament. The full story is told in *The Skilled Labourer* 1760–1832. Here we will only give an account of the treatment of a petition from the calico printers in 1804, because it shows the strength of *laissez-faire* prejudice,

---

[8] H. O., 42. 153.
[9] H. O., 42. 154.
[10] H. O., 42. 51.
[11] H. O., 42. 120.

for the petition received powerful support from a House of Commons Committee.

In 1804[12] a petition was presented to Parliament from journeymen calico printers in Lancashire, Derbyshire, Cheshire, Stafford, and in five Scottish counties, complaining of the excessive multiplication of apprentices which had become a great cause of unemployment. The men urged that the current price for the sale of goods was based on a wage of 30s. a week, which was the wage of adults, and apprentices were only paid from 4s. to 7s. The masters were, in fact, flooding the trade with cheap labour, and the journeymen who had served their apprenticeships found themselves deprived of employment. Under this arrangement the masters got all the benefits without observing any of the obligations of the apprenticeship system.

The petition was recommended to the House of Lords by so stern and uncompromising an economist as Lord King. The petition was referred to a select committee in the Commons, and the evidence that was given showed that there were some 900 apprentices to 1500 journeymen in Lancashire, Cheshire, Derbyshire, and Stafford. The sufferings of the men driven out of employment were made all the worse by the Combination Laws which had destroyed their benevolent funds. The committee adjourned without reporting, in spite of protests from Sheridan in the House of Commons,[13] but the minutes of evidence were published. Next year there was another petition without result,[14] but in 1806 the minutes of evidence already taken were referred to a select committee,[15] which reported in July. The Report,[16] which may be attributed with good reason to Sheridan, who had taken up the cause of these workmen in Parliament, is one of the most remarkable documents of the time, and the spirit in which economic topics are discussed distinguishes it from almost every other publication that emanated at this time from parliamentary committees:—

"Without entering into the delicate and difficult question, as to the distribution of profits between Masters and Journeymen, in this as well as the other mechanical professions, your Committee may venture to throw out, for the consideration of the

---

[12] February 22.
[13] *Parliamentary Register*, June 27, 1804.
[14] *House of Commons Journal*, March 1, 1805.
[15] *House of Commons Journal*, July 9, 1806.
[16] Report of Committee on Calico Printers, 1806.

House, whether it be quite equitable towards the parties or con-
ducive to the public interest, that on the one part there should
arise a great accumulation of wealth, while on the other there
should prevail a degree of poverty from which the parties cannot
emerge by the utmost exertion of industry, skill, and assiduous
application, and may, at an advanced period of life, notwithstanding perpetual labour, be obliged to resort to parish aid for
the support of their families. Is it just that such a state of things
should be permitted to exist? Is it fair towards the Landed Interest in these districts in which Manufactories are established,
that they should be called upon to contribute from the Poor
Rates to the support of the families of those who ought to be
enabled to derive a support from their labour, and who are at
the same time contributing to establish a fortune for the Principals of such Manufactories? The application of these remarks is
obvious: the utmost earnings of a Journeyman Calico Printer, as
appears by the Minutes referred to your Committee, does not
exceed 30s. a week, and the general average is about 25s. With
every consideration, then, for the risk of capital, the exertion and
anxiety of superior mind which may be supposed to belong to
the Principals of a Calico Printing Manufactory, your Committee submit, that in such a lucrative Trade 25s. or 30s. a week is
a very inadequate compensation to Journeymen: but how must
the House feel, when they reflect that even that compensation
is precarious?"

The Report concludes by declaring that either all restrictions
should be abolished or else additional restrictions about apprentices introduced, on the lines of the Spitalfields regulations. Under those regulations the proportion of apprentices to journeymen was 37 to 216, whereas in Lancashire, Derby, etc., it was
1 to 1. Next spring Sheridan introduced a Bill[17] to forbid a
master calico printer from taking more than a certain number of
apprentices, and from taking any without a regular legal indenture. His only support came from Peter Moore, the Radical
member for Coventry, a consistent advocate of the minimum
wage; he was opposed by Sir Robert Peel (who was himself in this connection a bad employer), Henry Erskine, and
Horner.[18] His Bill was rejected apparently without a division.

The weavers, who were originally a conservative element,
were always pressing for a minimum wage, and the treatment

---

[17] Printed March 25, 1807.
[18] *Parliamentary Register*, April 23, 1807.

of their case by Parliament had a great effect in embittering
and educating working-class opinion. A letter from the Stockport weavers to the magistrates tells the story of the conduct of
the House of Commons as that conduct appeared to the workpeople.[19]

The weavers said that their troubles began with the French
War. "The Weavers, urged by the difficulties with which they
were surrounded, took means of laying their case before the
Legislature and humbly prayed for protection from the ruin
which threatened to overwhelm them, they suggested the utility
of fixing a minimum on the price of their Labour but their
petitions were of no use to them and their applications of no
avail, the Weavers then imagined that if the apprentice Law was
enforced it might be of some benefit to their trade by restraining
the influx of hands, but as soon as they attempted to have re-
course to this measure the apprentice Law was entirely abrogated. The Weavers then turned their attention to the Law
which enabled Magistrates to fix the rate of provisions according
to the price of Labour, but no sooner did they seek the protection
of that salutory law than that law was quickly abrogated and
destroyed. . . . When the Weavers petitioned the Government
for bread it gave them a stone, or in other words by those of
whom the Weavers sought protection, they have been awarded
with punishment."

The hand-loom weavers never discarded the policy of State
regulation, and they were still pressing for it, many years after
the Reform Bill, with the help of John Fielden. The reason is
obvious. Hand-loom weaving was not a mysterious or difficult
art. It did not call for special qualities of mind or body: only
for personal industry applied for a very long working day in the
home of the workman and his family. Consequently it was the
natural refuge for the unsuccessful and the dispossessed of other
trades, and it was as true of this industry as of home-work industries to-day, that the workmen and workwomen could not
maintain their standard of life against a flood of immigrants.
Framework knitting was in the same position. Both hand-loom
weavers and frame-work knitters needed specially a minimum
wage, because the conditions of their occupations made effective
organisation almost impossible. For the spinners and the miners,
on the other hand, the chief means of success was full liberty to
combine. They could meet easily, they could picket, and, as they

[19] H. O., 42. 188.

were not living permanently on the brink of starvation, they could sustain a strike. They might hope indeed, when their organisation had developed its strength, to gain some control over the conditions of their employment, and the Lancashire spinners on one occasion demanded the right to submit three names for each vacancy in the mill.[20] But the spinners did not rely solely on combination, for they appealed to Parliament to legislate on the question of hours, and during the exciting years of 1831 and 1832 the agitation for the Ten Hours Bill was as living and eager an issue in the north of England as the Reform Bill itself.[21] The spinners held that the pressure of competition was so great that neither the power of the spinners nor the power of the good employers could secure the ten hours' day without an Act of Parliament.

By this time the outlook of rich and poor on the life of their times had become completely estranged. To the ruling class the laws that governed the economic world were simple. That world was under the power of a benevolent despot, capital. Where the conditions were favourable to production, capital would be encouraged, and men and women would be well off. There was no problem of distribution, for economic society divided its gains on lines of its own, and all that men and women had to do was to learn to keep their awkward hands off it. Life was full of hardships and inequalities, but political economy showed that there was a good reason for them, and that they were in fact inevitable. A man who knows that there is no escape from a burden is half-way to resignation; if the burden is on somebody else's back he is half-way to complacency.

The working classes were in a very different position. The practical difficulty of living kept them more or less captive to the facts of life and experience. Starting with this bias they found fault with the ideas of the governing class alike in respect of their logic and their justice. The manifestoes published from time to time by the working-class leaders are of great interest as contemporary criticism of the political economy described by Sydney Smith as a system of metaphysics.

In a document that combined good and bad reasoning, the Manchester weavers criticised in 1823 the fashionable belief

---

[20] Chapman, *op. cit.*, p. 213.

[21] It was an important feature of the contest between Sadler and Macaulay at Leeds at the election for the first Reformed House of Commons.

that the English manufacturers owed their success in the markets of the world to low wages:—[22]

". . . We cannot hear, without strong emotions, our Merchants boast their ability to undersell all other Nations, while that ability is acquired by reducing us to the Borders of Starvation, and keeping us but one remove from Slavery.—They boast of underselling foreigners, while foreigners oblige them to pay in the shape of duties what they unnecessarily take from our wages. The average Wages of some hundreds of Weavers, for 4 months, as proved from the Books of their Employers, is now in the Manchester papers: Their wages for that period was 4s. 10d. per week, to each. This may suggest to you the condition that Weavers' families must be in.—The application of many thousands of power-looms to weaving, at the time that many thousands of manual Weavers returned from the Army was altogether unnecessary because, by that Reduction the number of Weavers was more than sufficient to supply the demand. Power-looms by diminishing the demand for manual labour, has put the manual Weaver entirely in the power of his Employer. The Employers can throw their Weavers out of Employ when they please, without injury to themselves, while thousands are glad of Employ at any wages whatever. And Weavers residing in large towns from the number of one to twelve thousands, makes it impossible for them either to withhold their labour or to find other Employment. And their long endured poverty has made them incapable of removing to other places. Now, Sir, in this state of things, is it not evident, that Employers have more power over Workmen, than any class of men ought to have over others? I do not mean to insinuate that all our Manufacturers desire that gain, which cannot be had without keeping us at the starving point.—No, Sir, we believe that the greater number of them would rejoice to pay us well. But however good their wishes be, it is impossible for them ever to be realised, while the whole state of our Wages is determined by a few Competitors, who, to effect speedy sales reduce Weavers' wages.—Others discovering the means by which they are under-sold, are, as it were,

---

[22] H. O., 40. 18: Letter from Committee of Manchester Weavers. Philips had declared in the House of Commons that "the low rate at which we had been able to sell our manufactures on the Continent in consequence of the low rate of labour here, had depressed the continental manufactures and raised the English manufactures much more than any interference could do."

compelled to reduce Wages in their own Defence.—In our opinion, a Committee, of Masters, or of masters and Workmen, chosen by both, fixing the prices periodically, or as often as fluctuations in trade make alterations in the price of labour necessary, would put it in the power of honest Masters to alleviate the Distress of half a million. If, from 1d. to 4d. per yard, were laid on Cotton goods, and that added to the Weaver's Wages, he would not then be half paid as other Branches of the Cotton manufacture are, but still, this trifling advance which the consumer would never know unless by report, would keep the Weaver from pauperism—it would, in a great measure, keep Infancy and age from hunger—it would preserve youth from the demoralisation consequent upon being exposed to all the temptations of want, which has, of late, so crowded our prisons with juvenile Delinquents and too often furnished the platform with victims.—We only wish for such an advance, as the markets without the smallest stagnation can afford; and such as a proper and just regulation would soon produce.

"We are sending a petition to parliament; praying for a regulating Committee, such as mentioned above. We also pray for a tax to be laid on power-looms, which are now transferring labour from men to Children and Girls; and from Cottages to Factories. This by depriving parents of sufficient Employ, makes them dependent on their Children for support; which, as experience too tragically proves, deprives them of that authority over youth which is necessary to retard the progress of vice and to promote Virtue.—The evils of a Factory-life are incalculable.— There uninformed, unrestrained youth, of both sexes mingle— absent from parental vigilance; from Reproof and Instruction— confined in artificial heat to the injury of health.—The mind exposed to corruption, and life and limbs exposed to Machinery —spending Youth where the 40th year of the age is the 60th of the constitution, till at last themselves become dependant on their offspring or the parish. This, Sir, is no overdrawn picture, but, as may be easily proved a very contracted sketch of facts.

"In our humble opinion, the evils of multiplying power-looms, by first ruining half a million who depend on manual Weaving for support; and eventually those unhappy young people whom they now employ, are such as no human being can think are counterbalanced by any good expected from them. And if the Capitals now employed in power-looms, were applied the common way, the Manufacturer would have sufficient profit.

"The Weavers' Qualifications may be considered as his property and support. It is as real property to him, as Buildings and Lands are to others. Like them his Qualification cost *time, application and Money*. There is no point of view (except visible and tangible) wherein they differ. And when Buildings are removed, or Land engrossed for Roads, Streets or Canals, the proprietors are paid for them. Then, if two dependencies, of exactly equal value to the proprietors are sacrificed for convenience; does not equity require, that while the one is remunerated, the other ought not to be totally neglected?

"Sir, you have now read over the real causes of the tumult so often excited in our Districts; but Weavers too often imputed their misery to other Causes; and manufacturers understood their own interests too well to undeceive them.—Our petition will soon be before you in parliament, we hope the Justice of our Cause will be manifest."

The view, again, that economic law governed the distribution of profits, and that the working classes were receiving all that it was possible for them to receive from employers who might seem to be selfish, but were by a law of nature beneficent and public-spirited, was rudely questioned in a manifesto that was published in July 1818, called "The Mule Spinners' Address to the Public."[23] The Spinners' Committee afterwards repudiated the handbill. This remarkable address is headed with the text, "The Labourer is worthy of his Hire. Jesus," and proceeds, "We the most ingenious and industrious of his Majesty's loyal Subjects, yet the most abused, and confined in the iron Bastiles of Manchester, whose Factories are filled with an artificial Heat, the exhalations create a greater degree of warmth on the coldest day in Winter, than is known in the West Indies in Summer, so that our condition is worse, if we advert to the hours of labour, than even the Africans.

"Thus are our ungrateful Employers raised from the lowest Walks in Life, to sport in gilded Carriages—sit in the Senate of our Country—dazzle us with the splendour of their Equipages—their very menial Servants pampered by the Sweat of our wretched Bodies, and thus raised by our industry, from the lowest State, to outshine even the ancient Nobility, and fully verifies the Proverb, 'set a Beggar on horseback, and he will not know when to stop.'

"P . . . . d,[24] the Beggar-maker, who sits on the destinies of

---

23 H. O., 42. 178.
24 Probably Pollard, a big manufacturer.

the Poor, we have made a Man of him, whose Mother hawked
about the Streets a small Basket; on two Spinners being deputed
to ask for a small advance of Price, had the audacity to thrust
one from him with an Umbrella and discharged them both.—Is
not this more tyrannic than even the Dey of Algiers, he hears
the complaints of the people, then let us hear no more of Bar-
barian cruelty, for though we work six days and make long
hours, on an average the Mule Spinners cannot earn half a
proper subsistence, as their pale countenances will fully demonstrate, while their employers gain immense profits; we know this
from the prices of Cotton, Labour, and the Yarn when sold,
and we shall be obliged to publish them to the world, while
we are famishing, starved, and insulted.

"Spinners, let us swear to no man! but we declare before
God, our country, our wives, and children, we will not work
and see them starve; will they call this vagrancy and immure
our bodies in gaols? Unfeeling Tyrants! when we refuse to work
and starve, you say we are conspiring against the Government,
charge us with Sedition, send for soldiers to coherse us, and in
the Green Bag stile, assure the Governors we are plotting against
them; it is false, we are ready to protect our country against foreign and domestic enemies, but we will not submit to selfish
Trading Tyrants; they asserted in the House of Lords that our
employ was the most healthy followed, but Lord Liverpool de-
tected the trading liars, and said it was impossible: let these
miscreants remember what was done in France at the bridge of
Pont Neuf, by a fool of an officer beating an old man with the
flat side of his sword.

"We advise all professions who live by work, to stand up for
a proper remuneration for their labour, and then the poor rates
will lessen, and princely fortunes will not be so soon made by
the speculators who favour a few with good wheels and work, in
order to divide us and be a check against the less favoured workmen."

A good example of the spirit in which the working classes
regarded the fashionable explanation that low wages were a necessary incident of the warfare for the markets of the world is
provided in a series of resolutions drawn up by the frame-work
knitters of Leicester in 1817:—[25]

"That in proportion as the Reduction of Wages makes the

---

[25] H. O., 42. 160.

great Body of the People poor and wretched, in the same proportion must the consumption of our manufactures be lessened.

"That if liberal Wages were given to the Mechanics in general throughout the Country, the Home Consumption of our
Manufactures would be immediately more than doubled, and
consequently every hand would soon find full employment.

"That to Reduce the Wages of the Mechanic of this Country
so low that he cannot live by his labour, in order to undersell
Foreign Manufacturers in a Foreign Market, is to gain one customer abroad, and lose two at home.

"That if the Mechanics of this Country were to work for
nothing, it would not increase our Foreign Trade, as the Governments of other Countries must, of necessity, in order to protect their own Manufactures raise the duties upon our goods
in proportion to the cheapness that we can send them to their
Markets."

The secretary of a deputation that represented the men in
an interview with the hosiers, sent these resolutions to Sidmouth, sending also a letter in which he said that low wages
were due to the Combination Laws, that it was unjust for a
Parliament that legislated to keep up the price of corn to refuse
to legislate to keep up the price of labour, and that the Poor
Relief should be nationalised instead of being administered by
the parishes, in order to get rid of the vicious system adopted in
some places whereby the parish provided hosiers with cheap
labour. Two years later the same body of men challenged the
view that the capitalist's interest, as he conceived it, was always
the public interest, by describing the pressure of low wages and
long hours on the parishes, and showing that if this process
was carried further the parishes would have to take over the
manufactures or be ruined. The fears of the hosiers that higher
wages would drive the trade away they declared to be ground-
less, since no other country had the raw material. The reduction
of wages had lengthened the working day and increased the
number of people out of employment, thus throwing a greater
burden on the rates. "If the demand," ran one of the later resolutions, "is not equal to the supply, an advance of wages to an
amount that will enable single men at least to obtain a livelihood
by labour of twelve hours will tend to remove this evil, as there-
bye the hours of labour will be considerably diminished, and
consequently employment afforded to a greater number of hands,
while reducing the wages increases the hours of labour, and

throws a proportionate number of hands out of employment."[26] These arguments were presented to the local authorities as a reason for helping the men to keep up a standard of wages. The masters were then offering wages that made it necessary for a man to work fifteen hours a day in order to keep body and soul together.

By the end of this period scarcely any aspect of life or society or politics or economics looked the same to the two worlds. The ruling class assumed that any punishment was just if it tended to make property secure. A different point of view is reflected in a broadsheet picked up in the streets, professing to be the dying declaration of a Leeds man, hung for stealing a horse, in which it is stated that by this theft the man had saved the lives of his wife and four destitute children: "The laws that condemned me were made by the great, and have no other object than to keep the wealth of the world in their own power, and entail on others the keenest poverty and vilest subjection."[27] Romilly mentions that when Mrs. Fry visited the prisons she was surprised to find that the convicts thought the Government much more wicked than themselves: they took property, but the Government took life.[28] The Saints interpreted the message of religion as a summons to the poor to adapt themselves to the inconveniences of life with a pious gratitude, and to avoid the wicked counsels of Reformers, and as a summons to the rich to go regularly to Church, send Bibles to the heathen, and be gracious to their dependants. The Church interpreted its message as a simple gospel of subordination to authority. A working-class Reformer, thrown into prison in 1812, asked for a newspaper and was given the Bible instead. He read it with great interest, and wrote to say that after making a careful study of the books of Proverbs, Job, Psalms, Ecclesiastes, Isaiah, Jeremiah and Ezekiel, he had noted that all these writers appeared to represent the rich as oppressing the poor, whereas in England it was the poor who were considered as a burden to the rich.[29] It was from the gradual disillusionment produced by the experience of hardship and neglect, and the discovery that the world looked so different to rich and poor, that there developed the larger movements to be described in the next chapter.

---

[26] H. O., 42. 192.
[27] H. O., 42. 82.
[28] Romilly, *Life*, ii. 486.
[29] H. O., 42. 129.

CHAPTER XV

THE AMBITIONS OF THE POOR

As education of one kind or another led the working classes to look more closely into their misfortunes and their grievances, there developed two movements of a more general character: one, a movement for marshalling and organising the forces of the working classes as a whole for the economic struggle; the other, the movement for political reform. In these movements the sense of particular wrongs and injustices grew into a wider class consciousness; the workman thought of himself not as a weaver or miner who was ill-used by the manufacturer or the coalowner, but as the member of a great class that was being pushed deeper and deeper into the mire by the power of capital and the power of law.[1]

The first important effort to consolidate the working-class forces seems to have been made in August 1818. In the closing hours of the great spinners' strike of that year, a General Union of Trades was suggested as a last desperate manœuvre. Rumours of this new and dangerous development were sent up to the Home Office at the beginning of August, but the first definite news is contained in a letter, dated August 5th, from Mr. Norris, the stipendiary magistrate of Manchester, enclosing a handbill.[2] This handbill is addressed "To the Labourers of Manchester and its Vicinity." "Friends and suffering Countrymen," it begins, "to whose exertions and talents your Employers are indebted for every thing they possess above common labourers, and who, in the fulness of their gratitude for the Princely Fortunes received at your hands, cannot allow you a better name than that of Rascal, Ragamuffin, Vagrant or Pauper!" A comparison of prices was made in this handbill which showed that wages of 36s. in 1818 were equivalent to wages of 16s. in 1788.[3]

---

[1] See speech at public meeting at Bury, *United Trades Co-operative Journal*, May 1, 1830: "Sunk as they now were, they would continue to sink still lower in the scale of being, if a general effort was not made to protect themselves."

[2] H. O., 42. 179.

[3] The items are interesting, *e.g.*—

	Then.			Now.				Then.		Now.	
	£	s.	d.	£	s.	d.		s.	d.	s.	d.
House	3	0	0	8	0	0	Pork	0	3	0	8
Beef	0	0	3½	0	0	8½	Potatoes	0	4	0	11
Mutton	0	0	3	0	0	8	Milk	0	1½	0	3
Flour	0	1	4	0	3	2	Butter	0	3	1	4
Oatmeal	0	0	11	0	2	2					

The cause of the difference is attributed solely and entirely to the Corn Laws and the Combination Law, and a long passage sets out the evils and injustice of the Combination Law, declaring with rhetorical exaggeration, that "Before the enactment of the Combination Law, Labourers of all classes enjoyed the privilege of taking a part in regulating the price of their labour; labour being the commodity which they had to part with. . . ."

"The road is not long," continues the handbill, "to that respectable walk in society in which the Labourer ought to tread; tho' in the present state of things, I must confess, it is rather rugged; yet unless you not only make the attempt to regain that respectable walk; but also be determined to recover it, you may depend upon it, that both you and your children will be trodden into the earth by your interested and hard hearted Employers.—The first thing necessary to be done is to take your Masters' conduct for a model. They call their meetings, at which every one who has a labourer to oppress, most scrupulously attends; at which meetings whatever mode of oppression is agreed upon, it is as coldly, and as religiously fulfilled, as though they were doing that which was pleasing their Maker. Every branch of labourers, namely Husbandmen, Weavers of all classes, Dyers, Fustian Cutters, Calico Printers, Spinners of all classes, Hatters of all classes, Machine makers, Joiners, Bricklayers, Masons, Shoe Makers, Tailors &c. &c., in short every branch of Labourers necessary in every well regulated society, ought immediately to call district meetings, and appoint *delegates* to meet at some convenient central place, to establish such a connexion as shall be deemed necessary for the good of the whole, and also they should be empowered to agree to the following or similar resolutions:—

1. That Labour being the Corner-stone upon which civilized society is built, no able, active Labourer ought to be offered less for his labour, than will support the family of a sober and orderly man in decency and credit.

2. That whatever trade or employment will not leave profit sufficient to reward the Labourer, so as to enable him to live in credit, and respect, provided he be an able, active, and sober man, the loss of such a trade is a public benefit.

3. That any Employer offering to recommend a Labourer to an Overseer for Parochial relief as a part of the

reward for his Labour, is an insult, and such Employer
should be held up to public indignation.

4. That the earnings of the Labourer should increase in
the same proportion as the price of the produce of
the earth increases, and that whatever Law or Enactment tends to destroy that proportion, is unjust and
oppressive, and of such a Nature is the Combination
Law.

5. That Masters being permitted to lower the price of Labour since the return of Peace, is the cause why the
Public Revenue is so much diminished, many of the
necessaries of life being put under the Excise: the
Labouring class of the Community are unable to
purchase them so that private di[stress]⁴ is a public
loss."

On August 19 a meeting⁵ was held in Manchester, at which
representatives were present from the Calico Printers, Dyers and
Dressers, Hatters, Blacksmiths, Jenny Spinners, Cotton Weavers, Bricklayers, Fustian Cutters, Colliers, Sawyers, Shoe Makers, Slubbers, Mule Spinners, Machine Makers.⁶ They passed
resolutions, reported Mr. Marriott, J.P., "of a most unpleasant
description,"⁷ which were afterwards reproduced and circulated
on handbills. "At a General Meeting of *Trades*," begins the
handbill,⁸ "convened to take into consideration the Distressed
State and Privations to which the Working Class of Society are
reduced by their avaricious Employers reducing wages to less
than sufficient to support nature, or purchase the bare necessaries for our existence in the meanest way, although with great
economy and hard labour, therefore to render redress in such
cases of distress to any Body or Party reduced as aforesaid, we
propose the following Resolutions." Nine resolutions follow:—

---

⁴ Torn off.
⁵ For invitation probably to this meeting see printed bill:—
"To the ——. Gentlemen, you are requested to appoint proper
Persons to attend a General Meeting to be held at the Sign of the
—— on the ——. To take into consideration the propriety of forming yourselves into a society for the mutual support of each other,
and for establishing such a connection with other Trades, as may
tend to the good of all connected with the same " (H. O., 42. 179.)
⁶ H. O., 42. 180.
⁷ H. O., 42. 179.
⁸ *Ibid.*

1. A Union called a "Philantropic Society" is to be formed. Meetings are to be held every second Sunday in the month, attended by delegates from all trades with credentials.
2. Every trade is to raise a fund for the general benefit of all trades in the Union "and to enable the labouring part of the community to live in comfort and decency."
3. Any Trade that feels the necessity of an advance of wages must give notice to a meeting of delegates, and if their concurrence is obtained all other trades will support it.
4. No trade is to strike without informing and obtaining consent from the other trades.
5. The Society is to obtain legal redress for "any body of Workmen being oppressed or illegally used."
6. The Printing, etc., is to be paid for out of their separate funds.
7. A Committee of 11 is to be chosen by ballot, and is to go out by rotation every month so that the whole Committee is changed every three months.
8. "That in order to preserve decorum in this society or meeting of representatives, no person shall be allowed to advance any political or religious argument, under a forfeit of threepence for the first offence, & sixpence for the second which must be paid the night it is forfeited."
9. Representatives may alter and amend the rules provided that such alteration does not "act against" any trade or division belonging to the "General Philantropic Society."

The paper containing these resolutions was circulated also in the Potteries. An additional resolution dealt with the appointment of an auxiliary society in each town, and a list of the trades from which deputies had met was given.

The "Philanthropic Society" had a short life. On 26th August notices were still going out to different trades, urging them to appoint proper persons to attend a General Meeting "to take into consideration the propriety of forming yourselves into a Society for the mutual Support of each other, and for establishing such a connection with other Trades as may tend to the good of all connected with the same," but on 7th September Mr. Norris reported that the General Union seemed likely to be dissolved, and by the time the law-officers gave their opinion about the desirability of instituting a criminal prosecution for the publication of the handbill with resolutions, all danger from the Union was over.[9] Such a scheme, started towards the end of an unsuccessful strike, could hardly survive the suspicion and distrust that accompany failure.

In London, however, the scheme went on for some months longer. The spinners' delegates, who had come for the double purpose of collecting funds and starting the General Union, became associated with the more violent section of the Reform party, and reports of their doings were sent in by the Government agents.

The project seems to have hung fire, but in September it was taken up by the energetic John Gast, secretary of the Shipwrights' Club, afterwards the friend and ally of Place. He became chairman of the General Union,[10] such as it was, and in November a fiery address was issued to the General Body of Mechanics. After a denunciation of that "most partial and despotic law" called the Combination Act, the workers are addressed as follows: "The spirit of your fathers is fled—the hand of poverty has, in conjunction with methodistical cant and chicanery, benumbed your mental and physical exertions; the broad and malignant grasps of aristocracy, extended out by a cruel and overbearing number of Employers, have acted as an opaque body over the sun of your rights and independence—have intercepted all the cheering rays of social and domestic happiness, leaving you nothing but the winter of poverty and tyranny which has so long intervened between you and your rights."[11]

The writer urges the mechanics to subscribe a penny a week to redress grievances, and to help those who suffer from asking for fair remuneration. The rules of the society are to be agreed upon by a meeting of deputies, one from each trade. Beyond attracting the attention of Place, and hence causing the alliance between him and Gast, this project seems to have produced as little effect as the kindred scheme in Manchester.[12]

---

[9] They reported against prosecution, 19th October (H. O., 42. 181).

[10] H. O., 42. 180 (21st September).

[11] H. O., 42. 182.

[12] Webb, *History of Trades Unionism*, p. 106n., and pp. 76 and 95 for history of Gast.

A more deliberate and important effort was made on these lines, in 1830, when the National Association for the Protection of Labour was founded. The moving spirit was Doherty, who began by organising "The Grand General Union of Spinners" in December 1829, and then went on to establish this larger combination in the following summer. In 1837, when he had become a bookseller, he gave evidence before the Committee on Combinations, and told the story of its origin. He said the work-people had laid to heart the lesson of the failure of the strike of 1829. "It was then shown that no individual trade could stand against the combined efforts of the masters of that particular trade: it was therefore sought to combine all the trades." For this purpose he had borrowed some ideas from O'Connell's successful organisation in Ireland.[13] The Association anticipated in some respects the modern General Federation of Trade Unions: it was a combination of existing societies, each of which paid an entrance fee of £1, together with 1s. for each of its members, and 1d. a week per head. The several Trade Unions in a district were then grouped together into a branch.[14] The Association started with great promise. It enrolled 150 societies, and its income in the first nine months was £1,866.[15] The first societies to join were mainly connected with the textile trades, but they were soon followed by mechanics and coal-miners. The Association also had an organ, a paper called *The United Trades Co-operative Journal*, and after this paper had been suppressed by the Commissioner of Stamps, Doherty established *The Voice of the People* as its successor, a sevenpenny paper.

It is evident from the tone of speeches made at the early meetings, and also from the articles in these papers, that large and ambitious ideas were in the air on the subject of the organisation of the working-class movement. Thus one speaker at Manchester urged that the Co-operative movement ought to be based on the Trade Union movement, and he asked why the working classes, confronted with highly organised interests backed by the State, should not have their own Board of Trade and Chamber of Commerce.[16] In practice, however, the immediate object of the Association was strictly circumscribed: it was

---

[13] O'Connell was on the committee.

[14] Doherty's speech, *United Trades Co-operative Journal*, July 3, 1830.

[15] Webb, *op. cit.*, p. 107.

[16] *United Trades Co-operative Journal*, May 8, 1830.

limited to resisting reductions of wages. One of the speakers at a meeting at Bury declared that there had been a remarkable change for the worse in the conditions of the working classes during the last ten years, and that this would continue until the workers in the different industries united their forces for defence.[17] At the initial meeting at Manchester, the first resolution emphasised this aspect of affairs:[18] "That the miserable condition to which, by repeated and unnecessary reductions of wages, the workpeople of this country are reduced, urges upon this meeting the imperative necessity of adopting some effectual means of preventing such reductions, and securing to the industrious workman a just and adequate remuneration for his labour." The funds were only to be applied to prevent reductions of wages, and in those cases strike pay was to be 8s. a head a week.

The authorities soon took alarm, and their alarm was increased by a successful miners' strike at Oldham, in the autumn of 1830. Mr. Foster, the Manchester stipendiary magistrate, wrote in October that the power of the Union was a public danger, and that legislation was needed to put down picketing.[19] Sir Robert Peel, in replying, deprecated the use of military force, but thought it very possible that legislative measures against the proceedings of the Unions might be unavoidable. He was not very hopeful of Parliament. A few days later he ceased to be Home Secretary, and he left a note in which he recommended the whole of his confidential correspondence about the Union to the immediate and serious consideration of his successor at the Home Department. Foster wrote soon afterwards that it was almost impossible to trace the illegal acts to the Association itself, particularly picketing, and that it was very difficult to induce manufacturers to volunteer evidence.[20] The chief strength of the movement lay at first in Lancashire, Cheshire, Derby, Nottingham, and Leicester, but in the autumn Sir Henry Bouverie sent an alarming report from Rotherham, to the effect that the Yorkshire colliers were about to join,[21] giving an interesting account of the plan of campaign which the promoters were supposed to have formed: "The Leaders of these Unions have declared that they

---

[17] *Ibid.*, May 1, 1830.
[18] *Ibid.*, July 8, 1830.
[19] H. O., 40. 27.
[20] H. O., 40. 27.
[21] H. O., 40. 26.

will keep the wages of the men up to what they consider the fair price of labour, calculated, I presume, upon the profits to be made. Their system is to order the Hands in only a limited number of Mills to turn out at a time, in order that, until they shall have gained their point, they may be supported by the Funds of the Union. When they have got their wages increased to the extent of their demands, another set of mills are turned out, and so on, so that a constant state of irritation is kept up. The Turn Out of the Colliers is regulated much in the same way, but I am inclined to think that it has gone or is going beyond the wishes of the leaders, as, if it succeeds in its avowed object, viz. that of forcing the Mills to stop for want of fuel, the number of hands which will be turned out of employ will far exceed what the Funds of the Union will be able to support. . . . The leaders are men of much penetration." Bouverie adds that Doherty has £600 a year, and that the other officers are paid in proportion. "Mixed up with all this there is a strong and rapidly increasing political feeling." A week later Bouverie sent some further particulars.[22] He said that at the beginning of October the weekly receipts were £330, and the number of contributions about 80,000, but that there had been a great increase since, as many of the colliers had joined, and also many of the smaller Unions in Yorkshire at places like Bradford and Huddersfield.

Unfortunately the working classes were too poor alike in money and in the capacity for organisation and discipline[23] to sustain so ambitious and difficult a scheme, and though there was a wave of Trade Unionism through the northern and midland counties during the next two years, the Association itself came to an end. It was succeeded by the Builders' Union, from whose organ, *The Pioneer*, we have quoted some passages in an earlier chapter.

It has already been remarked that there was little sympathy with revolutionary ideas in Lancashire at the beginning of the French War. In 1801 the authorities were a good deal alarmed to find a printed paper in the Manchester market-place, encouraging seditious sentiments, and from that time there was always a certain political element in the industrial unrest of the north.

---

[22] H. O., 40. 26.
[23] *E.g.* there was a breach between the Lancashire and Nottingham branches (Webb, *op. cit.*, p. 109).

This particular paper professed to be an extract from a publication called *Les Ruines*, by M. de Volney, the famous traveller, who has been called the French Herodotus, describing a scene witnessed in a country on the shores of the Mediterranean.[24] Two bodies faced each other; the first large and poor, and miserable-looking; the second small, presenting "in the plumpness of their faces, symptoms of leisure and abundance." The first group was composed of labourers, artisans, shopkeepers, and all the professions useful to society; the second of the civil, the military, and the religious agents of Government.

A lively dialogue is conducted between the two groups:—

"*People.* And what business do you follow in our society?
"*Distinguished Class.* None: we are not made to work.
"*People.* How then have you acquired your riches?
"*Distinguished Class.* By taking the trouble to govern you."

The three divisions of the distinguished class each in turn attempts in vain to overawe the people.

"And the Civil Governors said, 'This people is mild and naturally servile; let us speak to them of the King, and of the law, and they will presently re-enter upon their duty. People! The King wills it, the sovereign ordains it.'"

The people, however, confound the Civil Governors by pointing out that the King's office originates with the people. The Military Governors then take their turn, and, stepping forward, say:—

"The people are timid, let us menace them; they only obey force. *Soldiers, Chastise this insolent rabble.*

"*People.* Soldiers, you are our own blood! Will you strike your brothers? If the people perish, who will maintain the army?

"And the soldiers, grounding their arms, said to their chiefs, '*We* also are the people—we are the enemies of ——'"

"Whereupon the Ecclesiastical Governors said: 'There is but one resource left. The people are superstitious; *we must* frighten them with the names of God and Religion. Our

---

[24] H. O., 42. 62.

dearly beloved brethren! Our children! God has appointed us to govern you.'"

But the people confound the priests by declaring they need no mediators, and after much dialogue of the following kind:

"*Priests.* Man is only born into this world to suffer.
"*People.* Do you then set us the example."

the priests too capitulate; the small group confess that their reign is over, since the multitude is enlightened, and both parties join together and live happily ever after. The paper ends, "The Voice of the People is the Voice of God."

From this time the Reform spirit is continually appearing and reappearing in the working-class agitations throughout the period. The weavers were apparently attracted to Parliamentary Reform for the first time in consequence of the treatment in Parliament of their petitions for a minimum wage,[25] and at the end of the war with Napoleon the Reformers found the cotton workers of Lancashire very ready to listen to them. The suspension of the Habeas Corpus in 1819 checked this propaganda, but only for a time, and it is significant that at Reform meetings in Lancashire and the north great stress was laid on the Combination Acts, workmen who wished to dissociate their enterprises from schemes of Parliamentary Reform being reminded that those Acts were passed by Parliament, and could only be repealed by Parliament.[26] When the National Association for the Protection of Labour was formed, politics were officially eschewed,[27] but *The Voice of the People* from the very first preached Radical Reform with great earnestness and ability, taking as its programme Universal Suffrage, Short Parliaments, and especially Vote by Ballot.

[25] See following volume.
[26] See meetings at Ashton, Blackburn, Manchester (H. O., 45. 85, 46. 10, 13, 15, 42. 188).
[27] The Mayor of Leicester, writing to the Home Office about a meeting of the National Association held there in September 1830, says that the speakers disavowed all political objects. On 30th August the editor of the *United Trades Co-operative Journal* advises a correspondent (a weaver) not to mix up political topics with his argument, since the law forbids us to discuss such subjects. See also prospectus in first number.

What was the attitude of the working classes to the Reform Bill, a Bill that left them in the cold, carried by a Government that spared no pains to remind them that in the Whig view they had no business with politics? Nobody was satisfied with it, but many accepted it, from the first, on the ground that, though it was a disappointment, it would pave the way to further reform later. Another section argued that it was bad and ought to be resisted. The first view was preached by Cobbett, who had of course immense influence in Lancashire, and it was supported by *The Voice of the People*. Doherty, though he took this view in his paper, expressed himself rather differently to Place in the autumn of 1831, speaking of the Bill as one that could bring no good to the working man, and arguing that the people ought to compel the Government by force to do what was right.[28] Henry Hunt took the view that the Bill was worse than nothing, and that the working classes were actually opposed to it. The working-class movement was organised in Unions, distinct in most places from the middle-class Unions on the Birmingham model. Many of these working-class Unions were founded by Owenite working men in London, who, breaking away from the detachment of their leader, started a Metropolitan Trades Union with the two objects of securing political representation for the working classes, and a shorter working day.[29] Hetherington and Lovett were leading spirits, and they drew up a programme embracing Universal Suffrage, Annual Parliaments, and Vote by Ballot, organised classes in different parts of London under leaders for discussing the works of Paine, Godwin, Owen, and Ensor, and gave themselves the high-sounding title of "The National Union of the Working Classes and others." Hetherington made a tour of the country, and similar Unions sprang up in many places, Manchester one of them. These Unions were a cause of great anxiety to the Government, and Place dreaded their influence on the fortunes of the Reform Bill. "The difference," he wrote afterwards, "between the Political Unions and the Unions of the Working Classes, was that the first desired the Reform Bill to prevent a revolution, the last desired its destruction as a

---

28 Wallas, *Place*, p. 263.

29 In this connection it is important to note that the agitation for the Ten Hours' Day was in progress, and that in Yorkshire it was a more burning topic than the Reform Bill. Many meetings were held at which the speakers agreed to leave the question of Reform on one side.

means of producing a revolution."[30] The Unions, imitating the
Reformers whom Pitt had extinguished in the early years of the
war, arranged a Grand Convention at Manchester to draw up a
Reform Bill.[31] In Manchester itself, the working-class Union
was stronger than the original Political Union: it had twenty-
seven branch lodges, with more than five thousand members.
The extraordinary Sabbatarianism of the time is illustrated by
the general condemnation of the Reformers for holding a meeting on a Sunday to protest against the death sentences passed on
the Bristol rioters. A second meeting was broken up by the authorities (it was alleged that some of the men had brought arms
to the first), the leaders were arrested, and four of them were
sent to prison for a year. In March the Government proclaimed
a General Fast, partly to please the Saints, and the working-class
Union, pouring ridicule on this way of treating a great political
crisis, organised a demonstration in London, which was attended
by 100,000 persons. At no stage was there any sympathy between the Government and the working-class Unions, though
Hunt became a convert to the Bill at the end; but if the re-
sistance of the Lords had provoked a revolution, the working-
class organisations meant to have a hand in it. In this sense they
counted among the forces with which the Lords had to reckon.
But it was the Bill and not the Revolution that the Lords gave
to England.

The history of the working-class movement in this period thus
exhibits the stormy and difficult birth of a social and a political
consciousness. After the Reform Bill and all its disappointments
(for if the working-class organisations derided it, there must
have been thousands of working men who shared Cobbett's optimism), the first finds its expression in the Owenite Syndicalist
conception of the "Grand National Consolidated Trade Union
of Great Britain and Ireland," and the second in Chartism. But
those are tragedies that belong to later history.

---

[30] Quoted, Butler, *The Passing of the Great Reform Bill*, p. 382.
This book gives the best account of the political agitation.
[31] *Ibid.*, p. 311.

CHAPTER XVI

CONCLUSION

An artificial atmosphere surrounds the life of the governing world. For that world is carrying on a system; it is responsible for the working of a machine; it has to consider the claims of precedent, routine, continuity, and the hundred and one ways in which an organisation is maintained and made secure; it asks of every proposal how it will affect the stability of a great scheme of law and administration. It is its instinct to judge problems and affairs first and last as the guardians of a great body of interests committed to its custody, whose duty it is to avert the immediate danger of disorder. Its reasons are reasons of State.

During the period we are discussing all the strength and power of this sentiment were concentrated on one aspect of civilisation. The classes that possessed authority in the State and the classes that had acquired the new wealth, landlords, churchmen, judges, manufacturers, one and all understood by government the protection of society from the fate that had overtaken the privileged classes in France. Property was the great civilising force of the world, "that great institution for the sake of which chiefly all other institutions exist, that great institution to which we owe all knowledge, all commerce, all industry, all civilisation, all that makes us to differ from the tattooed savages of the Pacific Ocean."[1] But the form that the world of industry was assuming—a form that the age accepted and admired—did not admit of a universal, or even a wide distribution of property. Hence arose the danger that the ignorant who suffered from its lack might lay reckless hands on the very institution which was the origin of all such happiness and well-being as society had achieved. And this population, which in fact owed everything to the principle of private property, but was easily blinded to that truth, was growing by great strides. The task of government in consequence was becoming more complex, more difficult, and more dangerous.

Different minds, of course, drew different practical conclusions. Anybody, said Cavour, can govern in a state of siege. A permanent state of siege was the vision of English society that inspired men like Castlereagh and Sidmouth. In their view, the

---

[1] Macaulay, Speech on the Reform Bill.

problem, though formidable in extent, was in character simple
enough. A small class was set to defend its own property and
that of a larger class against the turbulence of a large un-
propertied population. This mass of people was liable to be in-
fected with Jacobin doctrines, and if the State was to be made
safe from revolutionary agitation, it was essential that the proletariate should be excluded from all opportunity of discussion,
association, education, and remonstrance. The more the ignorant
masses seemed tempted by dangerous and seductive principles,
the more necessary was it to drive out that temptation by terror.
Bennet, reviewing the savage punishments inflicted on rioters,
summed up the methods of these statesmen in a bitter epigram,
saying that they had hung a woman to deter women, and a
child to deter children.[2] And to deter was the only recognised
duty of the State to this class. The suspension of Habeas Corpus
and the Six Acts were the concrete expression of the conviction
that any hardships inflicted upon the working classes under this
system should not weigh against the supreme importance of protecting property. It was shown that a man who had been put
into prison when Habeas Corpus was suspended was left there
for seven years without trial of any kind because the authorities
had forgotten all about him. A cynic might contend that the
fate of this man was in truth the fate of the working classes under Pitt and Castlereagh. The only problem in their view was the
problem of keeping the working classes out of mischief. Not,
of course, that these statesmen recognised their policy as a policy
of class selfishness: they would have said that they were preventing the working classes from hurting themselves and everybody else. And when the agitation for Reform revived, the opponents of Reform held that if the mysterious sanctity of
property was to be preserved, every brick and slate of the existing order must be kept in its place. To disfranchise Old Sarum
would be as direct an incitement to revolution as to countenance
the socialism of Thomas Spence or the blasphemy of Thomas
Paine. So far had the idea of property been separated from any
vital principle, that men ceased to ask its uses and had come to
worship an abstraction.

Other politicians, no less attached to the notion that property
was the chief interest committed to the care of government, took
a different view of the policy this duty demanded, and of the
measures it warranted. They did not admit that the rights of

2 House of Commons, July 16, 1812.

property set aside all other rights, or that it was just to make persecution part of the normal system of government. A man like Grey regarded the working classes as an element of danger in the State, but he would not admit that on that account they were to be refused all civil rights. Moreover, if it was bad morality, in his view it was bad policy. The motto of Castlereagh and Sidmouth was "Oderint dum metuant," but the opponents of persecution thought that property should be made less unpopular. Macaulay put their case in his clear and eloquent speeches on the Reform Bill. "To say that Old Sarum was the bedrock of property was not to make people think well of Old Sarum, but to make them think ill of property." Moreover, Parliamentary Reform on prudent lines would reinforce the guardians of property by associating a new and powerful body of interests with the government of the state. "At present we oppose the schemes of the revolutionists with only one half, with only one quarter our proper force." Bentham and his disciples, again, believed that if the political conditions of society were made more fair and more just, no fundamental antagonism would exist between the interests of property and the interests of the poor man. So long as all institutions in the state seemed to reflect the selfish privileges of a small class, the mass of men would be driven into a rebellious discontent. The formula that Bentham laid down, that each man should count for one, and no one for more than one, was an invaluable protest against the predominant passion for inequality, but he never thought out any method by which this principle could be reconciled with the shape that industrial society was assuming.

If we wish to understand the strength of this feeling about property, we have to keep in mind the influence of the Industrial Revolution on the imagination of the upper classes. We have seen what this Revolution looked like to the poor. In the educated world it gave form and substance to fixed ideas of subordination and discipline. If a great industrial scheme, increasing the scope and energy of human faculties a hundredfold, were introduced into the life of a group of colonists or settlers, living and working together on terms of equality and freedom, the new sense of power and confidence would belong to the whole community.[3] Each man would draw support and strength

---

[3] See Graham Wallas's *The Great Society*, p. 393. "If I try to make for myself a visual picture of the social system which I should desire for England and America, there comes before me a recollection

from association with his fellows in directing this new engine. Industry, with its new equipment and resources, might be expected to find a form that would do justice to the claims of human nature, giving responsibility, freedom, and a greater and nobler range of mind and will to all who took part in it. But the Industrial Revolution found England in the hands of an oligarchy, and of an oligarchy so free from misgiving about its capacity for government, that it resented even the smallest abatement of its control. The new industry increased human power to a remarkable degree, and it seemed to this oligarchy the most natural thing in the world that the economic should resemble the political structure, and that in the mill, as in the State, all this power should be concentrated in the hands of a few men, who were to act and think for the rest. Economic science seemed to add a sanction to the law of inequality, for it showed that the sovereign authority of capital was the condition of success in the world of trade. In industrial as in political life, the mass of men must be content with an obedience that asks no questions. Thus the new industry, instead of guiding mankind to a new experience of freedom, common to all classes, confirmed the power of the few, and made the mass of men still less their own masters.

The form which the new industry took satisfied the passion of the ruling group for inequality, but it made them more nervous as guardians of inequality as a principle, for though the Industrial Revolution had given to England a great and decisive instrument of progress, that instrument was dangerously delicate and fragile, since the workmen, whose labour was an indispensable factor, might break it to pieces. This atmosphere gave to the government of England in the early nineteenth century the character defined by Adam Smith in a passage in the *Wealth of Nations*: "Civil government, so far as it is instituted for the security of property, is, in reality, instituted for the defence of

---

of those Norwegian towns and villages where every one, the shopkeepers and the artisans, the schoolmaster, the boy who drove the post-ponies, and the student daughter of the innkeeper who took round the potatoes, seemed to respect themselves, to be capable of Happiness as well as of pleasure and excitement, because they were near the Mean in the employment of all their faculties. I can imagine such people learning to exploit the electric power from their waterfalls, and the minerals in their mountains, without dividing themselves into dehumanised employers or officials, and equally dehumanised 'hands.' "

the rich against the poor, or of those who have some property against those who have none at all."[4] It could not be said that this exactly described the government of France under Henry the Fourth, or that of England under the rulers who tried in the sixteenth century to check the enclosures.[5] At both periods there was an active feeling for the quality and character of the men and women who composed the nation and made it strong in war and peace. But in the period discussed in this volume the upper classes allowed no values to the workpeople but those which the slave-owner appreciates in the slave. The working man was to be industrious and attentive, not to think for himself, to owe loyalty and attachment to his master alone, to recognise that his proper place in the economy of the state was the place of the slave in the economy of the sugar plantation. Take many of the virtues we admire in a man, and they become vices in a slave. The courage to rebel against a powerful tyrant or an unjust law, the imagination that inspires a vision of a better society, the sympathy that prompts to acts of comradeship, the public spirit that drives a man to denounce abuses or to lead a movement, all these qualities make a good citizen, but a troublesome slave. And if you turn from the language of the Declaration of the Rights of Man to the language of magistrates' letters, or to the speeches of Pitt and Wilberforce, you realise that the war between England and France, which developed or degenerated into a war for power in Europe, corresponded to a deep and vital spiritual struggle within the nation. At the time when half Europe was intoxicated and the other half terrified by the new magic of the word citizen, the English nation was in the hands of men who regarded the idea of citizenship as a challenge to their religion and their civilisation; who deliberately sought to make the inequalities of life the basis of the state, and to emphasise and perpetuate the position of the workpeople as a subject class. The French Revolution, bitterly as it divided the French nation, made the French people self-conscious, giving it a new unity inspired by the term citizen,[6] whereas the Industrial

---

[4] Book v. chap. i.

[5] See R. H. Tawney's *The Agrarian Problem in the Sixteenth Century*, p. 376.

[6] Not that the French Governments succeeded in solving the industrial problems of their time. Those problems were less acute in France than in England, but the French intellect of the day was dominated by the reaction against the policy of monopoly, and com-

Revolution, that seemed to represent peaceful and constructive progress, inspired the separatist notion that the mass of men, women, and children were not the citizens of to-day or the citizens of to-morrow, but merely part of the machinery that the great industry plied and handled.

It followed that every effort of the working-class leaders to combat the mean temptations of a slave society, and to prepare a future less hopeless and degraded for their children, had to make its way against a ruling power that dreaded the development of the mind of the ruled. Place has left on record the change that the Reform agitation produced in the people of Lancashire: "One of its effects has been almost, if not entirely, overlooked. . . . It is that in spite of the demoralising influence of many of our laws, and the operation of the poor-laws, it has impressed the morals and manners, and elevated the character of the working-man. I speak from observation made on thousands of them, and I hold up this fact as enough of itself to satisfy any man not wholly ignorant of human nature as a very portentous circumstance. Look even to Lancashire. Within a few years a stranger walking through their towns was 'touted,' i.e. hooted, and an 'outcoming' was sometimes pelted with stones. 'Lancashire brute' was the common and appropriate appellation. Until very lately it would have been dangerous to have assembled 500 of them on any occasion. Bakers and butchers would at the least have been plundered. Now 100,000 people may be collected together and no riot ensue, and why? Why, but for the fact before stated, that the people have an object, the pursuit of which gives them importance in their own eyes, elevates them in their own opinion, and thus it is that the very individuals who would have been the leaders of the riot are the keepers of the peace. In every place as reform has advanced, drunkenness has retreated, and you may assume that a cause which can operate so powerfully as to produce such a change, is capable of producing almost anything."[7] Their concentration on the abstractions of property and order had so perverted the upper classes that kindly and humane men preferred the England of the "Lancashire brute" to the England of the Lancashire Reformer.

The worship of wealth as the only standard of success left

---

binations were made illegal, not as a measure of class warfare, but as a corollary from the declaration of the Rights of Man. See Fisher, *The Republican Tradition in Europe*, p. 173.

[7] Wallas, *Life of Place*, p. 145.

no room for the sense of joy in creation. It was an age of creation, but it was not the spirit of creation that men admired. It is one of the ironies of history that this age admired itself for every reason but the right one. What men praised was the great civil order which had survived all the storms of the Revolution, and had made property more secure than any other system in the world. The immense energy that might have created a society of free men was admired just because it had created a society in which so few men were free. Similarly a false value was put on all the discoveries and institutions of the time. To the modern mind the truest thing that was said about the Industrial Revolution was said by Doherty in *The Voice of the People*: that if life was to be enriched by the new industry, machinery must be made subordinate to the men who used it. The political economy of the age valued the new industry as offering rapid and tempting prizes to the spirit of gain which was regarded as the great motive power of human progress. The ideal workman was the man who set his heart on making money, and had no higher purpose in his toil and in his abstinence from pleasure. The religion of the age assigned one virtue to the working classes, the virtue of bearing with Christian patience "the inconveniencies of a lower station": inconveniencies that were steadily increasing. Economist and Evangelical alike judged every movement by the single standard of its reactions on the existing order. It was left to a few independent spirits to question this amazing complacency, to ask the Evangelicals whether ninety out of a hundred of their fellow-citizens had been born for no other purpose than to practise the virtue of resignation; to ask the economist whether the workman was to have no other god in life than the law of supply and demand, to be worshipped with impartial enthusiasm whether it found him employment or whether it put him in the workhouse; to ask the politician whether a government whose dominant object is to preserve its own existence fulfils any large or noble purpose in the world.

For three main schools combined to create the atmosphere of the Industrial Revolution. The political theory that was developed from the teaching of Locke acquired a new and sinister importance in this age, for that theory treated society as a community of shareholders in which a man's stake was his property. There was a large and increasing population of men without property. The economic theory that started with Petty and his contemporaries, and followed a course of its own through Adam Smith, Ricardo, and Malthus, growing into a more elaborate philosophy, assigned to this population the task of serving the masters of the great industry with a blind and irresponsible obedience. "The poor man," said a working-class paper, "is esteemed only as an instrument of wealth." The Commons of England, as Cobbett said, had become the labouring poor. Religion, in one form or another, might have checked this spirit by rescuing society from a materialist interpretation, insisting on the conception of man as an end in himself, and refusing to surrender that revelation to any science of politics or any law of trade. Such a force was implicit in the mediæval religion that had disappeared, good and bad elements alike, at the Reformation. Such again was the force, more passionate and direct, of that tempestuous religion that was sweeping over the battlefields of Europe; the spiritual message of the French Revolution, trumpeting its sacramental phrases across the world. But in England the religion that sprang from the Reformation, intensely individualist in its outlook, alive only at this time in the teaching of the Evangelicals and of the Methodists, tending to separate the world of the spirit from the world of public life, made no such claim for humanity. In the eyes of that religion the poor were only important as the servants of the will and intelligence of others, "a necessary part of the social system," looking beyond death for the happiness and dignity that they missed in this life. Thus the new system grew up, almost without challenge or protest, in the atmosphere of a discipline as rigorous as that of an army, for it seemed to the possessing classes that any acknowledgment of human rights would imperil its power, and even its existence. Hence it was that amid all the conquests over nature that gave its triumphs to the Industrial Revolution, the soul of man was passing into a colder exile, for in this new world, with all its wealth and promise and its wide horizon of mystery and hope, the spirit of fellowship was dead.

CHIEF AUTHORITIES

Home Office Papers in Public Record Office (referred to in this volume as H. O.).

Place MSS, in British Museum.

Journals of House of Commons.

Journals of House of Lords.

Reports of Parliamentary Debates in *Parliamentary Register, Parliamentary History, Senator,* Cobbett's *Parliamentary Debates,* and Hansard's *Parliamentary Debates.*

Annual Register.

PARLIAMENTARY PAPERS

Report of Committee on Woollen Manufacture, 1806.

Report of Committee on Calico Printers' Petition, 1806.

Report of Committee on Parish Apprentices, 1815.

Report of Committee on State of Children in Manufactories (Peel's Committee), 1816.

Minutes of Evidence before Lords Committee on Factory Bill, 1818.

Minutes of Evidence before Lords Committee on Children in Cotton Factories, 1819.

Report of Committee on Chimney Sweep Boys, 1817.

Report of Lords Committee on Chimney Sweep Boys, 1818.

Report of Committee on Artisans and Machinery, 1824.

Report of Committee on Combination Laws, 1825.

Report of Committee on Factory Children's Labour (Sadler's Committee), 1831.

First Report of Factory Commission (Commission on Employment of Children in Factories), 1833.

Second Report of Factory Commission, 1833.

Supplementary Report of Factory Commission, 1834.

Extracts from Information received by Poor Law Commissioners, 1833.

Report of Poor Law Commission, 1834.

Report of Committee on Accidents in Mines, 1835.

First Report of Children's Employment Commission on Mines and Manufactures, 1842.

There are in existence several excellent bibliographies for the period. The student may be referred to those published in:—

The History of Trade Unionism, by Sidney and Beatrice Webb.
A History of Factory Legislation, by B. L. Hutchins and A. Harrison.
La Révolution Industrielle au XVIIIe Siècle en Angleterre, by P. Mantoux.

The following list merely suggests some of the chief authorities for the use of the general reader:—

CONTEMPORARY AUTHORITIES

Aston, Joseph, *A Picture of Manchester,* 1816.
Baines, Edward, *History of the Cotton Manufacture,* 1832.
—— —— *History of the County of Lancaster,* 1824.
Bamford, Samuel, *Early Days and Passages in the Life of a Radical.*
Cobbett's *Political Register,* 1802–35.
Eden, F. M., *The State of the Poor,* 1797.
Engels, F., *The Condition of the Working Class in England in* 1844.
English Economic History, Select Documents, edited by A. E. Bland, P. A. Brown, and R. H. Tawney.
Fielden, J., *The Curse of the Factory System,* 1836.
Gaskell, P., *The Manufacturing Population of England,* 1833.
Pioneer, The, 1834.
Porter, G. R., *The Progress of the Nation* (Modern Edition, edited by F. W. Hirst).
Prentice, A., *Historical Sketches of Manchester,* 1850.
Romilly, Samuel, Life of, 1842.
Society for Bettering the Condition of the Poor, Reports of (5 vols.), 1795–1808.
Society for the Diffusion of Useful Knowledge, Publications of, *The Results of Machinery, The Rights of Industry,* 1831.
Taylor, W. Cooke, *Tour in the Manufacturing Districts of Lancashire,* 1842.
Tracts, Cheap Repository (the first in 1792).

United Trades Co-operative Journal, 1830.
A Voice from the Coal Mines, 1825.
The Voice of the People, 1831.
Wing, C., *The Evils of the Factory System*, 1837.

MODERN AUTHORITIES

Ashley, W. J., *The Economic Organisation of England*.
Bonar, J., *Malthus and his Work*.
Butler, J. R. M., *The Passing of the Great Reform Bill*.
Carlyle, E. I., *Life of William Cobbett*.
Chapman, S. J., *The Lancashire Cotton Industry*.
Cunningham, W., *The Growth of English Industry and Commerce*. II.
Dolléans, E., *Le Chartisme*.
Fortescue, J. W., *The History of the British Army*.
French, G. J., *Life of Samuel Crompton*.
Galloway, R. L., *History of Coal Mining*.
Halévy, E., *Histoire du Peuple Anglais au XIXe Siècle*.
Hobson, J. A., *The Evolution of Modern Capitalism*.
Hutchins, B. L., and Harrison, A., *A History of Factory Legislation*.
James, J., *History of the Worsted Manufacture*.
Lloyd, G. I. H., *The Cutlery Trades*.
Mantoux, P., *La Révolution Industrielle au XVIIIe Siècle en Angleterre*.
Meredith, H. O., *Economic History of England*.
Prothero, R. E., *English Farming Past and Present*.
Sadler, M. T., *Memoirs of Life and Writings of*.
Slater, Gilbert, *The Making of Modern England*.
Smart, William, *Economic Annals of the Nineteenth Century*.
Toynbee, Arnold, *The Industrial Revolution*.
Veitch, G. S., *The Genesis of Parliamentary Reform*.
Wallas, Graham, *Life of Francis Place*.
—— —— *The Great Society*.
Walpole, Spencer, *History of England*.
Webb, Beatrice, *The Co-operative Movement*.
Webb, Sidney and Beatrice, *History of Trade Unionism*.
—— —— —— *English Local Government—The Manor and the Borough*.

—— —— —— *English Local Government—The Parish and the County.*

Wedgwood, J. C., *Staffordshire Pottery and its History.*

A number of important books have appeared since this book was written on different aspects of the Industrial Revolution. A short list is given below.

Ashton, T. S., *The Industrial Revolution.*

—— —— *Iron and Steel in the Industrial Revolution.*

—— —— with J. Sykes, *The Coal Industry of the Eighteenth Century.*

Buer, M. C., *Health, Wealth and Population in the Early Days of the Industrial Revolution.*

Carr-Saunders, A. M., *The Population Problem.*

Chambers, J. D., *Nottinghamshire in the Eighteenth Century.*

Clapham, J. H., *The Early Railway Age.*

Cole, G. D. H., *Life of William Cobbett.*

—— —— *Life of Robert Owen.*

—— —— with R. W. Postgate, *Short History of the British Working Class Movement.*

—— —— *The Common People, 1746–1938.*

Cole, M. I., *Makers of the Labour Movement.*

Daniels, G. W., *The Early Cotton Industry.*

Dodd, A. H., *The Industrial Revolution in North Wales.*

Driver, Cecil, *Tory Radical. The Life of Richard Oastler.*

Fay, C. R., *Great Britain from Adam Smith to the Present Day.*

—— —— *Life and Labour in the Nineteenth Century.*

George, M. Dorothy, *London Life in the Eighteenth Century.*

Griffith, G. Talbot, *Population Problems of the Age of Malthus.*

Hamilton, H., *Industrial Revolution in Scotland.*

Lipson, E., *The History of the Woollen and Worsted Industries.*

Marshall, T. H., *James Watt.*

Pincbeck, Ivy, *Women Workers in the Industrial Revolution.*

Postgate, R. W., *The Builders' History.*

Redford, Arthur, *Economic History of England, 1760–1860.*

—— —— *Labour Migrations in England, 1750–1850.*

Rees, J. F., *Social and Industrial History of England, 1815–1915.*

Thomas, M. W., *Early Factory Legislation.*

Warner, W. J., *Wesleyan Movement in the Industrial Revolution.*

Wearmouth, R. F., *Methodism and the Working Class Movements of England, 1800–1850.*

Wadsworth, A. P., and Mann, Julia de L., *The Cotton Trade and Industrial Lancashire, 1600–1780.*

INDEX

Rich and Famous
Like My Mom

Also by Hila Colman
Diary of a Frantic Kid Sister
Nobody Has to Be a Kid Forever

Rich and Famous Like My Mom

HILA COLMAN

Crown Publishers, Inc.
New York

This book is for Ariana

Published by Crown Publishers, Inc., 225 Park Avenue South, New York, New
York 10003, and represented in Canada by the Canadian MANDA Group.
CROWN is a trademark of Crown Publishers, Inc.
Manufactured in the United States of America.

Library of Congress Cataloging-in-Publication Data
Colman, Hila. Rich and famous like my mom / Hila Colman. p. cm.
Summary: The overprivileged, lonely daughter of a famous and
popular singer seeks to find her own identity through friendship with
a street lady.
1. Homeless persons—Fiction. [1. Identity—Fiction. 2. Mothers and
daughters—Fiction.] I. Title.   PZ7.C7Ri 1988
[Fic]—dc19   87-27448
ISBN 0-517-56836-5   CIP
                                                               AC

10 9 8 7 6 5 4 3 2 1

First Edition

*Rich and Famous
Like My Mom*

Chapter One

I stood around playing with the bottles of lotions and jars of creams on my mother's dressing table, waiting for her to get off the phone. If she ever would. I don't know what that woman would do if she ever got stranded on a desert island. I bet she'd get the savages to string up wires and make a phone line. I giggled thinking about her in one of her bikinis lying on a rock talking into a Mickey Mouse phone surrounded by painted warriors dancing around her. No, *I'd* have a Mickey Mouse, she'd have a push-button.

"What are you laughing at?" She didn't wait for my answer. "Do I look that funny because I have these things on my hair?" She examined herself in her three-way mirror. "I suppose I do." She let out a deep sigh. "I look a mess. You're lucky, you'll never have to use hot rollers with your hair."

"No, I'll have to get mine straightened. I hate curly hair."

My mom laughed. She did have a great laugh. All the write-ups about her mentioned her laugh: "Deep, throaty, from-the-belly laugh. Philippa's whole face laughs, not just a sound from her mouth, but her eyes, her nose, her whole face crinkles up with a sudden joyousness. . . ." I read all her reviews, knew most of them by heart, and pasted them into a book with help from Agnes, our housekeeper.

"I'm not laughing at you," I said. "Just something I was thinking about. Are you going to take me out for dinner tonight?"

Mom looked woebegone. "My darling, I can't. I have to meet with Mike and some people; it's about the tour through West Germany and France. They want to include Italy, but I'm not sure I want to stay away that long."

Mike was her manager—a tall, skinny guy who thought he was my friend because he brought me expensive presents. Little did he know that I gave most of them away, but it wasn't his fault that I hated him. One part of me knew that he was innocent, he was just doing his job. But he was the one who was always dreaming up tours for Philippa and arranging them. Someday I was going to tell him to drop dead.

"Why do you not want to stay away?" I asked hopefully.

"Because I'm having that concert in New York,

silly, don't you remember? And I'll need time to rest and rehearse."

"Yes, of course. I keep forgetting."

"That's all right, sweetie. You don't have to remember." She got busy putting stuff on her face, covering it with some whitish goo. "How are things with you? How's school?"

"School's just great. I'm flunking math."

Even that didn't get a rise out of her. Any normal mother would have bawled me out or told me to get with it. But not Philippa, the great rock star whose records hit the top of the Top Ten regularly and sell millions all over the world. "Better luck next time, you can't win them all, darling," she said lightly. "Get yourself some new clothes, you'll feel better."

New clothes! I already had a closetful. Where did she think I was going? She was the one who traveled, not me. Except when she called up from some god-forsaken outpost clamoring for Western culture (last time it was Sri Lanka) and summoned me. "Cruishank (that's her lawyer) has a plane ticket for you," she'd say over thousands of miles of whistling wires. Not asking if I want to go, if I could go. It's supposed to be some great treat to visit my mom on tour in a bizarre place where the food is usually gross fish and chopped-up things that are scary. She shows me off to people whose language I don't understand while a smile freezes on my face. Once I was introduced to a boy who asked me what kind of contraceptives American girls used. I pretended I didn't know what he was

talking about, but when he got more graphic, I excused myself hurriedly. Another real nerd.

"How long are you going to be gone this time?" I asked dismally.

"Not too long. Four or six weeks, depending on whether I agree to Italy."

"It'll be spring when you get back," I said, looking at the early snow outside her window. For a while it would be pretty in the park. All our rooms except the library, Agnes's room, and the kitchen and pantry faced the park. Mom was pretty proud of that. She boasted that it was the best apartment in all of New York, and she was the one who had it.

"They weren't enthusiastic about having a rock star buy an apartment here," she said, followed by her deep laugh. "But I fooled them; I got it." I never knew what she did to "fool them," but she has her ways. My mom's full of schemes. She says if she wasn't thinking all the time she wouldn't be where she is. She has to think for everyone, she says—for her manager, for her lawyer, for the guys in her band. Maybe that's why she hasn't got much thinking left for me.

Okay, so I'm ungrateful. I suppose I should be deliriously happy because we have an apartment on Fifth Avenue with all those rooms facing Central Park, that I have a mom who's rich and famous, that I can buy all the clothes I want, all the toys I want (I've outgrown toys and dolls and all that stuff), all the computers I want (if I wanted them, which I don't), all the video tapes, compact discs. I could have a

roomful of electronic equipment, if I wanted. I do have two things that I love: all my books (I can buy anything I feel like), and Spenser, my horse, a beautiful six-year-old mare who's in a stable near Central Park West. I'm not allowed to go out in the park until the weather gets better, but now I exercise her in an indoor ring a few times a week. I love Spenser.

"That must be Frederick," Mom said when we heard the chimes of the doorbell. Frederick was her hairdresser.

"Why'd you fiddle with your hair if Fred was coming?" Her beautiful, thick black hair was all wound around little fat pink sausages.

"It was so wild; besides, I like fiddling, just in case."

"Isn't Amy going on the tour with you?" Amy was her personal maid and a kind of secretary, too.

"Yes, of course. But sometimes I want to do things for myself." She looked at me with her marvelous, dark brown eyes, lashes a mile long even without mascara. "I'm not as spoiled as you think I am. Don't forget, I once waited on tables. Before you were born, you're what—almost fourteen—and that was only sixteen years ago. We've come a long way, baby."

"I know." I gave her a hug. There were moments when I loved her so much I thought I would die suffocated with love. I wanted to climb all over her. I wished I was a baby again so that she could hold all of me in her arms, close to her. Sometimes I wished I was still inside of her, safe and warm, so I'd know where she was and she couldn't get away from me.

5

"Are you going out in the snow? Why don't you and Agnes go for a walk in the park? It should be pretty with the fresh snow."

"We may." But I had already decided I was going out alone. Not in the park (I wasn't allowed alone in the park), but I could walk on Madison, or even better, on Third Avenue, which was more interesting. There were more different kinds of people on Third; on Madison the women all looked alike in their mink coats and high boots, and the men carrying attaché cases. On Third, and even on Second, although those long, tenement-lined side streets were out of bounds to me, there were bag ladies, girls in tight jeans smoking pot in doorways, and winos sleeping curled up into balls of old clothes. I felt like doing something different today, even risky.

"I don't want you to be gone for more than an hour," Agnes said to me when she saw me snuggling into my fur-lined parka. "I think Sebastian should go with you, in this snow." Sebastian was our houseboy, a taciturn young man in his mid-twenties who came from some unpronounceable place in South America. He was okay, but I felt like being alone.

"Don't worry, I'll be okay," I said to Agnes. Whenever I went out by myself (not often enough), she made a big deal of it, as if someone was waiting outside the door to snatch me off for ransom.

"Just be careful. Don't talk to anyone, and one hour. Do you have your watch with you?"

"Yes. I'm not a baby, Agnes. I don't take candy from strangers."

"Don't be fresh with me, young lady," she said tartly.

The air was fresh outside, and the wet snow felt good on my face. I needed to calm my nerves. I hadn't told Philippa anything about what was bothering me. Somehow it hadn't seemed the right time—but then, there never was a right time to talk to Philippa. Just thinking bad thoughts about Philippa made me feel guilty because my mind told me that she had to do the things she did: she had to be busy with her work, she had to go on tours, she had to rehearse and rest, she had to make her records; otherwise we wouldn't have all the wonderful things that we had. What wonderful things? the other part of my mind asked bleakly.

Besides, there was nothing she could do about my problems. There was nothing I could do either. Except pay no attention. And go on hating Stacey Ford and Elaine Ross, and all the girls in my class who were planning a weekend skiing trip, deliberately talking about it in front of me, and no one, not one of them, ever suggesting that I come along. Only Elaine once said, looking at me over her glasses with her pale blue eyes, "You wouldn't like this place, Cassandra. It's a primitive kind of lodge, not the kind of elegant place you stay in when you go skiing with your mother." If she was trying to be friendly, I wasn't buying it.

"My mother doesn't ski," I said haughtily and walked away. Elaine wasn't as bad as the rest, but still she was part of Stacey's clique, and Stacey was obnoxious. I probably wasn't being fair to Elaine, but at that moment I didn't care.

I don't understand why they have to hate me because my mother is rich and famous. They're rich, too, but Agnes once explained to me their "rich" is different from my mom's. "Their daddies don't really have to work," she said. "They have inherited money from way back—their grandparents or great-grandparents. We call it 'old money.' Their daddies have seats on the stock exchange or are in investments, real estate, and banking. Your mama is self-made, she works hard for what she's got, and she doesn't come from their highfalutin society—she wasn't a debutante and she didn't have a coming-out party." Agnes laughed. "Your mama came out of nowhere, but she's better than any of them. Don't you ever be ashamed of your mom; she's the best."

Agnes had no business even suggesting such a thing. I would never be ashamed of my mom, but those girls really got me mad. When my mother had a new record out they weren't above coming around begging for autographed copies. I wouldn't have given them any, but Philippa always gave me a bunch to take to school.

"Look out, stupid. Can't you see where you're going?" The rasping, sharp voice stopped me, but I was sure the short, plump bag lady was the one who

had bumped into me. Who bumped who didn't matter. The bag full of oranges she was carrying was emptying into the dirty snow. "Now look what you done! A present from my friend the veg man." While she spoke she was busy unloading herself of various bulging plastic bags and brown shopping bags stuffed with what might have once been clothing but now looked soiled and raggedy. We both stooped over to recapture the oranges, but after picking up one or two she stood up to watch me gather up the rest.

"I'm sorry. I guess I was daydreaming."

"Hmmph," she snorted, and gave me a hard look from out of her small, piercing eyes. They were like bright buttons in her round face, hard-looking, as if to say, you dare touch me, I'll let you have it. I started to move away from her.

"You got any money?" she demanded.

"Not much. What do you want?"

"Don't you get an allowance? I ain't no beggar, but you can pay me for soiling my oranges. I don't like eating things soiled."

"They're clean inside. You don't eat the skins, do you?"

"Don't tell me what I eat. The skins got all the vitamins; in this cold weather I need my vitamins. Let's see, there was eight oranges. You can give me a nickel apiece, and you're getting off cheap. You got forty cents?"

I hadn't taken any pocketbook, but I found a

quarter in the pocket of my parka. "Here." I gave her a quarter. "That's all I've got."

"Ain't enough. You live around here; you bring me fifteen cents tomorrow. I'll be here, right on this corner, and don't you forget. My name's Mollie; everyone around here knows me. What's fair is fair," she muttered. "I ain't no millionaire, having my oranges ruined. I can catch my death of cold without my oranges."

"Where do you live? I can bring the money to your house," I offered.

"Where do you think I live? I live on this street. Usually there." She pointed to a doorway set back a little from the street, a door to a tailor's shop. "That's my place; everyone knows that. You be here tomorrow, hear?" She gathered up her bundles and went on her way. I stared after her. She lived in the street. I had never talked to anyone who lived in the street— I knew they were here, I'd seen old women and men huddled in doorways surrounded by their unsavory bags of clothing and food, but I never thought of them as the kind of people who worried about their vitamins. They seemed like people who were beyond caring about anything, who had given up. But that woman, Mollie, was so alive, so bristling with determination, knowing exactly what she wanted and out to get it. I had to admire her.

But she had spoiled my walk. I had planned to think about the girls at school and my mom going away and have a lovely time feeling sorry for myself.

10

When I'd had enough of that I'd have dreamed up some marvelous thing I'd do to make them all sit up and take notice of me. But that woman spoiled it all. I mean, I couldn't very well enjoy feeling sorry for myself when I had to think about what it was like to sleep in a doorway every night and eat orange skins to stay healthy.

I didn't even walk very long. Suddenly I wanted to get home and make sure of my room and my nice warm bed with my beautiful down comforter and all the cozy things I had. Also, I wanted to see Philippa. I needed her to give me a hug and hold me tight.

Frederick was still there when I ran into her room and flung myself into her lap. "Look out, Cassandra, you'll mess up her hair." Frederick stood hovering over her, tall and slick and slim, something like the long pair of scissors he held in his hand. "Watch out."

"It's all right," Philippa said, smoothing my hair. "What is it, baby? Is anything the matter?"

I shook my head. I didn't want to talk. I wasn't going to tell her about the bag lady—there was really nothing to tell. I just held on to her and let her hold me and smooth my hair and kiss the top of my head. I felt better when I got up, and I stayed and watched Frederick finish doing her hair.

He had given her a new haircut. Very straight on the sides, with only a little curl coming out over her cheeks, but a lot of soft, curly waves on top of her head. Her eyes were sparkling and she looked marvelous.

11

"Would you like Frederick to do something with your hair?" she asked me.

"No, no thanks." I looked at myself in the mirror, and wondered how my mom could have had anyone so funny-looking. I looked like her, that is, I had the same dark hair and dark eyes, but nothing in my face was straight. My nose had a little curve in it, my mouth didn't go in a straight line, and when I tried to make it straight I always broke into a giggle. Mom kept telling me I had a very interesting face, and that I would be a knockout when I grew up, but of course she had to say things like that because she was my mother. I think she was trying to convince herself that there was some hope for me.

"How about a short haircut?" Frederick asked, looking with some disgust at my shoulder-length black mess. "If I cut it short you would look like Liza Minelli."

"I don't want to look like Liza Minelli, but thank you just the same," I said politely. I love Liza Minelli, but I knew I would never look like her in a million years. I gave Mom another hug and a lot of kisses and left them to go to my room to think about the bag lady and her oranges.

Chapter Two

*A*t school the next day, I closed my ears to all the talk about the skiing weekend. I found out how to do that without even having to do anything so gross as noticeably walk away. I simply stared over their heads and thought about something terrific, like going to the Four Seasons for dinner with my mom. Their words fell on deaf ears.

That day, I also thought about Mollie, the bag lady. I wondered if she'd be there to collect her fifteen cents. When I got out of school, Adolph wasn't there. He was Mom's chauffeur and most days, to my disgust, he picked me up in her limo. It was stupid because school was only a few blocks from our house, but my mom was pathological about New York City streets. She was afraid of muggers, of kidnappers, of snipers—you name it and she'd have a story about

some horrible incident of someone getting knifed or strangled or chopped up that she had read about in the papers.

She had some crazy theory that walking the same blocks at the same time every day was the most dangerous thing. "If someone wanted to get you, that would be the time," she insisted. Inconsistent and typical of my mom, I was allowed to go out by myself for a short time *after* school. Nuts, but I wasn't going to argue about that. Finally I persuaded her that if she needed the car, I could walk home. I promised that I'd go directly home without stopping to even window-shop. It had been a hard struggle, but I'd finally won. Today was one of those times, and much as I wanted to go meet Mollie, I went home first.

Agnes and Sebastian, who had been told that I would be walking, were at the door waiting for me. That got me mad. "You don't have to hang around waiting for me, for heaven's sake. I wish I'd gone and had a soda."

Agnes gave a sarcastic laugh that I hated. "Sure, and we'd have the police out looking for you. You'd better not try anything like that, miss."

"I'll try anything I want," I said defiantly. I cared about Agnes, but sometimes she got on my nerves. I couldn't stand her hovering, as if any minute someone was going to snatch me away. "Anyway, I'm going out and I may be gone for a while."

"Where are you going?" she asked suspiciously.

"Just for a walk. It's a beautiful day and I don't feel like staying in the house."

"Then I'm going with you."

"Oh, no. Please, Aggie, I need to be alone. I'll be back in an hour, I promise. I'm just going walking."

She didn't look convinced. "All right," she said grudgingly. "But one hour, don't forget, or I'll be calling out an alarm."

I saw Mollie before she saw me. There she was, a short, squat figure, standing with her feet planted apart, her clothes draped around her loosely, looking as if she might have secret hiding places inside their folds—a little stolen tidbit tucked in here and there. As she had been when I first met her, she was loaded down with bundles and shopping bags.

"You're late," she said to me accusingly. "I've got a lot to do today. I can't spend my time hanging around waiting for a spoiled twerp like you. You got my money?"

"I thought I was on time," I mumbled, although I realized we hadn't set any time at all. I fished out the nickel and dime from my pocket and handed her the fifteen cents. I had been debating with myself whether I should give her more, and decided to add thirty-five cents so she'd have an even fifty cents. I gave her the extra quarter and dime.

"What's that for?"

"That's for you. I hope you don't mind."

She gave her contemptuous laugh that was more

like a snort. "Why should I mind? You got any more?"

I shook my head. "No, I'm sorry. But I can probably get you some more."

"Me and my friends, we can use it, anytime. But I'm no beggar, you understand that? I ain't one of them pitiful souls pretending they're blind or helpless making fools of themselves on the street to get a few pennies. No sirree, not me. I gotta go now."

"Where are you going?" The question popped out. I was dying of curiosity. Where would she have to be going?

"I gotta go take care of my sick friend, Edward. He's in a bad way and I'm worried about him. I can't stay here, gabbing with you." She picked up her bundles and waddled off down the street. I'd only been gone from home about ten minutes, so I took off after her.

I caught up with her at the street corner. She accepted as natural that I was alongside her and kept on with her mumbling conversation. "That Edward sure does worry me. He's got a heart condition and he ain't got no business living on the street. One of these days he'll get pneumonia for sure. It's a disgrace that he hasn't got a home. You'd think that in these United States there'd be a place where a man like him would have a roof over his head."

What about you? I thought to myself. The way she talked about her friend Edward you'd think she wasn't in the same boat. She had put down some of

her bundles waiting for the light to change, and she was having trouble gathering them all up again.

"I can carry some of these for you," I offered.

She snatched them up quickly. "Not on your life. You think I want someone to grab them from you and run? A little thing like you, you're just the kind they pick on around here. I can take care of my own things, thank you. No one's gonna meddle with me, they know me around these parts." She waddled across the street. She looked like someone who belonged in the circus, as if white birds or rabbits might suddenly fly out of her flouncy clothes; and with all her bundles around her she resembled a walking junk shop. I wondered what she had in all those shopping bags that was so precious.

She turned east at the corner and we walked one of those long blocks to First Avenue. I knew I was out of bounds but I didn't care. There was something about Mollie that made me want to follow her and try to get to her. If I got a bawling out from Agnes it would be worth it. Ahead of us we saw a small crowd gathered on the street, and the next minute an ambulance came tearing around the avenue. Mollie let out a shriek. "I knew it, I knew something was happening, I just knew it." With all her encumbrances, she picked up her skirt, which was down around her ankles, and much to my surprise, ran like a young girl to where the ambulance had come to a stop. "Wait," she yelled. "Wait for me. I'm going with him. . . ."

I ran after her. We were both breathless, but we

reached the crowd in time to watch the paramedics bend over the limp form of a man stretched out on the sidewalk. One young man in a white coat was giving him mouth-to-mouth resuscitation while the other was taking his pulse. I couldn't see the sick man's face, but he seemed to be gasping for breath, and his long, skinny body was shaking convulsively. Mollie had pushed her way through the crowd and was squatting beside him. "It's okay, Eddie, old boy, I'm here. No one's gonna hurt you, you're gonna be all right. You know me, Mollie, your friend, I'm here to protect you."

When the paramedics gently lifted the man onto a stretcher to move him into the ambulance, Mollie said, "I'm coming with him. I'm his nearest, I'm his friend, maybe his only friend. You're not taking him without me." Mollie could intimidate anyone. As I learned later, the toughest social worker was no match for her. She turned to me and dumped all her shopping bags at my feet. "Here, you take these to Bob's Sandwich Place, the corner of First on the next block. He'll keep them for me. Bob's Sandwich Place, you got that straight?"

She didn't wait for my answer, but jumped onto the back of the ambulance. I had thought she was an old lady, but the way she had run and now jumped up so easily made me realize she wasn't all that old.

Before I knew it the ambulance took off and there I was with all of Mollie's junk. I was in a daze. First she wouldn't let me carry anything and now she'd left

everything with me. She was bizarre. Some of the people standing around looked at me as if I was a weirdo, and one tiny woman, who looked as if she might blow away any minute, asked if I needed help.

"Mollie a friend of yours?" she asked suspiciously.

"Not really. We only met yesterday. But I'm glad if I can help her."

The tiny woman chortled. "No one can help Mollie much. The shelter people came to give her a bed, but she was back on the street in an hour. She doesn't want help. Surprised she trusted you with her belongings. Her things are mighty precious to her; after all, they're all she's got." She looked at me wistfully. "I can help you carry them."

I realized she probably expected me to give her something for carrying the bags, but I didn't have any money on me. "It's all right, I can manage." I felt sorry for her as she scurried away looking like some small brown animal you see in the woods. Another street lady, I decided, and suddenly it seemed to me that I was peeking into another whole world. There we were, Mom and me with Agnes and Sebastian and Adolph, and all the kids at school with everything we needed and wanted, and right on the street, under our very noses, were all these people living in their own world. It all seemed crazy to me. So many people, like shadows moving across a screen, living in the same city. Edward, dying, the tiny woman who knew Mollie . . . there could be hundreds of faceless people, but people who had lives, had thoughts and

feelings, but no connection with a life I could understand. I didn't think of big things then, like injustice, or that life wasn't fair, or any of that stuff. It just seemed nutty, as if everything had gotten out of whack. Like putting things on a seesaw where all of a sudden one side has it all and goes down, while the other flies up in the air with nothing. Anyone with any sense would want to even things out so that there'd be a proper balance.

I gathered up Mollie's belongings and trudged over to Bob's Sandwich Place. I must say, it wasn't easy. I felt like another one of the crazies walking up First Avenue with all that stuff. People looked at me as if I was one, and I was terrified that someone I knew might come along. If one of the girls from school saw me I'd die.

But I got there in one piece, or I should say me and a dozen pieces. The place was busy and I felt like an idiot trying to get to the man behind the counter, who had to be Bob. When he saw me he looked pretty surprised himself.

"Mollie, she said you knew her, she asked me to bring her things over here. She said you'd keep them for her."

He still looked surprised. "Mollie? Oh yes, the bag lady. What happened to her, where'd she go?"

"She went with a friend to the hospital. Where do you want me to put them?"

"I'll take them." He called to a girl at the other end of the long counter to make two hams on rye, heavy

on the mustard, and he took the bags from me. "I'll take care of them, don't worry," he said, still looking at me curiously.

"I'm a friend of Mollie's," I said, feeling that he needed an explanation.

"That's nice," he said, and he walked away with her stuff.

I left his store, knowing I was going to be late getting home, but I didn't feel like hurrying. I felt as if I was leaving a book in the middle, which I hate to do. I wanted to know what was going to happen next. Was Mollie going to come back to the street? Was her friend Edward going to die? I hated being left out. I knew I was unimportant to Mollie and her friends, just another rich kid in the neighborhood, one of those they probably hated, but I wanted to be involved with them. I wanted to know all about how they managed and lived. Where did they go to the bathroom, and how did they eat? Did they ever change their clothes or get undressed? In one of Mollie's bags I'd seen a toothbrush sticking out. It seemed incongruous—where on earth did she go to brush her teeth?

When I got home, Agnes was hysterical. "Where have you been?" she shouted at me. "I was ready to call the police. Don't you ever do that again, ever, ever."

"I didn't do anything. I'm sick and tired of being kept on a leash. I'm almost fourteen years old, and if I want to stay out all afternoon, I've got a right. I'm not doing anything bad."

"We'll see about that," Agnes said haughtily. "You and I will have a talk with your mother, and she'll decide what you can do."

I didn't answer her but went into my room and closed the door. I made up my mind that I had reached a new stage in my life. I wasn't going to be browbeaten by Agnes anymore. I was excited by Mollie and the people who lived on the street. They lived by their own rules, no one told them what to do, and I wanted to know more about them. If I couldn't stay out as long as I wanted, I'd never get to know them. I wasn't going to be treated like a baby anymore.

Chapter Three

*I*t was around one o'clock on Saturday that Agnes and I went into Mom's room for a discussion. Mom had done her workout and ridden her exercise bike for twenty minutes. Now she was sitting at the small table in her bedroom with her breakfast tray. Grape Nuts, bran, yogurt, and skim milk. Philippa was a health freak; she thought bacon was poison (animal fat), but once in awhile Agnes sneaked some to me. I could make a meal of it.

"We have a problem," Agnes announced. She looked particularly severe in a black dress with a prim white collar and cuffs. She could have been pretty if she didn't pull her hair back into a tight bun and if she used some makeup. In pictures of her when she was a young girl she was really attractive, but after she became widowed, she said, she preferred being plain.

She didn't want any man trying to mess around with her, she claimed, but the idea of Agnes with any man was unreal to me.

Philippa laughed. "You look so solemn, it can't be that bad. What's up now?"

"Your daugher, Miss Cassandra, is too full of herself. She thinks she's a grown lady already. She wants to go out in the afternoons, not tell me where she's going, and stay out as long as she likes." Agnes looked at my mother as if she had just explained that I had been caught sniffing cocaine or running off with a guy.

When Mom looked at me I had the feeling she was desperately suppressing a giggle. "That doesn't sound insoluble," she said. "Where do you want to go, Cassandra?"

"No place in particular. I probably won't even want to stay out every day. It's just the idea of Agnes watching over me like I was a two-year-old. The girls in my class go all over the city by themselves. It's ridiculous for me to be allowed an hour and for Agnes to have a fit if I'm a little late. It'd be easier for her if she didn't have to watch the clock for me."

"Don't you worry about making things easy for me," Agnes said tartly. "I'm getting paid for my job."

Mom sighed. She looked at me intently. "I suppose you are growing up, and I can't keep you wrapped in cotton forever. You should have your afternoons after school free, but I want you to tell Agnes where you are going, and to be home by five o'clock. And

stay in the neighborhood. I don't want you riding subways or buses. If you have a date with one of your school friends to go someplace, a museum or somewhere, see if Adolph can take you if it's not in walking distance. Okay?" She looked from Agnes to me.

"If that's what you want, Madam," Agnes said. She called my mother Madam when she was annoyed with her.

"That's fine with me." I threw my arms around Philippa. I didn't tell her that I never had dates with girls from school. If it made her happy to think she had a popular daughter, let her think that.

Agnes stomped off with her long nose twitching, a sure sign she was fuming over not getting everything her way.

"What are you doing this afternoon?" Mom asked me. I hadn't had a chance to try to find Mollie to know what happened at the hospital, so I'd intended to look for her. But if I had a chance to be with Philippa . . .

"Nothing, why?"

"I have some shopping to do. You want to come with me?"

"I'd love to." I adored shopping with Mom, although every place she went people recognized her and made a big fuss, asking for autographs and all that stuff. She said she hated it, but I knew she didn't; she loved it. But it embarrassed me. It seemed so silly to want someone's name on a piece of paper. "What are you looking for?"

25

"Johnny likes me in bright colors. He says I wear black too much—so I thought I'd get something new for the evening." She was looking positively coy, not like my mom at all.

"Is Johnny your new boyfriend?"

"Sort of. Do you like him?"

"I don't know him. I've only seen him to say hello." I'd gotten so I didn't take Mom's boyfriends seriously, mainly because she didn't seem to either. None of them lasted very long. Mom said it wasn't her fault that Mr. Right didn't come along. I had long ago given up asking about my father. She hated talking about him, and kept repeating that she'd told me everything there was to tell. It wasn't much: he was very handsome, she wasn't even eighteen when she fell for him, they knew each other two weeks when they got married. She got pregnant and he took off before I was born. "And let that be a lesson to you," she always said when she talked about him. "I was a very foolish kid, but I'm darn lucky that you came out of it."

"Where shall we go first?" Mom asked me when we left the house. It was a beautiful crisp day, the kind of day that makes New York all bright and shiny and full of excitement. The bare branches of the trees stood out against the gray sky. The people on the street were walking briskly, the women holding their furs wrapped around them against the wind. Mom had decided to walk, which suited me fine.

"Bloomingdale's," I said promptly, "unless you

26

want to go someplace else." Philippa had many of her clothes made for her by Dasha, an exotic-looking Russian lady who had a place on Madison Avenue. But today she'd said she wanted to go pick up something ready-made. I loved Bloomie's, especially on Saturday afternoon when everybody was there.

"We can try it," Mom agreed.

The store was jammed; you could hardly walk through the aisles on the main floor. Mom and I clutched each other's hands (neither one of us likes crowds). It's funny with Philippa; she loves her huge audiences but, like me, she gets claustrophobic if she's *in* a crowd. I could see her face getting tense and white and I was sure I looked the same. Anyway, we got upstairs and Mom led me to a designer's salon that was relatively empty and quiet.

Mom looked like nothing. She had no makeup on, and like me she was wearing jeans and a country jacket. A rather elegant saleswoman came up to us and asked if she could be of help, but the way she looked at us you could tell she was thinking: Why am I wasting my time on these two? This was a salon where the clothes were tagged in at least three figures.

"I'm looking for an evening dress, something in a bright color," Mom said.

The saleswoman motioned to a model who was parading around in a white chiffon gown. "Madam wants something in a bright color, will you put on the dress we have in apple green, you know, the off-shoulder one."

The model, a tall blonde with one of those frozen model smiles, nodded, and then she looked at Mom for the first time, and her face came to life. "You're, why you're Philippa, the singer, aren't you? You look just like her. . . ."

Mom nodded. "I'm afraid I am."

I thought the saleswoman was going to faint. She became all twittery and flustered, looking as if she didn't know whether to crawl into a hole or kiss Mom's feet. "Well, of course," she stammered. "I thought you looked familiar," she lied, "but I wasn't sure . . ."

After that the saleswoman was ready to hand the store over to my mom. The whole thing made me laugh, but Mom said she hated people making a fuss over her. "It makes me sick," she said to me, "people have such false values. They don't know anything about me except that I make a lot of money. I could be nasty, mean—they don't know the difference. Being rich and famous is what counts to them, not the kind of person you are."

"But you're not mean and nasty," I said, squeezing her hand. It was wonderful being out with her, but the trouble with me is, I can never enjoy anything one hundred percent. All the while I was with her, I kept thinking: Why isn't it like this all the time? If she was an ordinary mother we would probably go shopping together almost every Saturday afternoon, instead of this being something so special. In a week she'd be going away again and I'd be alone for weeks and

weeks. Sometimes I wondered if a treat was worth it; it just made all the other times worse.

The whole department came buzzing around Mom. She signed autographs, and the salespeople asked me the usual dumb questions. "How does it feel to be the daughter of someone so famous?" I felt like saying: It feels lousy, but I just smiled politely and mumbled an answer.

Mom finally picked out a smashing, strapless red gown. It was short and kind of draped around her middle, and with her bare shoulders that were always tan, she looked terrific. Of course she has such a fantastic figure, anything looks good on her.

"Now we have to find something exciting for you," Mom said when we left the salon.

"I don't really need anything," I told her.

"Of course you don't. But that doesn't mean you shouldn't have something. Something luxurious and unnecessary."

Agnes once said that my mother bought me a lot of stuff because she wanted to make up for being away and busy so much of the time. "You mean she feels guilty?" I remember asking.

Agnes didn't like the word *guilty*. "That's not it, exactly. She just wants to do everything for you that she can."

But I knew it was guilt, and I didn't want it. I didn't want her giving me things to make up for what she couldn't give, because the presents never made up the difference. I could have ten closetsful of clothes, but

I'd still miss her just as much, and feel left out of her busy life. There had never been a week in my life when my mother was there when I came home from school and I could talk to her and we had supper together. Never one whole week when that happened.

We went to the girls' department, but my mother didn't see anything that she liked and the clothes were too babyish anyway. But then, in one of the boutiques, she spied a suede skirt that she thought was divine. It was very elegant in a natural chamois color, but I could see myself scared to wear it for fear of getting it dirty. I really like clothes I'm comfortable in because I don't care about what happens to them. I don't feel right in expensive, elegant things.

"It's very nice but I don't want it," I said. "I'll never wear it."

"I don't know why not." My mother held it up against me. "With a pretty blouse or sweater, you could go anywhere in it. To a party . . ."

"I don't go to parties."

Philippa looked woebegone. "I don't understand you." She sighed.

How could you, I thought, you hardly know me. "You don't have to understand me," I said. Our day was being ruined. I could feel it slipping away like so much water running through my fingers.

My mother's large bright eyes gave me a puzzled look. "What an odd thing to say. Of course I have to understand you. You're my daughter, aren't you?"

"Maybe I'm my father's daughter," I said per-

versely, I don't know why. I'd never said anything like that to her before. All the while I wanted to be close to her I was pushing us apart.

Philippa didn't respond but I knew I had hurt her, and I was both glad and sorry. I wanted her to know that I didn't want her extravagant gifts, but I was sorry, terribly sorry, that I couldn't please her. We were miles apart.

The day was downhill from then on. It couldn't have been worse because, of all people, we ran into Stacey Ford and Elaine Ross, my enemy and her shadow from school, on the main floor of Bloomie's.

"Cassandra, how wonderful to meet you here." Stacey blinked her nearsighted eyes, looking at me as if I were her dearest friend whom she hadn't seen in ten years. The very girl who had passed me in the hall in school the day before and walked on as if I didn't exist! But she wasn't looking at me, she was looking at my mother, taking in her suede boots, her jeans, her country windbreaker. She was going to remember every detail to describe to all her friends . . . what the famous Philippa was wearing.

I mumbled an introduction to my mother, added, "Nice seeing you," and turned to go away.

But my mother, who could never miss responding to an admiring audience, said gaily, "I was just going to buy us some hot chocolate. Would you girls like to join us?"

They both nodded vigorously, and so there we were, the four of us ready to go someplace. I was

depressed beyond words. Mom found a taxi (she always does), and we went over to Rumpelmayer's on Central Park South. Stacey kept up a constant chatter, asking Mom all kinds of questions, even what she ate to keep her figure; she was obviously in seventh heaven. I could see her looking at me and thinking, how did Philippa ever have a lump like you for a daughter? Elaine was quiet and I suspected she was embarrassed by Stacey. I almost felt sorry for her.

While we drank hot chocolate and ate petits fours I had to listen to Stacey tell Philippa a bunch of lies about what fun we all had together in school: how strict but charming our Latin teacher, Miss Lent, was; the excitement of our last basketball game (I had never been so bored); and how the school really had such a good, friendly spirit. I never heard so much baloney.

When we dropped them at their homes from the taxi Mom said what lovely, charming girls they were. I was too exhausted just listening to Stacey to disabuse her of that notion and tell her what I thought of them. Hypocrites. They had made up their minds that I was spoiled and a snob, when they were the ones who cared about knowing someone famous, like my mom, but at the same time felt that neither she nor her daughter were "one of their kind." But I was glad that Mom didn't know how they avoided me because I was a dull mouse, the unlikely daughter of the outrageous rock singer. I was backward. Those girls were already dating while I still had to fight to go

out on the street alone. I wouldn't know what to do or say to a boy if one ever asked me out, which, thank God, there wasn't a chance of anyone doing.

Another Saturday night to stay home and watch TV with Agnes. Philippa was going out in her new dress. While I watched her getting dressed, after she'd had her shower, she must have caught a sorrowful look on my face. "What's the matter, baby? You look sad."

"When you were fourteen I bet you went out on a lot of dates," I said.

Philippa frowned. "They were pretty awful, honey. I didn't know nice boys the way you do. We didn't really have dates or have parties. I lived in a low-down neighborhood. Things were pretty rough."

"Rough how?"

"I can't explain, just rough. I wasn't very happy so I don't like talking about it."

She never did. She never wanted to talk about when she was growing up, about her parents or anything. She never knew her real parents and lived with foster parents until she left when she was only fifteen and struck out on her own. I never can understand why she keeps me so wrapped up when she took care of herself from the time she was fifteen. She says that's precisely why, that she knows how dangerous the streets are, and she wants my life to be totally different from hers. Boy, she sure is making it different. . . .

"Why don't you invite some friends over tonight?"

she asked, slipping the new red dress on over her head.

"I don't feel like it," I said. It never occurred to Philippa that her darling daughter had no friends to invite over. I was thankful that she didn't know.

She gave her hair a last brushing and put on ruby earrings that went perfectly with her dress. She looked gorgeous.

"How do I look, okay?"

"You'll pass," I said with a grin.

Johnny was in the living room waiting for her. He was older than she was, at least in his forties, I thought, maybe even fifty. He had a rather homely but strong, interesting face. A big nose, soft brown spaniel eyes, and a mop of graying hair. Well-built, tall, muscular but not fat. A nice, friendly, funny face. He looked at my mom with adoring eyes, and couldn't tear them away from her.

"Hi, Cassandra," he said to me.

"Hi." I liked him because he didn't give me presents or turn on the charm for me. Actually, he didn't pay much attention to me, which suited me fine. I couldn't stand some of Mom's friends, male or female, who fussed over me and made all the obvious dumb cliché remarks.

When Mom left I stood at the window and watched the wind blow the leaves around on the park side of the avenue. It had turned cold and much windier since the afternoon, and I wondered where Mollie was going to sleep for the night. I hoped she'd gone

34

to one of the shelters. I couldn't imagine anyone staying in a doorway all night. The thought made me shiver. Suddenly I wished I could go out to make sure she was all right, although I knew she would have put me down. But also I felt very good to be in my own, warm, beautiful house, and I ran back to the kitchen to find Agnes and get my supper on a tray so I could watch TV while I ate.

I thought, You are selfish, selfish, feeling so good to be here when there are all those people out on the streets. But what could I do?

Chapter Four

*M*iracles do happen and life can be full of surprises. What do you know, but in school on Monday, Stacey and Elaine actually came up to me and asked if I'd have lunch with them. I am such a nitwit, I should have been suspicious. But it came as such a surprise and they seemed so natural and friendly, I said "Sure" right away.

Stacey is very sharp looking, with a rather square face, a short nose, straight blond hair, and a tall, sturdy body. Elaine is much slighter all over. Her features are delicate: she is small-boned and very feminine, like a little doll. They both dress very modishly, either miniskirts and tights or long full skirts down to their ankles. They are very good at putting on makeup and obviously would die if they were seen without it. No matter how marvelous my

clothes look in my closet or even on me at home, they both manage to make me feel lumpy and dowdy.

"Your mother is fantastic," Stacey said when we had taken our trays to a table in the cafeteria. "She's so young and fun. You must have a marvelous time with her."

"We have a good time," I said modestly. When she's around, I thought to myself.

"What's it like to be the daughter of someone so famous?" I'd been asked that question about a million times by all kinds of people, but Elaine sounded as if she might really want to know.

Nonetheless, I gave her my stock answer: "I've never been anyone else's daughter so I have no basis of comparison. It's okay." I could have said, "What's it like to be the daughter of a cold fish like your mother?" whom I had met a few times on school occasions. But I didn't.

Anyway, it didn't take long before the reason for Stacey's friendliness came through. I was on the second half of my egg-salad sandwich when Stacey said casually, "I'm having a big party Christmas week. It's going to be at my grandmother's house or in a hotel, we haven't decided." Her grandmother had been a Vanderbilt and lived in a famous landmark house on Fifth Avenue. "You're invited, of course, and I thought it would be fantastic if your mother would stop by for a while. Maybe she would sing a song or two. . . . I mean, we're not asking her as a performer," she stammered, "but some of the parents

are coming, and if she could just come by for an hour or so, it would really make the party."

Her words, "You're invited, of course," made me want to laugh or throw up. Of course. I had never been invited to any of her parties and I knew already that I was not going to this one.

"My mother's not going to be here Christmas week. She's leaving on a tour and she'll be gone until sometime in January." I caught a quick glance of dismay between them. What were they going to do now, stuck with me without my mother?

"Oh, that's too bad," Stacey said sorrowfully. "She would have made the party. Well, you'll get your invitation in the mail, and I do hope you can come. Unless," and she looked at me hopefully, "you are planning to spend Christmas with your mother, wherever she is."

"You never know with Mom. I can get a call Christmas Eve to fly out someplace wild to spend the day with her."

"How exciting," Elaine said.

"It's interesting," I said.

I was glad when the lunch was over and we had to go to our classes. For the first time in my life, I was elated that my mother was going to be away.

That afternoon, after school, I went out with a strange new sense of freedom. I didn't have to be home in an hour! It made me sad to think that such a tiny relaxation of schedule could bring me such

happiness, but I luxuriated in it just the same. I walked quickly over to Third Avenue to look for Mollie. I found her squatting in her doorway, looking awful. Her ruddy face was drawn and haggard, and she looked like a very old lady.

"Hi," I said to her.

She glanced up at me with tired eyes. "What do you want?" Her voice had a semblance of her usual gruffness.

"Nothing. I was just walking by and wondered how you were. What happened to your friend in the hospital?"

"He's dead," she said flatly. "They're all going to die." She waved her arms toward the street. "People ain't supposed to live this way. Only rats survive in these streets and I bet they have a hard time. People need houses, food, nice warm kitchens, a stove to make a pot of tea. Every one of them is going to die, like poor Eddie."

"There are shelters, people can go there to sleep, can't they?" I asked gently.

She looked at me with disgust. "Shelters. You ever seen one of them?" She gave a harsh laugh. "They tried to make me sleep in one of them places. Sleep? The noise'd wake up the dead. Women fighting, screaming, them that get any sleep snoring their heads off, and the dirt. You can't believe the dirt. A disgrace, I'm telling you. No one cares about us, no one."

"I care," I said, embarrassed.

She pretended she didn't hear me. "You get an allowance?"

"Yes. Not much, two dollars a week."

Mollie snorted. "Your ma's sure knocking herself out for you, ain't she?"

"She says it's good for the soul not to have too much money to spend. Good for my complexion, too. I'd buy too much candy."

"What makes her think you got a soul?"

"Everyone has a soul," I said.

"Are you kidding? Most of the people in this world running around never came within a mile of a soul. They's just got bodies. Fat bodies, skinny bodies. If they'd got souls they'd not be fighting with each other all the time, an' my friends wouldn't be here on the streets. People'd be fat and healthy instead of mean and skinny."

"I don't think people are mean."

"What do you know? See that lady in that car over there?" She pointed to a chauffeur holding open the door of a long black limo for a woman wrapped in a mink coat. "How many houses you think she's got? She's got a house in the country for sure, maybe another one in Europe, say the south of France, she's got her duplex in New York, God knows what else— they're all empty except where she's living now and I bet that's got a dozen empty rooms. Would she give my friends a place to sleep, to rest their weary bones? You ask her, and you'll know what's mean."

I thought of our big, empty house up in Connect-

icut and I felt ashamed. "You could come sleep at our house if you'd like," I said blithely, wondering at the same time how I could get her past Agnes while my mother was away.

Mollie laughed, a deep belly laugh. "That's a good one. Your ma would love to have you bring me home. Oh boy, that's real funny."

"You don't know my mother," I said indignantly. "She's not mean, she'd let me, I bet; it's Agnes who would make a fuss."

"I don't know your ma and who Agnes is, and I care less. But neither one of them is handing out beds to the likes of me, even if I wanted it, which I don't. I don't want no handouts. I'm okay, I can take care of myself; it's the others I worry about. There's Fannie, who's got a terrible cough, and Mike, who's drinking himself sick with cheap wine, and some little kids just floating around. I could go on and give you lots of names, but it wouldn't do any good. Nobody cares."

"I don't believe that," I said. "I just don't believe that nobody cares. Some people do, I'm sure of that."

"You can be sure until doomsday, but that don't change nothing. I'm tired of talking," she said, and closed her eyes. I realized I was being dismissed, and I walked away reluctantly. For a second there had been a look on her face, or maybe it was in her eyes, that in a strange way reminded me of my mother. My mom had some of Mollie's toughness, as if she could fight the world, but at the same time a knowledge that

41

it would be a terrible fight and that she'd get hurt. They both made me feel helpless, that all around me people were hurting and I couldn't do anything to give them any relief.

A few days later I was sitting in Mom's room while she was packing. Actually Philippa doesn't do any packing. She goes through her closet and all her drawers and flings things on the bed. Then she goes through all the stuff on the bed and throws what she doesn't want on the floor. Then she may dart to her closet and pull out some skirts or pants she forgot about and add them to the pile on the bed. After much shifting and changing of what looks like one garment for another just like it, she yells for Agnes to come in and get everything neatly put into suitcases. Agnes furtively tries her own discarding, which drives Mom up the wall. "I don't care if I have a dozen suitcases," Mom would take a stand in front of her bed as if she were guarding home base and glare at Agnes. "My things make me feel secure when I'm on tour." Agnes had no answer for that.

She was still in the sorting-out stage when I decided to broach the subject that had been on my mind for the past few days: How was I going to get Mom to okay my inviting Mollie to the country for a weekend? I didn't like to tell outright lies, but I knew I was going to have to do a little embroidering of the truth. I had been trying to figure out how to do as little of that as possible.

"Mom, can I ask a friend up to the country for the weekend while you're away?"

"Sure, honey. A friend from school?"

"Well no, it's someone I met in the neighborhood."

Mom raised her eyebrows. "Someone in the neighborhood? A girl your age?"

"Not really. She's older. We met because I bumped into her accidentally and she dropped the bundles she was carrying. We got to talking, and we've run into each other a few times in the afternoon. She's very nice, I like her."

"Do you know anything about her? Where she lives or anything?"

"She lives in the neighborhood." So far I hadn't said one lie. "I don't think she has much money, or gets away much, and I thought she might like a weekend in the country." Lucky for me Mom never asked a lot of questions.

"I guess there's no harm in asking her. Adolph could take you up, and Agnes and Sebastian would go with you. You'd have to call Frank to turn up the heat in the house and open it up for you. I think he'd better air it a day or so before you go. Remember to tell Agnes to call him."

"Yeah." I was thinking how to get rid of Agnes, but decided to worry about that when the time came. "Tell Agnes it's all right for me to go up with a friend, please, so she'll know."

"Yeah, sure. Do you think I should take this?" Mom held up a very short black dress that showed off her

legs to perfection. "It's cut very low, you think it's too sexy? What do you think?"

"Since when are you afraid of being sexy?" My mom was as contradictory as Mollie. She oozed sex and at the same time could be a prude.

Mom laughed. "It's those Catholic audiences. . . . I'm not sure . . ."

"They'll love you no matter what you wear."

"I hope so." I couldn't believe her. She still got worried about being a success; every concert was a new hurdle for her. Here was this fantastic person, SRO (standing room only) every place she sang, tons of fan mail every week, and she still worried. She still wanted to hear from me, every time, how much her audiences loved her. Little me, her lumpy daughter.

I didn't go with her to the airport; I never did, I preferred to say good-bye to her at home. Those airports were depressing, everyone rushing around, lousy cafeterias, all too cold and impersonal. But when she left, the house was empty. It was different from when she was just going out, or away for a few days and I knew she'd be coming back soon. Wherever Philippa was, it was exciting, lively, last-minute dinners out, or like when she took me shopping with her. Or I could come home and find a party going. One part of her life was so disciplined, she said, with rehearsals and concerts and records, that she hated making plans for her free time. She liked to do things on the spur of the moment.

Not that I saw her that much. But at least when we

were in the same city, the same house, there were those chance, *unexpected* times with her. When she was gone there was nothing.

"Come on, cheer up." Agnes came into my room, where I was staring out the window. "Do you want to go to a movie this evening? Or buy one for your VCR? Don't mope."

"Maybe I feel like moping," I said. I didn't want Agnes to try cheering me up. I really wanted to be left alone. "I don't feel like going out. I'll stay home and read."

Agnes gave me one of her looks that said: Okay, if you want to be stubborn and miserable, go ahead. She marched out of my room with a hurt look on her face, but I felt too close to crying to go after her. I stretched out on my bed and thought about Mollie. I wondered if she ever got depressed.

Chapter Five

*M*ollie didn't get depressed, I discovered; at least I didn't see it in her, but she did worry. When I found her the afternoon after my mother left, she was sitting in her doorway with a tiny woman displaying a large, ugly bruise on her face.

I had bought a bag of cookies to bring to Mollie. "That's nice, that's real nice." She actually smiled at me, showing her missing front teeth. "This is my friend Eva," she said.

"How do you do," I said politely. Eva looked me up and down through swollen eyelids.

"I can't see good today," she said. "Had a terrible night."

"It was in one of them shelters you like so much," Mollie said disparagingly. "Some miserable woman beat her up, a little thing like her. It's a disgrace."

"That's terrible. I'm sorry."

"Sure you're sorry," Mollie said with disgust. "Everyone's sorry, but ain't nothing anyone's doing. More people living on the streets now, got no homes, and this country's the richest country in the world. Sorry ain't doing no good."

"I'm just a kid, what can I do?"

Mollie looked up at me. "Sure you're a kid, ain't your fault, I guess. Anyway, thanks for them cookies."

I stood awkwardly beside them, feeling as though I were about ten feet tall towering above them squatting on the sidewalk. I was longing to ask Mollie if she'd come up to the country with me some weekend, but I didn't want to ask in front of Eva. Eva had her head bent close to Mollie's and they were whispering together. I was about to walk away when Eva's thin voice piped up. "Hey, would you do me a favor? My kids are staying in one of them welfare hotels on Twenty-eighth Street. Could you go over and give them something for me? I ain't feeling good today an' I don't think I can make it there."

I thought quickly. I could walk there and back in about forty minutes, it was only around half-past three, so I could easily be home by five. Eva looked so pitiful I was glad to do something for her. "Sure, tell me how to find them and what do you want me to take?"

"Dan and Lisa, that's their names, they're staying with my friend Lily, a nice woman and a real good friend to my kids." She gave me exact directions to

the hotel. "They're in Room 214, you'll find it easy, on the second floor. Take them this." She dug into one of her bundles and brought out a soiled envelope. "You give this to Lisa, mind you, not to Danny but to Lisa, and tell her it's to buy them some lunch and supper. Tell them I'll try to get to see them tomorrow, that I ain't feeling so good today." She turned to Mollie. "You sure she ain't gonna keep this for herself?"

Mollie glanced at me. "She better not. No, she ain't no thief, I'm pretty good at judging character." Mollie looked at me sternly. "You take that right over there, hear. An' don't open it an' buy yourself some candy on the way."

I was furious and almost told Eva to keep her dirty old envelope, but the two of them looked so ridiculous in their tatty rags worrying about my taking Eva's money, I wanted to laugh. "Give it to me," I said, and took the envelope and hurried away.

I walk fast, so it didn't even take me twenty minutes to get down to the "hotel." It didn't look like a hotel to me. First I walked right past it and had to go back and make sure of the number. I thought hotels were elegant, like the Plaza, where my mom sometimes took me for lunch, but this was an old, grimy building you didn't even want to go into. Inside it was worse. The walls with the paint all peeling off were scribbled on; it was dark, and kids were running all over the place. I didn't dare go into the forbidding box that was the elevator, but found some stairs and walked up to the second floor. The smell was terrible. There

were torn bags of garbage outside the doors, the long hall was filthy, and through the doors I could hear a baby crying and a man and woman screaming at each other. I wanted to get out as fast as I could.

I ran down the corridor until I found Room 214, and knocked on the door. A woman who must be Lily opened it.

She sure was surprised to see me. "What you want?" she asked in a husky voice.

"I came to bring something to Dan and Lisa from their mother," I explained.

She stared at me, up and down, from my white leather boots to my fur-lined parka, and she burst out laughing. "Where little Eva find you? Where'd you get all them fancy clothes from; you rob a store?"

"Certainly not," I said indignantly. "They're my clothes. My mother bought them for me."

"Oh yeah . . . maybe she the one rob a store. What you got for Eva's kids? An' where is she? I can't keep them kids forever; I already got too many of my own in this room, four sleepin' in one bed and the rest on the floor. It ain't healthy, so many closed up in this box of a room. You tell Eva one more night and that's it. Give me what you got."

"She wanted me to give it to Lisa, please. Is she here?"

I'd been standing at the door praying that she wouldn't ask me to come into the room. There was a smell of old food, of urine, and of some decay that I didn't want to know about. I could see a lot of kids in

the room, and some little ones were hanging onto Lily's wide skirt, staring up at me.

"Lisa ain't here. I can't keep track of that one. She's out on the street somewhere. I'll give her whatever you got. If Eva thinks I want anything of hers, you tell her to shove it."

I think she would have slammed the door in my face if I hadn't handed her the envelope. I didn't know what else to do. "Please give it to Lisa," I said, and fled down the hall and down the stairs. I held my breath until I could get outside to the street.

I ran past the kids playing wildly on the street, and I didn't stop running until I was a safe few blocks away. Then I stopped, breathing hard. I felt as if I had just escaped from some dark, underground world, a nightmare world that I didn't want to know about. But then as I walked at a reasonable rate back to more familiar streets and neighborhood, I felt ashamed of myself. I had no reason to have been so frightened—just because those people were poor didn't make them evil. But that hotel was unbelievable, it was awful. I didn't want to be a snob, but the dirt and the smell had really made me feel sick. Yet my good clothes, and the fine underwear I had on, a cotton petticoat that cost $65 and that Agnes washed by hand and ironed every time I wore it, made me feel uncomfortable. I wouldn't have given them up for anything to live in that hole of a hotel, and those kids might not even want what I had, but all the same I felt like a ridiculous hothouse flower.

Mollie and Eva were where I had left them, each with a container of hot coffee and munching from a bag of donuts on the sidewalk between them. I gave Eva the message from Lily, and had to tell her that I didn't see Lisa but gave the envelope to Lily.

She grumbled a lot that I didn't find Lisa, and didn't say a word of thanks for my going there and back. "I don't know what to do with them kids if Lily won't keep them, I guess I'll have to go see her . . ." she kept rambling on, half talking to herself, until Mollie told her that Lily wouldn't throw the kids out. Mollie kept looking at me, and I had the feeling that some ideas were turning over in her mind that I didn't want to hear. I was scared she was going to ask me to take Eva's kids. I knew I couldn't, but I didn't want Mollie's look of disgust when I had to say no.

"Why can't Eva be with her kids?" The question popped out, although by this time I knew Mollie didn't like explaining things.

I didn't escape Mollie's look of disgust. "You see her, don't you? She can't stay in one of them shelters and her kids gotta sleep someplace. You think everyone's got a nice, cozy house with a momma and a daddy in it? Families is strewn all over the place, plenty of kids don't even know where their mommas and daddys are. Lily takes care of other people's kids all the time."

"I'm sorry," I mumbled, and excused myself and hurried away.

I made up my mind that day that I wasn't going to see Mollie anymore. What was the use? There was nothing I could do for Mollie, maybe nobody could, and as for her friends, I didn't want to get involved. I couldn't help them either. There were so many. All those people without homes living in that awful hotel, it was too much for me. Besides, they weren't even nice to me, and I was darned if I was going to be an errand girl for them and not even get a thank-you.

With Philippa away, I was terribly lonesome. Agnes said I was grumpy and I suppose I was, I felt at such loose ends. I decided to try again to make friends at school. The next day in the cafeteria, I took my tray over to a table where Stacey and Elaine, and another girl, Lori, were sitting. Feeling very courageous, I asked if I could sit with them. Lori politely made room for me.

"Is your mother making any new records?" Lori asked.

"No, not now, she's away on tour."

"That's why she can't come to my party," Stacey said, "but Cassandra is coming anyway." She said it with a forced smile.

I almost blurted out that I had no intention of going to her party, but I kept my mouth shut.

"What do you think about Mrs. Marconi's idea about working in soup kitchens?" Elaine asked Stacey.

I pricked up my ears. Mrs. Marconi was our social studies teacher, but we were in different classes. They

had her in the morning and I had her in the afternoon.

"I think it stinks," Stacey said. "Did you ever see one of those places? They're full of germs and diseases. Not me, thank you. Besides, Mrs. Marconi is a socialist, maybe a communist for all we know."

"That's ridiculous," I said. "Just because she teaches social studies doesn't make her a socialist."

Elaine giggled. "That's funny. Would *you* work in a soup kitchen?" she asked me.

"I'll wait and see what she says about it in my class."

Having lunch with them wasn't much fun. I ate my sandwich as fast as I could and left, saying I had to go to the library. But I kept thinking about the idea of working in a soup kitchen. If the school was doing it, and it was part of my social studies class, Agnes couldn't object. It was typical of Stacey to put it down, but I wondered what Mollie would think. She'd probably turn up her nose at soup kitchens the same way she did at shelters—she was truly a bizarre character. She wanted nothing to do with any part of the establishment even when it tried to help. There was something in me that responded to the way she thumbed her nose at everything in our whole society and yet managed to survive. A survivor like my mom, and I hoped I had some of that in me. To me she was kind of wonderful, and I thought, What a terrific person she could have been if she didn't have that mix-up in her personality. But I thought about Eva and her kids, and Lily and hers, and hundreds of

others who needed help and I resolved not to let Mollie and her hostility turn me off, not if I could really do something useful.

Predictably, in her second class, Mrs. Marconi brought up the subject of the homeless in the city. "I want to talk about a subject you young people probably know very little, if anything, about," she said. "Right in this city where all of you live in very comfortable apartments and houses, there are hundreds, maybe thousands, of young people like you, and old people, too, who have no homes. Some of them have places to sleep in shelters and hotels, and get food at soup kitchens, but that is not enough. The city is trying to build more shelters, and that is good; the shelters are fine, but in the meantime many people just live on the street or in subway stations, anyplace they can find." She looked around the room to see our reaction, I guess. Mrs. M., as we called her, was younger than our other teachers and she had a kind of eager-beaver attitude that was sometimes okay and other times annoying.

Right then, I was annoyed, because I didn't think she knew anything about the homeless. I put up my hand and spoke. "The hotel shelters aren't fine, they're pretty awful. Some people are afraid to stay in them."

Mrs. M. looked at me in astonishment. "How do you know so much about this, Cassandra?"

"I don't really," I stammered. "I went into one of those hotels once by mistake," I said. "It was terrible."

"That may be," she said as if she didn't quite believe

54

me. "In any case, I want to talk about the soup kitchens. I have a friend who has worked in one, and I thought it might be a project for you people after Christmas. I'd like you to think about it, and discuss it with your parents. I thought we could work out something so that those of you who want to could help out in one of the soup kitchens as a social studies project. In the meantime, I'll check it out with some of the people who run those soup kitchens and see what they think of the idea."

In any event, nothing was going to happen until after Christmas vacation.

Later on, after class, I ran into Elaine in the library.

"What did Mrs. M. talk about in your class?" she asked.

"I guess the same things she did in yours." She looked embarrassed. Maybe she didn't want Stacey, her idol, to find her talking to me. "She spoke about the soup kitchens."

"Are you going?"

"I might, if it goes through. I probably will."

She leaned toward me. Now I was sure she didn't want Stacey to come along and find her whispering to me. "If you go, I will." She seemed relieved to have gotten the words out.

I was as surprised as she was.

"Do you mean it?" I needed to hear her say it again.

She nodded. "Yes, I would like to. Don't say anything, not until it happens." She didn't have to tell me to whom I shouldn't say it.

"I won't breathe a word." Suddenly we smiled at each other, and her smile made me feel good. If she scrubbed off some of her makeup, I thought, she would be pretty. Maybe plain, but still pretty.

She left me abruptly, and I wondered, when it came down to working in a soup kitchen, if she would really do it. But one thing was clear: Stacey sure had a strong hold over her. It made me feel sorry for Elaine. I'd rather be alone than be that dependent on anyone, or that scared of their opinion.

Chapter Six

We had one of those unexpected lovely days you sometimes get in New York in early December, so I went over to the stable, and without telling Agnes I took Spenser out into the park. There is nothing like it: riding that horse by myself takes me into a world I don't have anyplace else. There is no one to tell me what to do. Spenser understands me; I hardly touch the reins and she knows where I want to go, and with only a small nudge of my heel she'll break from a trot into a canter. It's like being with a close friend you don't have to talk to.

I was riding along, lost in my thoughts, when suddenly, out of the bushes, a small rock came hurtling at Spenser. She jumped and reared up in the air and, taken by surprise, I slid off her back and landed in the dirt. I saw two small kids running. I was a mess,

but I wasn't hurt, so I scrambled up, threw Spenser's reins over a post, and ran after them. I didn't have to run far. Just the other side of the thick bushes there they were, two skinny little boys, no more than six or seven years old, standing beside a woman and a man on a blanket on the ground. A small, bedraggled family. The man was lying on his back, so I didn't get a good look at him, but the woman was sitting up, her hands busily trying to push her hair back under a soiled cotton kerchief. Her face was almost skeleton-like, her skin pulled tight over her cheekbones, and her eyes sunken into dark cavities. But she wasn't old. When she stood up and grabbed the two kids to her, she looked like a young girl.

"What'd you do now?" she asked the kids, holding each by the back of their shirts. Neither one had on a jacket.

"They threw a rock at my horse," I said indignantly. "I could have been badly hurt. They're lucky I'm okay."

Before she had a chance to answer a cop came through the bushes from the bridle path. "What's going on?" he demanded. "Is that your horse tied up out there?"

"Yes, it is. It's all right," I said hastily. "Nothing's happened." The kids looked scared and the young woman was biting her lips nervously. The man on the blanket had gotten up. He needed a shave and looked so sullen I thought he was going to beat up the kids, or the cop; I wasn't sure which.

"You're sure nothing's happened." The policeman was young, too, and he looked uncertainly from them to me.

"Yes, I'm sure." I turned to go, but the cop's voice stopped me.

"You people aren't allowed to sleep in the park. You can't stay here. I could take you in for being vagrants. Where do you live?" He seemed to know he was asking a foolish question.

"We ain't got a permanent address right now," the man said. He gave a twisted smile. "We'll send you a postcard when we get ourselves settled."

"Don't get fresh with me," the cop said gruffly. "Get along with you now. You can't live here."

"Listen, this park is free. It's daytime, we have a right to be here if we want. You can't order us out."

The young cop was trying to control his anger. "Just don't stay here overnight. You'll land in jail if you do." He turned and marched away. I followed after him. Neither one of us said a word as he got back onto his horse and I got back on Spenser.

But I didn't feel tranquil anymore. I kept thinking of that family. I couldn't imagine what it was like not to have a home—where did they brush their teeth, change their clothes, do any of the hundred things I took for granted? Did those kids ever watch TV? Did they have any toys? It was too much for my mind to comprehend. I leaned over to pat Spenser. I wanted to forget about that woman and man and the two little kids—what could I do for

them anyway? Nothing. Life wasn't fair—who said that? Had it been President Kennedy? I couldn't remember, but it sure was true. I mean, if I gave Spenser away, if I gave all my clothes and possessions away, it wouldn't help that family or anyone else. I'd just be another person on welfare or sleeping in the park. That was no answer. Something was cockeyed, but it was going to take a bigger brain than mine to figure it out.

The red-, round-faced doorman at home looked anxiously at my muddy khaki britches and jacket. "You have a tumble, miss?"

"Yeah, I took a slide, but I'm okay; it was nothing."

"Lucky you didn't get hurt." He nodded wisely, as if to say he knew that God looked after little misses like me. But he was a good sort and it wasn't his fault that he had to nod with his "Miss," "Ma'am," and "Sir," and be nice to everyone.

Agnes was less calm. "You take those clothes right off and get into a hot tub. The idea of you going out into the park without saying a word. God punished you, that's what. I don't know now if I dare leave you alone, there's no telling what you may do. . . ."

I wasn't paying attention to her usual ranting, until I caught her last sentence. "When are you leaving me alone?" I asked as casually as I could.

"I was thinking of going down to my sister's in Philadelphia. She's going into the hospital for some surgery and I thought she'd like to have me there. But now . . ." Agnes had pulled off my boots and

riding clothes and was running the water in the tub. "I'm not sure."

"That's ridiculous. Of course you must go. She's your only sister and she has nobody else. I'll be perfectly all right."

"Says you. Going out in the park in the middle of winter!"

"Aggie, it was a beautiful day. Besides, nothing happened. I took a little slide, that's all. It's just mud. I'm not even black-and-blue."

"That's not the point," Agnes said testily. I refrained from asking what the point was.

I had a lot of figuring out to do. With Agnes away for the weekend, this would be my one chance to get Mollie up to the country—if she would come. And if I could work it. I had to find a good reason for going.

I sat at my desk thinking about what to do, absently staring at the big calendar on the wall, the calendar I had marked off with where Mom was each day of her tour. The weekend Agnes was talking about, the second week in December, Philippa would be flying to Copenhagen to give a concert.

Suddenly a bell rang. The second weekend in December was when the big crafts show was held in Stoneridge, the town next to ours in the country. Mom and I always went to it and bought tons of presents for Christmas and the rest of the year besides. Real luck, that would be a perfect reason for going up there.

"I don't know," Agnes said. "I should stay home

and go with you. I don't like your going alone with Sebastian."

"I won't be alone. I'll take a friend."

"Who will you take?" Agnes demanded.

"I don't know, I haven't decided. If you stay home," I added meanly, "I won't go. I'll feel too guilty about your not being with your sister."

"Don't blackmail me," Agnes said severely.

I had to work hard not to show my anxiety in getting Agnes off on Friday. Purposely she took an afternoon train so she could see me after school before she left. I had to listen to her repeat all the things she'd already said to me a hundred times before: "Don't forget to pick up the grocery order at Gristede's, otherwise you'll have nothing to eat when you get up there; don't go off without telling Sebastian where you're going. I do wish you'd give me the name and phone number of the friend you're taking. Lock up when you leave here, and be sure to lock up, up there. Oh dear, I don't feel right about your going there without me."

"Please don't worry. I'm not a baby, you know, or maybe you haven't noticed. I can't give you anyone's name for sure because I'm not sure if my friend Mollie can come." (Agnes never remembered the names of anyone at school so "Mollie" didn't mean anything to her.) "I may even go alone, I don't mind."

She went on grumbling and worrying until she was

ready to go out the door with Sebastian, who was taking her to the train station. Mom's chauffeur, Adolph, was on vacation. Then in true Agnes fashion she threw her arms around me with tears in her eyes, as if she was going away for a year instead of a few days, and hugged me to her, telling me how much she loved me and how much she hated to leave me. I hugged her back, but gave a big sigh of relief when the door closed behind the two of them.

Alone at last, with nobody. I felt like jumping around the house like a wild one. It was a miracle that I had persuaded Agnes that I didn't have to go with her and Sebastian to the station, but that I really could survive for about an hour by myself. When Mom came home we were going to have a serious talk about this constant surveillance. I was much too old for that, and it was getting to be a big pain.

During the week, I had spoken to Mollie about coming up to the country with me, but I couldn't get a definite answer out of her. She mumbled about having a lot of things to do (I couldn't imagine what), and not liking to be around a lot of people, which was ridiculous, as she always had people around her on the street. I told her that there would be no one there, and I thought she would really like it. There was something about her that was so like a country woman—in the way she looked and the things she said, as if living on the street was being as close to the earth as she could get. I think that was what attracted me to her; she was the opposite of everything tinselly

and polished. She was crude, down to earth, bizarre but real.

Once I knew that Sebastian and Agnes had safely driven away, I put on my coat and flew downstairs to clinch it with Mollie.

She was in a state when I found her. "They've taken Eva's kids away and put them in some home. You know what them homes are like, and what is Eva supposed to do? She can't get them back, she's got no place to take them back to. It's a disgrace, a mom can't have a place for her own kids. An animal's got it better."

I had no way to comfort her. The whole situation was so hopeless: little kids without a home, teenagers, old people, a whole subterranean world living under my nose. But I wasn't going to be caught handing out dumb platitudes to Mollie like, Things will get better, or God will take care of it. "It's lousy," I said to her, "it stinks. But since there's nothing you can do about it, please come up to the country with me. It'll be just you and me and Sebastian, who will drive us. Be downstairs eight o'clock tomorrow morning, so we can get to the crafts show before the good things are gone." I repeated my address to her.

"I don't know, I'll have to see." She was putting on her I'm-a-very-busy-person airs which, I was beginning to learn, was her way of saying that she could lead her own life and get along without the rest of the world. It made you wonder.

By this time I knew I'd never get a straight answer

out of her. I could only hope she'd turn up the next morning.

Friday night was divine with no one to bother me. I took my own supper from the fridge: cold ham, lots of cheese and crackers, a huge plate of vanilla-almond ice cream, and a box of cookies. I had a new mystery to read and had a wonderful time. I went to bed around eleven and fell asleep right away. But I woke around five in the morning, and thinking about Mollie, and Eva and her kids, and all the people out in the light snow that was falling, I couldn't get back to sleep. I went into the kitchen. Sebastian was sleeping in Agnes's room; I could hear him snoring, and I ate some more cheese and crackers and drank a glass of milk. I crawled back to bed and tried to have happy thoughts (riding Spenser, playing tennis, visiting Mom) but I didn't really sleep. I was up and dressed by seven, an hour before Mollie might be downstairs.

I felt all nervous and jumpy, wondering if Mollie would show up, and then I stopped short: Hey, wait a minute, I thought, why are you so excited about taking an old bag lady with you? She's going to be a big nuisance and what makes you think you can trust Sebastian not to tell Agnes?

I had to stop to think about that. I wasn't really worried about Sebastian. I'd always felt that he was on my side when Agnes got persnickety. I could tell by the way he'd roll his eyes and the looks he threw my way. I thought he could keep a secret. Figuring out why I wanted Mollie wasn't as easy. I had to be

honest. I wasn't a do-gooder, and taking her over-night to the country wasn't going to change her life one iota. She'd go right back to her doorway on the street. I was doing it for myself.

There it was, as plain as could be: Mollie had something that was compelling. Nutty as she was, and living the way she did was pretty wild; she had stripped herself clean of all material possessions, and she was her own person. She had gumption, a fear-lessness that I envied. I seemed to be surrounded and invaded by a million anxieties that she was free of. The only thing she was afraid of was being closed in, and she would fight that off with all her strength. I guess I hoped that if I got to know her better, spent a little time with her, some of what she had would rub off on me.

Chapter Seven

I had a talk with Sebastian before I went downstairs. "If my friend shows up," I said to him, "please be nice to her. She's an older woman who's had a rough time, and I think a trip to the country will be good for her. She's . . ." (How could I explain Mollie?) "Well, she's different from the people we know, my mom's friends. She's a bit eccentric, but she's a good person." I didn't want to tell Sebastian too much. He's a decent sort, but not the brightest guy around, and he was unlikely to give much thought to Mollie. Sebastian was all excited about driving Mom's car (he adored it), and his main dream in life was to win the big lottery. "And by the way," I added casually, "I'd just as soon you didn't mention her to Agnes. If she asks you about my friend, just say she was okay, but that you didn't pay much attention to her. Okay?"

Sebastian grinned and gave me a wink. "Agnes and her questions. But don't worry, she won't get a word out of me." He giggled. "Be good for her not to know everything." I hadn't realized that keeping a secret from Agnes would give him so much pleasure, but now I knew he'd be mum.

The big question was: Would Mollie be downstairs? I had told her to come exactly at eight o'clock for fear that if she came too early, before I got there, the doorman would chase her away. I had begun to see how everyone in the city sidestepped the street people, avoiding them, not wanting them in sight.

I was downstairs a few minutes before eight, and no sign of Mollie. Sebastian had brought the car around and he was parked in front of the building, sitting in the driver's seat puffed up like a proud pigeon. He had gotten hold of a uniform, probably borrowed it from Adolph, so he looked almost like a real chauffeur, except that the suit was too big for him, so the result was pretty silly.

By ten minutes after eight, a quarter after, Sebastian was getting restless and said he thought we should leave. "I don't think your friend is coming. Do you want to telephone her?" he asked.

Of course there was no way to telephone Mollie, but I wasn't ready to leave without her. It was almost half-past eight when Mollie appeared around the corner. I don't know where she'd left all her junk, but she was carrying only one shopping bag. She wore her usual voluminous skirts but she honored the

occasion with a short, woolly jacket and an extraordinary black velvet wide-brimmed hat on her head. She looked like the Mad Duchess.

Sebastian's eyes popped when I greeted her, and I thought the doorman might have a heart attack when he saw me help her into the car. He closed the door behind us, shaking his head in bewilderment, as if the world had turned upside down for him.

"I don't know why I'm doing this," Mollie said, settling herself beside me on the seat, taking up more than half of it. "I have so much to do."

"What keeps you so busy?" I asked.

Mollie gave me a scathing look. "There are people who need looking after. I'm not like some people," she said, giving me another meaningful glance, "who have only themselves to think about, whose big worry is what new dress to put on. I have friends who depend on me."

"That's very nice."

"Nice? There's nothing nice about it. What do you know? Someone gets sick on the street, there ain't no doctor to call. I gotta go get medicine out of my friend at the drugstore, I gotta tell Eva where to find her kids; I know where's the best soup kitchen, not for me, but for others. I keep my ears open, I hear things, I know the street. I don't know what they'd do without me. There ain't no one to count on, them social service people, they know from nothing."

"How'd you learn all this?" I asked, not out of nosiness. I really wanted to know.

Mollie looked scornful. "By living. Experience, child, I got experience. I didn't grow up wrapped in cotton like some people I know. I lived. Ain't nothing you learn in school that counts. You got a lot of book learning I suppose, but you don't know nothing, not a thing."

"Maybe I can learn something from you," I said.

Mollie laughed, one of her deep belly laughs. "Yeah, I bet you could. But I ain't gonna teach you. You gotta learn for yourself. I'm talking about things no one can teach you, no one, not the best teacher in the world."

We didn't talk much after that. Mollie kept looking out of the window as we drove up the parkway. The trees had a light snow on them, and some were iced over with lovely icicles dripping from them. "It's real pretty," Mollie murmured. "Reminds me of when I was a kid." I was hoping she'd tell me something about when she was a kid, but she didn't, and I felt shy about asking her. I felt that any questions would make her shut up for sure.

"You ever been kissed by a boy?" she asked me abruptly.

I shook my head. "No, not yet."

"You got a real treat ahead of you. I remember my first kiss, I was about your age, maybe younger. It was on a bus. I don't even remember where I was going, but I do remember this boy sitting next to me. He had dark, curly hair and big dark eyes. We sat carefully, so we didn't touch each other, and then I dropped a box

of crackers I was holding. We both bent to pick it up, and *wham,* our heads clashed, and we both started to laugh. After that we talked all the way. He had to leave first, and before he got up to go, he turned around and smacked me with a kiss, right on the mouth. I was stunned, then he did it again, and I kissed him back. He got off the bus and I never saw him again. I think about him sometimes, what kind of a man he grew up to be, what kind of a life he's got." She giggled. "Probably got a lot of bills, kids, and a nagging wife. I guess I'm lucky he got off that bus."

Mollie became a different person. Suddenly she was someone who had had a life. She must have had a mother. Had she lived in a house, did she have sisters and brothers, had she ever been in love? I had to look at her differently. She wasn't just some flotsam floating on the street, she was a *person,* a person who had been born, taken care of as a baby, a human being with a life like other people. I wondered how and why she had ended up on the street, but knowing Mollie, I suspected I would never know. But all those other people, her friends on the street, the people in the welfare hotel, at the soup kitchens, they were all people who must have had lives too—what had happened to them?

As always, I felt excited when we got near our house. I loved that place. It was more home to me than the apartment on Fifth Avenue. My mom had bought it when I was three, when her new record had hit the

top of the Top Ten. It was an old house, 1830, I think, that Mom had remodeled with modern kitchen and bathrooms, but had left the good old parts alone.

It was a white, rambling house with a wide front porch, screened side porches, and shaded with beautiful maple trees. It had lawns sloping down to a stream with an almost natural large pool off to one side of it. Half the side of the pool was natural rock, the rest cement, and the water flowed in one side and over the spill on the other. The water was always stinging cold but marvelous. I was sorry Mollie wasn't seeing the place with the rhododendrons and azaleas in bloom, but under the snow it looked beautiful, too.

When Sebastian drove up to the house, I was waiting for Mollie to say something, but she was unusually quiet.

"Do you like it?" I asked.

Mollie grunted. "Where's around here to go for a cuppa coffee?"

"We have coffee in the house."

" 'Tain't the same. I like sittin' on a stool with other people around. Pretty lonesome here."

"That's what's nice about it," I said, "No neighbors, no one around for miles."

Mollie shivered. "Gruesome. You got ghosts here maybe?"

I laughed. "No, no ghosts." It occurred to me that maybe she was really frightened. "You're safer here than in a city apartment or on the street. Honestly."

"That's what you say."

Frank, who lived a couple of miles down the road, and who with his wife looked after the house for Mom, had turned up the heat so the house was toasty warm for us. As I always did, I ran from one room to another just to look at everything and make sure that nothing had changed. The house was filled with antiques Mom and I bought at auctions, or that we had picked up together driving around the country-side. The happiest times in my life had been in that house with Philippa, going on our jaunts together, or walking in the woods and swimming in the icy water, having our own picnics on the lawn under the big oak down near the stream.

I took Mollie upstairs and showed her where she would sleep, in a room next to mine that had its own bathroom.

"Is this okay?" I asked her.

Mollie held tight to her shopping bag. "I guess so."

"You can leave your bag here," I suggested.

Mollie hugged it to her closer. "No thank you. I'll keep it."

Soon after we arrived Frank's wife, Maggie, appeared with bags of groceries. I hadn't needed to bring stuff up from Gristede's after all. Maggie had everything we needed.

After Maggie gave me a big hug, I turned to introduce her to Mollie. Maggie gave her a cool hello.

"Are you going to be the new cook?" Maggie asked politely.

Mollie stared at her disdainfully. "Me cook? No thank you. I ain't nobody's cook. Never was, never will be."

"I beg your pardon." Maggie gave me a questioning look.

"Mollie is a friend of mine," I said, which only increased Maggie's bewilderment. She went into the kitchen shaking her head, as if to say this was all too much for her to understand. I suppose it was.

If I'd had any notion that Mollie was going to be impressed by Philippa's old house, her beautiful antiques and acres of lawns, a pond, and woodland, I was greatly mistaken. After I took her to her room, a lovely, high-ceilinged, large square room that overlooked the pond, and showed her the adjacent bathroom where she declined to wash up, I took her around the rest of the house.

"Your mom's so rich I thought she'd have pretty things. What's she want all this old junk for? She could go and buy herself a set of real nice new furniture. Some people don't know what to do with their money."

She didn't approve of the outdoors much either. I took her for a walk on a path through the woods. There was snow on the ground and on the trees and it was absolutely beautiful. Mollie hated it. It was too quiet. It was lonesome. There'd be wild animals, although I assured her she'd see nothing but squirrels

and maybe some deer if we were lucky. She couldn't wait to get back into the house. But inside she was just as restless and jumpy.

She refused to come to the crafts show with me. "Too many people," she said, "I don't like crowds."

"I thought you loved people," I argued. "You said it was too lonesome here, that you miss the street."

"This'd be different. Different kind of people, not my cuppa tea."

I didn't like going off without her, but I did want to see the show, so I left her in the kitchen with Maggie and promised that I'd be back in a little while. Sebastian was out cutting logs, but I got him to drive me to the crafts show.

It wasn't the same without Philippa. I felt lonely going around by myself. The few people from the village whom I knew and were there, only asked where my mother was. That's all they were interested in, no one cared about me. I didn't blame them.

I bought a pretty hand-knit sweater and some old wooden boxes and wondered why I had come up here at all. I felt foolish about having brought Mollie up. What did I think I was going to accomplish?

When I got back to the house, I felt worse. I found Mollie in bed, with all her clothes on, and a pile of blankets on top of her. She opened her slit eyes when I came into the room.

"What's the matter? Are you sick?" I was really worried.

She shivered noticeably. I felt she was doing it purposely. "I can't stand this cold. I ain't used to country houses."

I thought of her sleeping in her doorway in the city in all kinds of horrible weather, and I knew she was putting on an act. "It's not cold in here at all. The thermostat is set for seventy and the house is even warmer than that. What's really the matter? Please tell me."

"I want to go home."

Home? Where was home for her? "It's too late now," I said firmly. "We can go first thing in the morning if you still want to go. But we'll stay here tonight, and you're coming downstairs for supper. I'll get Sebastian to make a fire in the fireplace. It'll be toasty warm, I promise you."

She was like a child when I went back to get her for supper. I had Maggie fix trays for us so that we could eat by the fire. Mollie came down with a blanket wrapped around her, as docile as could be. I was afraid she'd complain about the food, but she cleaned up her plate. No one could resist Maggie's crisp, tender chicken, her tiny new potatoes and fresh salad. Mollie ate two big dishes of ice cream and about a dozen cookies, and promptly fell asleep in her chair.

I had to wake her up to get her to go upstairs to bed.

"I'd just as leave sleep right here," she said drowsily, curling up deeper into the chair.

"No, the fire will go out and you'll be cold. Come

up to bed." I practically dragged her up the stairs to the bedroom. But she was awake enough to bring with her the shopping bag that she had kept close alongside all evening. I couldn't imagine what was in it that was so precious, but maybe she had so few possessions that everything was important to her.

When I got her safely into her room I asked if there was anything she wanted, or if she needed any help. She opened one eye and mumbled in an aggrieved tone, "What would I need help for? You think I don't know how to take care of myself? I ain't a bum, you know, I'm a respectable woman. There's people who depend on me."

"I know, I know. Get a good night's sleep. I'm glad you're here." I didn't know whether to attempt to kiss her good night, but I decided she might not like it. It was hard to know how to behave with Mollie. In her own world she made sense, like really wanting to help the homeless street people around her, but as far as the rest of the world, she had some weird ideas. But I couldn't blame her for resenting the people who had so much of everything, and who didn't care about those who didn't.

I fell asleep the minute I got into bed. The day had been a long one, and I had to admit being with Mollie was tiring.

It was a little after midnight when an undefined noise woke me up. I sat up in bed trying to figure out what I had heard and where it came from. I realized I had heard the noise of someone walking, and a door

opening and closing. I wasn't scared, and thought immediately of Mollie. I went into the hall and, sure enough, the door to her room was open and she wasn't in the bed. Her bathroom door was open, too, and she wasn't in there either.

I went downstairs to see if she was in the kitchen, but the night light was on and no sign of her. She wasn't in any of the rooms downstairs. Then I began to worry, and wondered whether to wake up Sebastian, who was sleeping in one of the rooms behind the pantry.

There was a bright moon lighting up the lawn, and for no logical reason I went to the front door, and opened it to look out. I almost knocked Mollie over. There she was, huddled up in a blanket sleeping on the front steps alongside the door.

She was half-awake and furious when she saw me bending over her. "What you want? Can't you leave a body alone to get a night's sleep? Always nosying around. Go back to your bed and leave me be."

I didn't even try to get her to come inside. I went back to my own bed confused and very hurt. I was trying to figure out what I had done that was all wrong. Bringing Mollie up to the country was a disaster, that much was clear. But why?

I felt awful. There was no point in even trying to sleep. I sat up in bed to think: Mollie was a nut. I could accept that. But what was I trying to do?

I was trying to make myself feel good. There it was, clear as could be in front of me.

For her own wild reasons that I would never know, Mollie wanted to live on the streets. Obviously she didn't like houses and beds, and preferred a snowy doorstep outside. Maybe she had a notion of herself as being a good samaritan, or a saint, for the other homeless people. But she had little use for me because she could see that I wasn't doing anything to really help anyone—just sticking my nose into her affairs.

She made me feel like a busybody and a fool. I finally fell asleep thinking, to heck with her. I certainly won't bother Mollie anymore, and I'll forget the whole thing. The street people have gotten along without me, and they jolly well can go on doing so.

When I came downstairs the next morning Mollie was in the kitchen having coffee with Maggie. She was as bright and spry as ever. She didn't say a word about last night and neither did I. But I felt irritated and annoyed. Clearly it was my own fault for having cockeyed fantasies about bringing "poor Mollie" up to our beautiful country estate to give her a good time. What self-important rot.

There didn't seem much point in hanging around. Mollie wanted to go back to the city, so soon after breakfast we left.

"Where should I take your friend?" Sebastian asked on the drive home. He never called her by name. "Where does she live?"

"I think she wants to be dropped off at Sixty-ninth and Third," I told him. "She has some shopping to do."

Mollie didn't say anything but she gave me a wicked grin, listening to our conversation.

When Sebastian pulled the car to the curb at Sixty-ninth Street, much to my surprise, Mollie turned to me before getting out and with her most beautiful smile said, "It was a lovely trip, dearie. I'm glad to be home, but it was a nice change."

You just didn't know with her, what she was going to say next.

Chapter Eight

When we got upstairs we found cables from Philippa and messages to call the long-distance operator on the answering machine. The cables were Philippa's usual extravagant descriptions of where she went and what she ate and what she bought, the stuff most people put in letters. In one she gave a whole recipe to Agnes for a "divine country pâté." It must have cost her a fortune.

The last message was to call her in Paris at any time, and with the time difference I figured out it would be around two in the morning there, but she said "any time."

Philippa answered the phone quickly, and knowing my mom, even if she'd been asleep she was wide awake instantly.

"Darling Cassandra, where have you been? We've been calling frantically."

"I went up to the country, just overnight. How are you?"

"Exhausted, absolutely exhausted. Another concert tonight. But you must come over, I miss you. And I've met the most adorable young French boy, you've got to meet him."

"Why?" I asked stupidly.

Philippa laughed. "No reason, just for fun. But I want to see you. Can you come next weekend? You can fly in Friday and go home on Monday . . . missing two days of school won't hurt you."

"If you want me to."

"Is anything the matter?" Philippa had sharp antennae.

"No, of course not. We just got home and I guess I'm a little tired. But it sounds great."

It was a terrible week for me. Ordinarily I would have been excited about going to Paris to spend a weekend with Philippa, but that week I couldn't pull myself out of a depression. I avoided going anywhere near where I might meet Mollie, but I had one traumatic experience.

I was walking down Lexington Avenue when I saw a large woman with some kids around her. I could only see her back because she was bending over a litter can, going through it with her hands. It always made me feel sick when I saw people doing that, thinking of the horrible things that people threw

away into those cans and sad that anyone could find something they'd want.

When the woman stood up I saw that it was Lily, the lady who'd been taking care of Eva's kids. She had a dirty old pair of sneakers in her hands that she'd fished out of the can. She was examining them meticulously when I walked up to her. She didn't recognize me as I said hello. "Remember, I came to bring something to Eva's kids, over at the hotel?"

"Yeah, how're you doing?"

"I'm okay, how are you?"

"Not good. We left that rat hole, I'd rather be on the street than in that dive. They put Eva's kids in a home and I don't want my kids getting any drugs."

"Where do they sleep?"

"I take them to a shelter at night. They're supposed to find us a place to live, God knows when."

"I'm sorry."

She gave me a contemptuous look. "Yeah, I bet you are."

"Do the kids need sneakers?" I asked timidly.

She stared at me. "Listen, kid," she said, "what's I need is a job. I ain't crazy about living on welfare, it don't suit my personality. I needs a home an' a job. You got any ideas?"

"I guess I don't," I said and walked away. But she shook me up, she and her kids, the way they stared at me and my clothes. I left her rummaging through another litter can.

Agnes hated it when I went off to see my mother. She got nervous and fidgety, certain that Philippa wouldn't know how to take care of me (as if I needed taking care of). I think she was jealous of Philippa. For reasons only she knew, Agnes wanted to own me, perhaps because she never had any children of her own and she had started to take care of me when I was a tiny baby. I didn't like to hurt her feelings, but she got on my nerves telling me how to behave and what to eat. I had to laugh when she actually came out with the famous cliché, "And don't talk to strangers."

"It's not funny," Agnes said indignantly.

"But it is, terribly funny. You don't know how ridiculous you sound."

I was glad to get on the plane and see the last of her at least for a four-day weekend.

Amy, Philippa's secretary-maid, was at the airport to meet me. Philippa, she said, was at a rehearsal for that evening's concert. My heart sank. Another weekend to see Philippa without seeing her! We took one of the familiar crazy French taxis to the hotel—a small, lovely place on the Left Bank where Philippa always had a suite when she came to Paris. There were bedrooms for Philippa, Amy, and me, a large drawing room, and a balcony that overlooked the city rooftops. I loved it.

My room had vases filled with fresh flowers and a scribbled note from Philippa tucked into the mirror. She said for me to rest or go out for a walk with Amy, and she'd be back around five o'clock. It was only

around one then, so, since I'd been up for hours, and the time was all cockeyed, I lay down on the bed for a few minutes and fell sound asleep. A whole afternoon in Paris wasted.

Philippa woke me up with a hug and a kiss and scolded me for sleeping away the afternoon. I did feel stupid for doing that.

"We'll make up for it," Philippa said, looking me over. Agnes had put me in a long wool skirt for traveling, so I pulled it off and got into a black leather miniskirt, boots, a short fur jacket, and some chunky gold jewelry, and felt very Parisian. Philippa gave me an approving look. "You look marvelous. Come, we're going to meet the French boy I told you about, Anton; he's visiting his father here. He lives in Spain with his mother most of the time. He's a dear. He started a fan club, can you imagine? A fan club in Madrid." Philippa was like a kid about her fans; she never tired of their adoration.

Anton and his father were waiting for us at a table in the café. I wished it were summer so we could sit outside, but it was much too cold. I could see immediately that Anton wasn't the only one who was my mom's fan; his father, a terribly handsome man, couldn't take his eyes off her. Philippa seemed oblivious, and as usual took charge. She told everyone where to sit, threw a smile at a waiter who promptly came over. Philippa and Monsieur Carpentiere ordered wine, and sodas for Anton and me.

The conversation was the usual nothing. They

asked me about my plane trip, how I liked Paris, etc., etc. In a short while Philippa left with Anton's father, who was taking her to meet some big-shot agent, and I was left with Anton who was told to buy me supper and take me to the theater for Philippa's concert. He didn't look too happy about it. I wasn't either. My mother's idea of giving me a great time in Paris when all I wanted was to be with her.

I figured he was around seventeen, probably furious at being stuck with a kid like me. He wasn't nearly as good-looking as his father; tall and lanky, dark hair he wore quite long, a narrow, intellectual face, nice eyes and a good smile, when he smiled which wasn't often. He was the kind of character, I decided, who called top stars by their first names, saw and heard everything the minute it came out, very suave, probably thought everyone from the U.S.A. was a hick. Without saying a word, he made me feel like someone from the provinces.

Silently I swore at Agnes and Mom, too, who wouldn't let me grow up and become sophisticated.

"Do you like living in New York?" he asked politely, when we were alone.

"It's okay. I've never lived anyplace else so I have nothing to compare it with. We have a house in the country, but we only go there for weekends, and that's not too often anymore."

"I guess I've been to every important city in the world, but not New York. Not yet. I'll get there one of these days."

86

"You'll probably like it. People say it's exciting."

"It's a rich city, I hear, rich and glamorous."

"Not everyone's rich. There are lots of poor people in New York."

"There are poor people everywhere." He shrugged. "That's the way it is, nothing we can do about it."

"I think it's terrible. There should be something done about it," I said vehemently.

He gave me an amused smile. "Are you a crusader? Are you one of those kids who go on peace marches?"

"I've never been on one," I said, wishing I had been. I wanted to stick pins in his smugness. What on earth made Philippa think I'd like this nerd?

"I decided a long time ago to enjoy myself. To mind my own business and to have a good time."

"Do you have a good time?" I asked, not that I cared.

He gave his best pleased-with-himself smile. "Most of the time I do."

"That's nice for you." End of conversation.

We sat there sipping our sodas, while I was wishing I had never bothered coming. I always fell for the same bait when Philippa summoned me (which is what she did), and I came running, thinking I'd have time to spend with her alone, which was when we did have fun. I never learned that it always ended up the same way—Philippa having rehearsals and engagements and me left with some stranger I didn't give a hoot about and hardly seeing her at all. I kept telling myself that it wasn't her fault, but that didn't help.

"Where would you like to eat?" Anton asked.

"I don't care. This is your turf; you pick it."

He took me to a small restaurant a few blocks from the theater. It was very French and attractive, and the food was marvelous. I was sure Anton wished he were there with one of his girlfriends, it was the kind of place for a romantic, intimate supper, fresh flowers and candles on the tables.

Desperate to make conversation, I told him a little bit about Mollie. "She's weird," I said after telling him how I'd met her and what she was like. "She really wants to live on the street. I think it makes her happy to help other homeless people."

"You'd better be careful," Anton said in his accented English. "Aren't you afraid of getting AIDS?"

I was stunned. "What on earth has AIDS got to do with it?"

"A street woman. You don't know where she's been or who she's been with. I wouldn't go near her."

"That's the dumbest thing I ever heard. You don't get it by touching someone. That is really crazy." I couldn't believe that boy. I was sorry I'd ever mentioned Mollie to him.

Things went downhill from then on. Thank goodness we had to leave soon to get to the concert. Even stupid Anton couldn't spoil that for me.

Sitting in the audience at one of Mom's concerts was fantastic. They adored her: old people, young kids, poor, rich, long-haired musicians and beat-up hippie types, they went wild. They applauded and

stamped and stood up, and me with them. I wanted to stand up and shout, "She's my mom," but I just grinned and shouted louder.

Anton, who was supposed to be such a fan of Mom's, stayed cool, supercilious nitwit. He looked down his nose at all the clapping and excitement, but I told him in my own cool way that *my* mom, and all performers, loved audiences who responded with so much enthusiasm. He thought they were vulgar.

After the concert, I had to admit I was glad he was with me because we had a hard time getting backstage to meet Mom. The security guards wouldn't let us through, but Anton was able to explain in French who we were and argue until he convinced them to let us in.

As usual, Mom's dressing room was filled with flowers and lots of people I didn't know. Anton's father was there and everyone was speaking French (too fast for me to understand much), so after Mom hugged me and introduced me around, I sat over in a corner looking at a magazine. I wished we could go off together and be alone.

But that didn't happen. It seemed that Anton's father had reserved a table at an elegant restaurant and we were all going there (Mom and him, Anton and me, and two other men and a very pretty lady). Monsieur Carpentiere ordered shrimp and caviar and champagne (I had one glass), and it was *très gala,* but I would have preferred a hamburger and being alone with Mom.

By the time we got home, Mom was exhausted and went to bed. I was wide awake and stayed awake reading a paperback mystery I'd brought with me. It wasn't that good and my mind kept wandering. I thought about how Mom and I were each living in our own worlds. She knew nothing about mine and I didn't know much about hers. I wondered if she was in love with Anton's father. I hoped not, because I'd hate having Anton for a brother.

Mom got up around noon on Saturday. I spent the morning hanging around waiting for her.

"Did you have a good time with Anton?" she asked when she did get up and I was watching her get dressed.

I turned up my nose. "Not really." I could never tell Philippa how I longed to be with her. How could you tell someone, your own mother, that you wanted her attention, that you didn't want to be shunted off onto other people? I knew that Philippa loved me in her way, but her way wasn't what I dreamed of.

But it was a lovely day. We went out to lunch together to a great little café, and we did some shopping—Mom said I had to have a Paris outfit—and we had a wonderful time. We met Anton and his father again for dinner, but it wasn't so bad this time because the four of us were together. I wore my new clothes, which were a rather elegant white silk blouse and a black velvet miniskirt and jacket and gold earrings Mom gave me. Even sophisticated Anton admired the way I looked.

We got back to the hotel kind of early and I sat on Mom's bed and we talked. I asked her if she was in love with Monsieur Carpentiere.

Mom laughed. "Oh no, what made you think that?"

"The way he looks at you. I think he's in love with you."

"He probably looks at a lot of women that way. He's a very sophisticated man. But we're just friends. How do you like Anton?" She'd already forgotten our conversation that morning.

"I don't. He's very stuck-up."

"Don't make hasty judgments, honey. He seems nice to me."

"You like him because he's a fan," I said bluntly.

Mom laughed at me. "Of course, I love all my fans. Why shouldn't I? They keep me going."

"I'm a fan of yours. Do you love me?"

She leaned over and hugged me. "That's a silly question. But you're not asking seriously, are you?" Her bright eyes searched my face.

"No, not really." I buried my face against her and thought for a minute I might cry. Sometimes I did wonder about her loving me. It could be a nuisance for her, having me . . . but when she held me close I could push away those thoughts.

Chapter Nine

I wasn't looking forward to Christmas vacation. Not that school was so great, but Christmas wasn't the same without Philippa. She had a terribly busy schedule over the holidays, so there was no point in my joining her, I'd never see her.

Agnes asked me if I wanted to go up to the country, but I wasn't sure I wanted to be stuck up there with her. At least in the city there were places to go and things to see.

A few days before school vacation, Elaine was standing in line with me in the cafeteria. "What are you wearing to Stacey's party?" she asked me.

Her question came out of the blue. She'd always been friendlier than Stacey and some of the others, but she'd never asked me something intimate like that before. "I'm not sure I'm going," I told her.

"Why not?" She took a tuna-fish sandwich, cucumber salad, and a glass of milk. I took chicken salad and tomato juice. We both started walking to a table.

"Do you mind if I sit with you?" she asked.

"No, there's a table in the corner."

"Why aren't you going to the party?" she asked again when we'd sat down with our lunches.

"I'm not big on parties, especially when there'll be a lot of people I don't know."

"There'll be kids from school. You'll know them."

"I don't know them that well now," I said. "A party'll be worse."

"I thought maybe we could go together," Elaine said.

She took me by surprise. "Can I ask you a personal question? It's none of my business, but did you have a fight with Stacey?" I figured that was why she was making up to me, and I didn't want any part of it.

"No, we didn't have a fight. I decided we were seeing too much of each other. I think she got bored with me anyway. I've been shy about trying to make friends with you. I thought that *you'd* think it was because of your mother. But when you spoke up about wanting to work in the soup kitchen I decided I was being silly. That you were . . . well, that you were more regular," she added with a smile, and looked at me apprehensively.

"I'm glad you did." I realized I had never given her much of a chance because she'd always been with Stacey. "Do you think Mrs. M. will ever get that

project started?" I asked before either one of us got embarrassed.

"We don't have to wait for that." She opened her large canvas bag and pulled out some folders. They were about a couple of organizations in the city that helped homeless families. "We could go to one of these," she said eagerly. "They're asking for volunteers."

I picked them up and read that they wanted people to help in the office, to work in the soup kitchens, to raise money. They needed carpenters, electricians, drivers, all kinds of people. "I don't know what we could do," she said, "but we could find out."

"We could work in the office—I can type—or stuff envelopes, or work in a soup kitchen even if the class doesn't do it." I was very excited. "Let's go to one of these during vacation, do you want to?"

"I don't know if my parents will let me. What about you?"

"My mother's in Europe, so I can't ask her. I'll tell her about it when she comes back," I said with a grin. "What she doesn't know won't hurt her."

"I'll decide later whether to tell my mother or not. We could go and find out what it's all about first, couldn't we?"

"Sure." I had seen Elaine a thousand times, but I guess I'd never really looked at her delicate, pretty face before. She had a stubborn, defiant look I'd never noticed, and I felt that there was more to her than I'd ever given her credit for. I was glad that she

had broken the ice. "Let's make a date during vacation, and we can investigate."

"Before the party?"

"If you want."

"I'm hoping to convince you to come to the party."

When we left each other after lunch I realized I hadn't said a word to her about Mollie, and I was glad. I felt that Mollie belonged to me. I wanted to keep her to myself; besides, I decided she wouldn't like Elaine any more than she did me.

With Christmas coming, and all the stores decorated, people selling wreaths on the street, and the Salvation Army people singing on the corners, I thought about Mollie a lot. The city was glowy and alive, strangers smiling at each other carrying pretty packages, kids pressing their noses against toy-shop windows. The holiday spirit was everywhere, but I couldn't help thinking about Eva and her kids, and Lily and hers, and Mollie and all the people she worried about. Their Christmas had to be pretty awful.

Even if Mollie didn't have any use for me, I had to go see her. Not that there was anything I could do for her; I wanted to see her for my own sake.

She wasn't at her usual place, but I found her about a block away. She was talking to a young man slumped in a doorway. His hair was straggly and he needed a shave, he was leaning against a door with his legs in torn jeans stretched out in front of him. He had a

brown paper bag in his hand that held a bottle of liquor he was sipping from. Mollie seemed to be arguing with him.

"What do you want?" she said abruptly when she saw me.

"I just wanted to say hello. How are you doing?"

"I'm doing fine, just fine. But my friend here ain't so good. Come on, Lenny." She tried to pull him up but he didn't cooperate. "You need food. This stuff'll kill you, you gotta eat. I'll take you to the soup kitchen, come on."

The young man opened his eyes, looked at her for a minute, and closed them. "You're okay, Mollie, just leave me alone." He slumped down farther.

"Look at him," Mollie said with both pride and disgust. "He's got degrees from a university, he's got brains, and look at him, a no-good drunk. It ain't his fault, it's the people in big offices what done him in. . . ." She went on muttering and ranting about "the people higher up" who were rotten, greedy, and stealing from the poor. I could hardly hear what she was saying. She was crazy, but she really wanted to help her friends. I walked away, but I turned after a few blocks and came back. Mollie and Lenny were still there, but somehow Mollie had gotten hold of one of those big pretzels men sell on the street, maybe stole it, and Lenny was eating it. She was watching him with the satisfaction of a mother watching her kid eat up all his spinach.

"Where are Eva's kids?" I asked her.

96

She eyed me suspiciously. "Whadda you want to know for?"

"Well, it's almost Christmas . . . I don't know. . . ."

"Christmas, bah. Who cares about Christmas? Once a year they give you a handout, but you know there are 364 other days in the year, what about them? Don't talk to me about no Christmas. You go home, open up your presents, we don't celebrate no Christmas aroun' here." She looked at me contemptuously, flounced her skirts, and turned her back on me.

Even if she had told me where Eva's kids were, what could I have done about them? Or about any of them? I'd had glimpses of so many different people— the family in the park, Lily and her kids, Eva and hers, Mollie's friend Edward, who had died—there had to be hundreds more. A whole other world.

I called Elaine up when I got home, and we made a date for the next afternoon to go to one of the places that worked for the homeless.

Our vacation had started, and it was a couple of days before Christmas. When I was leaving the house, after my late breakfast, Agnes, of course, wanted to know where I was going.

"I'm meeting a friend from school," I told her. "I don't know what we'll do, maybe go shopping."

"Be home before it gets dark," Agnes admonished. "That's around five o'clock these days."

"Don't worry, I'll be home."

Elaine lived in an apartment house on Lexington Avenue, just a few blocks away. It was a bitter cold

day. I belted my fur parka tight around me, and was glad I'd put on leg warmers. The building was an old one, but the apartment was one of those large, old-fashioned places with high ceilings and huge rooms and wide halls. Her mother had furnished it very Spanish, with tile floors, Spanish furniture and rugs; it was very elegant.

Elaine introduced me to her mother, an older, plumper version of Elaine, with the same delicate features and pretty face. In her room, which was nothing like the rest of the house, but very modern with bright colors, she took a yellow sheet from her desk. "I wrote down the names of organizations I got out of the phone book. Here, look at it."

There was one on the Upper West Side, two up in Harlem, and one in the East Twenties. "The one in the East Twenties is the nearest. Should we go there?"

"Sure. Listen, I didn't tell my mother where we were going, so don't say anything."

"I didn't tell Agnes, our housekeeper, either. Mum's the word." We grinned at each other.

I wasn't sure why we were keeping this secret, except knowing Agnes, she'd find some objection. Anyway, it was more fun this way.

There was nothing furtive about the office we went to in the East Twenties. It occupied the street floor of an old brownstone, and the three women and two men working in it were friendly, but cool and efficient. They handed us a bunch of literature, and

when we stood there holding it, one of the women asked us if she could be of any help.

She was younger than the others, with a plain but nice face, and pretty, long black hair. Elaine and I looked at each other, and I spoke up. "We thought that maybe there was something we could do to help. Maybe over Christmas vacation we could work at something."

Mrs. Allison (we learned her name later) looked us over. "How old are you?"

"We're sixteen," I lied. It sounded better than almost fourteen.

"Do you think you could work in a soup kitchen? We need help there, especially over the holidays."

"Sure, that would be super. That's what we'd like to do." Elaine nodded her head in agreement.

Mrs. Allison looked at us thoughtfully. "How would you feel about going down to the Bowery? It's really quite safe, as safe as anyplace else. We need help there."

"I'd love it." That excited me. I'd never been in that part of New York, except once going to a Chinese restaurant with my mom in Chinatown, but it was at night and I just got out of the car in front of the restaurant and then back in afterward.

"Okay. Go down there tomorrow morning around eleven." She handed us a slip of paper with an address. "I suggest you take a bus or a taxi down, and Peter McDonald, he's in charge, will get you a cab to

take you home. He'll tell you what to do." She gave us a wide smile. "Thank you for being interested."

When we left, Elaine seemed nervous. "Do you think it'll be all right? I mean, going to the Bowery? Isn't that where all the bums and drunks hang out?"

"Nothing can happen to us. Not if we go right to the soup kitchen and home. We don't have to walk around there. I'm excited. It's more fun than going with the class, not so organized. Are you going to tell your mother?"

Elaine giggled. "To the Bowery, God no. She wouldn't let me go. I'll tell her I'm going to have lunch with you. You can say the same, that we're meeting for lunch. Okay?"

"Sure. Oh, this is fun."

Mrs. Allison neglected to tell us that this soup kitchen was run by a church and that Peter McDonald was a minister. Not that it would have made any difference, except we wouldn't have been so worried about going there. When we got out of the taxi in front of the old church and realized that was where we were going, we looked at each other with relief.

"No one can scold us for coming here," I said to Elaine, and she agreed.

Except for his turned-around collar, Peter McDonald didn't look like a minister. He was young, quite handsome, and right after we introduced ourselves called us by our first names and said to call him Pete. "Everyone calls me that," he said.

There was no mistaking the place. We had arrived before eleven and already there was a line outside waiting for the doors to the soup kitchen to be opened. Pete led us through the church to a large room adjacent to it that had two long tables set up at right angles to each other. In back of that room was a kitchen where two older women were working. Pete introduced us to Emily and Mary.

"The girls will help you with the serving," he said. "This way we can have two lines. Emily and Cassandra on one, and Mary and Elaine on the other. Tell me when you're ready for me to open the doors."

"Just a few minutes," Emily said. She was cutting off chunks from a large wheel of cheese, there were loaves of sliced bread, and huge pots of soup and coffee.

When Emily gave the word I got behind one table with her and Elaine went with Mary to the other. Pete opened the doors.

The room was filled in minutes. Pete had the people form two lines, and we began to serve. At first I was so busy and nervous filling plastic bowls with soup I hardly had a chance to really look at the people. But when I got more used to it and felt more relaxed, I was able to see the people as individuals and talk to each.

It was an eye-opener. These people weren't drunks and bums—they were ordinary people you could know. One old man with deep sunken eyes and a straggly beard looked at me and asked me if I studied

Latin. It so happened that I did and when I told him yes, his eyes lit up. "The most important language," he said. "I taught it once, a long time ago. People say it's a dead language, but it's not, it's the source." A man like that on a line for food! I wondered how it could be.

He wasn't the only one. A young girl, probably only a few years older than me, was wearing beat-up jeans and a designer scarf around her neck. I guess she noticed me looking at her scarf, and she laughed. "I picked it up on Madison Avenue." She added, "Some spoiled brat threw it away. My mother used to buy clothes in those fancy shops; she should see me now," she said with a bitter smile. "I don't care," she shook her head defiantly, "I'd rather be where I am than living with her." I would have loved to talk to her more. She had a wild look on her face, kind of furtive, as if she thought she was being followed, but defiant, too. She must have some story, I thought.

The three hours we were there flew by. At two o'clock they closed the doors and the food was gone. I wasn't the least bit tired, I felt exhilarated, as if a door had opened for me into another world. My feelings were so mixed, it seemed that so much that happened to people was a matter of chance. It wasn't my fault that I was Philippa's daughter; it was just chance that I was born to her. I could have been the girl who despised her mother so much she ran away. The whole idea of what happens to people was spooky. I didn't even want to feel sorry for the people

who came for food, it seemed patronizing to me—I guess more than anything I felt angry. It just seemed stupid for lots of people to throw food away—Agnes wouldn't keep any meat for more than a day; she insisted it would go bad, which was wrong—and for other people to go hungry. It made me mad.

Elaine and I went back to the soup kitchen the next day and the day after that. I felt that I was leading a double life, going down there (without telling Agnes where I was going), and then coming home to our elegant apartment. It was weird, like throwing a piece of bread into the ocean. I felt that what we were doing was so tiny compared to what needed to be done, I wanted to go around shouting at the top of my voice, "Let's do something big."

But we were only kids doing something small.

Chapter Ten

*C*hristmas was lousy. I spoke to Philippa on the phone, but that only made me more depressed when I had to say good-bye and hang up. Agnes gave me one of her speeches about how lucky I was and that I had no right to be depressed, which got me mad and made me feel even worse. I hate it when she tries to cheer me up, when I just want to be left alone. I wish she'd retire and go live with her sister, and not be on my neck all the time.

Somehow we got through the day and in the late afternoon Agnes and Sebastian and I went to a movie that was kind of funny.

Elaine persuaded me to go to Stacey's party. It was against my better judgment that I agreed. You'd think I was going on a trip to the moon, Agnes got so excited. She wanted me to go out to buy a new dress,

which I told her was ridiculous. "It's going to be a boring party, I won't know anyone, and no one will ask me to dance. I'd just as soon go in jeans," I told her.

The idiot took me seriously until she realized I was teasing her, but she didn't think much of my humor. When I picked out a long velvet skirt and a black, classic cashmere sweater to wear, Agnes gave me an argument again. "You're not going to a funeral," she said, "you should wear something bright. That's not dressy for a big party."

"I'll put on gold earrings." I wanted to be what Mom calls understated. I hated being overdressed, which was Agnes's style. She'd have me in some awful pink taffeta fit for a nine-year-old.

Of course Sebastian had to drive me there, only a short distance away, and he was to pick me up at midnight. At least I was able to pick up Elaine on our way.

It was a supper dance starting at seven-thirty, held in a very chic hotel on Fifth Avenue. Elaine and I were both jittery when Sebastian dropped us off.

"Have a good time, girls," Sebastian called out. "I'll be here at twelve."

"What if we want to leave before?" Elaine asked plaintively.

"You won't," Sebastian assured her. "You're going to have a good time."

"Says he," Elaine muttered.

After we left our coats at the cloakroom, we advanced timidly to the ballroom, where a lot of small tables were set around a dance floor, with a stage for the band at one end. The place was decorated with tons of flowers. There were also two long tables piled with gorgeous-looking food and sodas and fruit drinks. At the door we were greeted by Stacey and her parents. We all shook hands and Stacey's mother told us to go inside and help ourselves to food and to enjoy ourselves. My heart sank.

It was the first formal dance I'd ever been to, and thank God Elaine was with me. I never could have gone into that room alone. It seemed enormous (it really wasn't) and was filled with terribly chic boys and girls standing around in groups laughing and talking with each other. I didn't know one of them.

Not knowing what else to do, Elaine and I went to the food table, filled our plates, and went to one of the small tables and sat down. A few couples were at tables, but most of the kids were just standing around and talking. I felt conspicuously unattractive—I mean, two girls sitting by themselves eating right away could not be ragingly popular.

When the band started to play, and the dance floor got filled up, I felt worse. I was furious for having let myself in for this nightmare, and if I hadn't felt as sorry for Elaine as for myself, I would have let her have it for persuading me to come. We tried to talk to each other so that we wouldn't look like such a

disaster, but I guess we both felt too miserable to look lively.

"I bet if they knew that your mother was Philippa, they'd all come crowding around," Elaine said.

"Thank God they don't, and don't you dare tell anyone," I warned Elaine.

But I hadn't counted on Stacey. After the band had finished their first set and everyone was sitting at tables eating, the bandleader called a silence with a few drumbeats. "Our next song will be one of Philippa's," he announced, "and we understand that her daughter is here with us this evening." Everyone started searching the room, looking for who Philippa's daughter might be.

"Cassandra, stand up!" Stacey called.

I was stunned. Elaine pushed me to get up, and with my face flaming I stood up for a few seconds while there was a thunderous burst of applause. I could have killed Stacey.

I should have known. How I could have been so dumb as to have come, I'll never figure out. I had known from the beginning that the only reason Stacey had invited me was because of Philippa, but it never dawned on me she'd be so gross.

After one of the men in the band sang Philippa's song, a bunch of kids came over to our table. They asked for *my* autograph, which was ridiculous, so on little scraps of paper I had to write *Cassandra, daughter of Philippa*. I had to laugh at them, these

ultrasophisticated kids, being so banal and corny. Philippa would get a good laugh out of it, too, I knew.

But at least it made me feel better, and Elaine was getting a kick out of it. How could we be intimidated by such nitwits?

When the band started up again, a tall, skinny boy with longish hair asked me to dance. There were still some kids at the table, so I wasn't leaving Elaine alone. I was nervous that he'd be some exotic, wild dancer I couldn't keep up with, but it was okay. We got along pretty well. His name was Adam, he lived in Greenwich Village, and he'd met Stacey in Bermuda last spring vacation.

"But this kind of thing isn't my style," he said. "I'm not big on formal parties. I suppose you're used to them."

"Not me." I shook my head. "This is my first, and it may be my last."

He laughed. "You're for real. I thought you'd be stuck-up. I mean, with your mother so famous and all. But maybe that's a drag, is it?"

"Sometimes. I could kill Stacey for announcing it."

"You want to be known for yourself, not for being someone's daughter. But I'm afraid you're stuck, you'll always be *Philippa's daughter*."

"Not if I can help it."

When the dance was over Adam said, "Do you have to go back to that table? Can't we go someplace and talk?"

I looked around the room. I didn't see any empty table. "I don't see anyplace, do you?"

"There's a coffee shop down the side street. We could go there."

"You mean leave?"

Adam nodded. "Sure, why not? No one will miss us."

"I'd better tell Elaine." I felt excited. I ran over and whispered to Elaine that I was going out for a little while but I'd be back. She was wide-eyed.

"With that boy?"

"Only to a coffee shop next door. Don't get ideas."

We slipped out without anyone noticing. Adam said not to bother getting my coat, he'd give me his jacket and the place was just a few doors away.

It was cold out, and Adam wrapped his jacket around me and we ran to the coffee shop. Adam ordered hamburgers, French fries, and Cokes, and we both felt crazy, eating that ordinary stuff when there were shrimp and lobster salads and fantastic food at the party.

It was the best and most exciting time I'd ever had.

There was nothing stuck-up about Adam. He said the only reason he'd been in Bermuda was that his father had to be there for a business convention and so he and his mother had gone along. "We're plain folk," he said, "not like all you rich kids."

He wasn't all that plain. He went to a fancy prep school in New England, but he said his best friend there was a scholarship boy who lived in Harlem. I

told him about Mollie, and then we both laughed at how hard we were trying to impress each other with how *non-snobbish* we were.

I felt comfortable talking to him. "But if they hadn't made the announcement about my mother, you never would have come over to my table, and we wouldn't have met," I said to him.

"I don't know. I may have."

"You're being polite. I'm sure you wouldn't have. Two drippy girls sitting together, you'd have paid no attention."

"That's not fair. You're not drippy, not by a long shot. I'd have noticed you."

"Why?"

He scrutinized me. "You look different. You don't look like all the other girls."

I laughed. "Wow, that can mean anything. You mean different queer, a pointed head?"

"No, just two noses."

When we finished our hamburgers I said we'd better go back, I felt guilty about leaving Elaine. We really didn't want to go, but I persuaded him that we had to. Adam took down my phone number and said he'd call me. "Maybe we can get together before I go back to school," he said.

"That would be nice." Right away I wondered if he would call, or if I'd ever see him again. I made up my mind not to think about him, whatever happened would happen. Of course that was not the way it was going to be—I was going to think about him a lot.

When we got back to the party Elaine was dancing with a chubby blond guy and seemed to be having a good time. Adam sat down at our table with me, but it was different from when we were in the coffee shop. Maybe the atmosphere was constraining, but he became more stiff and formal and so of course did I. We did dance some more, but I was afraid that the vibes we'd had between us had disappeared. Elaine came back to the table with her partner, and when the four of us were there things got better. But it still wasn't the same as before.

It was a relief when it was midnight and Elaine and I excused ourselves and said we had to leave. Adam gave me a long look before we left, and said again that he'd call me, but I wasn't confident that he would.

"That boy likes you," Elaine said as soon as we were alone. "Do you like him?"

"I think I do, but I'm not so sure he likes me."

"He does, I can tell."

Since I wanted to believe her, I certainly didn't put up an argument, but I had my doubts.

Sebastian asked if we'd had a good time, and to my surprise when I told him yes, I wasn't making it up. I really had had a good time.

The next morning I woke up thinking about Adam, and in spite of feeling silly doing it, I hung around the house hoping he would call. The only one who called was Elaine. It was a gorgeous, clear bright day

outside, and Agnes kept nagging me to go out with her, but that was the last thing I felt like doing.

By midafternoon, though, I got tired of making a fool of myself, and told Agnes I was going out for a walk, *alone*. When I got outside I thought about Mollie.

I hadn't seen her now in several days, and I had hardly been thinking about her. I felt terrible at how easily and quickly I could forget about people like the homeless when having a good time. I'd been so involved with myself I'd even put the soup kitchen out of my mind.

When I found Mollie she was more than ever like the Mad Duchess, carrying on, talking to herself about one of the shelters being closed down and more people put out on the street. It was hard to tell if she knew what she was talking about, but she was agitated enough for me to try to get a straight story out of her.

"Don't interrupt me," she said when I questioned her. "I'm telling you, just listen. They closed up that place because they said there was too much drugs, but I'm telling you that ain't the reason, they just don't want to pay for any heat. Nobody cares what happens to people, you hear, nobody gives a hoot."

"But what will happen to the people? They're not going to just let them live on the street."

"Says you. Where else? Anyhow, I can't stay here gabbing with you, I got plenty of things to do. I got a sick friend I gotta take care of." She kept shaking her head, and with her shawl wrapped around her, she

picked up her shopping bags and started down the street. I went with her.

She walked about a block and a half to where a woman, perhaps a little younger than Mollie, with flaming red hair, was squatting in a doorway surrounded by her shopping bags. "How are you feeling?" Mollie asked.

"Terrible. I think I'm gonna die." The woman did look very pale.

"You ain't gonna die. You gotta go to the hospital, they'll give you something."

"No thank you, I ain't going to no hospital. You can't make me."

Mollie, who had paid no attention to me, now turned to me, knowing full well I had followed her. "What can you do with a simpleton like this one? I don't like hospitals no more than she does, but sometimes you can't choose. You call an ambulance."

"No-o-o," the woman screeched. "I don't want no ambulance. Just leave me alone. If the Lord wants me to die, I'll die."

"Pay no attention to her," Mollie ordered. "You go to the phone booth and call an ambulance before her appendix busts, that's what's ailing her."

"You don't know nothing, you ain't no doctor," the red-haired woman screamed. But her face was contorted with pain. I didn't know what to do, whether to obey Mollie or stay out of it.

"What you waiting for?" Mollie screamed at me. "Go."

I went to the phone booth on the corner and dialed 911, and asked for an ambulance to come in a hurry. I couldn't believe it was me, little Cassandra, mixed up in this drama on the street. It seemed like forever before an ambulance came screaming around the corner. The paramedics jumped out, examined Mollie's friend, and against her whimpers that she didn't want to go, bundled her into the ambulance. Mollie watched with satisfaction as they drove away.

"I don't know what these people would do without me," she muttered, and I had to agree with her. But there were all those thousands of people Mollie wasn't there to take care of, that nobody was taking care of. Mollie sat down in the doorway her friend had left, ignoring me. I walked on, I knew when Mollie'd had enough of me. I was just like all the other people going by, women in their mink coats and warm boots. Most of them didn't even glance in Mollie's direction, they didn't know or want to know that she existed. But she was there, and all the different people I'd seen through Mollie's eyes. People without last names, like the faces you saw in a crowd for a few minutes that then disappeared.

Chapter Eleven

*A*dam called me the next morning and we made a date to do something that afternoon. I played it very cool with Agnes, but privately I was terribly excited. I didn't know what we might do, but I didn't care.

Promptly at two o'clock, as he said he would, Adam appeared. He looked adorable in jeans and an L. L. Bean hunting jacket. Agnes, of course, made a big to-do about our getting back by five o'clock, before dark, which embarrassed me no end.

Adam caught on to her, so we didn't spend any time hanging around the house, but went downstairs.

"What do you want to do?" he asked me.

"I don't care. Whatever you want."

It was too cold to stand around so we went into the park and walked to the zoo. We both loved the

apes and baboons, and stood watching them for a long time, stuffing ourselves with the peanuts Adam had bought. The afternoon flew by and it seemed like no time when it was close to five and we had to go home.

Adam came upstairs with me. Agnes made hot chocolate and I put on some of Philippa's tapes while we drank the cocoa and ate a bunch of cookies.

Adam's not the kind of boy who talks a lot or tries to impress you with what he knows, but not talking doesn't get sticky. He didn't make me feel that he was having a bad time because I wasn't being brilliant or witty. The way he looked at me and just kind of smiled made me feel good, and without words said that he liked to be with me as much as I liked being with him.

Up in the house he did talk more, and told me about his older brother and kid sister, and his parents. It sounded as if they had a good time together. He had a lot of cousins, and they went away for weekends skiing together, and on picnics in the summertime. Adam really liked his family, he made them sound as if they were quite special, and I could tell he was proud of them. He didn't make me feel exactly jealous, but I did envy him all the fun he had with his own sister and brother and cousins.

"I can't imagine what it's like being an only kid," Adam said. "I don't think I'd like it, it must get lonesome."

"It does," I agreed. "But a lot of kids don't get

116

along with their brothers and sisters; they fight all the time. I wouldn't like that."

"Neither would I." Adam gave me that nice smile of his. "I guess we just have to be satisfied with what we get."

When he left he said he'd write to me and I promised that I'd write back. Agnes was in the foyer when we said good-bye, and I think that if she hadn't been there, he might have kissed me. Agnes sure is a pain.

The big news came from Philippa after Christmas vacation was over. She was coming home earlier than planned, because the maintenance and technical staff at the opera house in Italy were on strike, and so she canceled her concert. Philippa wouldn't cross a picket line. I was thrilled.

Her plane was coming in on a Tuesday, and I insisted on staying home from school. Agnes said that Philippa didn't expect me to be at the airport on a school day, but I refused to listen. "She's my mother and I want to meet her and you can't stop me," I said.

Agnes tightened her lips and said in the cold tone she uses to put me down, "You are too full of yourself these days. I don't know what's come over you."

"Growing up, that's all," I said, as curtly as she. "I'm not your baby anymore."

Agnes turned around and went out of the room. I heard the door to her room close, and I wondered if she was going in there to cry. I almost went in after

her, but I restrained myself. I *was* growing up and she had better get used to it.

Of course Agnes came to the airport with me, there was no way out of that one. I adored airports when Philippa was coming home. It was as if all the noise and excitement in the airport was an introduction to the electric excitement Philippa brought with her, something like the advance publicity that came before her concerts. When I saw her plane coming in, landing on the field and taxiing to a stop, I thought I'd burst with my feelings. Philippa didn't know it, but when she was away I often had horrible fantasies of terrible things that could happen to her: an awful automobile accident or a fire, or some crank shooting people on the street, or a hijacker of a plane. But when she came home I felt we were safe for a while. It was a tremendous relief.

She looked fantastic. She had on a shiny black suit with a very short skirt, some fur draped around her shoulders, and her face was tan, although how she got a tan in Europe in midwinter only God knows. It was probably new makeup. Of course people were recognizing her, but in airports they're usually in a hurry and don't bother her much. Her retinue was with her—Amy, her manager, Mike, and a public relations lady. When she saw me, she ran and I ran, and we hugged each other hard. She held me away at arm's length to look me over. "Good God, I think you've grown again. You're going to be a tall woman. Very elegant, too." She laughed. "Imagine me with an

elegant grown-up daughter." A few people clustered around for autographs and, as always, Philippa in her gracious way wrote her name for each of them. We were walking through the waiting room to go to the car, when what had looked like a bundle on a bench turned into a person with a head and a face, and eyes that looked directly at me. "Why, hello, miss," a rather nasal voice said. "How you doing?"

I had been hanging on Mom's arm, and I stopped dead, and she stopped with me. I was looking at Eva, Mollie's friend. It was so incongruous seeing her there, so far from the streets at home, in this bright, glittery place. "Hello, Eva," I said. "What are you doing here?"

She had been curled up like a ball on the bench, surrounded by the usual shopping bags, and now she straightened out and sat up. "I gotta right to be here, it's a public place," she said defensively, as if I'd challenged her.

"Do you know this woman?" Mom's dark eyes were wide with astonishment. Mike was tugging at her to move on.

"Yes, I do know her. Eva, this is my mother, Philippa. Are you okay? What *are* you doing here?"

Mom acknowledged the introduction with her famous smile, and shook Mike's arm away.

"It's safe here," Eva said. "It was Mollie's idea, she said I'd be better off here where it's warm. I ain't strong like she is, my lungs is weak, I can't take the cold. And I can't take them shelters."

"Where are your kids?" I asked.

"They's in a foster home. When I get myself together I'm going to find a nice little place where we can all be together." Eva looked at me with her weak eyes, and I was sure that she knew as well as I did that that would never happen.

"Take care," I said to Eva.

A small group had gathered around Mom, and now Mike did propel us away. "Where on earth do you know that woman from?" Philippa asked me.

"I'll tell you later," I whispered. Agnes, of course, was hovering around and I didn't want to tell Philippa about Mollie in front of her. Adolph was waiting outside with the car and Mom got in back with me. She told the others to get a taxi because she wanted a chance to talk to me. I gave her a hug for that.

"So tell me what you've been up to," Philippa said as soon as we were under way. "I want to know everything, don't leave anything out."

"I don't know where to begin," I said. "I guess I'll start with Mollie." I told Philippa about meeting Mollie, about her introducing me to Eva. I didn't tell her about going to the welfare hotel, I didn't think she'd like that. But I did tell her about Elaine and me working in the soup kitchen, and how many of the people there were ordinary people, not drunks and dope addicts. "It's awful, Mom," I said. "Can you imagine not having a home, a place to live? The shelters for the homeless are terrible, so a lot of people just live on the streets. It makes me feel sick

just thinking about it. I wish we could do something."

"But you said your friend Mollie wants to be on the street. You can't help people who don't want to be helped."

"That's just Mollie. She's nice but a nut. People like Eva would like something."

"Let me think about it," Philippa said. "What else has been happening?"

I told her about Stacey's party, but not that I went off to a coffee shop. But I did tell her about meeting Adam. I was surprised by Philippa's reaction.

"You're a little young to start dating," she said.

"Mom!" I shrieked. "I don't believe you. You, of all people. Most of the girls in my class have been dating for at least a year. You're as bad as Agnes."

Philippa laughed. "You see I know what goes on, so I'm talking from experience. I don't mean you shouldn't go out with a boy, but not too much," she added with a grin.

I snuggled up close to her. It was marvelous to have my mother home.

Two days later, Philippa said that she wanted to meet Mollie. I was deliriously happy, but nervous too. Mollie was so unpredictable, heaven knows what she might say to Mom. Insult her, maybe.

Anyway I took Mom down the street that afternoon to where Mollie hung out. She wasn't there, but we found her a few blocks away in her usual tizzy. At first she barely looked at Mom, she was all excited about

some street vendors who'd been arrested for peddling without a license. "The nerve of them cops," Mollie said. "People wanting to make an honest living. They ain't hurting no one, people getting robbed every minute and them cops bothering good, honest folks. It's a disgrace."

Mom agreed. "You're right, absolutely right." Mollie looked at her then.

"Who are you?"

"This is my mother, Mollie. She wanted to meet you."

Mollie looked Philippa up and down. She was wearing jeans and a suede jacket, and had a woolen scarf around her neck. "She ain't nothing much. I thought you was rich," she said to me. "She don't look like nobody's mother."

Philippa and I laughed. "Well, she is my mother, believe me."

"I'm glad to meet you," Philippa said. "Cassandra's told me a lot about you. What do you think anyone can do to help people who need a home?"

Mollie gave Mom a look of disgust. "Build them houses. It ain't complicated, the government's got plenty of money. They should take care of people."

"That would be nice," Mom said, "but it's not that simple. In the meantime maybe some people could help. Maybe I can do something."

Mollie looked skeptical. "What can you do? You ain't nobody."

Philippa laughed. This was a new experience for

her, but she seemed to enjoy it. "We'll see. Maybe I can surprise you."

"Nothin' can surprise me, not after all I've seen. I've seen everything."

"Well, good-bye for now. Take care." I was afraid Mom was going to kiss Mollie, which Mollie wouldn't have liked. But she didn't. We walked away, arm in arm.

"What do you think you can do?" I asked when we were out of earshot of Mollie.

"I've been thinking," Philippa said. "I've got to talk to Mike about it . . . I've been thinking maybe I could give a concert for the homeless. Cancel the small concert that was planned for the spring and get a much larger hall. We could give all the money to an organization that could take it and use it for providing what they need."

I stopped in the middle of the street. "Mom, that would be fantastic. Would you really do it?"

"Why not? If I can get Mike to arrange it."

As we walked I kept looking sideways at my mother. She really didn't look like anything much in her jeans and casual jacket, but I realized how terrific she was. She didn't moon about things the way I did, she took action. I knew that nothing would stop her. She'd convince Mike to have a concert, and she'd insist that it could be done and that there was time. My mom wouldn't take no for an answer. It struck me how weird it was that Mom's drive (and her talent, of course) led her to be what she was, while Mollie, with

the same kind of toughness, landed on the street because of her crazy quirks. I felt that I was learning something from the two of them. I guess one was a constructive drive and one was destructive, and people had to choose between the two. I put my arm through Philippa's and held on to her tight—I didn't have her talent, but I could go straight to good goals, the way she did. Right then and there I vowed, to myself, that I'd try not to feel sorry for myself anymore when she had to go away. I'd always have what she had to give me, and I darn well better not forget it.

Chapter Twelve

*T*hings really got hectic after that. As I said, when Philippa made up her mind, there was no stopping her. That very evening she had a conference with Mike and the publicity people. She let me sit in on it.

Mike said it was impossible. "Where do you think we can find a hall big enough during spring vacation?"

"I'm sure you can," Philippa said calmly. "New York's a big city. It doesn't have to be a concert hall. A large, empty theater would do. There's got to be something. I know you can do it, Mike."

Mike looked as if he was going to scream at her, but he closed his mouth in a grim line instead.

"Should we do any advance publicity?" a young woman from the public relations office asked.

"What's the good of publicity when we don't have a place?" Mike yelled.

"I just thought to drop some hints to a few columnists, so word gets around that something's in the works. I don't see that it can hurt." She looked wistful.

"And then if it doesn't come off?" Mike looked around at the group with a glare.

"It will come off," Mom said firmly. "I think some word can be dropped, just as a teaser."

Mike shrugged. "It's on your head."

They talked a lot. About publicity, about how much the tickets should be, about Mom's program, about how much money they thought they could raise after expenses.

"I'll take care of some of the expenses," Mom said. "I want there to be a really substantial amount left to give away."

"Where are you going to give it? Go out on the street and hand out dollar bills?"

"There's got to be someplace to give the money," Mom said impatiently. "Don't put this project down, Mike."

"You want miracles," he said tartly.

"I know of some organizations," I offered mildly. "I went to visit one when I worked in the soup kitchen."

Mike's eyes almost popped out. "You worked in a soup kitchen? I thought I'd heard everything, but this beats all. So tell us about it," he said, sounding quite patronizing.

"She *can* tell you about it," Philippa said, putting

126

him in his place. "If it wasn't for Cassandra there wouldn't be any concert, I probably wouldn't even know about all the homeless people in this city. I am very proud of my daughter. She can give you the names of the organizations she knows about and you can check them out."

"Yes, ma'am," Mike said curtly.

I still had the piece of paper with the names Elaine and I had copied off and I ran and brought it to Mike.

He accepted it with a bow. "I still think it's impossible to get a hall. It's a great idea for next fall, but Easter vacation . . ." He threw up his hands in despair.

"Cassandra and I want to do something now, these people are suffering. Next fall is too late. Okay?"

"I'll do my best," Mike said meekly.

By a miracle, it seemed, something was canceled, and Mike got Madison Square Garden for a Monday night during spring vacation. Mom hugged him so hard he said it hurt. But that meant selling thousands of tickets.

From that day to the day of the concert, things went wild. Of course Mom had been involved in big, important concerts before, but I had never been part of it. She'd been terribly busy and I knew lots was going on, but I'd always been on the outside. But this one was different, and Mom understood how much this meant to me.

It was fantastic in so many ways. Of course I was deliriously happy that Mom wanted to do this for the

homeless people, but that wasn't all of it. I felt, in a funny way, that she was doing it for me, too, really for us. It was like Mom was saying, I know it's hard for you having a mother like me, not like most mothers. I'm self-involved, I'm busy with my career, I don't spend much time with you, etc., etc., but I do love you, and I want to do this because it's something we are doing together, something we both are touched by and want to do something about.

Mom would never say all those things, and I'd be embarrassed if she did, and I wouldn't say them out loud to anyone, but I have a nice, warm feeling inside because I think it's true for both of us.

So I didn't mind that Mom was busy most of the time with meetings, with okaying publicity, with re-hearsing her program, with going for photographs and having interviews, all the stuff and hard work that goes on before a concert.

But this time she kept including me. She'd show me the press releases and ask my opinion; she'd ask me to pick out the best photo, she discussed the program—and she listened to me. It was great, for the first time in my life I felt that Mom and I were in the same world. That she wasn't off someplace (even when she was home), and that I was living in my own world even when we were in the same house.

I was involved. I made a poster and put it up in school, and I arranged with the school office to sell tickets. It was fantastic. The tickets kept getting sold out and I had to bring in more. I think everyone in

the school and their cousins, uncles, and aunts bought tickets for this concert.

"I should put you on the payroll," Philippa said.

When Agnes kept on with her mumbling "That girl is too full of herself" it was marvelous that Philippa was there to hear her.

"Our little girl's growing up, Aggie," she said. "And I think we have to let her."

Agnes had no answer for her.

The day I got a letter from Adam, I couldn't wait to show it to Philippa that night. It wasn't a love letter or anything like that, but it was a nice letter, and ordinarily I would have kept it to myself. But now I wanted to talk about Adam with Philippa, like she was a friend, not just my mother.

"Do you like him?" Mom asked me. We were sitting in her bedroom, I was sprawled out on her bed and she was in her chaise.

"I think so. I don't know him very well. I mean, he's not a boyfriend or anything like that."

Mom laughed. "You have lots of time for boyfriends. Do you want to invite him to the concert?"

"You mean to come with us?"

"Yes, to be your guest."

"That would be fantastic. He'd love that."

"Then write and ask him."

Philippa was like that. Everything was simple for her. I'd agonize for days, should I ask Adam or shouldn't I? Maybe that's part of growing up, being

able to know how you feel and make decisions without torturing yourself about whether to do something or not. Or maybe it's Philippa, I don't know.

The day of the concert, the big problem was to get Mollie to come. Philippa and I had talked about it and talked to her. We both felt that she should be there, as she was the one who had started the whole thing. If I hadn't bumped into Mollie, and gotten to know her, and been exposed to what was going on right in my own city, under my nose, the concert wouldn't have happened. It was creepy to think of how accidental everything was.

The first thing that morning I ran to my windows and pulled back the curtains. There was a real smell of spring in the air coming up from Central Park; the sky was hazy but the sun was trying to come through. It was going to be a good day. Philippa was still in bed when I went into her room, but when she saw me she sat up and was wide awake.

"I'm going down to find Mollie," I said. "I'd like to get hold of her and keep her with us all day so that she doesn't disappear before tonight."

Mollie had said that she didn't need no concert, and that she wasn't going to sit in a stuffy hall and listen to music. Of course we told her that Madison Square Garden wasn't stuffy, and that she would like the music, but she wouldn't listen. But I wanted so much for her to be there, I wouldn't give up trying.

130

Mollie was in her element, putting on a show of what she thought of "fancy people showing off" to give "handouts" to poor folk, when, in her opinion, the government should take care of people having "a decent house to live in."

"But the government does a lot," I pleaded with her. "No one's giving a handout, Mollie. Mom's concert will give money to an organization that is putting pressure on the federal government, that is monitoring the welfare hotels, that is working for change. Beside, we want you there, you'll enjoy it. If it wasn't for you it wouldn't be happening."

Mollie smiled coyly. "I'll think about it." I realized that she wanted to be coaxed, and so I coaxed and pleaded, until I got a promise out of her that she'd be downstairs at our building at six o'clock. She adamantly refused to come upstairs. The concert was scheduled for seven-thirty, but I wanted to get there early, before the mob.

It was a wild day. The phone rang constantly, people came in and out to see Mom, and I worried about whether Mollie would appear or not. Adam came over around five-thirty, which was nice. I hadn't seen him since Christmas vacation, but our letters made me feel that he wasn't a stranger. Yet, seeing him made me feel shy—I kept trying to remember what I'd written, hoping I hadn't said anything too dopey.

Adam and I went downstairs around a quarter to six to wait for Mollie. I kept running to the corner to see if she was in sight.

"Who is she, anyway?" Adam asked. "What's so important about her?"

I reminded him she was the one I'd told him about at Stacey's party, and that it was because of her this whole thing was happening.

When Mollie came waddling down the street, I was afraid Adam was going to laugh. She had on a straw hat, trimmed with flowers, her usual full skirts and shopping bag, and a bunch of half-dead daisies tied to her front. Mollie was dressed up. But Adam was super. He kept a straight face, gave a half-bow when I introduced him, and offered to carry her shopping bag, which, of course, Mollie wouldn't let out of her hand.

Adolph was taking Mom down later, so we hailed a taxi. Mollie was very nervous in the taxi. She kept looking out of the window as if she were afraid we'd hit something, but every time the meter jumped she beamed. I think she wanted the ride to be very expensive. When we got stuck in traffic, she sat back and said, "It's gonna cost you a lot of money just sitting here."

If I'd thought we were going to escape the crowds getting there early, I was mistaken. There were lines around the block and cops were all over the place keeping people in order who had come just to watch the celebrities arrive.

The mayor was due to come, and everyone of any importance in the city: a couple of senators, film and stage stars, musicians, politicians, plain millionaires.

The place was electric with excitement, as if the whole city had turned out to honor my mom, and also to want to be in on the act of doing something for the homeless. It was like suddenly Mom had woken everyone up (as if they hadn't known anything about it before!) and they wanted to show their faces so they wouldn't be left out. I don't want to sound mean, but some of the newspapers had said the same thing. But maybe that's how big things happen; someone has to make a noise.

I got nervous when I saw the crowd and hoped we wouldn't have any trouble getting in. Fortunately I saw one of Mom's publicity people and I grabbed him and he got us through a side door.

We had seats way up front, and I think Mollie was beginning to enjoy herself. She kept looking around that huge auditorium and saying, "You think all them seats gonna be filled?"

"You saw the crowd outside, half of them won't even be able to get in."

"Your mom gonna sing in front of all these people? She got nerve; she ain't scared?"

"She gets nervous, but she's used to it. She's been doing it for years."

We had quite a wait, but I wasn't going to leave my seat and leave Mollie alone, so the three of us sat there while the place got filled up. Adam was really good-natured about staying with me, but he amused himself by bringing us sodas and snacks.

I would have liked to be outside to see all the

celebrities come in, but I was able to spot some of them and point them out to Mollie. She wasn't much interested. When the mayor came to his box a lot of the audience pointed and clapped and cheered, but Mollie was contemptuous. "He looks just like anybody else," she said. "What's so special about him? I bet he never slept a night in one of his shelters. He should try it."

Finally the lights were dimmed, and the concert began. The curtain went up on Mom's group onstage, playing her opening number. They were dressed in their spangled jackets and sleek black slacks, and watching Mollie's face I had to smile; she was as smug as could be, looking as if the whole thing was of her doing, and that they were performing just for her. To a degree she was right. When Mom came out in her simple, straight, brief black satin dress, the audience went wild. She looked like a kid up onstage, and it seemed crazy that this huge mob of people were clapping and cheering her. She gave her great smile, took hold of the mike, and began to sing. The place became quiet as a tomb.

She was fantastic. My mom doesn't make a lot of grimaces when she sings the way some performers do. She's just natural, as if she were singing because she was happy having a good time in her own living room. I think that's why people loved her so much. She made you feel good, glad to be alive. But she could also make you feel sad, like when she sang a blues song, it made you feel that out there in the

world people were lonely and yearning for something impossible. Then she'd change the mood and sing a happy song, but always there'd be something in her program to remind people that somewhere there were those who were hurting.

They wouldn't let her stop that night. Mom just sang and sang until she couldn't sing anymore. Mollie had tears in her eyes when Mom took her final bow. I wanted to think that tough Mollie had been moved, but I really think she was overly pleased with her own success. She claimed the evening as her own.

Adam, Mollie, and I went backstage to Mom's dressing room, and the grand finale of the night was Mollie being introduced to the mayor. She shook hands with him and looked him over, and gave him a piece of her mind.

"You gonna do something about what's going on in the streets?" she demanded. "I'm telling you, it's a disgrace. Them shelters ain't fit for goats, let alone little kids. You should be ashamed."

He took it good-humoredly, and said that if there were more people like Philippa around there'd be nobody without a place to live.

Mom's friends wanted her to go partying, but she said she'd come home with us. It was just our own family and Adam and Mollie who came home in the limo. I was torn between wanting Adam to come home with us and wanting Philippa to myself. Ho-hum, I thought, this is something new. Suddenly I saw a flash ahead into the future: I was going to want

to be with someone else (the someone looked very much like Adam) more than wanting to be with Philippa. No fooling, I guess I was growing up.

But that night Adam said he had to go home, so I didn't have to decide about asking him. But I had a good feeling about other nights when we could be together, and, miracle of miracles, I wouldn't be lonesome for Mom. So we dropped him off, and, of course, when we got to our house, Mollie wouldn't come upstairs.

She thanked Mom politely for the evening, but she was still skeptical. "Hope it does some good," she said.

We watched her go off down the street, still holding on to her shopping bag (she hadn't let go of it all night).

Philippa was holding my hand. "You love that woman, don't you?"

I hadn't thought about her that way. "Yes, I guess I do." But I turned and gave Mom a hug. "But not the way I love you. I'll never love anyone the way I love you."

Mom hugged me, too. "That goes for me, too," she said.

When we went upstairs, I thought: This is a turning point in my life. Philippa and I were close, but I also felt free in a new way. I could count on her loving me, but I didn't have to count on her for my life. Maybe it was Mollie's independence, or Philippa's tough determination, that somehow had rubbed off on me. Maybe it was my having had a hand in doing some-

thing big and important like this concert. It could even be that Adam had something to do with it. But for the first time I thought: Wow, I'm going to have choices and make my own decisions—I'm going to control *my* life, too.

I was glad Philippa had decided to come home with me. We went upstairs and Mom opened a bottle of champagne and we had a drink to Mollie and her friends, while privately I raised my glass to my own future.

FIC   Colman, Hila.
COLman
        Rich and famous
        like my mom

$10.95   21.67